The Memory of Trade

Patricia Spyer

The Memory of Trade

Modernity's Entanglements on an

Eastern Indonesian Island

Duke University Press   Durham & London

2000

For my parents,

Dick Spyer and Helen Spyer-Stetson

Contents

Illustrations

Preface

What is one to make of queries posed to a nineteenth-century naturalist by the natives of a far-flung archipelago when they resonate across time with those posed by their descendants to a twentieth-century anthropologist? And what is one to think of this gap of more than one hundred years when, echoing their forebears, these descendants still insist on probing an outsider for the whereabouts of some long lost kin? What kind of uncanny space—neither "here" nor "there," "then" nor "now"— is opened up by such queries that are so heavy with loss and longing? Of what desires, expectations, imaginings, and historicities is such a space made? And how is one to understand the positioning of peoples who alienate their most intimate ties to far-off places while keeping the foreign close at hand as something to which they are beholden? What, in other words, is the status for these people of the faraway and the nearby when neither ever settles without being immediately inhabited and unsettled by the other. This book navigates the fraught junctures opened by these different queries and historicities as it explores the fissured construction of community among the pearl-diving peoples of Aru in the southeast Moluccas of Indonesia. More specifically, it considers the dilemmas, ambivalences, and compromises that describe Aruese people's engagement and location of themselves vis-à-vis two imaginary elsewheres—the "Malay" and the "Aru." If with respect to the former gloss for the beyond of commerce, state, and church, Aruese do not feel entitled to full citizenship, they increasingly figure the latter designation for custom's space apart as the ever vanishing past of a "foreign country" (see also Ivy 1995; Lowenthal 1985). This book traces, politically and historically, the sometimes fluid, at other times rigidified contours of these Malay and Aru elsewheres, together with the responsibilities and difficulties that arise for Aruese within a predicament where no steady circuit of communication or identity can ever be established with either.

Ethnographically speaking, the book's point of departure is what I theorize as a situation of "entanglement." I use the concept of entanglement to characterize the double predicament of these Aruese collectors of sea products for the international market. Positioned on the one hand by the archipelago's centuries-long engagement within extended networks of commerce and communication and, on the other, by modernity's characteristic repressions and displacements, Aruese make and manage their lives somewhat precariously within what they often seem to construe as a dangerously widening if still enticing world. By documenting not only the particular expectations and strategies Aruese develop in their dealings with this larger world but also the price they pay for participation therein, this book also speaks to the problems that peoples in the frontier spaces of modern nation-states commonly face elsewhere.

In focusing on the construction of community in a small-scale place, this book follows the tradition of classic ethnography, as it also does in invoking a wide range of practices and cultural forms to make its argument. I do not believe it necessary to rehearse once again here the criticisms of this ethnographic tradition that have already been so well articulated by others (Clifford and Marcus 1986; Fabian 1983). Indeed, one of my aims has been to recover the ethnographic impulse, the fine-grained analysis, and the close knit between theory and ethnography that distinguished some of the most outstanding examples of this genre. At the same time, the differences between an earlier ethnography and my own should be clear. A modest point I make in this book, for instance, is that the community at stake in its pages is in a crucial sense compelled in imagining and constructing itself to imagine and construct the much larger world around it. Simply put, such a community does not overlap with the bounded "societies" of an older anthropology devoted to the documentation of places like Aru (Strathern 1988), which assigned native alterity to a timeless topography (Fabian 1983; Thomas 1989). Arguing instead that Aru's "runaway topographies" are inherently fissured (chapter 1), their presence ongoingly haunted by their absent elsewheres, this partial writing of Aru therefore assumes entanglement and modernity as its preconditions. In Appadurai's formulation, this book is most aptly described as one possible "ethnography of the modern" (Appadurai 1996, 182).

Aru is a low-lying archipelago made up of six large central islands and multiple smaller ones clustered under the Bird's Head of New Guinea in the southeastern part of the Moluccas. During the mid- to late 1980s, when I spent the bulk of my time there, the entire archipelago constituted a single subdistrict (I. *kecamatan*) within the southeast district (I. *kebupaten*) of the province of Maluku. Although administrative plans were under way at this time to divide the subdistrict into two, the fact that this had not already been done in an archipelago of Aru's size—some 180 kilometers from north to south and 80 kilometers wide at its widest part—in contrast, for instance, to its neighbor Tanimbar, speaks perhaps better than anything else to the marginality of these islands within both the provincial and the national settings. The archipelago is further administratively ordered into some 122 *desa*, or village, units, which range in size from approximately eighty to one thousand inhabitants. Some of the largest of these villages are located on Barakai Island in Aru's southeastern Backshore, where the majority of the archipelago's pearl divers and collectors of sea products reside.

I have lived in Aru a total of about two years, including a preliminary visit in 1984, a twenty-one-month stay from 1986 to 1988, and a brief return in 1994. Early in 1986, when I set out on a trader's boat from the capital Dobo for the islands off of Aru's southeastern coast, I followed a trajectory that in part recapitulated the historic voyage in 1857 of England's great naturalist Alfred Russel Wallace. Stopping at times to take on copra, collect firewood and water, and once when we ran aground, the boat to Barakai charted a winding course through one of the riverine channels that snake through the larger islands of the archipelago to open out into the seas off its eastern coast. Apart from the continual hum of the boat's motor and the modest Christian steeples and silvery domes of rural Indonesian mosques, the glimpses of gardens cleared out in the bush, of villages set back from the river on inclines, of Aruese in canoes, and even traders in motorboats resonated for me with scenes depicted by Wallace and other nineteenth-century visitors in their writings on Aru. And I had a hint of how my own arrival had already been prefigured by the comings and goings of countless others—especially the traders who have long plied the saltwater channels connecting the archipelago's Front- and Backshores, but also the Dutch colonial officials and other Europeans whose interest in Aru peaked in the second half of the last century and, more recently, the government officials who occasionally travel to the Backshore to take censuses, collect taxes, or prepare its inhabitants for national elections, along with church representatives and the odd visiting dignitary.

The impression of a place somewhat delicately poised in the midst of an ongoing if erratic sea traffic was rapidly established for me in the context of my own arrival on Barakai Island. No fewer than three boats mediated my entry in Bemun, one of this island's five communities. Like virtually all others who journey to the Backshore, I arrived on the boat of an ethnic Chinese trader who had relatives and business on Barakai. Along with the boat's crew, two bureaucrats from the subdistrict office—who took the opportunity of my trip to categorize the island's predominantly ethnic Chinese storeowners into tax brackets—were my escorts. Shortly after I climbed the stone steps up to Bemun, built like many Backshore villages on a cliff overlooking the sea, I was officially welcomed into the community in the "customary manner" by its two main *adat*, or "customary," officials, known as the Prow and the Stern. As a pair, the officials form the "two halves" of a boat anchored at the center of village space in the house altars of these men, which once a year in the context of the community's annual performance sets, as it were, sail. Besides the trader's motorboat and custom's own vessel, the news that had spread across the island forecasting the arrival of a white woman heading for Bemun had set off a flurry of speculation in the community centered on a third boat. More particularly, the rumors that preceded me triggered retellings of the history of a great foreign ship that had sunk long ago in the seas off of Barakai. Along with its important cargo, the ship carried what is most aptly described as a Portuguese civilization hero. The *portugis*, as he is locally known, lived for many years following the shipwreck among Bemun's ancestors until, taking along an Aruese wife, he left in a trader's junk for his faraway home across the sea.

Much as I myself, tracing the well-worn path between Aru's Front- and Backshores, recalled Wallace's visit to the islands, so too the triad of boats that effected my entry to Barakai evoked for many of its inhabitants other arrivals that for them have assumed a paradigmatic importance. Not long after I was given the customary reception of persons who plan to reside in the village for some time, I was inundated with questions regarding my own background and somewhat more cautiously pressed for any information that might have revealed a relation to the aforementioned portugis. Chapter 3 considers several divergent tellings of the so-called great ship's history and takes up this concern among Bemunese with its imagined contemporary after-effects. Suffice it to say here that one figuring of my status as a new outsider took place in the effort to link me to this much-storied foreigner who is commonly held to have introduced to Aru some of the most privileged tokens of civilization—notably clothing and a colonial staff of office along with the collection of pearl oysters and, therewith, commercial relations.

As with other exemplary outsiders commemorated, for instance, in song, the Portuguese civilizer's importance derives especially from his connection to trade. Besides this European, the figure of a Chinese merchant fleshed out in the status he wields and the expectations he elicits is codified in a popular Barakai song that is sung on formal occasions like bridewealth exchange as well as more informally, for instance, as a lullaby. Setting the scene for the merchant's arrival, the song opens with the sweet sound of a small gong wafting across the waves breaking in front of a village and announcing to it a trader's junk from Dobo. The next image is that of a delegation rowing out to the junk to fetch "our *tukang*"—here a high-ranking person with special skills—who addresses them in Chinese. The song ends with the Chinese merchant striding into the village under the shade of his great status umbrella.

The last in the series of boats mediating my introduction to Barakai was custom's own vessel. Like the Portuguese ship and the trader's junk but much less explicitly, the boat whose beginning and end coincides with the two altars presided over by the Prow and the Stern assumes the role once a year of the Malay outsider. In so doing, and in opposing itself to an Aru "inside," this boat links Bemun to a larger world beyond the archipelago. By extension, it also identifies the community with trade and circulation. If the brief sketch I have just offered seems to suggest an island community simply waiting on and welcoming a stream of illustrious outsiders, then this is far from the case. As the site where the community's adat achieves its most concretized expression and the ancestors are invoked, the altars of the Prow and the Stern do, indeed, on first impression appear to crystallize a pristine Aru. Yet figured as a boat, the custom that today is increasingly ensconced as codifying a self-contained Aruese culture implicitly gestures to a Malay beyond from whence the ancestors of the Bemunese community are believed to have come. If by and large Bemunese look to the arrival of outsiders and are hospitable to their others, their own assertion of a foreign provenance lays a claim to possessing worldliness, alterity, and far-reaching knowledge. Out of the charged interactions and negotiations with these shifting figures of Aru and Malay—positively construed as celebrated custom or cosmopolitan traveler and negatively, as backward primitivism versus coercive violence—the fissured construction by Bemunese men and women of their community emerges as a genealogy that refuses to settle.

Early in January 1986 I arrived at Barakai Island, remarkable even in Aru for its centuries-long intensive involvement with commerce that continues to this day and for the related requirement placed on its inhabitants of engaging with a heterogeneous, fluctuating stream of multiple outsiders. While the peoples of all five Barakai communities dive for pearl oysters and collect sea products for trade, I selected Bemun as a place to live because of what I perceived at the time as its particular specificity. I was taken by the attractive location—elevated on a cliff overlooking the sea—of this village that, unlike the other Barakai villages, was also known for a steady supply of fresh water as well as for its towering mango trees, which cast a deep shade throughout most of Bemun. Beyond comfort and beauty, what intrigued me most was the conversion of the entire community to Catholicism, in 1976–77. With only a few exceptions, all of Aru's Backshore pagan communities became at least nominally divided along religious lines when forced in the mid- 1970s to convert to what the Suharto government defined as an *agama*, or "world religion." Since this time, on Barakai, for instance, the communities of Longgar and Mesiang comprise Catholics, Protestants, and Muslims; that of Apara, Protestants and Muslims; while the wholly Muslim affiliation of the inhabitants of the former traders' stronghold Gomogomo largely predates the conversions of the mid-1970s. In collectively opting for the Catholicism of the Sacred Heart Mission,[1] Bemunese also chose the religion that represents the only real alternative in Maluku to the dual hegemony in this province of the Protestant Church of the Moluccas (I. Gereja Protestan Maluku, or GPM) and Islam. Additionally, Bemun counted among its inhabitants those Aruese who had held out longest against the pressures of Dobo bureaucrats who had taken it upon themselves to convert Aru's remaining pagans so that, by having a religion, they might participate in the country's 1977 elections. With an agama to declare on their citizen's identity card and therefore a double conversion to both religion and citizenship within the Indonesian nation-state (Spyer 1996b), Aru's Backshore peoples would qualify for participation in the country's crucial ritual of national elections or, as it was sometimes also called, a "democracy party" (Pemberton 1994, 5). As I later discovered, this insistence on maintaining a certain unity in the face of outside pressure had much to do with Bemun's annual performance.

During my first year in Bemun, I lived with the daughter of one of Bemun's schoolteachers—who, although her family originated from the neighboring Kei Islands, had been raised in the village—along with her Bemunese husband and their three young sons, his Bemunese mother and Longgarese father, and a varying number of their kin from either Bemun itself, the other Barakai communities, or occasionally from Kei. In many respects my residence with this family represented an ideal living situation for my first year on Barakai, providing intensive, ongoing exchange with the different personalities, projects, concerns, and sometimes tensions of a three-generation household, an optimal setting for informal immersion in the Barakai language as well as an immediate ready-made connection to one of Bemun's largest kin groups, the Jonjonlers, and to the kin group of the houseowner's father in Longgar. After a six-month interruption of my research from late December 1986 to June 1987 imposed by the government's requirement that I leave Aru during Indonesia's 1987 elections, I resettled in the village council house. There, on more neutral ground unidentified with any particular kin group, I hoped that all my friends, acquaintances, and whoever else wished to visit me would feel less encumbered by the etiquette and politics that for some had occasionally made it less than comfortable to casually drop by my former home.

My companion in the council house, Birgita Gomarir, had become my main assistant during the course of my first year on Barakai and would continue to work with me through my return visit there in 1994. Together with another woman in her mid-thirties, Kabet Kobawon-Anggrek, Gita had appointed herself within days after I arrived at Bemun as a language teacher, and she rapidly became a lively, intelligent, and delightful all-around companion. While Gita had divorced her Longgarese husband some years back and seemed determined to preserve her independence, Kabet was one of only two Aruese women I knew who had married a Chinese trader and, in her case, one from a prominent Dobo family. When I settled in Bemun, her husband had already died some twelve years before, shortly after the couple had their first child, but she continued to reside in the remnants of the former tradestore with her half-Chinese daughter and a second husband from Kei. While Gita and Kabet regarded each other as friends, each of these women represented one of the two largest *fam*, or extended patrilineal kin groups, in Bemun, the Gomarir and the Jonjonler—who much like the two families dominating the action in a classic soap opera continuously intermarried, intrigued, and rivaled each other.[2] While many of the people I spent the bulk of my time with and was most intimate with on Barakai came from one of these two fam, some of my most taxing moments in Aru were spent sorting out and negotiating my attention and, occasionally, loyalties, among their respective members. Besides these two younger women, I had warm and familiar relations with several older women including Gita's mother, commonly known by her teknonym, Gita ken ma; Kabet's mother, Abu Meme; and her younger sister, Abu Sabuan. While, at marriage, both the latter had become members of their husbands' fam, they wielded considerable influence in their fam of birth as the sisters of some of the most prominent senior Jonjonler men. I also developed close ties with several of these men as well as with several senior Gomarir men, especially Gita's father, the Stern; his younger brother Bemun's headman; and their aged but still feisty father. Acquiring relationships with younger men took more time and commonly occurred within the wider framework of my friendship with another person in the man's family like a sister or wife. Besides having ties with the members of these two fam and with other Bemunese dispersed across the remaining nine fam of the community, I spent a great deal of time with Bemun's traders, especially its two tradeswomen, as well as with others in Longgar, Apara, and to a lesser extent Mesiang and Gomogomo. From my conversations, exchanges, and commercial transactions with all these persons, I gained much insight into the ambitions and expectations common among Aru's trading community, the toil and troubles of running a tradestore, the traders' attitudes toward their Barakai clients, and, importantly, their management of the latter's debts.

I asked and received permission from all persons mentioned in this book to use their names and to write about the particular events I describe here. A few incidents that I regard as sensitive, either politically or personally, I have chosen to omit from the book entirely or have sufficiently altered and disguised so as to make the identification of the persons involved unlikely. After considerable thought and these necessary adjustments, I have largely retained the true names of the persons whose stories, comments, observations, and lives I draw on here as well as the names of the places in which they live. A source of pride for many Bemunese and at times an important ingredient in island politics was the fact that I had selected their community over the others on Barakai as a place to live and that, via this book, as they imagined it, the name of Bemun would travel far and wide. Other Barakai women and men as well as Aruese elsewhere also generally expected their contributions to be acknowledged and their names recognized in what I would come to write. To try to account individually for all these persons here would be impossible, and in choosing to refer to people by name rather than pseudonym I have probably mentioned fewer persons than I might have otherwise. While I applaud and adhere to a politics of writing sensitive to the privacy and safety of the persons and places it describes, I have found myself increasingly uncomfortable with the personal and at times historical erasures that such writing often leaves as its trail. In choosing then to name some of the persons and the places I came to know best in Aru, I have done so with the conviction that this choice has been both respectful and wise.

Although I lived in Bemun, all of the Barakai communities with the partial exception of Gomogomo, located on its own small island across a narrow strait facing Mesiang, are closely knit by marriage ties, kin relations, and economics. Probably the most telling example, which also suggests a historical depth to Gomogomo's difference, is the annual ritual cycle in which the four communities located on Barakai itself each hold in sequence a performance to open the diving and trade season. When I write therefore of Barakai, my observations pertain most directly to my experience in Bemun, Longgar, Apara, and Mesiang. At the same time, I believe that many of the things I say in this book apply more generally to Aru's Backshore peoples, who much as those on Barakai have long been entangled in erratic if persistent commercial relations and who, as anyone else in Aru, have had to shape their lives within successive colonial and postcolonial situations.

Today all five Barakai villages are located on the coast—Longgar and
Apara high on rocky cliffs like Bemun, and Mesiang and Gomogomo
low-lying and directly adjacent to the beach. In contrast to the other
Barakai peoples and with important ramifications up to the present,
today's Bemunese and Mesiangese trace their ancestry as communities to
a prior residence in the forest, at a remove from the hustle and bustle of
coastal trade. At the same time, when people on Barakai spoke not of villages but of fam, they did so in very much the same terms as all other
Aruese I met with in 1984 and later—with reference, that is, to their
earlier migrations from elsewhere. As I was also told in the different
places where I traveled in the archipelago, the various fam found in Aru
all derive from one canonical event, namely, the mythic shattering of
the paired islands of Karang and Enu at the southernmost extreme of
the archipelago as the impetus to the exodus of Aru's ancestors and
their subsequent travels and dispersal throughout the island group. The
names of many of Aru's fam codify these ancestral wanderings. For
instance, the fam Agujir is said to have come to Barakai after an initial
residence in Ujir in northwest Aru, that of Gomarir to have spent some
time on the Backshore island of Mariri before settling on Barakai, while
that of Jerwi, its name a synopsis meaning "the jer shell is gone," is held
to have embarked on its migrations in the islands without the jer shell
commonly used to bail bilge water on Aruese boats. Many fam names
recur in different parts of the archipelago; the Bemunese Jonjonlers, for
example, regarded themselves as related to the Jonlers of the Batulay
area. On Barakai at least, there was not, however, any elaboration of such
putative fam origins or travels. At most, migrations were mentioned in
passing and their discussion either limited to a brief explanation of
the fam's name such as those I gave above or of its totemic emblem—
commonly a kind of fish or a bird species identified with the shifting
border between sea and shore like the pelican, different kinds of herons,
or sandpiper-like birds. Occasionally, people would bring up the migrations in order to position their fam with respect to one of the three larger
collectivities that are held to comprise all Aru peoples and, like fam, to
be an effect of the common yet internally differentiated exodus from
Karang-Enu. Fam on Barakai, as in many other parts of Aru, thus fall
into one of the triadic divisions of the people of the front, the middle, or
the back as a consequence, as I was variously told, either of having been

among the first, the middle, or the last boatloads to abandon the ancestral home, or of the fam's position in one of these boats itself—at its front, middle, or rear.

The above is not intended as a preliminary overview of Barakai social organization. Whenever the ancestral exodus and its effects were invoked, it always seemed to have more to do with the aim of asserting a certain commonality and shared experience among all Aruese than of inscribing differences among fam or other categories of related persons. On Barakai, the most visible importance of the fam and its sphere of action lies in those formalized exchange events in which a core group of senior men, their sons, and married sisters, with a shifting contingent of supporters, briefly achieves the coherence of a group as it works toward specific goals. Although a knowledge of how exchange works on Barakai has been crucial to understanding some of the practices I describe in this book, for instance, the transactions of divers with undersea spirit women discussed in chapter 4, I only speak in general terms in its pages about marriage and the related practice of bridewealth exchange (for a more detailed discussion of these matters, see Spyer 1992). If I bring up here these mythic travels and ancestral scatterings, it is to foreground the mobility and dynamics that Barakai peoples (and other Aruese) place at their beginnings and, in so doing, to convey the sense of a world beyond that seems to hover at the contours of their conceptions of community and self—somewhat like a boat buffeted by the sea that keeps it adrift. It is this world and these dynamics that I explore in this book.

Fieldwork in Aru (1984 1986–88, and 1994) and archival research in the Netherlands (1987) were made possible by financial support from Fulbright-Hays Dissertation Fellowships, the Wenner-Gren Foundation for Anthropological Research, the Institute for Intercultural Studies, the Southeast Asian Council of the Association for Asian Studies, with funds from the Luce Foundation, and the Netherlands Foundation for the Advancement of Tropical Research (WOTRO). Research in Indonesia was carried out under the kind sponsorship of the Lembaga Ilmu Pengetahuan in Jakarta and the Universitas Pattimura in Ambon. In addition to the generous support of these institutions, I also wish to acknowledge the earlier support of a Charlotte W. Newcombe Dissertation Fellowship, a William Rainey Harper Fellowship from the University of Chicago, and funds from the Committee on Southern Asia, also of the University of Chicago.

From the very beginning my interest in Aru was stimulated and encouraged by Susan McKinnon and James Collins, and I have benefited over the years from their sound advice, generosity, and friendship. The bulk of the materials on which this book is based and some of its parts first took shape as a dissertation at the University of Chicago (Spyer 1992). There I had the excellent fortune to study with Bernard Cohn, Nancy Munn, Marshall Sahlins, and the late Valerio Valeri. The scholarly dedication, utter seriousness, and intellectual creativity of these teachers has been an inspiration ever since. Of the many contributions made by others at the University of Chicago to this book, I acknowledge especially Jean and John Comaroff and Elizabeth Traube. James J. Fox also lent his advice and assistance to this project at an early stage, and I thank him for it.

This book was reconceived and, to a great extent, rewritten in the Netherlands at the Research Centre Religion and Society of the University of Amsterdam, where I have been since 1993. I extend my heartfelt thanks to Gerd Baumann, Birgit Meyer, Peter Pels, Peter van Rooden, and Peter van der Veer for the scholarly rigor and warm support with which they have shared with me their criticisms and suggestions, and for their collegiality and friendship. Peter van der Veer deserves special mention for his unflagging attention to the progress of this book and his more general enthusiastic support of my work. Among my new Indonesianist colleagues in the Netherlands, my exchanges with Jan Breman, Henk Schulte Nordholt, and Leontine Visser have been especially stimulating and pleasurable.

I am grateful to the many friends and colleagues who warmly and unfailingly have offered their advice, criticisms, and support over the years, particularly Inge Boer, Suzanne Brenner, Mariane Ferme, Janet Hoskins, Marilyn Ivy, Webb Keane, Laura Lewis, Ruth Mandel, Annelies Moors, John Pemberton, Adela Pinch, Danilyn Rutherford, Laurie Sears, Mary Steedly, and G. G. Weix. Portions of the manuscript were commented on by Gerd Baumann, Inge Boer, Webb Keane, Prahbu Mohapatra, Birgit Meyer, Peter Pels, Peter van Rooden, and Peter van der Veer. Webb Keane's common scholarly interest in Indonesia and his friendship throughout many years has been an immense source of pleasure and our exchanges an ongoing intellectual stimulation to my work. I note also my special indebtedness to John Pemberton for the candor and energy with which he read the entire manuscript of this book, offered crucial commentary for its revision, and lent throughout of his warmth and friendship.

I am most indebted to Rafael Sánchez, who read and commented at length on virtually all of the earlier and later versions of this book, and always gave generously of his insights, intellectual creativity, and critical powers. His ability to travel with my words does not cease to astound me. It is with the utmost gratitude that I acknowledge here his unabiding support and invaluable contributions.

In Indonesia, I relied on and enjoyed the generosity, hospitality, companionship, and assistance of many people, much too numerous to be named here. Special thanks are due to Bapak Camat and Ibu Leatemia, Ibu Sely and Bapak Nahbot Unwawirka, Anis and Bolo Unwawirka, Bapak D. and Ibu J. Oat, Richard and Judith Manuputty, Bapak Edi Masinambow, Thontji Galongguga, Javed Kamarmir, Matias Tunjanan, Pendeta Remalise Manuhutu, Incebencang, Apong, and Toko Surabaya. Members of the Sacred Heart Mission offered generously of their knowledge, time, and resources in Ambon, Aru, and the Netherlands. I thank especially Bishop Andreas Sol, Pater Segers, Pater van Lith, Pater Scheurs, and Pater Akeboom. I must also acknowledge the kind assistance of many officials at the *propinsi, kabupaten, kecamatan* and *desa* levels as well as the captains and crews of the numerous boats in the Moluccas that I traveled on, especially Captain Erenst Marthing and Nikki, Ganá, and Teka. I also express my profound gratitude to Birgita Gomarir, Sabuan Jonjonler-Tebwayanan, Iskia Tebwayanan, Senin and Helena Kobawon, the late Isau Kobawon, the late Bebi Jonjonler-Kobawon, Kabet Kobawon-Anggrek, Bobi Rahail, Magar and Gongon Gomarir and their sons and sons' wives, Sijor Gomarir, Matagwa Jerwi-Gomarir, Lakulu Kobawon, Stephanus and Tangwa Liubun-Ho, Ika and The Dian Cu-Eddiwisman, Bapak Guru Hurlean, Bapak Guru Ngutra, Lawa and Boi Jonjonler, and Magar Jonjonler. I must also mention Lena Gomarir-Lengam, Dima Lengam, my *joli* in Mesiang, Amasi ken ma, and the *kepala desa*s of Longgar, Mesiang, and Apara. To all of these people and to many, many more, I extend my deepest appreciation.

Some passages and sections of this book have been published elsewhere. Most of chapter 2 appeared in Spyer 1998b (reprinted by permission of Routledge), part of chapter 3 in Spyer 1999, parts of chapter 4 in Spyer 1997, and parts of chapter 5 in Spyer 1996a (the latter both reprinted by permission of the American Anthropological Association). I had assistance in producing the maps from Germen Boelens and Hans Straver of the Landelijk Steunpunt Educatie Molukkers in Utrecht. The maps are adapted from the Atlas Maluku published by the LSEM in 1998. Figure 3 is reproduced by permission of the Royal Tropical Institute, Amsterdam, and figure 5 comes from Pater van Lith MSC's own collection of photographs of Aru, for which I thank him. All the other photographs are mine.

Lastly, I want to thank Ingrid van den Broek for her kindness and dedication during the production of this book and Jasper Klapwijk for his excellent technical assistance. The editorial devotion, good humor, and friendship of Ken Wissoker were crucial to this book's revision and completion, and I offer him my most heartfelt thanks.

A Note on Language, Translation, and Orthography

The linguistic landscape of the Aru Islands is a highly complex one, made up of either twelve distinct if related languages (Hughes 1987) or five different languages that are further fragmented along dialect chains (Collins 1983). Apart from my own efforts with Barakai, the language spoken by the approximately three thousand inhabitants of the island of the same name in southeastern Aru, only the language of the Dobel area in central-eastern Aru has been the focus of serious study—since the mid-1980s by members of the Summer Institute of Linguistics (SIL). All languages spoken in Aru belong to the Austronesian phylum, with the closest cognatic languages found in the neighboring archipelagos of Tanimbar and Kei. Two dialects are distinguished on Barakai, one spoken in the community of Mesiang and the other by the peoples of the four remaining Barakai villages—Bemun, Longgar, Apara, and Gomogomo. Local language use is strong, although all islanders are also fluent in Aru Malay or the archipelago's version of the regional dialect, Ambonese Malay. Additionally, Barakai islanders are taught the national language, Bahasa Indonesia, in schools and are regularly exposed to it through government programs, speeches, and rituals as well as through the national media. Because of the long and extensive history of the island's engagement in international trade, Barakai people have had frequent opportunities through the years to speak Malay with outsiders. The Dutch colonial officer Bik, for instance, had no problems communicating in Malay on the island when he visited there in 1824 to install local chiefs (Bik 1928 [1824]). This interaction presumably explains the marked tendency to incorporate Malay words and even entire phrases into Barakai conversation. Notwithstanding this flexibility and interaction in speech, islanders strictly differentiate between *gwerka lir*, or

"Aru speech/language," and *mala lir*, or "Malay speech/language," with the latter comprising any of the variants on the continuum between the local Aru Malay and the national Indonesian. I have chosen in this book to follow this Barakai usage. While "B" before a word or phrase indicates the Barakai language, "I" includes anything from Aru Malay through the Indonesian that is spoken in the contemporary setting of the Indonesian nation-state, while Malay applies here exclusively to the colonial lingua franca. In the Barakai language as in Indonesian, I follow the new Indonesian orthography (*ejaan baru*) with one important addition in the case of the former: é as in the English "say" is used, for instance, in the Barakai *alé*, or "empty," to distinguish it from the unemphatic English mid-central vowel as in "the." Words and phrases taken from Dutch, the language of Indonesia's former colonizers, are preceded by "D."

Aruese use kin terms, personal names, and, after the birth of a couple's first child, teknonyms to address and refer to each other. Thus, Aruese commonly speak of X ken pa (or Xem) or so-and-so's father and X ken ma (or Xjin) or so-and-so's mother. After the birth of their first grandchild they would be referred to by the child's name as Abu X.

All translations from Barakai, Indonesian, Dutch, and the occasional French are my own.

1 Introduction:

Runaway Topographies

A number of the natives gathered round me, and said they wanted to talk.
Two of the best Malay scholars helped each other, the rest putting in hints
and ideas in their own language. They told me a long rambling story; but,
partly owing to their imperfect knowledge of Malay, partly through my
ignorance of the local terms, and partly through the incoherence of their
narrative, I could not make it out very clearly. It was, however, a tradition,
and I was glad to find they had anything of the kind. A long time ago, they
said, some strangers came to Aru, and came here to Wanumbai, and the
chief of the Wanumbai people did not like them, and wanted them to go
away, but they would not go, and so it came to fighting, and many Aru
men were killed, and some, along with the chief, were taken prisoners, and
carried away by the strangers. Some of the speakers, however, said that he
was not carried away, but went away in his own boat to escape from the
foreigners, and went to the sea and never came back again. But they all
believe that the chief and the people that went with him still live in some
foreign country; and if they could but find out where, they would send for
them to come back again. . . . They had sought for them everywhere, they
said—on the land and in the sea, in the forest and on the mountains, in the
air and in the sky, and could not find them; therefore, they must be in my
country, and they begged me to tell them, for I must surely know, as I
came from across the great sea. . . . And then they told me that a good
many years ago, when the speakers were boys, some Wokan men who were
out fishing met these lost people in the sea, and spoke to them; and the
chief gave the Wokan men a hundred fathoms of cloth to bring to the men
of Wanumbai, to show that they were alive and would soon come back to
them; but the Wokan men were thieves, and kept the cloth, and they only
heard of it afterwards; and when they spoke about it, the Wokan men

denied it, and pretended they had not received the cloth;—so they were quite sure their friends were at that time alive and somewhere in the sea. And again, not many years ago, a report came to them that some Bugis traders had brought some children of their lost people; so that they went to Dobbo [*sic*] to see about it, and the owner of the house, who was now speaking to me, was one who went; but the Bugis man would not let them see the children, and threatened to kill them if they came into his house. He kept the children shut up in a large box, and when he went away he took them with him. And at the end of each of these stories, they begged me in an imploring tone to tell them if I knew where their chief and their people now were. (Wallace 1962 [1869], 357–59)

When I reread Wallace recently I was arrested and unsettled by this passage, which I had overlooked during my earlier forays into the existing literature on the Aru Islands—what Michel de Certeau calls a "library navigation" (de Certeau 1986).[1] Here was Alfred Russel Wallace, the great English naturalist and author of *The Malay Archipelago: The Land of the Orang-Utan and the Bird of Paradise*, on the evening of April 28, 1857, having a "grand consultation" with some natives of the Aru settlement of Wanumbai. Here at the far end of a small tributary that branches southward off of the Watulai "river" to burrow itself deep into the forested interior of Maikor Island, Wallace would suffer greatly from ulcers on his feet caused by pernicious insect bites. Here, too, he would obtain several specimens of the fully plumed Legless Bird of Paradise (*Paradisea apoda*), thus fulfilling one of the main objectives of his visit to these islands (see Quammen 1996, 88–96; Swadling 1996, 127). Although unremarked in later biographies, in Wanumbai Wallace was also the select audience for this remarkable story that, he writes, had evidently been plotted beforehand by the inhabitants of this modest settlement of hunters and small-scale horticulturalists (Wallace 1962 [1869], 357).

Uncannily, this story resonates across a span of more than one hundred years with tales told to me by Barakai islanders of some long lost kin across the sea and of their ongoing and repeatedly thwarted attempts to send to their Backshore relations boxes of clothes. Let me be clear from the start. I am not interested in documenting the resilience across time of what Wallace positively embraces and normalizes as "tradition." Nor is my aim the historicist one of extracting the truthful kernel of a locatable

1. Map of the Aru Islands with Mr. Wallace's routes.
Reprinted from Wallace 1962 [1869], 338.

happening from within the shell of the tale. To be sure, as Wallace speculates, there may be a historical memory at work in the story told to him
as in the one I heard a good century later. It is, for instance, not unimaginable that such stories might have first taken shape in the wake of the
seizure of Aruese to work as slaves on the nutmeg plantations of the
neighboring Banda Islands in the latter half of the seventeenth century.[2]
Or they may betray Aruese knowledge or, less likely, experience, of how
Europeans occasionally took with them a handful of natives for exhibition back home (at one point when Wallace realizes that the endless

stream of visitors to his hut had come especially to look at him, he reflects on how just a few years before he had been "one of the gazers at the Zulus and the Aztecs in London" [ibid., 349]). Seen in this light, the Aruese anxiety about their lost ancestors might be regarded as a local gloss on a civilizing story that draws out its underside of native expropriation and loss. As Benjamin observed, "There is no document of civilization which is not at the same time a document of barbarism" (1969, 256).

Notwithstanding the differences separating Wallace's "grand consultation" and the stories of misplaced kin told to me, the uncanniness that comes from their juxtaposition should be neither dismissed nor shied away from. I am intrigued by the persistence in Aru of what appear as related tellings. Rather than being some complacent continuity, I argue that their repetition speaks to a chronic and fraught structure of expectancy on the part of Backshore Aruese vis-à-vis a highly elusive elsewhere. Token today of a particular politics of difference characteristic of modernity, this elsewhere emerges out of the cultural and commercial entanglements that must form the starting point of any discussion of Aru. The particular dynamics of these entanglements in the archipelago have, I believe, only intensified a common effect of colonialism—the perception that the world in certain crucial respects resides in another place, more often than not across the sea.[3] Problematically, it is the sense of a haunting by a desired and elusive elsewhere to which one is connected that conjoins the imploring tone with which Wanumbai men beseeched Wallace for the whereabouts of their kin to the adamant insistences voiced to me that Bemunese relations *must* still be there, across the sea, and to the instructions I was given on all my departures from Aru to track them down (chapter 3). As I will argue, this haunting also crucially speaks to a feeling of incompleteness that is resolved in myriad ways that I explore in the following chapters. Yet if perhaps in Wallace's time the sense of a fragile affinity to an indeterminate elsewhere was singular, on Barakai today it doubles. In local terms one could say that the sense of an elsewhere applies to both the Aru (B. *gwerka*) and the Malay (B. *malayu*), with the understanding that the two are by no means at all times either equivalent or opposed. A central challenge of this book is to understand how what is being imagined here might inform, modulate, and largely motivate some of the practices and subjectivities that today are especially salient on Aru's Backshore.

To risk stating the obvious, Aru's entanglement within a larger world and its modernity shade imperceptibly into each other. If entanglement refers to a longer durée involving, among other things, Aru's long-standing if shifting position within global trade, modernity reveals itself more recently in the archipelago as the discursive effects of Dutch colonialism and Indonesian postcoloniality. Between entanglement and modernity there is therefore a difference in both level and chronology that I maintain throughout the book. While entanglement serves as its theoretical point of departure, I reserve modernity for the subsequent mapping out of specific discursive moves and erasures in the day to day of Aruese lives. Put otherwise, if the contrast between the Malay and the Aru can only emerge in a situation of entanglement, the asymmetrical valuing of this contrast itself is a consequence of modernity. Specifically, the latter is an effect of the forms of power and knowledge wielded today by, especially, the Indonesian government and before it by the Dutch colonial one and the displacements and hierarchies that both of these in interaction with Aruese called forth and put into place.

Take, for example, the designation of the southeastern islands where I worked in the archipelago as Aru's "Backshore" (D. *Achterwal*) in opposition to the northwestern "Frontshore" (D. *Voorwal*) identified with the island capital Dobo. Already in the precolonial Malay world a distinction was commonly made between the more cosmopolitan peoples of the coast and those of the hinterlands. The famous Pigafetta, for example, wrote of the north Moluccan island Halmahera that it was inhabited by Moors who controlled the coast and heathens who lived in its interior, "a division of power," a well-known historian of Asia adds, "which the Europeans found to be quite common throughout the East Indies" (Lach 1965, 596). As far as I know, however, it took the Europeans, in contrast to the peoples before them, to elaborate fully the moral-political dimensions of such difference, which they then, indeed, often bolstered with religion. Much like its contemporary Indonesian successor "backcountry" (I. *belakang tanah*), today's most current name for Aru's eastern parts, the Dutch "Backshore" bore both topographical and derogatory connotations. Beyond designating the archipelago's east coast and outlying islands, these terms have been successively assimilated to the Dutch and Indonesian words for "backward" (respectively *achtergesteld* and *terbelakang*).

I have nevertheless opted in this book to maintain this nomenclature, since it encodes a history and positioning that Aruese have for long had to negotiate and that is central to the argument I develop here. Whatever the limitations and possibilities that Aruese themselves may have discovered in these terms, they cannot therefore simply be written away. At the same time, it is worth noting that I never heard a "back-country" Aruese object to this description of their home, and notably it is the one that they themselves normally use. But I invoke this nomenclature here less to defend my own use of it than because it vividly concretizes the difference between modernity and what I call entanglement. It also confirms just how intimately these two are related insofar as both exemplify moments of capitalism's culture. In repeatedly making its own mobile landscape, capitalist modernity inevitably marks out its fluctuating backcountries and shores and, in the context of colonialism and postcoloniality, the structures of sentiment to which this topography corresponds.

While frequently opposed, the Malay and the Aru share their common emergence out of specific "structures of feeling" that pervade the imagining of community on Aru's Backshore (Gupta and Ferguson 1992, 8). Notwithstanding some important gendered differences, the relations that Barakai women and men largely construct with, respectively, the Malay elsewhere of church, state, and commerce or the Aru elsewhere of a customary past tend to be disturbed by distance, ambivalence, and frustrated desires. If the former is the sometime object of seduction and danger, it just as often invites a cautious disavowal by Aruese of the things that the church, state, or island traders would put upon them. And if the Aru is annually celebrated as the charged source of a highly compromised communal identity, it also—notwithstanding appearances— implies an indirect refusal of "the spatial incarceration of the native" (Appadurai 1988) or of the move that would fix Barakai women and men as backward, Backshore primitives standing in for the persistence of primordial "custom" (I. *adat*).

Such evasions by the islanders should be understood as the effects of their negotiations with a certain politics of difference and of the inevitable contradictions in which people manage and make their lives rather than as evidence of "indigenous resistance." Repeatedly in such diverse settings as the telling of island histories, divers' transactions with seductive undersea spirits, intervillage disputes over sites of collection, ritual performances, and interactions with church and state representatives Barakai women and men problematized and unsettled the integrity of the "us" and the otherness of the "them." Along with a specific historicity, the concept of entanglement captures the predicament of these Barakai Aruese as they repeatedly confound any attempt to separate unproblematically "inside" and "outside," "here" and "there," "us" and "them." These kinds of separations form the foundational ground on which theories of resistance and political revolutions necessarily reside but are inadequate to understanding the banality of the day-to-day concessions and entangled solutions that are the basic stuff of Barakai peoples' lives.[4] Any attempt, therefore, to reduce these lives to the terms of a strict oppositional logic risks either aggrandizing power or romanticizing resistance (Abu Lughod 1990), while at the same time glossing over the complexity of the partial, provisional inhabitings by Aruese of two intertwined, incomplete, and, at times, antagonistically related elsewheres.

Rather than an oppositional stance, at issue here is what Homi Bhabha has called "the uncanny of cultural difference": that which transpires when, abandoning all its usual essentialist trappings, cultural difference enters the fray of provisional and hybrid accommodation and "as the strangeness of the familiar . . . becomes more problematic, both politically and conceptually . . . when the problem of cultural difference is ourselves-as others, others-as-ourselves, that borderline" (1989, 72). The shifting negotiations with the Aru and the Malay that surface in and shape the strategies and expectations of Barakai women and men mean that neither achieves the status of a full-fledged representability; neither the Aru nor the Malay is ever successfully stabilized or made fully present in topography, as a crucial marker of community on the Backshore or as a definition on which women and men can draw to define and position themselves. Beyond such determinations, the Malay and the Aru also shatter the topography that in any simple sense might be seen as underlying the contrast between center and periphery, metropolis and margins. Yet at the same time, the shifting accommodations of Barakai women and men with these alternatives confirm modernity's success in effecting its characteristic displacements. Backshore Aruese do not feel themselves entitled to full citizenship in, as it were, the Malay, while the

Aru that they annually invoke in performance is increasingly figured there as the disappearing past of yet another elsewhere. Hybridity here comes with a cost and is no easy compromise solution. The fluctuating and vexed connections that Barakai women and men forge with what they see as, respectively, the Aru and the Malay serve then as a corrective to theories of hybridity that celebrate its liberating and subversive potentials without also tallying its costs. Across the different chapters of this book, I explore these alternative, intertwined dimensions to the makings of a community that imagines itself as provisional, internally rent, and somehow beholden to and bereft of identity vis-à-vis its elusive Aru and Malay partners.

A preliminary mapping is necessary. In what follows in this introduction I conjure poetically a series of scenes emergent under conditions of entanglement. In so doing my intent is to evoke some of the complexities that correspond to the existential predicament from within which Backshore Aruese conduct their lives. While largely historical, I have selected these particular scenes of entanglement for their relevance to contemporary conditions in Aru. The first scene calls up the dramatic fluctuations of trade's on- and off-seasons in the island capital in the latter half of the nineteenth century. Wallace serves again as guide, since his stay in the archipelago in 1857 spans the period of extreme quiet preceding the arrival of commerce to Dobo and its bustling heights when anyone who was himself not a trader became unimaginable (Wallace 1962 [1869], 329). The second scene follows commodity circulation both on Aru's Front- and Backshores and looks at the commercial division of labor between coastal and interior peoples on Barakai itself. "Super Sharks," the third and last scene of entanglement homes in on the bust and boom cycles that have long described Aru's trade in the luxury products such as bird of paradise, mother-of-pearl, and shark fins for which the archipelago to this day is known. In the two sections that follow these scenes, I begin to map out the topographies of desire that are woven through their different entanglements. "Trading Cities" asks about the less visible aspects of trade and the desires, expectations, memories, and imaginations inherent to the institution of the market. The section that succeeds this one considers how the especially restless form of consumer desire and the sense of scarcity fostered under capitalist regimes takes a specifically Aru form when cross-cut by the debt relations that commonly bind Aruese to

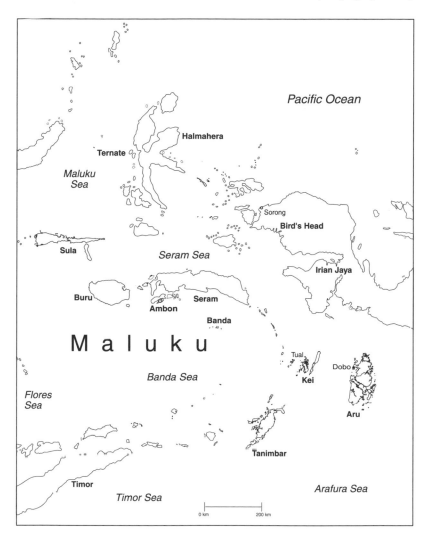

2. Map of the Moluccas and Irian Jaya

foreign traders. All these different sections build on each other, each successive one providing additional depth and filling out the initial differentiation of on and off trade seasons in the nineteenth-century island capital with which I began. The final section returns to the present, to the Aru and the Malay, and the position of Barakai within the Indonesian nation-state under the former regime of the country's recently deposed President Suharto.

Dobo, 1857

Toward the end of June during his second residence in the Aru capital, Wallace describes how the Chinese traders in Dobo killed for their farewell party the pig that they had been fattening since their arrival to the archipelago at the onset of the trade season—"for how could the Chinamen exist six months without a feast of pig?" (1962 [1869], 335)—and how he partook of its pork along with a bowl of bird's-nest soup that little impressed him. Along with the "growing porker" (ibid.), Wallace's two residences in Dobo, separated by his six-week stay in Wanumbai, frame the unfolding activities of the 1857 Dobo trade season. With much vivid detail, Wallace documents the transformation of the forlorn spit of land—"desolate in the extreme" (327)—on which he landed in early January into the "full to overflowing" trading community of Aru some six months later (361). And just as quickly as the pig met its final destiny, so, too, the mass exodus of fifteen Makassar praus on July 2, one of which bore Wallace, and in their wake some hundred smaller boats from the Moluccan islands of Seram, Goram, and Kei, whose crews catered to the various needs of the trading community, brought an abrupt end to the season. It would have meant a sudden draining of Dobo of all the sights, sounds, and amusements that were so meticulously recorded by Wallace and that had animated the Aru capital during the previous months as part and parcel of the great "shuffle of things" in this far corner of the Netherlands East Indies (Bacon 1594 in Pels 1988, 103). Since the stores, warehouses, and makeshift dwellings that had been erected early in the season would now be abandoned or dismantled—the latter with an eye toward business the following year on the part of the headmen of the communities surrounding Dobo, who charged land rent and anchorage money, and of the renowned carpenters and boatbuilders from neighboring Kei (Bik 1928 [1824], 44; de Hollander 1898, 525)—barely a ghost of the former trade entrepôt would have been left behind. Only the graves of the twenty-odd people who had passed away during the 1857 season would have betrayed the capital's recent bustling commerce: the simple fenced-in carved wooden headposts of the Muslims along with the fancier solid granite tombstones inscribed with red, blue, and gold characters and brought from Singapore by some of the wealthier Chinese (Wallace 1962 [1869], 366).

"Dobbo, in the Trading Season." Reprinted from Wallace 1962 [1869], 360.

One of the things that struck Wallace most about Dobo was the highly diverse and cosmopolitan character of the trading community that annually gathered in this remote outpost "to look for their fortune" or, as he further clarified this expression, "to get money any way they can" (335). A few of Dobo's notables he singled out for closer inspection, including an old Buginese *hajl* who customarily made an evening round of the town "in all the dignity of flowing green silk robe and gay turban" and tailed by two boys who carried his sirih and betel boxes (335), the Javanese who acted as master of ceremonies for Dobo's cockfighting ring (363)—a chief nightly entertainment along with football and the music of tomtoms, Jew's harps, fiddles, and "melancholy Malay songs" (362)—as well as "spruce Chinamen" in blue trousers and white jackets who sported long queues braided with red silk and socialized in the mornings and evenings (335).

But for the most, Wallace had little to say in favor of Dobo's population. What surprised him was less, in today's terms, its multicultural composition than the peacefulness with which its "motley, ignorant, bloodthirsty, and thievish" members went about their own affairs (336). Wallace registers the effect of the Dutch presence in the islands and the acknowledgment of this authority by Aru headmen and the "chief traders of the place"—who jointly were responsible for keeping order in the absence of colonial representatives. Yet he singles out trade, in a formulation strikingly reminiscent of Mauss, as "the magic that keeps all at peace" (336; cf. Mauss 1967 [1925]). But if one confronts Wallace's account with other nineteenth-century sources from approximately the mid-century on, especially those of the government commissioners charged with settling disputes on their (usually) annual visits to the islands, then it would seem that the combination of commerce and "civilization" can just as easily be seen as aggravating rather than alleviating strife and violence.

Along with the regular tensions that appear to have accompanied trading in Aru, repeated mention is made of conflicts among Aruese over access to sites of collection (Mailrapport 1880, 6392: no. 128+, ARA; van Hoëvell 1890, 25), between these collectors and the traders over debt payments (Bleeker 1856, 92; van Eijbergen 1866, 239), and regarding accusations by Aruese men of the traders' mistreatment of their women and other abuses (Brumond 1853, 78, 293; van Doren 1854, 38–56). In the mid-1880s another source of discontent and frequent disturbance for the already volatile Aruese diving population was added when Sech Said Baadilla, the lieutenant of the Arab community in Banda, received permission to dive for pearl oysters off of Aru's Backshore and around the same time Australians also began to fish in this area. In 1893 the colonial government published an ordinance punishing diving by outsiders within Aru's territorial waters—reckoned as three English sea miles from the coast—which were reserved for the local population's own habitual collection of oysters, mother-of-pearl shell, and trepang (Beversluis and Gieben 1929, 190; van Kol 1903, 223). It is clear that at times Backshore communities received some sort of retribution from these companies for fishing in their territory, and I was told on Barakai of some large "manila" gongs that in this context had been given to several communities as a payment.[5] Since, however, two warships were regularly dispatched to keep the peace on the Backshore during the diving season and a colonial source directly attributes the placement of a *controleur* in Dobo in 1903 to the repeated conflicts between Aruese and the pearling companies, it is doubtful how forthcoming or effective such retribution really was (Beversluis and Gieben 1929).[6]

Between the 1880s and 1915 several full-fledged revolts broke out on the Backshore that took a variety of forms and coincided not only with the arrival of the pearling companies but also with the consolidation of Dutch rule in the islands (van Hoëvell 1890, 27).[7] If the colonial presence was crucial in sparking this kind of resistance, the forms that these movements tended to assume were, explicitly or implicitly, thoroughly wrapped up with the workings of trade in the archipelago. Thus, the most violent and extreme of these movements called for the banishing of all trade from Aru along with the larger colonial apparatus as the precondition for clearing the way for a mass return of dead ancestors to the islands. Others envisioned the exile of only a handful of trade's main representatives or the rectification by the colonial authorities of some of the most egregious of the latter's abuses.

While such confrontations had everything to do with trade, they also must have repeatedly hindered and disturbed it—as, indeed, they at times do today (chapter 3). In the same way conflicts as far afield as British India could also reverberate in Aru—albeit more mildly. The colonial officer van der Crab, for instance, notes a three-year hiatus between 1856 and 1859 in the import of elephant tusks to Aru, which Buginese traders in the islands attributed to war in the British colonies (van der Crab 1862, 89). Given the importance of this "medium of payment" (D. *betaalmiddel*) in island exchange, the halt in its import must have affected not only the balance of trade but also such things as marriage, in which the payment of a tusk by the groom's to the bride's people formed a prerequisite for the union of at least some Aruese couples.

Much the same can also be said of the products collected by Aruese, the prices, availability, and demand for which tended to vary greatly. Van der Crab remarks regarding the trade statistics of 1859 that the price of mother-of-pearl had risen considerably in recent years, owing to the relatively new demand for this product in Europe in addition to the older China market. Yet he also notes that, by contrast, the trepang price had failed to reach its former heights as a result of "the disturbances in China [which] cause this article to rise and fall in value" (1862, 90–91). Price fluctuations were often dramatic in Aru, for a host of reasons, not all of which were directly market-related. Depletion of the pearl and trepang banks is one reason frequently given (de Hollander 1898, 520; van Hoëvell 1890, 30), "bad faith and laziness" on the part of the local population is another that traders gave to at least one colonial official (van der Crab 1862, 85), while the "conniving" practices of Buginese and Chinese traders are factors that the colonizers repeatedly singled out (van Eij-bergen 1866, 223, 239; van Hoëvell 1890, 38). Warfare was another recurring source of disturbance.[8] All of this makes it both difficult and ill-advised to try to write any predictable pattern into the annual shift of on and off commercial seasons in the archipelago. Such seasonal fluctuation was always subject to interruptions, shifts in consumption and collection patterns, depletions, and delays that necessarily made trade a much more erratic and often violent business than the even, harmonious exchange idealized by Wallace.

Every House Is a Store

A recurrent source of mild shock for European visitors who stopped in Aru before the turn of the century was the quantity, variety, and especially the luxury of many of the articles to be found in Dobo stores. They seem to have been especially taken aback because quite a number of these goods were purchased not only by the traders but by Aruese themselves. "As strange as it may seem," writes van der Crab in 1862, "that butter, sardines, saucis de Boulogne, dessert biscuits and other European provi-and are imported to Aru in relatively large quantity, it is nonetheless true that, besides the traders, several natives buy such things, maybe at times out of curiosity for the contents or taste or to become the owner of the decorative tin or glasswork in which they are contained; several dozen bottles of champagne were in 1859 rapidly dispensed with" (90). After two months' residence in Aru's capital, Wallace could confidently declare, "Every house [is] a store" (1962 [1869], 335). In addition to the more mundane things desired by Aruese like "knives, choppers, swords, guns, tobacco, gambier, plates, basins, handkerchiefs, sarongs, calicoes, and arrack," some stores also had tea, sugar, wine, biscuits, and the like for the traders, while others "were full of fancy goods, china ornaments, looking glasses, razors, umbrellas, pipes, and purses, which take the fancy of the wealthier natives" (ibid.). At least since Wallace's time, perhaps as much as a century earlier, and up until the Second World War, bronze gongs, elephants' tusks, and porcelain—or "the wealth of the Aru people"—also formed part of the cargo that regularly arrived at the archipelago (ibid., 368; Earl 1853, 103; Sperling 1936, 149).

Along with the abundance and variety of goods found in Aru, the cheapness with which many articles of European manufacture could be obtained in the islands did not go unremarked in the accounts of visitors. An Englishman noted with some delight in 1898: "In all the stores you can buy European articles—for instance straw hats, soap, cotton clothes, canvas boots, plates and dishes, gaudy colored handkerchiefs, and even clothes are to be purchased for very moderate sums considering the great journey they have made. I bought some long, cane deck chairs and many other little knick-knacks of European manufacture" (Cayley-Webster 1898, 198). Some forty years earlier, Wallace's assessment of the same situation was more sober. Following a long aside on what can only be described as the discontents of modernity, the naturalist concluded that his reflections had been triggered by the observation "that in one of the most remote corners of the earth savages can buy clothing cheaper than the people of the country where it is made; that the weaver's child should shiver in the wintry wind, unable to purchase articles attainable by the wild natives of a tropical climate, where clothing is mere ornament or luxury, should make us pause" (1962 [1869], 364).

Nor was the circulation of such articles limited to Dobo and its immediate surroundings. Some Aruese came in from the "back of the country" with the produce they had collected during the previous months to sell to the traders in the capital (ibid., 329). Others, notably those of the so-called trepang communities of Barakai Island, waited until the traders came to them (Bik 1928 [1824], 73).[9] Dobo was, as one Dutchman put it, the locus of "the wholesale trade" (D. *groothandel*), but traders in the capital commonly sent their representatives across the archipelago in small native craft—usually purchased in Kei en route to Aru or from Kei islanders who came to Dobo during the trade season (Earl 1853, 103; van Hoëvell 1890, 38)—to obtain Backshore luxuries directly at the sites of collection (de Hollander 1898, 525). Such emissaries were called in Malay *toekang petak* (ibid.). Translated roughly, this term means the person in charge of a "compartment" or "cabin," perhaps because the goods used in payment for trade products were kept in such places on board their boats. These petty traders usually stayed several months on the Backshore from their arrival sometime in February to the end of the diving and collection season in May or early June. As early as 1824, Bik mentions three Chinese agents of Makassarese merchants who by late April, when he arrived at Barakai, had already spent two months in Apara buying trepang (Bik 1928 [1824]). In 1862 the Barakai community of Gomo-gomo boasted in addition to its eleven traders—five Buginese and six "Malays"—and their appointed head—a man named Laibo—the crews of all these different traders' boats, who came predominantly from the Moluccan island of Goram and from Buton off of south Sulawesi (van Eijbergen 1866, 320). All together these people numbered approximately one hundred. Although the main concentration seems to have been on the southern tip of Barakai in the contiguous villages of Longgar and Apara, the traders spread themselves out across the different island communities. In 1888, for instance, two "Makassarese" or "Buginese"—undoubtedly traders—are listed as residing in Mesiang (population 135), while there were twelve such men and seven women in Longgar (population 230), seventeen men in Apara (population 197), and nine in Bemun (population 85) (van Hoëvell 1890, 11).

A look at the names of the traders who were compensated for damage to their houses and wares in a court trial held in June 1893 following a rebellion on Barakai suggests the high diversity of the island's trading population. Quite a number of the names are Chinese, while the title *daen* (properly *daeng*) before proper names indicates a Buginese origin. One name, Abdul Salam, is probably Arabic, while a few others like "Honey" (*Madoe*) and "Rat" (*Tikoes*) are presumably nicknames. According to the report, the traders due to receive compensation included nine resident in Apara (Abdul Salam, Langale, Batjo Kalankarie, Daen Pawara, Ingtai, Palalo, Manloeka, Moesa, Tamalaga), eight in Longgar (Tan Kwan Tjai, Oei Hie Hoan, Seng Tjoan, Daen Baoe, Madoe, Wa Kasso, Daoeda, Sempo), seven in Bemun (Daen Paliwan, Tonga Patola, Salewa, Tikoes, Palarie, Wanalisa, Batjo), one in Mesiang (Daen Mangesa), and only two in Gomogomo (The Thie, Daen Matola) (Mailrapport 1893, 6503: nos. 858+, ARA).

Along with the simpler goods brought by these traders to Barakai, tusks, gongs, porcelain, and cloth made their way to the Backshore, while alcohol was another crucial and probably early ingredient in commercial exchanges. Trade ties that may have had greater or lesser political significance also linked the more shifting settlements of the Barakai interior to the coastal communities of the island's collectors and thus to chains of commerce and communication that radiated out from Dobo to the far extremes of the archipelago. The colonial official Bik, probably the first Dutchman to visit Barakai in a very long time, summarized this relationship: "Behind the village the land is fertile, the inhabitants plant some rice, lots of maize, tubers, sugarcane, and make oil, which articles they supply to the trepang villages, who plant nothing, and through which they obtain their share of the cloth, arak, gongs, etc.; that the traders retail out to trepang villages like Affara [sic], Longar [sic]" (Bik 1928 [1824], 73). Another colonial official suggested that some of the interior peoples were subject to the coastal trading communities whose inhabitants were all divers and who possessed the richest pearling grounds of Aru (Brumond 1853, 75). Whether the latter indeed once exercised some authority over the horticulturalists of the interior, the ongoing importance of a ceremonial cycle that today links four of the five Barakai communities suggests that they may have been joined by more extensive connections in the past and, if so, that these probably turned upon the relationship between coast and interior. While all four participating villages—Mesiang, Bemun, Longgar, and Apara—have been located on the coast since the early nineteenth century, the annual performance dramatizes the interconnection between them as that of former forest peoples represented by the contemporary communities of Mesiang and Bemun versus those of Longgar and Apara, whose inhabitants can claim ongoing residence on the coast. My guess is that the sequence of performances that today annually inaugurates the diving and collection season on Barakai formerly played a part in the political organization of regional trade (chapter 4).

As early as 1735, treaties were signed by the "headmen" (M. *orang kaya*) of three Barakai communities—Longar (Longgar), Afairat (Apara) and Oeree (Vree), as well as by the community of Krey (Krei) on Trangan Island with the Vereenigde Oostindischen Compagnie (VOC), or Dutch East India Company.[10] According to the terms of the treaty, the summoned headman promised "as loyal subjects" to deliver all the hawksbill shell and mother-of-pearl shell that they collected to none other than the Honourable Company (*Corpus Diplomaticum* 5, vol. 96: 232–33).[11] The signing of these treaties followed several decades in which the VOC searched the archipelago for things of commercial value while at the same time attempting to bring Aru within the monopolistic orbit of the Banda Islands. The VOC's primary aim during the previous century had

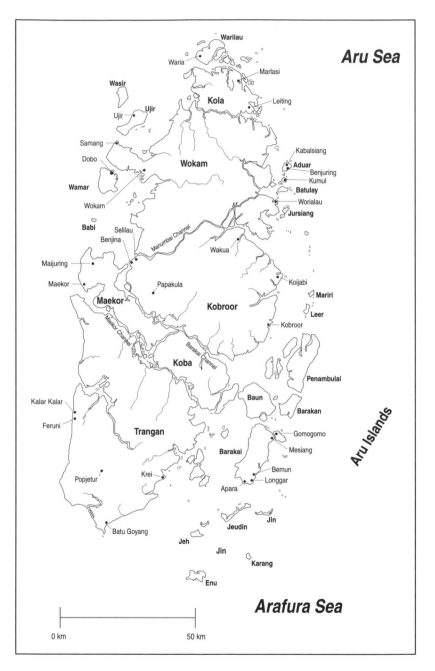

3. Map of the Aru Islands

been the imposition of a trade monopoly in the Moluccas with a special focus on Banda, the renowned source of nutmeg and mace, in addition to Ambon and its surroundings, where cloves were found and subsequently cultivated under the company's direction (Chauvel 1990, 16–23; Hanna 1978). In 1623, less than twenty years after Aru's official "discovery" by the Dutch in 1606 (Riedel 1886, 248), the VOC wrote into the treaties they signed that year with "all kings" (D. *alle connighen*) a prohibition for Aruese on traveling or trading in places other than Banda and Ambon without a company pass (Stapel 1943, 32–40; *Corpus Diplomaticum* 3, vol. 91: 180).[12] Presumably the lack of success of these agreements led to their reiteration in 1645, when again local headmen were committed to trading exclusively with Dutch-governed Banda.

By 1635 the VOC began to encourage Christian proselytizing in Aru in the hope that this contact would contribute to the reestablishment of old commercial ties between this archipelago and Banda (Meilinck-Roelofsz 1962, 222; Wurffbain 1931, 102). Portuguese sources mention Aruese who traded sago and birds of paradise alongside them in these spice islands. But all the old trade connections between Aru and Banda were brought to a dramatic halt by the extermination of almost the entire Bandanese population in the first quarter of the sixteenth century by Governor General Jan Pieterszoon Coen (Swadling 1996, 30; Villiers 1981, 736).[13] The renewal of this trade under a VOC monopoly would have enabled the Dutch to cut down on the high costs of importing food supplies from Java to Banda through the import of sago and garden produce from Aru (Swadling 1996, 30; Bickmore 1868, 249; van Leur 1955, 141; Riedel 1886, 248). It would also have assured the Banda nutmeg plantations of a steady supply of slaves (Meilinck-Roelofsz 1962, 222; Riedel 1886, 248).

Company and Christianity worked hand in hand in Aru. A *cranck-besoecher* appointed by the Dutch Reformed Church to assist sick members of the community with solace and prayer apparently spent much of his long residence in Aru combing its beaches for "rarities or sea crops" and was the first to report the presence of pearl oysters in the archipelago.[14] The report also mentions the ignorance on the part of the local population regarding this "preciosity of the sea," while the absence of local divers was noted shortly thereafter (Coolhaas 1960–1979, vol. 3, 16 December 1660: 315–16; ibid., 25 January 1667: 530). Until 1724, when the first mention is made of thirty mother-of-pearl shells from

Aru, hawksbill shell, coconut oil, and slaves were the main "products" collected by the voc sergeant posted in the archipelago (Generale Missiven VII 1713–25, 30 November 1724: 711). Beginning in the 1720s, Dutch traders from Banda also began to look for trepang in Aru (Swadling 1996, 153).

Recent archeological investigation on Barakai has uncovered trade entrepôts or distribution centers of considerable size that date from the late eighteenth to the early and mid-nineteenth centuries. The Australian team that carried out the research postulates an early-nineteenth-century date for the site Sirlasi, the ancestral village of the inhabitants of Longgar, Apara, and Gomogomo, on the basis of the ceramic and glass bottle assemblage found there (Veth et al. n.d.). Finds at Sirlasi included a glass bottle with a round lozenge that reads "John Alberty Vieux Cognac 1815 Bordeaux" in addition to Dutch and Chinese porcelain sherds, mangrove shellfish, and occasional dugong bones (ibid.). Another site of archeological investigation on Barakai, the cape Goljurun to the north of Bemun, was probably abandoned before Sirlasi and thus as early as the late eighteenth century. Today, the Bemunese community claims Goljurun as the site of their ancestral village Wanusumor or, in Malay, Seltimor. For this reason the cape receives a share of white plates in the communal distribution of plates that concludes Bemun's annual performance (chapter 7).

When Bemunese themselves occasionally spoke of the sites, they repeatedly stressed the large and impressive size of these ancestral communities and the number of their inhabitants. In their references to migration and settlement, women and men would usually name sites in the forest, each linked to a fam whose members gardened and who gravitated around a large coastal "city." According to most Bemunese, their ancestral community of Wanusumor was just such a city. It was so densely populated, some claimed, that its inhabitants brushed shoulders as they passed each other on the pathways that coursed through the city, and if all these people cried out in unison, the reverberations of all these voices conjoined caused leaves to fall from the city's many trees.

It would, indeed, be difficult to exaggerate the intensity and amount of seasonal traffic on Barakai during much of the nineteenth century. Take this description of the lively scene of collection recorded by a colonial officer who visited the island in the 1820s:

Vorkay [*sic*], an island lying exposed to the ocean at the southeastern extremity of the group, is of great importance from its pearl fishery. At a distance of eight miles to the eastward lay several smaller islands, between which and Vorkay the trepang banks are situated. At low water hundreds of men, with their wives and children, may be perceived wading from Vorkay towards these islets, (the water being only two to three feet deep), carrying a basket on their backs, and having in their hands a stick provided with an iron point. When the water is deeper than this, they make use of canoes. For fishing on the banks situated at a greater distance, the Arafuras use a prahu, constructed for this purpose in which they embark with the entire family. They have great beams, and the stern runs up a high curve, while two planks project forward from the bows.[15] . . . The prahu is propelled by a large sail made of rushes which folds up like a fan, (in a manner similar to the sails of Chinese junks), set upon a tripod mast of bamboos, while it is steered by two rudders.[16] (Kolff 1840, 175–76)

Although, following the annual departure of the traders, there must have been the expectation among the islanders that the next year they would again return—not the least because of their own debts with the latter—it is not clear when men and women would begin to collect sea products. Today, for instance, owing to climatic conditions that seem to have been the same a century ago, diving begins with the onset of the west monsoon in early October and ceases sometime in April, when the arrival of the east winds makes the seas off of Barakai cloudy and rough. Several sources claim that collection began before the traders arrived to the Backshore. Others suggest that the men would only dive and the women and children gather sea products on the tidal flats after the traders had paid the price of trepang and mother-of-pearl with goods given to them on credit (Bik 1928 [1824], 702)

Inevitably there were lulls and interruptions in trade and probably even entire seasons in which for whatever reason no collection took place. While commercial activity must have sporadically abated, this remains largely unmentioned in the sources, which tend to document the high moments of commercial exchange. Not surprisingly, these were also the times when government officials would have had most to gain by their input and control over activities in the archipelago. Not all such commercial traffic would have had the same implications for Barakai peoples. Unlike the trepang and mother-of-pearl booms of the nine-teenth century in which—whatever else one might say about the rela-tions between the islanders and the traders—Barakai women and men were actively engaged, the arrival of the pearling companies meant more than anything else their systematic exclusion from the most lucrative forms of commerce in the archipelago. When in 1905 the colonial gov-ernment leased rights to dive off of Aru to the Batavia-based but in reality Australian Celebes Trading Company, which had merged with the Baadilla brothers, 150 loggers and seven schooners manned by a crew of some fifteen hundred persons populated Backshore waters (Beversluis and Gieben 1929, 192). A negligible few if any of these people were Aruese (ibid., 195; Merton 1910, 144). With all the fluctuations in commercial relations described above, the engagement of Barakai islanders in trade, while overridingly intensive, was therefore also at times dramatically challenged and undermined.

Super Sharks

I heard little about shark fins during my first year in Aru in 1986. When I returned to the islands after a six-month break in July 1987, people talked of nothing else.[17] One government official in Dobo claimed that there were now over two hundred motorboats in Aru. Just a casual impression of the activity in the capital suggested that all of these were somehow engaged in shark fishing. Since I had left the islands the previous Decem-ber, the local price of fins had soared 150 percent from Rp 30,000 to Rp 75,000 for the white or so-called Super shark, and Rp 65,000 per kilo for the black shark.[18] Everywhere, along the docks and in back of the traders' houses, men were at work constructing new and larger boats—a given trader's second, third, or even fourth. These would soon augment the already heavy traffic plying the Arafura Sea between Aru and the Indone-sian province of Irian Jaya in western New Guinea in pursuit of a com-modity that had taken on boom proportions in the archipelago. In al-most every store I entered in Dobo, one or more persons—the trader, tradeswoman, members of their family, and often young boys employed for the task—were furiously making or repairing shark nets. When the work had been briefly laid aside, the floor was often treacherously thick with the fine white cord and the sturdier green and blue ropes of half-finished nets. Signs of sharks, in short, were everywhere: tail and dorsal fins drying in low piles in the sun, their smell permeating the capital's streets, houses, and stores; all the busyness and labor on boats and nets; the new consumer goods in the homes of Dobo traders—especially TVs, VCRs, and bedroom sets with multiple pieces—and on the wives a surplus of shiny gold. The Primadonna movie theater, as its name suggests the first of its kind in the archipelago, had also been opened with shark money by one of the capital's most prominent ethnic Chinese traders.

Only later would the repercussions of the boom reach the Backshore, although rumors were already rampant when I arrived there of traders who had become fabulously rich overnight, of the different takes in kilos, of Super versus other sharks, and of the boats the traders had built and the commodities their wives had bought. All of this talk circulated along-side the stories of the handful of islanders who had worked on the boats and had made it all the way to Sorong in Irian Jaya. On my next visit in 1994, the effects of the fin boom and especially its dramatic follow-up—the boom in pearl oysters and their subsequent decimation by disease—were readily apparent on Barakai. As the shark population around Aru had begun to dwindle within only a few years, most traders redeployed their newly acquired boats for pearl diving, in what now became a much more technologically assisted and intensified mode of collection. In a decided departure from older practices and relations that until this time had linked the Barakai traders to the islanders who dove off of their boats, they now—almost exclusively—employed men from Kei and south Sulawesi. These men were willing to spend several weeks at sea and to work with oxygen tanks. Some traders still reserved a boat for the more traditional diving of the islanders who shopped at their stores. Many more did not, which meant, in turn, that Barakai families had to build or purchase their own small motor-powered vessels in order to continue diving.

In part the exclusion of Aruese was self-imposed. While some Barakai men had tried their hand at shark fishing, many complained of the long stretches away from home. In addition to this common objection, most men had several others to add when it came to diving with tanks for a trader—the oxygen tanks were considered unsafe and the dangers of this type of diving greater than those of "natural" diving, which was the customary mode on Barakai. But men singled out especially the long hours and the hold the trader had over them once they were at sea as this type of diving's greatest drawback. "It's not even dawn yet and you're already diving," one man said of why he preferred to stay at home. By the same account, the relative control the traders had over divers from elsewhere as opposed to Aruese was for them a clear advantage. Still, many complained repeatedly about *deba-deba*, as the new divers were called, who "ran away" before paying their debts.[19] In an attempt to increase their authority over these divers, Aru's traders initiated regulation after regulation, including photographing and fingerprinting the deba-debas, registering them with the Dobo police, housing them all together in Backshore villages during the "off" periods, and, last but not least, materially indebting the divers to themselves. From early 1991 on the situation suffered a dramatic turnaround when Aru's oysters began to die by the hundreds from a mysterious disease.

I will have more to say about the deba-debas, the pearl oyster disease, and the implications of outside competition and the ecological devastation of the oyster beds for Barakai peoples (chapter 4). Here, I merely wish to foreground the shifts in collection patterns according to the whims of several fashion-driven luxury product markets, the erratic rhythm of bust-boom cycles, the crucial ecological dimension to Backshore collection, and the necessary adjustments, realignments, and refigurings of Aruese within this mobile and highly complex entanglement of sociocultural, politicoeconomic, and ecological conditions. In the relatively short ten years between my first and most recent visit to Aru (1984–94) I saw how Barakai islanders abandoned the collection of agar-agar, or Eucheuma seaweed, when a price drop in 1987 meant that the traders would no longer buy it.[20] I saw also how they negotiated the effects of the fin boom, including the initial reorientation of the traders away from diving and subsequently the radical redefinition of diving itself in the face of shark depletion. I saw, as well, how the ensuing marginalization of Aruese with respect to their characteristic form of livelihood sparked a minor renaissance in traditional boat building, how the kinds of debts the traders were willing to contract with islanders changed, how money transactions as opposed to credit became more common, and how by 1994, in the wake of the oyster disease, trepang replaced pearl oysters—practically if not symbolically—as the privileged object of Backshore collection.

While the rhythm of such shifts and redirections may in recent times have intensified through technological innovation and mounting irreversible ecological destruction, the fits and starts of the ten years between 1984 and 1994 were hardly exceptional for Aru. All the luxury products for which this archipelago has long been renowned—notably birds of paradise, edible bird's nests, trepang, mother-of-pearl shell, shark fins, and pearl oysters—have gone through bust and boom cycles, and in several cases more than once. Beyond these relatively short-term dramatic shifts, longer cycles of trade have implicated Aru for centuries in chains of commercial relations that extend far beyond the archipelago.

In *Plumes from Paradise*, Swadling maps outs the long-term trade cycles for outer Southeast Asia and their impact on New Guinea and the neighboring islands until 1920. While the earliest period of trade is not directly relevant to the theme of this book, it is worth noting that already in the context of the first cycle identified by Swadling, from approximately two thousand years ago to 250, C.E. birds of paradise were the main products sought by specialist traders in the region as well as the first to go through a cycle of boom and bust (Swadling 1996, 15–16). From about 300 C.E. until another plume boom in the late nineteenth and early twentieth centuries, bird of paradise were a subsidiary product within the now more important spice and aromatic bark trade. Nonetheless, Portuguese records mention birds of paradise skins traded in 1500 C.E. to Persia and Turkey, where they were used to decorate the headdresses of important officials (ibid., 62). Plumes and birds from Aru brought to Banda and exchanged there for textiles subsequently made their way to Melaka and from there to different parts of Asia, where they were brought by Bengali merchants. For example, plumes of the Greater Bird of Paradise, only found in Aru, probably first reached Nepal through this early trade and there became a crucial symbol of royalty (ibid.).[21] A seventeenth-century source reports the failure of VOC attempts to involve Aru more directly in the spice trade by inducing the inhabitants of Aru's west coast to plant nutmeg trees in exchange for some kind of honorarium (Wurffbain 1931, 100).

During Swadling's third long-term trade cycle, dominated by the collection of marine products for China, Dobo developed into a major trade entrepôt from the early nineteenth century as the source of several of the most sought-after products. Around the time world spice prices fell in the mid-seventeenth century, China under the recently established Manchu rule became a market for new trade products from Southeast Asia, especially mother-of-pearl, trepang, and edible bird's nests. The demand for these products was, in part, a stimulus for the great diaspora of Makassarese and Buginese throughout the archipelago in the late seventeenth and early eighteenth centuries (Curtin 1984, 158–78). Besides Buginese and Makassarese, who proved stiff competition for the voc in Aru, Europeans were also engaged in the marine product trade in the archipelago. In the early eighteenth century, for example, Aru's trepang trade was dominated by A. J. van Steenbergen, the resident of Banda, who deployed no fewer than seven trading vessels in the islands (Swadling 1996, 154). By the mid-eighteenth century the English also joined in the search for luxury goods desired by the Chinese. For them this search amounted to a desperate attempt to find a substitute for the silver that the Chinese demanded to the exclusion of virtually all else in exchange for their tea—the object of the newly acquired luxury taste of the English (Sahlins 1994; Swadling 1996, 277). In 1816, when following a brief British interregnum the Dutch regained the Indies and the recently established colonial government abandoned the former monopolistic trade practices of the voc, conditions were ripe for Dobo's ascendance in the luxury product trade. When the ban on emigration in China was lifted in 1860, large numbers of Chinese headed for Nanyang, the region they called the Southern Ocean. Along with such prominent cities as Singapore and Makassar, places like Dobo also became linked to Chinese trading networks. In fact it was largely as a result of the "silent wars" between England and the Netherlands in the nineteenth century over the control of trade in the Malay archipelago that these overseas Chinese were able to consolidate their influence (Post 1991, 70). Only with the arrival of the steamship and the founding of the Koninklijke Paketvaart Maatschappij (KPM) in 1888 were the Dutch able to direct inter-island trade toward places more profitable to themselves like Batavia and Surabaya in Java and away from the English competitor Singapore (ibid., 79).

If from the early eighteenth through much of the nineteenth century Dobo was a major entrepôt in the outer archipelago for China-bound marine products, it retained its importance in the context of the fourth and last of Swadling's long-term trade cycles. New or increased European interest in such Aru products as bird of paradise plumes, mother-of-pearl, and pearls, as well as in copra and minerals found elsewhere, predominate in the last trade cycle she identifies (Swadling 1996, 278). The plume boom together with the glorification of birds by European visitors to Aru at the expense of the archipelago's human inhabitants is the focus of the following chapter (chapter 2). Taking here "the pale poetic pearl" as an example, it is clear that if the price of mother-of-pearl rose according to novel French fashion demands in the late nineteenth century, the arrival of the pearling companies as this century drew to a close came in the wake of a new technological discovery (Melville in Joyce and Addison 1993, 193). In 1890 Mikimoto Kokichi successfully cultivated the first pearl, thereby founding an industry that to date has had profound implications for life in Aru. By the turn of the century, in the opinion of one historian, Dobo was a "paradise for adventurers, smugglers, and prostitutes" (Post 1991, 75) and in the words of another, "a new Klondike." (Clarence-Smith 1998, 38).[22] A small indication of the impact today of the recent boom in Aru's oyster industry is—as at the beginning of the century—registered in the numbers of prostitutes who in 1990 "expanded" to Aru from their home base in Batu Merah, Ambon.[23] At the height of the boom there were over two hundred women working in Dobo, while in 1994 in the wake of the oyster disease more than one hundred still remained in the capital. "Payment in Pearls, Not Money" proclaims one Surabaya newspaper sensationally, thereby drawing out the clandestine magicality that already infuses this and other kinds of commercial transactions (*Surabaya Minggu*, 4 March 1990).[24] As one of Aru's most prized commodities, pearls in all their alluring beauty crystallize in the newspaper article's title the magic secularly attached to this trade.

Trading Cities

In *Invisible Cities*, Italo Calvino writes of Euphemia, a trading city in the great country of Kublai Khan where merchants gather to exchange their wares at every solstice and equinox. Yet beyond the traffic in pistachio nuts and poppy seeds, or the transactions of bagged nutmeg for bolts of muslin, there is an implicit, more covert dimension to the trade of these men: "You do not come to Euphemia only to buy and sell," writes Calvino, "but also because at night, by the fires all around the market, seated on sacks or barrels or stretched out on piles of carpets, at each word that one man says—such as 'wolf,' 'sister,' 'hidden treasure,' 'battle,' 'scabies,' 'lovers'—the others tell, each one, his tale of wolves, sisters, treasures, scabies, lovers, battles. And you know that in the long journey ahead of you, when to keep awake against the camel's swaying or the junk's rocking, you start summoning up your memories one by one, your wolf will have become another wolf, your sister a different sister, your battle other battles, on your return from Euphemia, the city where memory is traded at every solstice and at every equinox" (Calvino 1972, 367). How does one think a marketplace?[25] How does one think the contribution of memories and imaginations and the structuring of feeling, desire, and expectation that are the less visible aspects of the traffic in things and the workings of trade? How does one think all of this in relation to a trade that has none of the regularized, idealized equivalence of Euphemia but is instead a hierarchical and fraught terrain where more often than not Aruese collectors get the raw end of the deal? And finally, how can one begin to ponder and engage the lives of women and men that in certain crucial respects are both radically detached from and dependent on an international and increasingly globalized market?

The marketplace, according to Stallybrass and White, is often the epitome of "local identity" at the same time that such identity would be continually undone by the movement of things and persons that defines the market's very life and existence (1986, 27). Rather than the deceptive self-sustaining locus of a stable identity, the marketplace and, by extension, market sites like Aru's Backshore are intersections and crossings of ways. They are at their very core beholden to and subject to a "beyond." Although the bulk of the markets Stallybrass and White use as examples tend to be more physically delimited and permanent than the seasonal and relatively dispersed thoroughfare of Aru's Backshore, they argue that the problematic familiarity with which most people know their own market may in fact inhibit its adequate understanding. "The tangibility of its boundaries implies a local closure and stability, even a unique sense of belonging, which obscures its structural dependence upon a 'beyond' through which this 'familiar' and 'local' feeling is itself produced. Thus in the marketplace 'inside' and 'outside' (and hence identity itself) are persistently mystified" (ibid., 28). In other words, the market is fissured in two important senses: first, by its intimate and elided relation to an

"outside" or "beyond" and, second, by the "inside" disruptions, depletions, and diversions that are themselves the signs of the market's imbri-
cation in faraway processes of consumption and production, extended
networks of trade and communication, global economic flows, as well as
more immediate ecological circumstances.

In economic terms Barakai women and men represent the supply side
of a volatile luxury product trade. For this reason, they are necessarily
attuned and responsive to remote places where the value of what Backshore Aruese collect is to an important extent defined by abrupt and
faraway shifts in fashion and taste. At the same time, the comings and
goings of traders figure much more prominently on the Backshore than
in the kinds of marketplaces discussed by Stallybrass and White. Stories
in which the islanders alienate their own means of reproduction, in
which a crucial interlocutor is absent and evasive, or that link the coming
of things to the alienation of close kin as a kind of fissuring of the self
seem to speak, among other things, to the socioeconomic conditions in
which Backshore lives are played out and to a certain mystification of
"inside" and "outside." And they do so in a language heavy with loss,
longing, and expectation. Some of the most nagging questions I grapple
with in this book first emerged out of listening to these stories. Why
should such a sense of loss be engraved so deeply? Why should identity
be pinned onto the gap opened up by an absence? How should something perceived as so intimately close come to seem so far away? And why
does the double preoccupation with connection and deficit appear so
inextricably entangled? I begin here to address the problematics opened
up by these questions by offering a few orienting remarks.

A particular configuration of circumstances and discursive effects—
only in part subsumable under the category of the socioeconomic—
abets and molds the production of a pervasive thematics of expectancy,
loss, and desire. This thematics informs and contours the two elsewheres
of Aru and Malay and provides the persistent tropes that shape such
things as the telling of histories and migrations, intervillage conflicts
over diving grounds, confrontations about ritual authority, and gender
relations. In the context of the annual performances that open trade on
Barakai, this thematics surfaces in the overriding sense of longing, exile,
and memory that lends these performances their compelling quality and
structures the actions, recollections, and feelings of participants. Subse-

quent chapters situate ethnographically the thematics I outline here. Suffice it to say for the moment that a number of different factors collaborate in overdetermining Backshore understandings of community and self so that they appear disturbed and haunted by an abiding sense of lack and incompletion. Seen in this light, absence surfaces in essentially two ways: as a self that is in part lost, alienated, elsewhere, and "beyond" or, from a slightly different angle, only present as a partially depleted, hollowed out, and provisional arrangement. The differences, entanglements, slidings into each other, and stark stand-offs of Aru and Malay are only one possible albeit pervasive way of addressing and figuring these depletions.

The makeup of the marketplace and the accentuation of its intrinsic beyondness by the dynamics of Backshore luxury trade contribute structurally to the production of a fissuring of community and self that is permeated by a strong sense of deficit. Siegel's work on the position of speakers of a lingua franca or the position of a not fully inhabited "I" sheds light on another aspect of this production. Although Siegel develops his argument with respect to circumstances different from those in Aru, it is nonetheless helpful in thinking through some of the predicaments that often pertain in commercial settings. Drawing on Maier's important work on the first writings in the Malay language under Dutch colonial rule in the Indies, Siegel describes how the lingua franca *melayu* developed in the interspace between speakers and was produced by their mutual mimicry and the reciprocal adoption of linguistic forms (Maier 1991; Siegel 1997). At this stage of its production, the lingua franca is neither tainted negatively nor is it positively legitimized by the in-built authority that comes to speakers of a first language and that lends them both a sense of mastery and the conviction that they have a place in the world (Siegel 1997, 16). As opposed to a mother tongue, which a speaker authoritatively embodies, a lingua franca offers—I would add, even compels—"a certain excursion, if not into a new identity, at least away from an old one" (ibid., 15). Add to this structural consideration a discursive one—the Dutch insistence that the first language of native Malay speakers was not in fact a language and that they therefore did not have the possibility of communicating with authority (ibid.). The position of the "I" in melayu was thus doubly destabilized: first, as a lingua franca and, second, as the lingua franca spoken as a first language by colonial subjects. By definition, as colonial subjects these women and men could never fully inhabit the places that their colonizers designated as proper, legitimate, civilized, and, in certain important respects, essentially European and white (chapter 2). As Siegel writes, echoing Maier, "one could only know [as the angst-ridden speaker of the lingua franca low Malay] that being in the world meant being nowhere locatable" (ibid., 17).

While noting these inherent limitations, Siegel advocates a shift in perspective to the possibilities made available to speakers of a lingua franca: specifically, the impulse it gives to search for a new identity, something that in the Indies took the form of an immense literary exploration and linguistic experimentation—a "staggering polyphony and heterogeneity in printed materials" (Maier in Siegel 1997, 17)—together with the formation of new ethnically unmarked audiences. Both the negative and positive dimensions of lingua franca are consistent with my own insights on the dynamics of commercial settings. Regarding the first, it is the structural incompleteness characteristic of the "I" of a lingua franca speaker as further enhanced and brought out by colonial repression and asymmetry that is relevant here. My point of departure is this kind of displacement rather than the production of the lingua franca in the interspace formed by speakers who, much as in Calvino's Euphemia, adopt and trade words, commodities, and the memories thereof on equal terms. As for those aspects of linguae francae that open rather than close off possibilities to their speakers, then especially the requirement of an excursion that distances or detaches them from an older identity and entails the concomitant production of a novel space resonates with what goes on among Backshore Aruese. There among the collectors of sea products for the international market, this space corresponds, I argue, to the "beyond" that they commonly associate especially with trade, missionization, and the Indonesian nation-state—or with what Barakai women and men gloss as the Malay as opposed to the Aru.

Let me pursue for a moment the analogy of language. When, in addition to a lingua franca, people also habitually speak a "local" language (I. *bahasa daerah*), then the question of their mutual relation and respective identities may arise. Keane, for instance, asks what shape the latter assumes once people begin to think of themselves as intrinsically linked to the "local" as opposed to—or, I would add, alongside—a national or international linguistic alternative (Keane 1997a). Similarly, what on

Barakai has come to be called the Aru has been discursively cordoned off and localized as the repository of adat, or customary practices (cf. Hoskins 1993). Under Dutch colonial rule adat was an alibi for customary or primitive law held to take slightly different forms in different communities. Subsequently, and especially since the mid-1960s under Suharto's New Order government, adat and its more elite cousin kebudayaan, or "culture," have been valorized as the locus of tradition (chapter 5; cf. Pemberton 1994). If a lingua franca opens for its speakers the possibility of a "beyond," it also points to something prior, an older identity, that its speakers would have left behind when they ventured into new linguistic spaces. Among Backshore pearl-diving communities, this prior and partially abandoned place of an older identity has come to be filled by the Aru as the site of an increasingly localized "custom" (I. adat) or "tradition" (I. tradisi). In sum, the analogy of a lingua franca applicable to commercial conditions as well as specifically to the Aruese distinction between the Malay and the Aru further brings out how the sense of a "beyond" emerges alongside an equally distanced space imbued with logical priority and therewith pastness.

On the Backshore, the close identification of adat with the "local" has succeeded in contaminating it with associations of primitivism and backwardness, as something out of sync with the former Suharto government's heavily prioritized national program of development and, more generally, with modernity.[26] One corollary is the recent official designation of virtually all Aru communities as "villages that have been left behind" (I. desa tertinggal). Beyond the discursive effects that position Backshore Aruese negatively with respect to development and modernity, the understanding that Barakai women and men have of themselves further enhances their ambivalent stance toward the Aru. The fact that they see themselves as travelers and outsiders, as people who hail from elsewhere, contains an implicit claim to knowing the world, to a certain savvy and familiarity with its ways, and at times even to an affinal connection with the Malay. This attitude stands in the way of an uncomplicated identification with the Aru. Because of their assertion of an outside provenance, the connection that specifically Bemunese annually establish with the Aru is derivative and rests on a somewhat tenuous genealogical claim: because many years ago their ancestors forged a connection to Barakai by killing the first autochthone they encountered on the island (a cassowary), Bemun's performative assertion to a place on Barakai rests not only on a connection to the ancestors but, via them, also to an animal. If somewhat in "stranger-king" fashion the Bemun community annually legitimizes its occupation of the village site and surrounding territories, the claims they make to this land are never consolidated through, for instance, marriage with original island inhabitants—in contrast then to Sahlins's famous example (1985, 73–103). Instead, genealogy remains at a remove, with the Aru, conquered in its emblematic cassowary form, banished to the wild rather than appropriated by Bemunese (chapter 6). Hence, with respect to the Aru just as the Malay, albeit for different reasons, Bemunese rather uncomfortably see themselves more as strangers than as kings.

A Pearl Worth Half Your Tribe

Thomas Hobbes observed, already long ago, that "by desire, we always signify the absence of the object. We may need something that we already possess, but we cannot be said to desire it. If desire is felt it is because of a lack" (Hobbes in Xenos 1989, 4). I have focused on the market as an institution and on its fostering of a sense of beyond among Backshore Aruese collectors. Here I consider the workings of the commodity itself and specifically how the complex and volatile commodity world in which Barakai has long been inserted contributes to the double production of desire and deficit. The production of consumer desire, or, in economic terms, the introduction of a notion of scarcity, has long been regarded as intrinsic to the operation of capitalist economies (Sahlins 1972; Xenos 1989). As a particular form of sentiment, however, consumer desire has always assumed different shapes at distinct historical moments and in disparate places. By the second half of the nineteenth century, aggressive insistence, codified expectations, and a taking for granted on the part of Aruese characteristically accompanied trade in the island capital.

> Living in a trader's house everything is brought to me as well as to the rest—bundles of smoked tripang, or bêche de mer, looking like sausages which have been rolled in mud and then thrown up the chimney; dried sharks' fins, mother-of-pearlshells, as well as Birds of Paradise, which,

however, are so dirty and so badly preserved that I have as yet found no specimens worth purchasing. When I hardly look at the articles, and make no offer for them, they seem incredulous, and, as if fearing they have misunderstood me, again offer them, and declare what they want in return—knives, or tobacco, or sago, or handkerchiefs. I then have to endeavor to explain, through any interpreter who may be at hand, that neither tripang nor pearl oyster shells have any charms for me, and that I even decline to speculate in tortoiseshell. (Wallace 1962 [1869], 329)

The passage betrays a comfortable familiarity on the part of Aruese with trading procedures and products—hence the anomaly with which Wallace confronted them when he resisted their commercial overtures in the form of precisely those goods that at the time took the fancy of Dobo traders. And hence, presumably, their own consuming passion for things like handkerchiefs. What Greenblatt calls the European dream, endlessly reiterated in the literature of exploration, of grossly unequal exchange along the lines of "I give you a glass bead and you give me a pearl worth half your tribe," is alleged to have led a brief historical existence in the archipelago (Greenblatt 1991, 110; cf. Pietz 1987, 41). Thus, in 1890 one Dutchman complained that since the natives were already well acquainted with the value of pearls, the days in which one could obtain the most beautiful of pearls for "an apple and an egg" were over (van Hoëvell 1890, 33).

From the available literature, it is impossible to know whether this prelapsarian fantasy ever took place in Aru or if it should simply be regarded as the retrospective projection of a high-ranking Dutch colonial officer. In view also of Thomas's astute observations concerning the liberal tendency to take "the irresistible magnetism of whites' commodities" for granted, one should avoid reading too much into either the pressing demands of Aruese vis-à-vis Wallace or their alleged naïveté in supposedly handing over their most precious trade products to obtain mundane European commodities like "apples and eggs" (Thomas 1991; 1992, 22). It is true, as has often been noted, that capitalism operates and expands by inciting an especially restless form of desire. At the same time, it is equally true that the forms and finalities of capitalism are never knowable or determined beforehand (Sahlins 1994). Just as one may not legitimately presuppose any natural "propensity to truck, barter and exchange one thing for another" (Smith 1976 [1904], 17), so, too, the cravings for particular things or for things in general are neither inborn nor—when and where identifiable—eternal and unchanging; indeed, such a static condition would be fatal for the capitalist economy, whether in its mercantile, industrial, or late industrial version. While Aru in most respects is what economists would regard as an entirely untapped market (although perhaps not an immediately attractive one), a kind of consumer desire has at times been consciously fostered by strategies like the commodity aesthetics deployed by some traders today in Backshore stores or by the alcohol addiction promoted by their predecessors in the past. Perhaps more perduringly, the relatively inchoate consumer desire that one finds today on the Backshore emerges in the context of more subtle exchanges and processes such as the tendency especially on the part of Barakai women to emulate the ethnic Chinese traders (chapter 4).

Like the international trade that excites it, the desire that today suffuses commerce on Barakai articulates itself less as a need or wish for particular things than as a more diffuse sense of deficit and longing. This desire is as mobile and dispersed as the undersea that provides the islanders with the main products of Backshore trade and that itself is a space simultaneously set off from and entangled within the debt bonds that link the islanders to their traders. When desire does crystallize forcefully in the actions and expectations of women and men, it does so not in the guise of a consumerism fixated on fulfillment through the acquisition of specific store-bought things. Instead the products that Barakai islanders themselves collect in the context of their debt ties to traders fetishistically condense all the seduction and, importantly, also the dangers identified by them with the Malay. Holding out the promise of excess, the enticing undersea spirit women who provide male divers with pearl oysters ensnare them in twinned relations of erotic expectation and debt. Beautified in return by the gifts of store-bought jewelry that Barakai men cast for them into the sea, these spirits personify a quirky twist on what is commonly understood as commodity fetishism (chapter 4). At the same time, these fantastic figures hint at the intimate footing with which Barakai islanders commonly confront the Malay, at the enticing aura that surrounds it, and at the coercion that, along with its temptations, is unavoidably part of the Malay's manifestations.

Runaway Topographies

Conjointly, Aru and Malay are figures for negotiating and recasting the various structural conditions and discursive circumstances that I have outlined above. They yield shifting configurations of community that cluster and fissure around a sense of beyond as well as around deficit and lack, and are fostered by the specific makeup and operation of the market, an erratic luxury product trade, the lingua franca–like "I" of commercial settings, the diffuse longing and indebtedness that permeates Backshore trade, as well as the crucial discursive effects of Dutch colonialism, missionization, and in the post-Independence period especially the former Suharto government's policies and programs. Rather than a foundation for the emergence of a sense of community or even multiple communities, the Aru and the Malay are figures of entanglement that achieve their most compelling realization for Bemunese women and men in the context of their community's annual performance. The figures chosen at this time of year as emblems of the Aru and the Malay are telling for the overriding movement and flight that in this setting animates each of them. Recalling the important tracing by Bemunese of ancestral ties to other Moluccan islands, the Malay is here a boat with curved prow and sternboards. Yet the Aru, too, asserts a genealogical connection in the shape of the first autochthone sighted by the ancestors on their arrival to Barakai—the cassowary known among the island's hunters for its especially shy, elusive, and flighty disposition.

The annual realization of the Aru and the Malay in their emblematic forms of cassowary and boat topographizes a space of flight in which Bemunese women, men, and children simultaneously take on the roles of both autochthone and outsider in a dramatic game of hide and seek. If the annual performance inaugurates the season of trade, it also, as I will show, inaugurates a space of commerce and translation in which the operative modes for Bemunese are exchange and a hospitality toward their others. It would be a mistake, however, to romanticize this openendedness and translatability; its very possibility rests on an act of violence and usurpation: the performance concludes with the radical exile of the Aru in cassowary guise along with the repression of all its material signs and memory. Thus, the dark underside to the space of commerce and translation that sets the terms for Bemun's engagement within increasingly globalized circumstances is, on the one hand, the violence of the community's own exclusion and marginality vis-à-vis the Malay and, on the other, the requirement of a forgetfulness toward what they see as their own Aru past.

Forgetfulness of one's past is, indeed, the price that many so-called indigenous peoples must pay for a legitimate place within the nation-state and a stake within a larger world. On Aru's Backshore, however, this price has not been fully paid—one reason, I believe, why Bemunese women and men continue to find relevance in the fraught difference of the Aru and the Malay. In the context of their annual performance, dramatization makes palpable the heavily debated and practiced flux in which both elsewheres are continually repositioned vis-à-vis each other. At the same time, such ongoing assessments and ambivalences regarding the imagined repertoire of conceptions of community are only possible because Barakai Island and Aru's Backshore more generally remain unevenly integrated within the Indonesian nation-state.

Until the recent monetary crisis and the ensuing political upheaval that precipitated President Suharto's resignation on May 21, 1998, the "success" of the New Order regime that he inaugurated in the wake of a coup and terrible violence in 1965–66 had been widely proclaimed by politicians and academics in the United States and Europe. While economists and political scientists have tended to focus on the country's growing prosperity, the impressive rise of a middle class, and the general political stability of this Southeast Asian "tiger," increasing numbers of anthropologists have analyzed how culture itself became harnessed under the New Order to the state project of forging a unity out of the country's remarkable human, linguistic, and religious diversity. John Pemberton's groundbreaking book *On the Subject of "Java"* is the most original and sustained discussion of how normative concepts like "traditional values," "ritual," and "cultural inheritance" were deployed by the Suharto regime in its dominant interest of fostering stability and order. To my knowledge it is the only study of contemporary Indonesia that interrogates the ways in which the implicit taken-for-grantedness of "culture" secures the repressive normality that for so long and until recently underwrote the New Order's much celebrated apparent "success." Regarding Aru, Pemberton's book has been especially stimulating in helping me think through the implications of the phantasmatic forms of New Order self-reproduction as they also touched and quietly transformed places quite different and distant from Java (chapter 5).

Still, the New Order's ability to penetrate and alter the most intimate aspects of day-to-day existence varied considerably across the great span of territory claimed by Indonesia. The state's capacity to reach into the backcountries and uplands of the archipelago's many islands transpired through such means as the national school system, government development programs, rural health clinics, in- and out-migration, as well as through the national media such as radio and only recently television. Probably the single most important factor contributing to the gradual and intermittent New Orderization of Aru's Backshore as I knew it between the mid-1980s and the mid-1990s has been the unremitting and discrete spread of the national language, Bahasa Indonesia, especially through schools, tradestores, churches, village meeting halls, and the national media. In many of what Tsing calls Indonesia's "out-of-the-way" places (Tsing 1993), these more subtle forms of state penetration seem to have remained largely unregistered in the popular imagination, which has tended to foreground the more obvious if equally baffling and oppressive forms of state authority.

Among the Meratus people of Kalimantan studied by Tsing, for example, the extractive and violent forms of state intrusion took shape at times in rumors about headhunters in government employ. It was said that they roamed the mountainous terrain where Meratus live in search of heads to lay at the foundation of the many edifices constructed as part of Suharto's national development program (Tsing 1993, 85–91). A popular story from Anakalang, Sumba, explains both the origins of Java's exclusive hold on the Indonesian presidency and the president's own authoritative presence throughout the archipelago. In brief, the story reports the birth in Anakalang of an unusual rooster that crowed so unabatedly and so loud that it was heard in Java, drawing a prospective buyer to Sumba (Keane forthcoming, 29–30). A deal was struck with the Javanese in which in exchange for the rooster the Sumbanese received this man's gold ring along with the multiple gold offspring it ceaselessly produced. Yet if the Sumbanese thereby appear to have retained some value for themselves, the rooster's alienation from their island seems also, it is tempting to suggest, to have entailed their own alienation from authority—or, more specifically, in Siegel's terms, the alienation of the very possibility of communicating with authority from Sumba or, for that matter, as Sumbanese. For Anakalangese, according to Keane, the story explains why all Indonesian presidents come from Java as well as why they can always be heard, even in the country's most remote and tucked-away corners.

On Aru's Backshore, too, as elsewhere in Maluku, rumors occasionally crop up of government headhunters on the loose, while the Indonesian word for government, *pemerintah*, has assumed a talismanic force and decisiveness all its own—as when, for instance on Barakai, its powers are invoked in pat and unnegotiable statements like "the government decides" (I. *pemerintah putus*). Yet to some extent in contrast to many other peoples who populate Indonesia's more remote parts, the women and men who live on the Backshore have, within recent memory, come into very direct and dramatic confrontation with state authority in the context of their own conversion in the mid-1970s. The process of forced conversion was often violently coercive; many, for instance, on Barakai remember armed policemen in church ensuring the attendance of recent or future converts, or being threatened with branding as a "communist"—the declared enemy number one and recurrent specter of the Suharto regime—if they refused to comply. Pagan Aruese were also often caught in the cross fire between the proponents of the different faiths dominant in Maluku and in heated competition at this time in Aru: Islam, the Sacred Heart Catholic Mission, and the Protestant Church of the Moluccas.

There was little room for resistance, although what room there was appears to have been claimed to the fullest. One recurrent strategy throughout the Backshore and an instance of what I call a runaway topography was the prevalent practice on the part of pagans to convert serially to the available agamas—sometimes moving through all three local options until at least provisionally settling on one. One pensioned government official whom I interviewed in 1994 about the conversions glossed this phenomenon in Maluku Malay as *berlumba-lumba*, a verb that describes the innocuous play of porpoises as they frolic in and out of waves, moving in rapid succession from one place to another. I raise this example of what I have elsewhere termed serial conversion in order to nuance and qualify my argument regarding the New Order's uneven and intermittent presence on the Backshore (Spyer 1996b). If, as I claim, government penetration is in some respects limited, I have no intention to offset the confrontations Aru's Backshore women and men had with the extreme violence and coercion of the Suharto regime. In ways that they cannot forget, its representatives (and others) intervened irrevocably in their lives. Notwithstanding the state's menu of possible "religions," the official repertoire unwittingly inaugurated a space of flight or serial conversion somewhat beyond the state's reach. Sliding among the official slots while never pausing too long in any of them, Aruese could transform and negotiate their subject positions and identities as a result of choices they made within a framework that was not of their own making.

Much as is the case with their engagements—however fraught—with the Aru and the Malay, the example of serial conversion offers a glimpse of how in spite of oppression and violence Barakai islanders, along with other Backshore Aruese, retain a measure of ability to map out and inhabit their own runaway topographies.

2   The Legless Paradise

At the height of its power and imperial glory—a moment that some in Holland still like to recall as a time in which "something great was done" (*er wérd wat groots verricht*)[1]—the former Netherlands East Indies came to be referred to with increasing familiarity by the Dutch as an "emerald girdle" (*gordel van smaragd*). Although the immediate referent of this precious chain was the glittering band of glassy green islands that trace out an arch across the great Malay Sea, a more fitting description could hardly have been found for the close links between conquest, clothing, and booty, or between the fashioning of gendered subjects and imperial design. In studies of colonialism, sexuality, and subject formation, much has been made of the capacity of cloth to embrace, shape, and subjugate persons and populations—with special attention usually paid to the so-called civilizing import of European forms of dress and comportment (Cohn 1989; Murra 1989).

Aru was no different in this regard, especially toward the late nineteenth century, as commercial traffic increased and colonial rule tightened its hold on these islands. Focusing on accounts left by European visitors of Aruese made up in quasi-metropolitan forms of dress, on the one hand, and the lavish descriptions of the archipelago's birds of paradise, on the other, suggests how the island's native population became defined in colonial sources by a general lack and insufficiency. In brief, Aruese did not wear the clothes the colonizers gave them with the authority that these clothes—as privileged tokens of civilization—allegedly contained. The striking juxtaposition of birds and men that crops up repeatedly in the nineteenth-century sources also reveals how colonial authority became naturalized in Aru at the expense of the island's inhabitants. While depriving them of authority, this kind of strategic description incorporated Aruese within the imperial administrative topography of the Netherlands East Indies.

This chapter tracks one possible genealogical strand to the sense of deficit that today informs Barakai islanders' experience toward what they call the Malay, of which Western-style clothing is one of the most salient markers. While this chapter sounds out this deficit in the writings of Europeans who visited Aru from about the mid-nineteenth to the early twentieth century, in subsequent chapters I continue to explore why many of Barakai's women and men are haunted, among other things, by the lingering sense that the clothing they wear as Aruese is somehow inappropriate or by the relative assessments they make of their own modernity vis-à-vis that of the other Barakai communities.

If cloth had a particular role to fulfill abroad in the elevation of colonial subjects to the heights of European civilization, at home and especially as the nineteenth century progressed, it had also come into its own. Draperies, carpets, and fabrics with heavy folds and multiple accoutrements wrapped and sheltered an increasingly private and prosperous bourgeois world. In France, as most elsewhere, this was "the age of the *tapissier*," "the heyday of trimming," and the day that the tassel can be said to have "arrived" (Corbin 1990, 369). In the Aru Islands, on the fringes of the fashionable world, this was also the time when feathers of the famed Greater Bird of Paradise were exported—especially to France—in unprecedented numbers. It was simultaneously the highpoint of European travel to these far-flung parts. What such meant in Aru was that in addition to the regular coterie of colonial officials—including what the Dutch in their usual no-nonsense manner termed "controllers" (*controleurs*)—and the archipelago's trading community, naturalists of different breeds and persuasions flocked to the islands to take in and as often as not take out Aru's unusual, hybrid fauna and to a much lesser extent flora.

Reigning supreme among Aru's natural attractions was that Greater Bird—once known simply among Malays as God's bird (*manuk dewata*) and subsequently known among Europeans as the Legless Paradise (*Paradisaea apoda*)—which increasingly was relinquishing its feathers to fashion and the habits and habitat of which already seemed to prefigure such a fate (cf. Savage 1984, 35–38). It is the male bird that is by far the most splendid. He lives permanently in towering "display" trees where—when the season for such shows comes around—he puts on a magnificent production for the females of his species, displaying thereby only

Natives of Aru shooting the Great Bird of Paradise.
Reprinted from Wallace 1962 [1869], 336.

one of many strategies through which a bird can market his reproductive charms (Purcell and Gould 1992, 76).[2] In the late-nineteenth-century sources on Aru, descriptions in naturalists' accounts of Aruese in various modes of dress are almost on a par with those of birds and their plumage, in terms of the regularity with which they appear and the extraordinary detail of their documentation. And if somewhat less attuned to the charms of the archipelago's birds, the colonial officials who came to Aru also seem to have felt compelled to record the look of its inhabitants. More than a curious parallelism, this twofold preoccupation with the appearance of Aru's birds and that of its human population points to a conundrum whereby colonial authority was caught in a double bind: on the one hand, its reproduction demanded the preservation of a strict demarcation between colonizers and colonized; on the other, the dynamics of colonial rule constantly threatened to blur such a divide, as it also presumed the fabrication of colonized others in its own imperial image.

Although such a conundrum was intractable in actuality, it nonetheless offered many possibilities to the imagination. While testifying in its very instability to the power of the dilemma, the alternation in colonial accounts between paradise's birds and its all too human inhabitants was one way of playing out this problem in the imaginary register, with results that, if nothing else, were both emotionally and aesthetically satisfying. The shifting gap between birds and men corresponds to a fetishization of nature that, in turn, facilitates the naturalization of colonial authority in Aru. Along the way, it offers a glimpse of some high imperial imaginings of class, gender, and race.

The 1870s, 1880s, and 1890s especially witnessed the elaboration by the different European powers of a " 'theology' of an omniscient, omnipotent, and omnipresent [Imperial] monarchy" for their colonial possessions (Ranger 1983, 212), which went together with a hypertrophy of the aristocratic and seignorial trappings of command and rule.[3] This was a time when antique conceptions of patrimony and privilege were resurrected in remote corners of the European empires, when the full-blown capitalism of the metropole flaunted itself abroad (but not at home) in "feudal-aristocratic drag" (Anderson 1991, 150), when following a code of courtliness and glory, colonial officers "dressed [themselves] to kill in bed- or ballroom" and "armed [themselves] with swords and obsolete

industrial weapons" (ibid., 151), and when the dominant authorial position of European travel writing was the decisively gendered "monarch-
of-all-I-survey" mode (Pratt 1992, 213). Beyond the golden feathers of the
Greater Bird of Paradise or the birds that between the 1880s and 1920s
nested in their entirety on European women's hats,[4] either in itself sufficient to tickle the stereotypical fetishist's fancy,[5] the fetishism on the part
of the colonizers of their own imperial forms of power and privilege
emerges clearly out of the juxtaposition of the late-nineteenth-century
descriptions of Aru's birds and those of its human inhabitants.

There are a number of good historical reasons, having to do, among
other things, with the fault lines of class, race, and gender as these both
conjoined and divided European metropoles and their colonies, that
help to explain what Anderson has aptly termed this "Tropical Gothic"
imaginaire at the apex of European imperialism (1991, 151). One such reason was the enormous power that high capitalism had given the metropole and the concomitant surplus of neotraditional capital that became
available for investment in the colonies. Another reason was the rising
numbers of bourgeois and petty-bourgeois men in the colonial service
who were encouraged to lord it over the subjugated peoples, following a
principle of colonial racism according to which class difference at home
became subsumed—though by no means effaced—within the idea of an
all-around European racial superiority: "the idea that if, say, English
lords were naturally superior to other Englishmen, no matter: these
other Englishmen were no less superior to the subjected natives" (ibid.,
150).[6] At the same time, the last decades of the nineteenth century were
also the moment when many European powers were pressed to make
their colonies look more legitimate, respectable, and even benevolent. In
so doing, they often bolstered their claims with quasi-aristocratic, regal
expressions of patrimony—the kind of attitude that the imagining of the
Indies as an emerald girdle so thoroughly captures. Shortly after Princess
Wilhelmina's coronation as queen in 1898 was celebrated amidst much
feudal fanfare in the colonies, the so-called Ethical Policy (Ethische Politiek) was enunciated in the Netherlands East Indies in 1900. The following year the queen herself, in her annual oration before the Dutch parliament, spoke of the "debt of honor" that the Netherlands in something
quite like a gesture of noblesse oblige wished to repay for what by then
amounted to three hundred years of exploitation.

In the Netherlands East Indies, as elsewhere, this was then the moment when the objects, rituals, and routines that articulated, legitimated, and produced the colonizer's position vis-à-vis their colonized subjects became matters of a heightened and even tropical Gothic obsession.[7] By the second half of the nineteenth century in Aru, along with all the attention bestowed on the archipelago's birds, lengthy descriptions of Aruese in "native," "national," or "European" styles of dress are a regular feature of both travelers' and official accounts of the islands. For the most part, the kinds of clothing encountered in Aru could be cast comfortably within the increasingly standardized genres of customary and folkloric otherness available at the time. Yet what seems to have made for a somewhat distinct and at times unsettling experience for visiting Europeans were those moments when they felt their own gaze turned back on themselves, when the gaze, as it were, became a "look" as Aruese appeared before them in European guise.

Clothing Paradise

As in other colonial places, the *mission civilisatrice* in Aru, involving naturalists, colonial administrators, members of the Indische (Protestant and state) church, and self-styled wanderers, entailed gestures of a practical and more often than not godly kind. Nomination was the christening act par excellence (Greenblatt 1991, 52–85; Pratt 1992). If it was especially in naming that the religious and territorial projects of Europe initially tended to come together, from the eighteenth century on it was nature itself—revealing through study and knowledge the handiwork of God—that increasingly became the object of attention. A century later, following the publication of Darwin's *Origin of Species* (1859) and—more relevant here—Wallace's *Malay Archipelago* (1962 [1869]),[8] evolutionists and creationists would wage battle over the source of the excessive beauty of creatures like Aru's paradise birds: How could such extravagance be earthly? Was the challenge posed by the latter? How could their showy garishness or that of, say, peacocks, hummingbirds, or orchids exist in the world other than as part of a divine plan to edify humanity? (Quammen 1996, 610).

Another prevalent gesture with which divinity had long been interwoven was the colonial practice of giving cloth or clothes to local rulers and the more extended, open-ended effort to encloth persons and even entire populations. More explicitly borne out in the association between the robe and the priesthood, between "men of the cloth" and the service of God,[9] the primacy of clothing in the often godlike authorizing actions of Europeans was rooted not simply or always in moral or chaste ideas about personhood and propriety but, equally importantly, in the fact that "God Himself 'clothed' the earth in the process of Creation and that he manifests himself 'clothed' with honor and majesty, who coverest thyself with light as with a garment" (Psalm 104.12 in Perniola 1989, 237). More than the familiar story of Creation and its aftermath in which the substitution of clothing for nudity follows the original sin, at issue here is the important relationship between Christian thought and certain notions of European statecraft and political theory that from the late Middle Ages on posited a close connection between divine or divinized kingship and the mantles of authority and rule (Kantorowicz 1957; Marin 1988; Wilentz 1985). It is this genealogy especially that accounts for the long tradition in the Indies of handing out cloth or clothing to subjugated peoples in order to consecrate and give substance to the officializing gestures of colonial politics.

One of the most common acts of rule in the former Netherlands East Indies on the installment of a headman was the bestowal of cloth (sometimes but not always in the form of a flag) and/or clothing, which commonly accompanied an act of appointment, and often a silver- or gold-knobbed staff of office. Dating from the time of the Dutch East India Company and continuing throughout the colonial period, such ceremonies of investiture displayed not only a remarkable persistence over time but also a certain uniformity across the archipelago. For example, the objects presented by colonial administrators in the 1890s to Aru chiefs on their official installments were virtually the same as those given in 1623 by Jan Carstensz, the commander of the *Pera*, when he was dispatched from the Moluccan capital Amboina to Aru with the mission of establishing ties of "friendship" with "all kings" (D. *alle connighen*) (F. W. Stapel 1943, 32–40; *Corpus Diplomaticum* 3, vol. 91: 180). Nor were such gestures limited to the Dutch. A good century later, de Bougainville interrupted his circumnavigation with a stopover on the island of Buton just south of Celebes, where he left some gifts of cloth (and accepted a deer), made certain that another cut of cloth—the flag of the French nation—was displayed and made "known," and commented as well on local attire (de Bougainville 1982 [1771], 377). Such scenes of encounter and exchange were often the stuff of serious competition among European nations, although there was considerable divergence both among individuals and at different historical junctures in the scrupulousness with which these ceremonies were carried out.

Besides the trail of cloth left behind after such official moments in the Moluccas, where—as in other parts of the Indies—the costumes, flags, and gifts of fabric tended to be "preserved with the greatest of care as heirlooms, and used only on official occasions" (Kolff 1840, 229–39; cf. Merton 1910, 119), a formal decision to import cloth into Aru was taken in 1761. By the mid–nineteenth century cloth and clothing were being imported to the islands in impressive number and variety.

In an article on the "State of Imports and Exports to the Aru Islands, during the Year 1849," cloth heads a double list of imports compiled by the commissioned official for the archipelago and subdivided into "Goods of European Origin" and "Goods of Asian Origin" (Bosscher 1853). Some ten years later cloth continues to prevail in a detailed list drawn up by another colonial official and again subdivided, with "European cloth" comprising "unbleached cotton—Madapolam, the brand NHM [Nederlandsche Handels Maatschappij] is carefully watched out for, the Belgian and English Madapolams have less value—, chintzes of various sorts, blue cotton of various sorts, red Adrianopol cotton, slendangs, abdominal belts and the like, headcloths of various sorts, sarongs of English and Dutch imitation, kodie, thread and unspun cotton" (van der Crab 1862, 87–88). Under the heading "Cloth from elsewhere, outside of Europe" are found "sarongs: Java, Buginese [South Celebes], Gorontalo [North Celebes], and Bengal, kodies, Tjindees, gingans [sic], and other fabrics" (ibid., 88). During the latter half of the nineteenth century, only alcohol occasionally rivaled cloth's precedence on the list of imports to Aru.

Notwithstanding the insistence on separating goods of European provenance from those of Asia or "elsewhere," the lists testify not only to the complex circuits traveled by cloth as it made its way from diverse sites of "origin" to Aru, but even more to the prolific hybridizations that characterized colonial cloth production.[10] Chintz, from the Hindi *chint*, is a famous example. But what is one to make, for instance, of European batiks; NHM, Belgian, or English madapollams; sarongs of English and Dutch imitation; or ginghams "from elsewhere, outside of Europe"? Such examples underscore the import of attending to the complicated crisscrossings and crossovers characteristic of cloth production within the larger colonial situation that comprised not only "elsewhere" or Europeans in "elsewhere" but always and inevitably Europe or the metropole itself. It is important to recall, for instance, that the intensive dissemination of cloth in a place like Aru was only possible as a consequence of the revolution in cloth production that was occasioned as much by the colonial enterprise itself as by an "industrial revolution" that traditional historiography records as exclusively European in origin (McKendrick 1982a; Mukerji 1983). Along these same lines, it is probably not for nothing that Adam Smith's famous example of the division of labor was none other than a pin factory (1976 [1904], 89) or that a coat makes such an early appearance in Marx's *Capital* (1967 [1867], 41).[11] Likewise, it is crucial to recognize that at the same time that Aruese ornamented and outfitted themselves in the garb of European and Eurasian civilization, their own islands were being stripped of the luxury articles of fleeting European and Asian fashions.

One account has it that during the fin de siècle feather craze that overtook Europe, three thousand bird of paradise skins were being exported from Dobo annually (Quammen 1993, 38). In the 1880s a self-styled "naturalist's wife" writes of her distress on seeing in the port of Makassar a cargo from these same parts comprising "2000 skins of the orange-feathered bird of paradise, 800 of the kingbird, and a various lot of others" (Forbes 1987 [1887], 36).[12] In New Guinea, no fewer than three European nations—the Netherlands, England, and Germany—vied for the privilege and profit that would come from the plumes destined for European women's hats.[13] At the height of this trade, between the 1880s and World War I, up to eighty thousand birds were killed and exported per year from Dutch New Guinea alone, while the ban on hunting in 1924 together with the change in fashion left behind a ghostly landscape of abandoned settlements that had arisen or boomed during the great feather hunt (Purcell and Gould 1992, 76).[14] Nor, incidentally, were the naturalists themselves always circumspect in their own collecting, and for some like Alfred Russel Wallace collecting provided a primary source of income. Thus, Wallace financed his expedition to the Malay archipelago by collecting for museums and private individuals with a passion for natural history. Seen in this light, Aru was not only a crucial case for the formulation of his theory of nature but also the place where he accumulated the most lucrative collections of his eight-year travels (Quammen 1993, 38).

Rather than insisting on what risks becoming a fairly seamless story of imports and exports or of commodities and their conspicuous collection, I focus in what follows on one of this story's most striking denouements: the dressed aspect of Aruese as it appeared to visiting Europeans. A look at some of the descriptions left by nineteenth-century travelers to Aru of "native," "national," and "European" attire suggests that appearance was, indeed, all-important. In focusing on this dressed aspect of Aruese, the accent here is on the embodiment and fit of costume, understood as embracing not only cloth but anything else that either accompanied its transmission or became part of its trappings in Aru.

Following the contours of cloth on Aruese bodies compels at the same time several critical moves. It means, first, leaving behind the museumizing that all too long has hung up the history of cloth, making of it an endless stream of death-dealing descriptions of disembodied dress and technologies of production. For if, following Barthes, "it is impossible to conceive of a dress without a body . . . the empty garment, without head and limbs . . . is death, not the neutral absence of the body, but the body mutilated, decapitated" (Barthes in Gaines 1990, 3), it is also true that after a death, cloth—having once received a body—can never be neutral again (Stallybrass 1993). Indeed, it may be more saturated with life than ever before. My point is that, as the next best thing to bodies, life and death tend to commingle in cloth in an often uncanny fashion. One guiding assumption here is that this uncanniness is itself an effect of modernity insofar as the latter introduces a novel sense of timing in which "old" and "new," "traditional" and "modern," and perhaps even the living and the dead become clear-cut alternatives as they are made to jostle for places in the positioning of things. Another assumption is that historically the perceived relations between human bodies and clothing has been highly variable. The fact that, in the language of nineteenth-century English tailors, clothing retained the "memories" of the bodies it had once contained—most obviously in the creases left behind by them in sleeves (Stallybrass 1998)—suggests a deeper connection or more intimate embeddedness of human bodies in the clothes they wore than is possible in the present fast-paced times. Today, perhaps more than at any other moment, only death seems to stay the frenetic donning and discarding of clothing that both materially and socially registers fashion's compulsive swings. Another example of a marked historical difference in the relations between bodies and clothes is seen when modern medicine begins to emerge and some of the first anatomical drawings depict human skin as itself a kind of bloodless, luxurious fabric that can be folded back to reveal the wondrous secrets lying within (Perniola 1989, 250, 258–59). Note that the approach taken here also departs from the kind of perspective that sees cloth as always already more than skin-deep, embedded as it is held to be in underlying meanings that model and color the more superficial phenomena of the sloppy and slipshod everyday, as I turn to engage the "look" of Aru as it was received and recorded by nineteenth-century visitors to the islands.

The Standard Adult Male Specimen

Not unlike the pursuit of birds of paradise in their customary habitat, Wallace opined—expressing a view that was increasingly shared by others in an age that witnessed the beginnings of ethnologizing if not anthropology proper—"one must see the savage at home to know what he really is" (1962 [1869], 332). If the two forms of description privileged in late-nineteenth-century writings on Aru—namely, those of birds and their plumage, especially birds of paradise, and those of Aruese in different kinds of dress—are set side by side, then a funny thing happens. This juxtaposition makes clear that the "savage at home" in his natural setting, as it were, bears a marked resemblance to the bird of paradise as he is also captured in his characteristic surroundings. This striking overlap becomes even more blatant when one considers the gendered dimension of these descriptions. Thus, writers often insisted on the dramatic difference in appearance between native men and women or, likewise, between the male and the female of a given bird species. The former's flamboyance, exuberance, and bejeweled beauty contrasted sharply with the aspect of the latter—inevitably drab, less decorated, and easily overlooked.

It was almost a golden rule in the creation of natural collections that the unmarked and prize specimen was always the adult male, while the female sometimes did not even warrant a description (Pratt 1992, 64).[15]

After a lavish passage devoted to the "King Bird of Paradise," Wallace begins his short aside on what I would call the Queen by observing that "the female of this little gem is such a plainly coloured bird, that it can at first sight hardly be believed to belong to the same species" (1962 [1869], 427).[16] Regarding another "rare and elegant little bird" found in neighboring New Guinea, Wallace writes that the female of this variety much resembles that of the King, and "we may therefore conclude that its near ally, the 'Magnificent,' is at least equally plain in this sex" (ibid., 428).

A similar sexual dimorphism in decoration was extended to so-called savages as these were observed "at home."[17] Again Wallace, with characteristic confidence, notes that "the men, as usual among savages, adorn themselves more than the women" (ibid., 355), while another visitor frequenting Aru at the absolute fin de siècle notes that "the Aru women wear a considerable number of ornaments, but the men, like all true Papuans, wear by far the greater number" (Cayley-Webster 1898, 207). Likewise in Tanimbar, southwest of Aru, the aforementioned "naturalist's wife" noted that the women "do not dye their hair as the men do, and give little time to its arrangement" (Forbes 1987 [1887], 169). "The gay young beaux [in these islands] spend much time in arranging the hair; those to whom nature has given only straight locks use a crimping instrument. Just behind the postholder's house stood a long unused prahu, in which rain-water collected, and this was the village mirror. It was an unfailing amusement to me to watch the row of youths standing there in the morning, tying with utmost nicety, and apparently with great vanity, the different coloured bandages, one just edging over the other to see that the well-combed locks were properly confined" (ibid., 160).[18] At a time when in Europe men, at least of the "better classes," went about only in black and gray, thereby displaying "a drabness that caused Baudelaire to exclaim that the male sex looked as if it were always in mourning,"[19] and women bedecked themselves with plumes and could also claim "perfume, makeup, coloring, silk and lace" as their "exclusive province," at such a time nature as Aru and culture as—of course— France seemed to stand each other off in customary fashion (Corbin 1990, 488).

But unlike the changing fashions of the metropole, whatever the peoples of Aru or their neighbors chose to wear is inscribed either in essentialized gendered differences analogous to those that in nature distinguish male and female bird species, in the unchanging rules of custom, or in another timeless primordialism—the nation. As so often in colonial and subsequently some anthropological accounts, native custom appears carved in stone, as a kind of idol that the savages bow before in fear and unwavering submission. One Dutch official writes, for instance, that some traders claimed that they had suggested to the men of Aru's Backshore that they should make their women wear sarongs. The men, however, had rejected this proposal on the grounds that their mothers had not worn sarongs either, and furthermore they feared a divergence from custom would elicit punishment and cause their villages to die out (Brumond 1853, 291). The following suggests, however, that the stubbornness with which Backshore Aruese allegedly held to their own ways was probably at least as much a pervasive reluctance to accept the ways of the Europeans and the traders as their own: "Although the inhabitants of the backshore possess enough means in their pearl banks to supply themselves with better clothing, they remain stubbornly attached to their national costume. They seem to have a distinct prejudice against clothing, and only the heads dress themselves, for better or for worse, upon visits of officials" (van Hoëvell 1890, 22–23).

Whatever their own reasons might have been, it is clear that the inhabitants of Aru's Backshore, at least in part and at certain historical moments, resisted some of the things that the colonials would put on them. It is also clear that they busied themselves refashioning cloth into those cuts that most pleased them. A brand consciousness of sorts was already in place in that, for example, NHM madapollam was preferred over Belgian and English variants. Predilections for particular colors or cloth patterns observed among the Frontshore Aruese were duly noted, while more dramatic alterations documented in descriptions of what in the late nineteenth century came to be called "the national costume" (D. nationale kleederdracht) testify as well to the creativity on which cloth could count in Aru (van Hoëvell 1890, 22–23).

When reading through the nineteenth-century sources on Aru, it is often hard to be certain what "nation" was in fact conveyed by the local costume. If Backshore Aruese were at times not overly eager to accept the staffs of office offered to them by the colonial government and persisted as well in adhering to their own styles of dress, the Dutch flag nonetheless

provided the design for men's loincloths—and one, I was told, that remained popular until the Japanese occupation of the islands during
World War II.[20] Then, for obvious reasons, the so-called flag loincloth
(B. *gom lulub*) boasting the red, white, and blue stripes of the Dutch
national banner was rapidly abandoned. Striped tails, however, continue
to decorate the loincloths worn by men during adat feasts.[21] In a place
soon to be designated the "Tropical Netherlands"—reiterating the Dutch
Islamicist Snouck Hurgronje's famous vision that foresaw "only Oriental
and Occidental Netherlanders"—it is no surprise that the colonizer nation increasingly—if not consistently—assumed the place of an original
with the colony defined as its copy (Snouck Hurgronje in van Doorn
1994, 60).

This kind of imaginary goes at least some way toward explaining the
workings of a prevalent process of recall in which, for instance, a colonial
visitor was struck by "the costume of a Dutch Fisherman" (D. *het cos-
tuum eenen Hollandschen visscher*) unwittingly reproduced, as it were, in
the clothing worn by an Aru chief (Brumond 1853, 252–53). Similarly, a
fleeting sense of a familiar fashion might also be felt in the "look" left by
an Aruese. Anna Forbes, the naturalist's wife, mistook at one point a
group of Aruese pearl divers for women—a mistake, she explained, "due
to the arrangement of the hair; for their immense mops of frizzy locks
were gathered behind in a large chignon or knot, while the short escaped
hair formed a fringe, the whole coiffure being an untidy copy of the fashionable style I had left behind in England" (1987 [1887], 129). In the latter
half of the nineteenth century, fashion reigned supreme in metropolitan
capitals, while the rural countrysides of European nations became the
site for a nostalgic folklorization of, among other things, costume.[22]
Abroad, however, identifications of fashion and folklore remained limited to such ephemeral feelings of déjà vu, both generally giving way in
the colonies to more timeless readings of local custom or of native life
lived out in more positively or negatively valued states of nature.[23]

Imaginary Heads and Mock Chiefs

Like some other colonials, the Dutch made much of mimicry. At the
same time they also often feared it as something that could easily get out

of hand and, drifting from the original, take on, as it were, a life of its own. A clear instance can be traced in the concerns and correspondence about the circulation of the staffs of office topped by the silver or golden "apples" already admired by de Bougainville at the end of the eighteenth century. Tokens like these together with acts of appointment and flags assumed an almost talismanic importance for the Dutch around the turn of the century, the time that across the Malay archipelago witnessed the transformation of a colonial project into a properly imperial one. In Aru, the location of staffs of office within different settlements pinpointed for the Dutch their influence in the islands and formed part of a wider process through which different "landscapes" (D. *landschappen*) were mapped together as a whole.[24] The importance of disseminating such tokens of Dutch rule in marginal places was repeatedly reiterated by the colonial authorities (Mailrapport 1885, 6448: 342+, Afschrift no. 1002, ARA). By the same token, the Netherlands East Indies government confiscated all flags, acts of appointment, and staffs of office when it chastised a rebellious village (Mailrapport 1887, 6460: 342+, Afschrift no. 1002, ARA).

As in the regional center Ambon, where the staff of office was always returned to the colonial government on the death of the office holder, thereby assuring the authorities the opportunity to give it out again, so too should have been the arrangement in Aru. Here, however, the staff together with the office it embodied appear to have been passed on from father to son, causing the Dutch to bemoan their inability to control the excessive circulation of the staffs. Through a kind of crazy mathematics, the prolific passings on had—for them at least—the unfortunate consequence of multiplying the number of native chiefs (Mailrapport 1880, 6392, ARA). One might suggest, drawing on Marc Shell's insights regarding tromp-l'oeil and fake money, that the counterfeit, having an inflationary value, always robs its subjects of their originality (Shell 1992, 23). Indeed, from the perspective of colonial bureaucrats, the unauthorized multiplication of chiefs produced an untidy and troubling situation in which "one finds in addition to the true heads, a multitude of imaginary heads, still armed with the staffs of office of their forefathers, even though [their] family has not exercised authority for a long time" (Mailrapport 1876, 6042, Afschrift nos. 486+, ARA). Presumably it depends on whose authority one is talking about. In New Guinea as well the presence of "mock chiefs" was reported and described by one Dutchman as "founded on the idea that any foreign strand dweller would think himself the lord and master of every living thing in the interior."[25] Although this represents a different possibility built around the coastal-hinterland distinction that was prevalent throughout the Malay world, the lingering sense left by the specter of a multitude of imaginary heads and mock chiefs is that of a landscape drifting from the intended Dutch one, an alternative administrative vision disruptive of their own mappings and much closer to a mockery than a mimicry of themselves.

Indeed, the fine line between mimicry and mockery runs like a red thread through the descriptions of Aruese as they appeared before nineteenth-century visitors in quasi-European dress.[26] One of the problems must have been that the islanders—made over in something akin to metropole mode—seemed to stand before the Europeans as an unsettling, slightly skewed copy of themselves as well as of the "civilization" they had come to convey through clothes.[27] I suspect that the sheer materiality of this "meeting ground"—the mere physical fact of being confronted with native bodies contained in one's own colonizer clothes—is one aspect of the discomfort that seems to filter through the writings of these Europeans. Given that their visits coincided with the high point of colonial racism, when the divide between the colonizers and the colonized became increasingly construed as founded in the physiognomic, material differences between the races, this particular form of contact may have had profound unsettling effects.[28] Following this line of argument, savage bodies in civilized clothes would defy the distinction that, in part, determined the double list of European cloth and clothing versus the same kind of thing imported from "elsewhere" that underwrote the constant concern on the part of colonials with categories like métis, indo, "Brown Gentlemen" (Stoler 1992), and so on, and that caused, more diffusely, an "invisible line" to be imagined obsessively as cropping up wherever and whenever the twain would meet (Pemberton 1994, 96–101). A major conundrum faced by colonials in the Indies lay, for instance, in what the authorities called "artificially fabricated Europeans" (kunstmatig gefabriceerde Europeanen), or persons who elicited the fear that a copy could be taken for the real thing, that, more concretely, "children were being raised in cultural fashions that blurred the distinction between ruler and ruled" (Stoler 1992, 531). Clothing was, indeed, as Stoler suggests, critical in all of this, as borne out by the notion in French Indochina, for example, of "an indigène in disguise" or the accusations of

Annamite women who had lived in concubinage of clothing their métisse daughters in European attire, "while ensuring them that their souls and sentiments remained deeply native" (ibid.). Such, indeed, are some of the colonial contradictions that help to reveal the cracks in modernity's mirror (Dirks 1990, 29). Was it then not only in the moves of mimicry but perhaps even more in the close physical envelopment of native bodies by European clothing that the contamination of the colonizer by the colonized could most concretely be felt? Taussig's insistence on the necessary collaboration between copy and contact, on "the magical power of replication" whereby the image affects—or even contaminates—what it is an image of, is, I believe, also relevant here (Taussig 1993, 2). Let me consider, then, some of these contaminations and the ways in which Europeans, in turn, attempted to contain them.

The Tooth of Time

Like Macaulay's translator and other mimic men, Aru chiefs—and more those of the Frontshore than the Back—could in Homi Bhabha's words be called "the appropriate objects of a colonialist chain of command, authorized versions of otherness. But they are also . . . the figures of a doubling, the part-objects of a metonymy of colonial desire which alienates the modality and normality of those dominant discourses in which they emerge as 'inappropriate' subjects" (1994, 88). This kind of doubleness can be discerned in the colonial attitude toward Aru chiefs in quasi-European clothes as perhaps the privileged site where copy and contact, containment and contamination accompany each other and ambivalently collide. In ceremonies of investiture, Aru "savages" were turned into "true heads" as the appropriate objects of a colonial chain—or even girdle—as well as the concrete investments of a "civilization" that was held to emanate outwards from Europe to the farthest corners of the globe. By extension, the chiefs were also those persons who most often faced the Europeans in their old hand-me-down clothes, motivating thereby and once again, colonial gestures of containment.

In their writings, European visitors to Aru deployed a number of strategies that were aimed at displacing and disarming the apparition of Aruese as quasi-metropolitans, an apparition that proved disorienting to their own imperial pretensions—if perhaps only in passing. Thus, one move made repeatedly by the colonizers when describing Aruese in European-style clothes was to highlight the discomfort with which such dress was worn, in an effort, I suspect, to disguise from themselves their own sense of being unsettled by the clothing's off-centered look. As Freud would claim, what we tend to see as other and outside of ourselves more often than not dwells within, while what appears most uncanny or *unheimlich* is commonly quite familiar and close to home (Freud 1955). Some of the late-nineteenth-century writings deploying strategies of dis-placement and containment probably say more about a sense of out-of-placeness experienced by visiting Europeans than about the islanders themselves. Beyond the colonial racism that underwrote the rift running between native bodies and civilized clothes, I believe the Europeans may also have faced in the distorted look reflected back to them by Aruese their own off-center subject positions—as colonials far removed in every possible respect from the fashionable, tone-setting, and policy-making metropolitan centers of Europe, and as persons who could pretend to aristocratic privilege when abroad but could never escape from their class origins at home. These positions and others may have been brought home to them—if only fleetingly—in the *unheimlich* apparition of Aru-ese in cast-off, quasi-metropolitan clothes.

Shoes, as perhaps the quintessential marker of the shod and unsavage Western world, were often marshaled forth in colonial writings to make a comforting point (see also Schulte Nordholt 1997). "The Orang Kaya [or headman]," writes one European visitor, "paid me a visit directly I let go the anchor. He was dressed in a black coat and hat with white trousers and boots, which kept him in a constant state of unrest the whole time he was on board" (Cayley-Webster 1898, 203). At other times, a rejection or absence of shoes was simply noted (Brumond 1853, 252–53; Riedel 1886, 258).

Another strategy that seems to have been prevalent among Europeans when sizing up Aruese outfitted as their quasi-metropolitan selves was to stress that the "savages," in multiple ways, fell short—in clothes too big, loose, long, or simply silly—of that which they were (allegedly) trying to imitate.

Already from afar, several cannon shots rang out toward us; when we arrived, the Orang kaya awaited us with his following on the bank. . . . A small, puny little man with a dried out and sallow face, he was decked out in a red general's uniform. The tails of the much too wide frock coat hung to his heels, while the broad golden collar enclosed his head far above the ears, leaving scarcely an opening through which one could discover his insignificant little face. The pants, richly decorated with braid, hung with many pleats on his boots, which surely each could have accommodated two of his feet. . . . In one hand his staff of rank with the golden knob held by its middle stiffly against his nose, in the other a red handkerchief completed the highly remarkable portrait of the great man. Immobile, he awaited us in this pose and received all greetings: his face remained entirely unaltered; a hand and stiff bow, worthy of the greatest monarch, was his response to all. (Brumond 1853, 81)

Described in the fullest of detail, every aspect of the "great man's" attire as well as the stiff embodiment with which he wore it is, to paraphrase Bhabha, "not quite, not right."[29]

Ever both amused and scrupulously observant, Anna Forbes, the naturalist's wife, writes of her encounter with some Aruese who stopped by her ship to report the murder of the son of "the Rajah of some place in the neighborhood."

I could not refrain from laughing aloud at the ludicrous appearance of the group before us, but was soon checked when I saw their really sorrowful countenances. . . . The old chief wore bright green trousers, a long black coat, and *over* this a *kabia* [her emphasis] or native jacket of bright purple satin with inch-wide gold-thread stripes, and a very dirty and starchless collar lay untidily on his neck. Another had trousers of bright scarlet, with large butterfly pattern, a faded green silk coat brocaded with large gold flowers, and a shabby grey felt hat; and another a long surtout coat, with a much worn black satin vest, wrong side out, over it. Two others were not so abundantly clothed, for one suit served them both. It had evidently descended to the present wearers from some passing vessel where the theatrical entertainments had been whiling the tedium of a voyage, for the coat had a blue tail and a red, and the trousers one leg of green and the other of yellow. Somehow the man with the trousers looked much better clad than the man with the coat. These garments formed doubtless the entire wardrobe of the village, accumulated during who knows how many generations. (Forbes 1987 [1887], 134–35)

More than the fit or the embodiment of the clothing, Forbes focuses repeatedly on the wrongness with which the tenue is put together—a vest worn "wrong side out"; a kabaya pulled on—oh my goodness!—*over* a long black coat; or a costume, already theatrical in design, harlequin-like, and split, *again* split to be shared between two "savages"—just as, she speculates, the entire wardrobe seems itself to have been pieced together from the scraps of clothing accumulated through the ages in one Aru village.

One of the concrete effects of the writing strategies that I have so far considered—the lack of a "fit" between Aruese and European clothing or the wrongness with which it was worn—was to impose a distance between "savage" bodies and "civilized" clothes. Or, put otherwise, everything in these late-nineteenth-century descriptions happens as if a very visible line had been drawn between Aruese and the kinds of figures they cut in European clothes. The distance thus effected highlights the difference between Europeans, who wore their clothes—and especially when abroad—not simply as a sort of "social skin" but even more as a civilized one (Turner 1980), and Aruese, concerning whom and quite concretely a slippage served to separate them almost physically from the costumes that they created with the colonizer's clothes—at least, that is, if one takes the Europeans at their word.

Nor is it surprising that in the context of the thoroughly modern endeavor constituting late-nineteenth-century colonialism, fashion figured as another prevalent mode invoked by the Europeans to make more or less the same important statement. Following this fashion statement, time served as the raw material with which distinctions of dress were marked and made, and thereby as a way of denying the coevalness between colonizers and colonized through the medium of their very clothes (Fabian 1983). If the colonizers always ascribed one or another "traditional" outfit to the natives, the move that would deny coevalness through contrasts in European costume was maybe even more effective or, at any rate, differently so than when the natives appeared in their own alleged timeless attire. The crucial difference between customary native garb and a costume configured after the colonizer is that the latter—whatever else one might say—was always anachronistically at a once or twice remove from the latest colonial, not to mention metropolitan look. Importantly, this was not that different from the colonizer's own sartorial position vis-à-vis the European metropole.

A particularly telling passage from one Dutchman's piece on the "Religious Practices in the Residence of Amboina" notes: "The Christian natives in Ambon are now wild about these high silk hats. They show off with them on Sundays, when they go to Church, to funerals and on festive occasions. They are usually overly old examples that have suffered from the tooth of time, so that like shoes they are sometimes shined with polish, but it does look distinguished, and the man who can get hold of such a gem is more than a little proud of it!" (de Vries 1921, 112).[30] Sometimes insisting on a separation between colonized bodies and civilized clothes gets the better of European writers, as here where the Sunday best worn by Ambonese Christians separates from their bodies in a fetishistic turn in which clothing and churchgoing come entirely apart, thereby allowing a hat to wander off by itself. Following a slippage that betrays how the author may himself have lost a stable position from which to speak— and that ensues from the recollection of the *shining* sometimes given to high silk hats—the hat takes on a life of its own, "but it does [apart from Ambonese bodies] look distinguished." Not unlike paradise's birds, the antique silk hat, transfigured into a precious "gem," becomes both elusive and something to be eagerly pursued and possessed.

When taking a look at the time that the Europeans threaded through clothes, it is important to realize that Aruese, like the Ambonese Christians captured in the above quote, were regarded as always already out of date and—what is more—doubly so. Both overly old and out of fashion, their costumes were literally and metaphorically gnawed by the "tooth of time." Besides the issue of time itself, one crucial, material consequence of the quick turnover characteristic of what Barthes called "the fashion system" (1967) is that "a disproportionate volume of cloth ends up in the ragbag or as hand-me-downs"—or, indeed, I would add, as something to be given away in the colonies (Schneider and Weiner 1989, 11). Even in this century and culminating in the conversion offensive launched in Aru by Dutch missionaries in the 1960s and especially mid-1970s (Spyer 1996b), boxes of clothing containing the cast-offs of Catholic families in the southern Netherlands were shipped in to be distributed in the islands. Another consequence of "the cult of the transitory"—the essence of fashion and, more generally, "[capitalist] modernity"—is that its built-in momentum for making things obsolete simultaneously promotes both desire and a disdain for material goods (Lefebvre in Lears 1994, 385). And if the fluctuations of desire that make up fashion were felt

Regent in official costume (1919). Courtesy of the Royal Tropical Institute, Amsterdam.

over and over again among Aru's Backshore communities of collectors, fashion's flipside—disdain, derision, or a more mild ironic amusement—tends to describe the tone of the Europeans as they took in the look of the Aruese. Fashion, as is well known, once passé very rapidly looks ridiculous.[31] One can at least speculate that this attitude may not have been wholly lost on the Aruese. In colonial accounts, therefore, fashion could readily be called on to make precisely those kinds of statements that many scholars of colonialism today regard as typifying the colonial attitude toward colonized peoples. For like history and like time, fashion belonged to the colonizers and never to the colonized, and, consequently, just as Aruese and other others were by definition always out of history and out of time, so too, and even more concretely, were they always out of fashion (cf. Dirks 1990, 28). At the same time, it is possible to suggest that through their own creative configurations of costume and their refashionings of a retroactive colonial or even company "look," Aruese and others in confronting the Europeans with their own cast-off and hand-me-down clothes turned, in a fashion, the clock back at them.

The Legless Paradise

The overinvestment in vestment characteristic of these late-nineteenth-century colonial accounts—again, and crucially, only rivaled by the drawn-out descriptions of the splendid, bejeweled birds that made of Aru a kind of paradise—and the compulsion on the part of visiting Europeans to embellish their writings continually with descriptions of dress describes a kind of obsessive desire that both makes for and repeatedly motivates a fetishistic focus on a given thing. But only rarely in the colonizers' accounts did clothing truly take on a life of its own to become a full-fledged fetish on a par with paradise's birds. Instead, whether for Europeans paradise was linked to cloth or, inversely, prefigured in the romantic desire of keeping such "civilization" afar, in the various colonial readings of the relation between "civilization" and cloth, cloth repeatedly served as a border, a "civilizing" skin that, depending on one's inclinations, could be filled in favorably or not. In clothing paradise and in playing God going about the important business of Creation, the Europeans also created a conundrum for themselves. The act of clothing their colonized subjects in the garb of quasi-metropolitan "civilization" seemed to imply for the colonials that they themselves might not be fully installed in their own clothes. Yet not doing so seemed to suggest much the same thing. In other words, given the close creative fit between colonial authority and "civilized" clothes, there was simply no way for the Europeans to retain full authority over their colonized subjects and simultaneously carry out their "civilizing" mission to its logical implications—that is, the making over of these same subjects into a mirror, a tropical reflection of themselves. Although offering in its materiality the promise of fulfillment, clothing then was always made to point beyond itself to a "civilization" that could never be fully attained.

Yet if Aruese in quasi-metropolitan clothes might be seen in some sense as a concretization of the colonizers' "civilization" as well as—in being unfinished and fragmentary—its negation, so too, though somewhat differently, might those birds who from the beginning provoked the association between this far-off archipelago and paradise. If one considers, for instance, the names that the Europeans bestowed on the most flamboyant of Aru's birds, then the utopics of an imperial design begins to emerge. Because the first of such birds arrived in Spain from the Moluccas legless—as purely a splendid and preserved skin—the belief spread that lacking apparently any means to alight on earth such beings could only originate in paradise. Hence also Linnaeus's commemoration of this old legend in the name the "Legless Paradise." Later nomenclature continued the paradise theme while at the same time providing it with more earthly dimensions. Following this vision, paradise was a place presided over by kings wielding an authority that was immediately manifest and provided with substance in the resplendent showiness, Gothic theatricality, and glittering presence of their royal highness. As Purcell and Gould write about the birds named for kings: "The name chosen for Birds of Paradise reinforce their gaudy majesty. Most were given monikers to honor various European monarchs" (1992, 69). In addition to the lofty leglessness of "paradise" himself, there is the somewhat lesser though equally regal King Bird of Paradise, the King-of-Saxony Bird of Paradise, and the Blue Bird of Paradise or *Paradisaea rudolphi*, named after the only son of Emperor Franz Joseph, the Archduke Rudolph of Austria (ibid.), as well as others whose names reflect a more generic royal splendor like the "Magnificent." Some names simply invoke the patrimony of kings. Thus, if the descriptions of birds of paradise left by nineteenth-century travelers to Aru and neighboring New Guinea commonly rely on a language of opulence and treasure to convey the breathtaking beauty of these creatures, at least one species was actually named after a jewel: among French authors, the so-called Lesser Bird of Paradise is known as "Le petit Emeraude" (Wallace 1962 [1869], 423). As the classic exception that proves the rule, perhaps the best example of the kind of royalty repeatedly assigned to paradise's birds is the *Diphyllodes respublica*, named by the French ornithologist Charles Louis Bonaparte, who also happened to have been a nephew of the lesser, more farcical emperor, Napoleon III. In his own words, the French ornithologist chose this name because "I have not the slightest regard for the sovereignty of all the princes in the world." As Purcell and Gould explain, however, "he also thumbed his nose at earthly governments, selecting his label in mock honor of 'that Republic which might have been a Paradise had not the ambitions of Republicans, unworthy of the name they were using, made it by their evil actions more like a Hell' " (1992, 69–70).

On either side of the turning of the present century and at the height of its power and glory, a certain telos underwrote the imagining of the

Netherlands East Indies as an archipelago of imperial proportions and design. Traced out in the glassy brilliance of the Indies as an "emerald girdle"—as simultaneously a possession and a prize—this kind of imaginary had its refractions even in Aru, located, as it were, at one far end of the imperial chain. If, for Europeans, the Legless Paradise embodied in its disembodied skin the ethereal heights of a fully dressed beyond, the men and, even less, the women of Aru, could never approximate the exalted "civilization" that the Europeans hid in their clothes. Indeed, one might say that the repeated distancing of natives from their "civilized" clothes had as its counterpart a colonial reverie of a legless paradise from which all Aruese had been excluded. More specifically, a fetishized and thoroughly tropical Gothic vision of civilization in which obsessions about endlessly proliferating heads thought to make a mockery of colonial rule could be displaced momentarily by those splendid birds that as surrogates for European monarchs displayed civilization in its most exuberant, exalted, and authoritative excess. It is through this particular fetishization of nature as a displaced thoroughly tropical Gothic civilization that colonial authority came to be naturalized in many of the late-nineteenth-century writings on Aru.

The definition of Aruese in terms of a lack or of Aru as a legless paradise—an empty land of abundant natural wealth and beauty—is only one possible genealogy to the feeling of deficit that chronically imbues Barakai islanders' understandings of themselves and their communities. While the provenance of this feeling is complex and multiple, women and men on Barakai today seem to have largely internalized an outsider's look at themselves in their own ambivalent evaluations of their not-so-distant pagan past and the clothing to which this past corresponds. This sense of deficit is at the juncture of different historicities—some more determinate, others less so. It is impossible to know precisely what and how much contemporary sentiments owe to the colonial *imaginaire* that I have sketched in the preceding pages or, if lacking such historical depth, they should simply be understood as the effect of a much more recent overdetermined confluence of Protestant and Catholic missionization, the coerced conversions of the mid-1970s, and the former New Order's prejudices and programs directed at "left behind" communities. With these uncertainties in mind, I turn now to the women and men of Barakai who first spoke to me about their clothes and inadvertently encouraged me to investigate their history.

3 The Great Ship

"Save your old clothes and make a garden," a woman admonished a small gathering of her kin and neighbors as we sat over coffee one evening in February 1994, "because we won't be going to the store and we won't be buying new clothes. The oysters are gone and soon there will be no more *pencarian* [the collection and trade in sea products]." In an immediate sense this woman's words spoke merely of the latest in a series of ecological disasters that have struck Aru's Backshore over the last one hundred years. In 1994 the double devastation of the archipelago's pearl oyster beds through a combination of overexploitation and disease threatened to make these the most recent addition to the archipelago's long list of rapidly dwindling marine and land species. But beyond the summing up of a bad situation, this woman's warning also proclaimed a strategy of last resort. Evoking a scenario that Bemunese only fall back on in times of extreme duress or war, saving old clothes and making a garden means retreating into the forest and laying down the life of consumption and commerce in sea products that on Barakai is subsumed under the Indonesian word *pencarian*.

The space that opens up between saving old clothes and making a garden, on the one hand, and buying new clothes and pencarian, on the other, is a field of arguments and possibilities. Within such a field the local significance and value of either one of these options is variably defined in reference to a wide range of situationally appropriate strategies. As stark alternatives they dramatize the opposition between the lack that Bemunese often identify with the Aru and the concomitant surplus of the Malay. In this chapter I consider how the Aru "inside" and the Malay "outside" are realized and variously played out in different situations around the recurring dichotomies of forest and coast, male and female, darkness and light, ignorance and knowledge, and in the elusive space of a pagan elsewhere versus the coercive yet tantalizing materiality of "external" practices—especially those linked by Barakai islanders to trade, the Indonesian state, and the church.

Yet whichever meanings are assigned by Bemunese men and women to either the Aru "inside" or the Malay "outside," neither of these imaginary locations appears to offer them a stable ground or place of repose. None of the above categories bestows on these locations the solidity of a foundation or offers an unproblematic solution insofar as both the Aru and the Malay are always haunted, compromised, and undone by the intrusion of their other. There is then no satisfactory place from which Bemunese might begin to debate their position within a larger world, although different persons within the community, and notably women versus men, may conceive for themselves varying points of departure. Thus, if the break signaled by the activities of making gardens and saving clothes is a recurring strategy on Barakai, the forest into which Bemunese retreat is also the ambivalent site of their "backward," ignorant, and pagan past. And if the Malay subsumes all the fascination and desire of the islanders for a dynamic world of circulation and possibility, it is also for them inextricably bound up with coercion. Incompleteness and ambivalence trouble both these alternatives. I explore here how Bemunese women and men navigate the fractured social landscape that I began to map out in the preceding two chapters, by focusing on such vexed sites as the forest, clothing, trade, and religion as they emerged in the histories told to me of a great sunken ship, in intervillage rivalry over collection sites, and in the story of religion's arrival on Aru.

Standing on One's Own Feet

Probably ever since the early nineteenth century, when some of the ancestors of the present Bemun community first turned their backs on the forested interior of the island to establish a more permanent settlement on the coast and engage directly in trade, the "forest" has served as a backdrop, a reminder of a life that had been, and one that this small Backshore community continues to memorialize in its annual celebration. Besides the hiatus between 1973 and 1976, when, as it is often told, the men of Bemun did not dive for oysters and their women dared not venture into the shallows to fill their headstrap baskets with trepang, eucheuma seaweed, or the odd pearl oyster exposed at low tide, there were several other times in living memory when community members had felt sufficiently put upon or provoked to abandon their coastal settlement. Then, too, the forest had provided a place of refuge where Bemunese families made gardens and saved old clothes, until the worst of whatever first drove them there had once again passed them by. At least since the Second World War and probably earlier, Bemunese residence in the forest as opposed to on the coast has heralded hard times and, to some extent, a return to a former existence. More recently under Suharto's New Order as elsewhere in Indonesia Barakai's forested interior has been increasingly burdened with notions of backwardness and primitivism, figured in the rhetoric of the regime as the repository of a pagan past to be left behind by progress (see also Tsing 1993). While further complicating the Bemunese relation to their past, such official representations are also refracted within intervillage politics on Barakai Island.

In recent memory, the last occasion on which Bemunese withdrew into the forest occurred in the mid-1970s in the context of what was often termed a "war," which had erupted between them and the neighboring community of Longgar over diving grounds. During my first months in Bemun, allusions to the war clouded my initial impressions of a relatively peaceful place that, it seemed, only the occasional illicit romance, ill-advised marriage proceedings, or spat over sago palms would passingly disturb. It took, however, quite some time, a good half year or more, before anyone would talk at length with me about the conflict. While at first I heard relatively much—here and there and in passing—about the three-year break with pencarian when Bemunese largely withdrew into the forest, I heard almost nothing about how or why the war had happened. More fleshed-out accounts of the conflict over rights to the diving grounds off of Barakai were presumably seen as volatile. The number of Longgarese married and resident in Bemun, including the grandfather in the house in which I lived at the time, and my own still unknown disposition were undoubtedly factors as well.

When I did finally hear of the conflict, the emphasis was less on the war as I might have imagined it but rather on the "history" (B. *sejara*) that had backed Bemun's position in the conflict, together with this history's song. Although on first hearing they seemed only related to the

Backshore village in northeast Aru

war of the mid-1970s and the community's claims in this context, both the story and the song codified for Bemunese the history of a great foreign ship, its capsizing off of the island, and the confiscation of its cargo by Bemunese ancestors. As I gradually came to understand, the history of the ship—above and beyond the court decision in Bemun's favor in the regency capital—contained in fact for many on Bemun's side the clinching argument against their opponent. Before turning to the ship's history and song, however, I sketch in brief some of the background to the rivalry between Bemun and Longgar along with the tensions that preceded and, I believe, in part prefigured the outbreak of the confrontation between them in the mid-1970s.

As far as I could make out, no single incident appears to have set off the Longgar-Bemun war in the early 1970s. In the aftermath of a confrontation in late 1966 over the establishment of a Catholic mission school in Bemun, tensions had troubled the relationship between the two communities for some time. Problems probably existed before then and at least since Independence, when Bemun was granted an administrative status on a par with that of its neighbor—that of a "village" (I. *desa*) under its own headman (I. *kepala desa*). Previously, under Dutch colonial rule, they had been ranked in relation to each other with the headman of the smaller community Bemun (I. *orang tua*) answerable and subordinate to that of the larger Longgar (I. *orang kaya*). Since the early 1920s, moreover, when the Protestant Church of the Moluccas (Gereja Protestan Maluku, or GPM) founded an elementary school in Longgar, those Bemunese who wished to send their children to school had depended on that of their neighbors. Whether or not Longgar had felt its historical superiority vis-à-vis Bemun eroded with the institution of village headmen of equal rank after Independence, such feeling seems to have crystallized when the latter community attempted to establish its own mission school.

One of the grievances on Bemun's side most forcefully articulated in the official correspondence about the school conflict, sent by this community's headman and by representatives of the Catholic mission to Dobo and the regency capital in Kei, emphasizes how the Longgarese would prevent the smaller community from "standing on its own feet" (I. *berdikari*). The Longgar position, by contrast, laid out in its correspondence, suggests that Bemunese persisted after Independence in their dependency on the former Dutch colonizers. The allusion here is to the hierarchy of the Sacred Heart Catholic Mission, active in Bemun, in which the most important positions, such as bishop of Ambon and head of the mission station in Dobo, continued to be occupied by Dutchmen.[1] A closer look at the correspondence about the conflict over Bemun's school suggests, indeed, that it was the independence of the smaller village from the larger one and, by extension, its elevation to an administrative status of equal rank that presented a problem for Longgarese. Statements in the correspondence from Longgar's side reinscribe hierarchy into the relation between the two communities by contrasting, for instance, the "high" educational certificates of Longgarese schoolteachers with the rank of "frying pan's buttock" attributed to Bemun's teacher or by branding Bemun's school a "chicken coop." Additionally, the Longgar correspondence displaces the dependency of Bemunese that they seemed to want to continue vis-à-vis themselves onto an inappropriate colonial locus. Rather than upholding the red and white flag emblematic of the Indonesian nation-state, one of their letters accuses, the Bemun community supported a Dutch school and therewith the tricolored flag of the country's former colonizers.

On March 7, 1967, the regency court in Tual, Kei officially "decided," as it was put in Bemun, recognizing the community's schoolhouse as an SD Nasional R.K., or national Roman Catholic elementary school.[2] The important place assigned to the "desire" of the "Bemunese people" in this decision may have been a response to the repeated references in the correspondence from Bemun's side to the "Presidential Instruction Regarding Compulsory Education and Self-Reliance" (I. *Instruksi Presiden mengenai Wadjir Beladjar dan Berdikari*)—more literally, the Duty of Education and Standing on One's Own Feet (I. *berdikari* or *berdiri di atas kaki sendiri*) (letter of 18 March 1967 to Director of GPM Protestant Schools in Aru from District Head, MSC archives, Bishopric Ambon). Indeed, most Bemunese remembered their own stake in the conflict as simply their desire as a community for a certain independence, commonly phrased as "standing on one's own feet." Be that as it may, according to the Bemunese who spoke to me of the events leading up to the war, their community had barely begun to fulfill this duty when it was swept, as it were, off its feet again, as the ongoing hostile stance of their neighbors took a dramatic turn for the worse.

Around 1973 the men of the larger village allegedly began arming themselves and threatening with physical violence Bemunese who dove for oysters or otherwise exploited the seas off of Barakai. Invoking the *sejara*, or history, of Bemun's provenance in the forest, the Longgarese argued that the contemporary descendants of this former interior community had no right to fish or otherwise profit from the sea. Most emphatically, they could exercise no claims to the pearling grounds where men from both Longgar and Bemun customarily dove during the west monsoon. Numbering in population at this time under half the size of Longgar, the smaller community seemed initially to succumb to the force of its own past, retreating largely into the forest to take up gardening and sago palm exploitation on a full-time basis. Eventually, Bemun filed a court suit against Longgar in which it claimed first rights to the disputed Barakai diving grounds and argued that its ancestors, as first comers to the island, had in fact granted those of Longgar permission "to exploit jointly the diving grounds belonging to the above-mentioned plaintiff with the people of Bemun . . . that in fact the tidal flats of the plaintiff are only bordered by those of Apara and Mesiang, but because of kinship and brotherhood the plaintiff does not request exclusive rights but only that the disputed diving grounds be shared" (letter of 24 June

1974 sent to Bapak Ketua Pengadilan Negeri Tingkat II in Tual, undersigned headman of Bemun).

Beyond the generalized bullying by Longgar that most Bemunese say they suffered when they spoke either of the war in the 1970s or of the conflict over Bemun's school some years before, the immediate impetus to filing the suit was in some accounts the confiscation of a Bemunese woman's canoe by a group of Longgarese men. Caught out alone on the tidal flats one morning, the woman is said to have been forced to surrender her canoe to the men, who claimed she had no right to be there. Her husband, a man from the Kei Islands resident in Bemun since 1959, was one of the main instigators of the court case against Longgar, together with the Keiese teacher who had been harassed during the conflict over the school and the village headman and his staff. It may not be coincidental that the few Keiese living in Bemun should have been the ones to rally the villagers to legal action against their neighbors. As people who have been driven to search far and wide for a more hospitable living environment than their own barren islands, Keiese tend to be better versed in the bureaucratic discourse and routines that mediate the movement of persons throughout the archipelago and typify exchange with state authority in Indonesia. They are significantly the main low- and middle-ranking government officials in Aru, while Ambonese from the provincial capital and Javanese from the nation's center fill the higher posts. Following local stereotypes, Keiese also enjoy a reputation throughout the south Moluccas for strong resistance against oppressive government and military figures, an image that stands in sharp contrast with that of Aruese as timid and silent before authority.

Even for the woman whose canoe had been confiscated (and eventually returned) and her Keiese husband, the history backing Bemun's claims in the war with Longgar appeared more important than the court case in Tual. Long before I heard from her or anyone else how her canoe had been seized as she was out gathering seaweed, she and others had already told me of the great ship's history, its related song, and how the latter had been deployed as a weapon in the war. Perhaps the overriding importance of the history versus the court decision—at least in retrospect—had to do with the efficacy attributed by many Bemunese to the singing of this history's related song at one of the war's most heated moments and its devastating success in thus allegedly parrying an agressive advance of their neighbors. Or it may have had to do with the difference for them between an abstract bureaucratic procedure in a faraway regency capital where few Bemunese had ever been, on the one hand, and the immediate relevance and more far-reaching ramifications on Barakai, on the other, of their own connection to the great ship.

The decisive confrontation in which the song of the great ship was launched took place in Bemun itself at the height of the conflict. One day in the mid-1970s, some men from Longgar apparently walked into Bemun brandishing weapons and poking fun at the villagers' forest and, by extension, allegedly backward origins. Provoked by the taunts and threats, a group of Bemunese women is said to have spontaneously formed on the spot and, facing the men, to have countered this challenge with one of their own—a song about the arrival of foreign clothing to Aru and an allusion therewith to the history of a great sunken ship. Most Bemunese eventually referred to this event when they spoke of the inter-village confrontation over diving grounds. Some claimed that it turned the tide of the war by setting the various differences straight with what they called "sejara" and—equally important—by causing the Longgar men who had come to harass them to return shamefacedly to their own village. Others also acknowledged the force of sejara, while adding that the sheer size of Longgar together with the alleged arrogance of its people did not allow it to be so easily daunted. For them it was not until after the government decision that made official the joint exploitation of the diving grounds by the two communities that Bemunese could again take up diving and seasonal trade.

The Forest and the Trees

Like many songs sung on Barakai, the song of the great ship (B. *kapal jin ken sab*) can either be sung on its own or called on to bestow authority on one or another telling of the "history" with which its status has become more or less loosely intertwined. Thus, while what is widely known on Barakai as the "song of the great ship" makes no mention of a ship, a canoe, or even the sea, it has over time and through various circum-stances—including the Longgar-Bemun war—come to be closely linked, though perhaps only passingly, to the so-called history of the great ship

(B. *kapal jin ken sejara*). Beyond its title, then, the song with which an ad hoc gathering of Bemunese women asserted their community's claims to the Barakai seas—a riposte so devasting that it is alleged to have sent the blustering Longgarese bullies straight back home—turns entirely on the excitement, desire, and fascination generated by the arrival on Aru of a cargo of "Dutch" or, less specifically, "foreign" clothes.

Kapal ken Sab	[*The Song of the Great Ship*
Ban wo i	The bird has one plume
dua selnen abel	the lord within the village
tur gwagwa daririn	they run to and fro excitedly
daririn dev jurtai	they exclaim over the clothes
Jin kut mate	The first time we set eyes on such things
seen gwadin	only now for us
seen jurta	only now clothes
Seen jurta	Only now clothes
jurta dua	the clothes of the lord
jur kaka dawe dal Gwerka	they take them all around Aru
Gwerka jurta Walad	Aruese with foreign/Dutch clothes]

At least since the mid-1970s, when the song served as a weapon in the intervillage war, the frenzied excitement of Aruese triggered by the sheer novelty of the clothing, the fact that the clothes are foreign in origin and belong to a high-ranking person or "master/lord" (B. *dua*), and, last but not least, the title by which the song is generally known on Barakai have evoked for many islanders—and certainly Bemunese—the "history of the great ship."

Along with its relatively codified connection to this history, the great ship's song also seemed to conjure for many Bemunese other ships with other cargos that much more recently have either run aground or been seized by Indonesian authorities in the seas off of the archipelago. In particular the Taiwanese shrimp trawlers that regularly trespass into national waters tended to come up in the conversations with women and men that spun out of the great ship's song. The all-around excitement, sense of discovery, and animation captured by the song were the same as the emotions that take hold of the islanders when one of those ships arrives, confided one woman named Ama Tiong. And she then went on to list for me some of the articles salvaged from the most recent of the arrested and temporarily abandoned vessels off of Barakai—"so and so's Supermie [noodles]—where do you think she got all that?—Lim's monkey, oil drums for ovens, and lots of tin cans." Besides these relatively unusual happenings, people derive a more minor thrill from scavenging the Barakai shore during the off-season, when the east monsoon brings what others might see as miscellaneous flotsam and jetsam but among which islanders find—if they are lucky—the uprooted trunks of great New Guinea trees that make the sturdiest of canoes, oil drums that once sawed in half and fitted with a sturdy lid are the only ovens available to bake the closely evaluated cookies and cakes that are served on Barakai by both parties to a marriage negotiation, as well as more modest prizes like plastic containers, the odd tossed or swept away sandal, chunks of styrofoam, rubber tire, ends of twine, and other things potentially put to multiple good uses.

But that the great ship's song resonates with contemporary realities as well as more generally with the fact that all things good and bad come to Aru via the sea does not explain the momentous effect that the singing of the song allegedly had in the war. What is it about the ship's song that, according to many Bemunese, had the power to deflect the claims of their Longgarese neighbors and dispatch them back home? To answer this question it is necessary to unravel the significance the song has in connection to sejara, or history, as understood on the Backshore. Classified locally as a "proof," the song's main import in the conflict was that of material witness to the sejara with which it was held to be entangled (cf. Hoskins 1993, 120; Keane 1997b). As a "proof" the song also condenses all the crucial emotions that Bemunese commonly identify with the founding moment of the ship's arrival and that individuals in the community draw out and develop in their own strategic tellings of its history.

Recall that in the war both the Longgarese and, subsequently, the Bemunese called on sejara to justify their position in the conflict. First, the Longgarese appealed to the history of the former forest residence of Bemun's ancestors as the basis for the exclusion of the latter's descendants from the disputed diving grounds. When Bemunese women spontaneously sang the great ship's song as a counter to their neighbors' accusations, they, too, invoked a sejara so forceful that it was supposedly enough to shame their opponents. In the narrative of the great ship that follows below, shame or embarrassment is the main sentiment identified by the storyteller with the ancestors of the contemporary Longgarese. On the Bemunese side of things, much of the storyteller's effort in depicting her own ancestors goes into displacing the negative content of their prior forest existence away from herself and fellow Bemunese and onto their neighbors. Conversely, some of the main sentiments that Bemunese ancestors express vis-à-vis those of Longgar in this ship's history are superiority and triumph. All this, in turn, is alleged to be intimately linked to the ship's song and, by extension, spun out of all the acquisitiveness and excitement provoked by the arrival to Aru of the master's new clothes. This particular ship's history radically revalues Bemun's position with respect to its neighbors and, even, the rest of Aru.

In its capacity both to act as a witness and to codify a particular repertoire of sentiments, a "proof" such as the ship's song, a special object, or a feature of Barakai's natural scenery has an objectified, thing-like character. This character, in turn, rubs off onto the sejara to which the "proof" is attached. In the hands of a skilled storyteller who rallies the various "proofs" that, familiar to her audience, texture and inbue her tale with the appropriate authority and sentiment, a given sejara acquires a certain objectivity. Barakai *sejara*, a cognate of the Indonesian word for "history" (I. *sejarah*), should therefore be understood not only as designating a "history" but also as the referent about which a history is told—not only, then, discourse, but also the discoursed world.[3]

For the above reasons, sejara on Barakai sometimes seemed to stand on its own as if endowed—in and of itself—with a compelling and decisive force. I was told that simply by "knowing" a particular "history," a woman or man could set it to work by invoking it verbally with reference to an immediate, practical goal. Speaking one day of sejara, a man from Mesiang, which together with Bemun claims first residence on Barakai, explained how his community had repeatedly invoked this history of early settlement to give its soccer team an edge in the archipelago-wide matches held annually during the 1970s in the island capital. Although the team no longer exists and the island-wide competitions have, for whatever reason, long been abandoned, it was this "history," according to him, that accounted for Mesiang's unchallenged status as archipelago champion throughout the 1970s.

But if, as this Mesiangese implied, sejara, to be efficacious, must be invoked by the appropriate persons or groups with specific objectives in mind like winning a soccer match, acting against sejara needs no such mediation. Sago palms planted by neighboring villagers on land claimed by Bemunese were said by the latter to have withered and died without any intervention on their part. The work of the wrong hands in the wrong place, their very presence was, according to these Bemunese, an act against sejara. Other Bemunese maintained that during the time they spent sitting out the war in the forest while the Longgarese dove alone in places that until then they had exploited together, the latter encountered considerably more sharks than shells. Again, what their neighbors had done by excluding Bemunese from Barakai waters went very much against sejara. When provoked as in such circumstances, sejara is seen as capable of coming—aggressively and powerfully—to its own defense.

Although on Barakai sejara was widely spoken of as endowed with a force that allowed it to be harnessed and deployed in the projects of the right persons or groups or that even—when sufficiently challenged—could make it act on its own, often it was simply recalled and told. Depending on its contents, telling sejara—or listening to it—was seen by many Bemunese, young and old, as an engaging way of whiling away an evening in a more or less intimate circle of family and friends. At other times, although the difference was not always so clear-cut, sejara was related, usually by older women or men, more self-consciously as something that should be passed on to one's children or to interested, sympathetic outsiders like myself.

Yet telling sejara as opposed to a story (B. *tekun*) is a somewhat tricky business. The telling of sejara, like the tales known on Barakai as tekun, which also happens to be the generic term for "spider," is more often than not a loose meandering process of unfolding not unlike the notion of spinning a yarn. But if in tekun, as the name for these spidery stories suggests, the attention is directed toward the teller and the deftness with which she develops her story and crafts its idiosyncratic texture and shape, in sejara the emphasis necessarily also falls on the range of authorizing "objects" that a teller manages to trip up and entangle within a given history to lend it validity and weight.

The most appreciated local raconteurs of history moved adroitly back and forth between the unfolding of sejara, which commonly has a winding story line of sorts—given that it is usually supposed to explain something like how such-and-such came to pass or why this or that is as it is today—and forays beyond the web of their own tale into the larger world where the "objects" that service the history as "proofs" can be located and caught up within the flow of their story. Through such moves the sejara itself becomes sedimented within a wider landscape of knowledge and experience that is familiar to the speaker and her audience alike. In the same way that, in a walk along the beach or when crossing the elephant grass toward the gardens, a villager might gesture toward a waterfall, an unusual outcrop of rocks, or an out-of-the-ordinary tree and in passing say something like "that has its history" (B. *ai ken sejara*), so, too, in an inverse move, will the teller of sejara undergird her account with some matter-of-fact summary statement along the lines of "it has its song" (B. *ai ken sab*), or "sign" (B. *ai ken tanda*), or simply "proof" (B. *ai ken bukti*), the latter being a gloss for songs as well as signs held to be inscribed in the natural scenery of Barakai Island as well as beyond it.

Frequently, the person recounting sejara will spell out the more precise location of a given "proof": "You know that deep, black pool in the forest beyond Abu so-and-so's old garden—the coconut palms and mangos are still there—well that's where she vanished, that bamboo clump on the side is what remains of her hair." These sedimented sites buttressed a woman named Puasajin's telling of the sejara explaining why women from her family should not marry the men of a particular Mesiang fam, more specifically, the tale of an ill-fated, abusive union from which an ancestress only managed to extract herself when she was engulfed by the Barakai landscape instead of overwhelmed by the husband pursuing her. Or in the case of the histories spun around the great ship, an undersea site called Chiselhead is usually mentioned as the spot where the ship would lie petrified beneath the Arafura Sea, at the same time as its name would commemorate the tool with which the ancestors carried out their civilizing if somewhat dubious deed of downing it. On Barakai then, sejara is always an argument about place. It is an argument that being localized and objectified in an array of tangible and privileged "proofs" endows the history told with a certain transcendent pastness. At the same time it molds the landscape in which the events related could convincingly have taken place.

Just as histories told on Barakai seem to have a certain permanence through their embeddedness in things that have "always been there, from a very long time ago," so too do songs, by being articulated in a linguistic register that stands somewhat apart from that of the everyday (see also Keane 1997b, 41). Because of the predominance in many songs of archaic constructions and even unintelligible foreign words, they often seem to participate in the very histories they are sung by islanders to recall. Beyond what were seen as such obvious signs of age, the widespread distribution throughout the Backshore of a well-known repertoire of songs sung on occasions like marriage, which bring large numbers of people from different places together, may also contribute to this general perception of songs as antique and unchanging. At such gatherings songs are remembered and sung, usually with the various parties and persons present first running through the gamut of the most widely shared and codified of songs; then, as the night wears on and drinking loosens tongues and spirits, newer compositions will sometimes take shape. Yet even the most innovative of such newly formed songs will necessarily have a familiar ring to them for Backshore listeners and remain, to a greater or lesser degree, suffused with a sense of sejara. Built up as they usually are out of short, already codified song "tips" (B. *sab ken toh*) and "trunks" (B. *sab ken un*) that are flung as offerings into the common pool of smoke, alcohol, and recollection by the most prominent of a night's singers or proposed from the sidelines by lesser-voiced younger men and, to some extent, women, they almost always comprise one or more stanzas already known to some people or that at least sound as if they should be.[4]

When speaking of innovation in the case of either Barakai songs or sejara, it is just as important to see the forest as—dare I say—the trees that emerge out of the different conjunctions of "trunks" and "tips." Admittedly, as cultural theorists increasingly insist, tracing out the distinctive turns of phrase, form, intent, and situation with which women and men distinctively story and shape their necessarily myriad renderings of "history," "experience," and so on takes one importantly, away from the totalizing distance of a single voice and vision, and presumably nearer to what positioned persons often feel most partial and passionate about (Haraway 1991). Yet doing so should not mean losing sight of the various criteria and conventions regarding the authority, credibility, modes of evaluation, or debatability that on Barakai, at least, make for all the difference between a just-so spidery story and something that might pass as sejara, or between a song sung simply for the pleasure it gives and one put forth as a "proof." Rather than adjudicate between them, it is necessary to take account of both the particular positionings from which people inflect and shape narrative forms and the more obviously codified values and discourses that they share with others—and, indeed, often feel partial and passionate about. Just as certain songs evoke bygone times even as they are performatively embedded in novel projects, so, too, sejara more generally is continually storied by different persons in new ways out of, into, and across the Barakai landscape. Yet while sejara and their related songs are therefore always expansive and innovative, they are not so without limit. Put somewhat differently, in Appadurai's formulation, the past of sejara is a "scarce resource" (Appadurai 1981).

Like the history of the great ship that follows, sejara is not infinitely susceptible to invention but rather "scarce"—inflected, for instance, by the state classification of Backshore communities as "left behind," by the realities of seasonal trade and the collection of sea products within an increasingly global economy, and by the memories of coercion and violence that accompanied recent pagan conversion in Aru. Invention is further curtailed by the criteria—aesthetic and otherwise—that influence such things as how a song should sound on Barakai, when and who should sing it, and what might serve respectively as its "tip" or "trunk." The notion that sejara is "scarce" as opposed to subsumable to and infinitely pliable within the political designs of those who invoke it should, however, not be taken as an appeal to any temporal baseline or assumed bedrock of "experience" or "context." Nor is it meant to suggest that sejara, as told by different persons, would simply mirror male, female, or other allegedly stable social "identities" or "points of view," although it clearly refracts the varying, divergent partialities and positions such persons may contingently assume.

As told to me by Abu Sabuan, the woman whose canoe had been confiscated by Longgarese in the mid-1970s, the great ship's history was dramatically delivered and bore the marks of her own sejara-telling idiosyncrasies. In addition to being told directly as the sejara that had bolstered Bemun's position in the war against its neighbors, it also spoke eloquently to the kinds of concerns and activities that tended to preoccupy Barakai women more than men. In the emphases, arguments, and repetitions with which Abu Sabuan patterned her history, it hints at some of the shifting times, spaces, and interlocutors in relation to which, I suspect, it was generally spoken. In her sejara the vexed sites of forest, trade, clothing, and religion all appear, while the submerged presence of state and church can be clearly felt.

Abu Sabuan's Great Ship

We sat one afternoon—me tape recorder in hand and she worrying once in a while that barking dogs or restless chickens might spoil my re-cording—during the lazy midday lull when most people lie around cat-napping, combing each other's hair for lice, or drowsily exchanging a few words, together on a mat in the run-down former tradestore whose owner—Abu Sabuan's elder sister's daughter and a frequent companion of mine—was off elsewhere. By this time, almost a year after I had come to Bemun, I had already heard of the great ship, its sejara, and related song—not surprisingly, given that the stir of my own arrival set off a flurry of sejara retellings and even more truncated synopses given by several prominent senior Bemunese men for my own edifying benefit. In the earliest references I heard of the ship, made almost exclusively by the important men who monopolized my attention during the first days following my arrival to Bemun, the image repeatedly presented was that of the authority rescued from the ship—the colonial staff of office that had been concealed in the great vessel's hold—and, as I later under-stood, the authority these men claimed for themselves from the Malay and thus, by extension, from outsiders like myself. Beyond their instruc-tional purpose, some of the very first of these sessions either concluded or began with a string of questions and assertions. As in Wallace's case more than one hundred years earlier in another part of Aru, all of these re-volved around the possible existence and whereabouts of kin (and ini-tially my own possible connection to them)—great, great, great, great-grandchildren, as it was commonly put. These would have been the offspring of the shipmaster's son, the sole survivor of the sunken vessel, and a Bemunese ancestress who after marrying in the village set off together in a trader's junk for (usually) "portugis." When I left Bemun as the community readied itself for the 1987 elections and, again in 1988, to return to the United States, several senior men also dispatched me with directives—again, regarding the ship's contemporary after-effects. They wanted me to track down their long lost relatives in Europe.

When I returned to Bemun the first time in the wake of the 1987 elections, I felt that I should do my best to bring back something portugis. And so I returned to Barakai with glossy brochures from an Amsterdam travel agency picturing boats beached under twisted nets on "portugis" shores, sun-washed scenes of fishing, *marisco*-rich dinners, and ruddy fisherfolk faces. But the pictures lacked the sympathetic magic I had, back in Holland, imagined they would have as I carefully picked out those travel vignettes that, however far removed from it, appeared most akin to the life I knew on Barakai. Yet even for those men who had initially prodded me for information about portugis or emphasized their special link to these staff-wielding first comers in a stream of trading outsiders[5]—and who would send me off again with the same instructions in 1988—or for those women—Abu Sabuan, her elder sister's daughter, and a few others—who spoke to me in the months following my arrival of the ship, the brochures, while passed around and looked over closely, did not have the effect I had hoped they would have.

Instead of triggering the shuttle movement of a sejara that might have inscribed portugis more insistently in Backshore topography—or vice versa—the same kinds of questions posed to me earlier were again reiterated: Had I heard anything in Holland or perhaps elsewhere while I was gone about anyone from Aru, or perhaps anyone from "the village of the east" (B. *wanusumor*, Bemun's main ancestral village) who had made it to portugis? Had I heard of any Backshore descendants living there, had I heard no names, no remarks, no stories told of them? And then after the questions came the insistences similar to those voiced by some of Bemun's senior spokesmen during my first weeks in the village when it turned out I came partly from Amerika, partly from Belanda but definitely not from Portugis: There *must* be some great, great, great, great-grandchildren, there just have to be some, they must be there. "Now," Abu Sabuan began,

> they saw this ship so they went out to the sea.[6] They saw this ship and went to the seashore. And, at this time, they wore those things, they wore barkcloth.

So, they saw this ship at sea and then they convened a meeting. They held a meeting and then the villagers went out to cut rattan on the island's sheltered, lee side. They went to collect rattan like that in order to make a raft. After they made the raft they then chose three men to go look at the ship. They selected those who would go first.

The men tied those things together, and they did this at the place called Top of the Cave. At the Top of the Cave they tied those things together, those ends of rattan. They kept tying them together on and on like that until they reached the side of the ship.

They boarded the ship and everyone was asleep.

After that they dove into the sea so that they could damage the ship [i.e., chisel a hole in its hull]. They kept on doing this, doing it like this—one man would surface, when one of them was tired he would surface, then another man would dive again. They kept on doing this over and over until just before daybreak the ship sank [B. *etulé*, to sink due to a hole].

When the ship began to sink, the men yanked the rattan rope [to notify those awaiting their return in the village that they had finished their task and were ready to head home]. They cast off the rope [away from the ship] so that those at home in the village would know.

So that their women would know they were coming home. So that they could go home and sleep in the village. Those three people had finished the job, and now they could go home.

[At this point Abu Sabuan backed up in her sejara to give some detail about the goings-on on board the ship itself.]

It was like that and then they moved to the rear of the ship, see. They yanked [the rattan rope] to go home then they went there [to the rear of the ship] and waited. They waited and a little later the ship began to sink.

Then the ship's master awoke and said, "Go make a place for the child— go make it." So they [the ship's crew] made a place for him to stay. They finished making it and he was up in the mast [Abu Sabuan and Gita described it as a little room at the top of the ship's mast, something like a crow's nest].

Well, then they cast off [the rattan rope] so that the people in the village would know, see. So then they went home to our ancestral village—the Village of the East.

So they [the three men] went in that way—they pulled, they arrived [at the village], and they spoke like this, "Hey, it would be better if tomorrow morning we went again because the ship master's son is there, they put him up in the crow's nest."

They went. So the next morning they went. They finished eating, they had slept, using that rattan they went out again.

They took the raft. They did not take canoes but they took the raft. They went and they arrived and then they took the child.

They took him and they put him on the raft and he said, "There are things down there, you know. Down below."

["The child said that?" I asked.]

Yeah, he said that. He said, "There are things down there. So you go dive for them. There are things, all kinds of things—palm wine and beer, all kinds of things. There, down there. Food, so you go home and get some canoes and then come back. There are things there."

They went to get canoes, see. Great big canoes and then they returned. They returned with the child.

They dove and dove but the ship's cargo was too much for them.

[Abu Sabuan at this point in her story shifted from sea to shore and from the activities of men to those of women to describe what was going on with the things that had been retrieved by the divers from the ship.]

Well, then the women would lay the things out to dry in the sun. They would retrieve something and then they would lay it out in the sun.

As they were laying things out in the sun like that, they felt pity for those people, those neighbors. They felt pity for the Longgarese.

So they said, "It would be better if we went to tell them so that they can go dive for themselves."

Like that, see. They went and they [the Longgarese] weren't wearing cloth loin coverings [but rather barkcloth]. They [the Bemunese] went and they had seen that clothing [from the ship], so they went wearing it, see.

They went and they were drunk [from the alcohol retrieved from the ship]. They were drunk and they were singing as they went there [to Longgar]. They were singing that song—the ship's song.

So they went and the others were ashamed. So they [the Longgarese] said, "Hey, where did you get your emblem (B. *somin*) from?"

They said emblem, see. These clothes they called their emblem.

So they said, "Well, we have come to call you. Don't run away for we have come to call you so that you can dive for yourselves. Because we took a lot but we couldn't . . . [the implication being that the ship's cargo had been too vast for them to retrieve everything]. So you go dive for the remainders."

So they went to dive for the remainders.

As for the child, well the village then looked after him. Not just one person looked after him but all of the villagers together.

And he [the child] saw that they threw away those things. Those pearl oysters.

So he said, "If you find them, well stop eating them and instead collect and save them. You look out to the shore and I will find a way. I will go find a way for you. You save those things."

Well, until they [the Europeans] went to war [the Second World War], those things, those pearl oysters, they would take the pearls and wear them.

So he said, "Save them, save those things. Don't do that. Stop eating them like that and save them instead."

They collected them, see. They collected them until he grew up, until they gave him a wife. They gave him a wife. So he took a wife from the Walwi family. They took her. They took her from the Walwi family. Her name was Bilé.

They stayed on [Bilé and the shipmaster's son]. They stayed on like that and then they made a trading junk, see. They made a trading junk. He went away with his wife. He took her and off they went.

In order to find a way for those things. Those pearl oysters.

Like that and he said to his wife, he said, "It would be better if we left." And that was good because the village had paid for the wife. They paid for her. He went away with her.

[This sounded like a resolution of sorts—off they went, which was a good thing since the village had paid for Bilé's brideprice and since the shipmaster's son had to "find a way" for the pearl oysters collected by the ancestors—but Abu Sabuan was not finished. First, she went back to the ship to retrieve from it another important article for her sejara that the divers had salvaged from the vessel.]

And they dove and they found the gold-knobbed staff (B. *tongka masne*). It belonged to the ship's master, a gold-knobbed staff. A woman or a man took it . . . who knows where they put it, that staff.

[After a short pause she resumed her story again, this time to locate the shipwreck at a specific named site in the Barakai undersea.]

It went down there—Chiselhead. The people who were on it turned into stone. The ship turned into stone. Its name is Chiselhead because they used a chisel on that ship, see. So they called it Chiselhead.

[Finally, she concluded with a summary of the import of the ship's sejara for her community as well as for Aru more generally.]

He took those pearl oysters across the sea and he brought these clothes. And these [clothes] are in Aru because of this village. Because of this ship. They wear clothes because of this village. They all wear clothes because of this village. Because that person carried those pearl oysters across the sea and only because of this are things as they are. Because they [foreigners] came again. That's how it is that people wear clothes—because of this village.

The above sejara provides a beginning to the ending proclaimed by a Bemunese woman at the opening of this chapter—"Save your old clothes and make a garden, because we won't be going to the store and we won't be buying new clothes. The oysters are gone and soon there will be no more pencarian." Endings such as these are dramatically salient in times of war—the three-year interlude spent "in the forest" during the conflict with Longgar or the Japanese occupation of Aru during World War II, when islanders said they buried their most prized possessions in the forest and women recalled desperately piecing together scraps of clothing and tattered garments to clothe especially their unwed daughters.[7] Given Aru's long-standing entanglement with a wider world of trade and colonialism, one might assume that such markers have delimited experience already for several centuries in the archipelago. Beyond such times of conflict, the rhythm of fits, starts, and depletions that describes the bust-boom swings, the rags to relative riches or riches to rags momentum of Backshore trade is also one of repeated new beginnings and greater or lesser endings.

In positing a beginning to trade and "civilization," Abu Sabuan's sejara is one possible narrativization of the foundational moment that crystallizes in the great ship's song and therewith of the modernity that the vessel's violent seizure sets in motion. At the same time, her account betrays the indeterminacy that for Bemunese informs the relationship of an Aru "inside" to a Malay "outside" as a difference that is itself opened up in the sejara with the departure and deferred return of the shipmaster's son and his Aruese spouse. This moment captures a historic and, on Barakai, recurrent gamble: will the portugis "civilization" hero find a way for "those things, those pearl oysters" with which the ancestors entrust him as he sails from Aru shores, and will other foreigners, indeed, flock year after year to trade on the Backshore, thereby allowing contemporary islanders to find some recompense for those first privileged tokens of their pencarian that in ancient times were carried away from Aru in a trader's junk? The lack of specificity of the Malay "outside" also explains the impulse of Bemunese occasionally to debate the national origins of the great ship. Although the prevailing interpretation is "portugis"—thereby linking the vessel to those Europeans who throughout Malaku occupy a mythical place of precedence in a long line of colonizing powers—speculations periodically arise that the ship might have been English or Spanish. Before I return to the indeterminacies, doubts, and delays that inform the relationship of the Aru "inside" to the Malay "outside" at the conclusion of this chapter. I would like first to specify further the context of Abu Sabuan's telling and to explore how the fraught topoi of forest, clothing, trade, and paganism—and therein the prevailing Backshore relations with church and state—surface in her sejara. I will along the way also have occasion to remark on the story's gendered specificity.

Modernity's Clothings and Unclothings

Against the looming backdrop of the forest and the buying or saving of clothes, I aim in the remainder of this chapter to pursue several threads in Abu Sabuan's history. I will take a few detours in which I confront this sejara with other tales and rumors in order to draw out and develop my argument. Recall first the immediate setting of this particular telling. Recall that bolstered by the force of its sejara the great ship's song had for some the power to deflect Longgarese arguments against Bemun's claims to commonly exploited diving sites and to shame thoroughly at least some of the most belligerent of its neighbors. This woman's story should therefore be seen as articulating a claim or, more precisely, a counterclaim that is intended to offset the arguments launched in the mid-1970s by Longgar. Recall also that the sejara was told to me, a European "outsider," in the abandoned front room of a former tradestore, in a village officially classified as having been "left behind," on the "Backshore" of a south Moluccan archipelago, and in a country run at the time by a government that styled itself not only as a "New Order" (I. *Orde Baru*) but also as a "Development Order" (I. *Orde Pembangunan*). This government had, furthermore, named all its cabinets "Development Cabinets" (I. *Kabinet Pembangunan*) and liberally attached the appendage "Development" to its institutions, social programs, and guiding constructs. And finally, it stood under the nation's first and only "Father of Development" (I. *Bapak Pembangunan*), President Suharto (Heryanto 1988, 11).[8] In a subtle and pernicious fashion, the implications of these "Developments" were not lost on most Aruese. Abu Sabuan's account bears the unmistakable traces of the official governmental designation of Bemun as "a village left behind" as it also stands witness to the forced conversion of Aru's pagans in the mid-1970s.[9]

In Abu Sabuan's *sejara*, the clothing, the alcohol, the song, the sentiments the clothing provokes, and the gendered division of labor set in motion by the ship are all part of the same package. As in other tellings of the great ship or, more generally, in conversations with women and men about the arrival to the islands of "Malay" (B. *malayu*) as opposed to "Aru" (B. *gwerka*) dress, or, for that matter, of "religion" (I. *agama*), the coming of such things effects a radical break. Sometimes this break is storied across a series of starkly delineated contrasts that variously make their way into the tellings of women and men—a world already opened versus one as yet closed, enlightenment versus darkness, intelligence or shrewdness versus stupidity, progress versus primitivism—or, more discursively, as above, where the dramatic difference that clothes make stages itself in the sentiments the clothes provoke, in the sociological effects they have in the story, and in the turns of phrase and language through which Abu Sabuan crafted her account.

"They saw this ship and went to the seashore. And, at this time, they wore those things, they wore barkcloth." Sunk by ancestors in the era of darkly shrouded ignorance that for most Backshore peoples—and perhaps especially those whose former forest habitation is occasionally flung by neighbors in their faces—remains the most readily available representation of their pagan past,[10] the great ship with its immense cargo of clothes and alcohol, and its savvy shipmaster's son opens up a whole new world that splits the work process along gendered lines and creates differences between those Aruese who can claim first access to cloth attire as their distinguishing mark or emblem and those who (as yet) cannot. In a remarkably economic fashion, Abu Sabuan's sejara subsumes all the main ingredients of a complex history of trade and colonial and postcolonial predicaments. The ship's arrival introduces the motivation to dive—first when the ancestors chisel a hole in the hold of the ship, subsequently when they retrieve its cargo, and finally when they collect the pearl oysters with which the portugis fills his trading junk. Along with the shipmaster's son, who directs Aruese energies to pen-carian and whose departure opens up a space for trade, the ship brings clothing, alcohol, and a colonial staff of office to the archipelago. Beyond pointing to the consumption of clothing and alcohol as important in-dices of commercial engagement,[11] the sejara also intimates how the dif-ferential embodiment of the master's clothes by distinct Aruese commu-nities introduces hierarchy and the potential for conflict among them.

In Abu Sabuan's particular take on trade and Backshore beginnings, the gendered division of labor introduced by the ship assumes a pro-nounced and reiterated prominence, translating into men's diving and women's care for clothes as well as neighbors. In the more truncated versions of the ship's sejara that were told to me at the outset of my resi-dence on Barakai by several prominent Bemunese men, the gilded staff of office figured more centrally than it does in Abu Sabuan's account. Misplaced or not, because of its official function under Dutch rule as an *objet chargé* of colonial authority (chapter 2; cf. Hoskins 1993, 127–37), the staff could be conjured up as the authorization of Bemun's long-standing connection to and, crucially, claim over important outsiders— whether portugis shipmasters, their sons and great, great, great, great-grandchildren, or recently arrived anthropologists like myself. Unlike these men, who tended to subsume such Malay tokens within the au-thority they wielded locally as, for instance, adat officials, Abu Sabuan, like many other women comprising the generation of Aru's first con-verts, more easily took to and appropriated the new values associated with the "outside" Malay. Women are, for instance, much more actively involved than men in the organization and dissemination of the new Catholic religion in their community for reasons that I discuss below. More generally, when the rift between the Aru and the Malay is dramatically asserted in the community's annual celebration, this difference becomes gendered as "male" versus "female." In its context women as opposed to men are also relatively Malay and are often seen as embodying the latter's disruptive forces as they undermine the essentialized Aru space that the male-dominated performance aims to establish.

Cargo and the gendered work required to retrieve it go hand in hand in Abu Sabuan's history with the sheer surplus of the ship's contents piling up narratively in the repetitive actions of male and female ancestors, with the repeated diving of the men alternating with the repeated laying out of wet clothes in the sun by the women, in the big canoes especially brought in to convey the salvaged goods, in the cargo that proved to be too much, and in the condescending invitation extended to Longgarese to dive for the "remainders" (B. *ken sisa-sisa*). Indeed, the combined labor of ancestral women and men extends as a clothes-line that effects a sharp divide between the past and the present, between primitivism and the celebratory boisterousness that comes with a good set of Malay clothes, as well as between the neighboring communities of Longgar and Bemun, here ranged relationally on a devolutionary "civilization" ladder. By articulating their claims as a first and privileged access to the world of trade, cargo, and international relations opened up by the ship, those Bemunese who invoked its song or sejara with reference to the war implied that their community's historically forged affinity to all of these things could displace their neighbors' denunciation of themselves as backwards. The story shows that even as former forest peoples Bemunese would not have been left behind by the civilizing momentum identified on Barakai with the *malayu* coast. Suffused with the unease widespread among Bemunese of being labeled primitive or "left behind," Abu Sabuan's account also speaks to the increasingly pervasive sense on Barakai in the mid-1980s that, like it or not, those practices that stood out as "pagan" or incompatible with Suharto's "development" plans had to be altered, taken distance from, or in the worst of cases "cast off" (B. *detebeen*). In other words, the rift that runs complexly through Abu Sabuan's sejara between Bemunese and others and that is variously bridged, opened up, and negotiated in her account is a rift that runs much deeper than one woman's recollection of an intervillage confrontation more than ten years back.

If the novelty of the clothing and the frenzied desire it sets off speak

loudly and clearly through the ship's song—"they run to and fro excit-
edly, they exclaim over the clothes, the first time we set eyes on such
things"—in Abu Sabuan's story the sentiments and implicit assumptions
that come with a "civilized" sartorial economy are already naturalized
and taken for granted. Laying out the wet clothing in the sun, the women
are overwhelmed by feelings of "pity" for their neighbors, who, unlike
themselves, do not as yet have Malay as opposed to Aru clothes. Decked
out in their new outfits and drunk with celebration, these women and
men set off for Longgar to invite its inhabitants to partake of the "remainders" left behind after their own plunder of the ship. Yet as this
civilizing mission approaches the village, their neighbors caught, as it
were, in their barkcloths are overtaken by shame and run to hide. Before
beating a retreat, however, they call out to ask where the Bemunese
obtained their distinguishing emblem.

In my experience, little reference was made to these emblems, or
somin, on Barakai, and the sociological relevance of these totemlike emblems that serve to distinguish among fam and especially larger named
clusters of fam seemed negligible. *Somin* also surfaced as the name for
the three groups resulting from the foundational division of Aru peoples
in the wake of the mythic diaspora from Karang-Enu into "those of the
front" (B. *selmona*), "those of the middle" (B. *tuburjuer*), and "those of
the rear" (B. *selmuri*) and as the term for the carved animals and birds
that decorate the sterns of indigenous boats (B. *belan*). When a person
dies on Barakai, her relatives will usually stamp her corpse with four
charcoal images of her kin group's emblem as the crucial insignia that
will allow the dead person's ancestors to identify her on arrival in the
afterworld. In other parts of Aru like Batulay, people sometimes place
images of their emblems in their gardens as a discouragement to thieves,
while on Trangan the social importance of somin seems to be greater
than on Barakai (Manon Osseweijer, personal communication).

Abu Sabuan's appeal to this term in her story has the effect of under-
scoring Bemun's inalienable claims to the master's clothes, which they
therefore possess as a community much like a group is identified by the
totemic emblem that distinguishes it from others. Here, too, the somin
serves as a mark of distinction in Bourdieu's sense (Bourdieu 1984).
Hence, Abu Sabuan's metalinguistic aside: "They said somin. These
clothes they called their somin." Besides bringing out the "distinction"

these clothes bestow on their original wearers, she also, I believe, high-lights the modernity embodied when they are worn rather than loin-cloths or other markers of pagan backwardness. Especially striking in her account is the conjunction of, on the one hand, the condescending invitation to Longgarese to profit from the ship's "remainders" and, on the other, the assertion put in their mouths that the attire that Longgarese receive from their neighbors, being a somin, cannot but substantiate Bemun's inalienable claims to the world of the ship.[12]

Like religion in much of Indonesia and dramatically so on Aru's Back-shore, Malay clothing draws a sharp line between those who already have it and those who as yet do not. Hence, the pity felt by Bemunese women for the ways in which their neighbors still went about. Hence also the immediate desire on the part of these same neighbors to run and hide when confronted with the specter of "civilized" clothes—as if they could already know what not (yet) wearing such clothes implied, or as if their own primitivism could only be produced in the very face of Malay civilization. As implied by the future anterior that pervades this *sejara*, positing a has-been in reference to what will be the case (S. Weber 1991), it is, indeed, the rhetoric and radical revisions of modernity that are at issue here. Differentially brought out as "development" and "progress" and, most pointedly in Aru's recent history, as the having or not having of a religion, this rhetoric decisively inflects the identities and stakes in many different conflicts and situations on Barakai. A popular take on the arrival of religion to the archipelago highlights the material and coercive means of agama's dissemination and has the virtue of bringing out the religious politics woven through Abu Sabuan's account. At the same time the story complicates the stark oppositions that structure her sejara, making room for a more pliable agency.

What's in a Pocket?

In one distant prereligious past, goes the story occasionally told on Bara-kai, the very difference between Muslims and Pagans emerged out of an accident of dress, following from the apparently trivial circumstance of the having or not having of a pocket. Familiar in its characteristic synop-tic form across the island, the story zooms in on that decisive moment when two Aruese ancestors—one wearing a so-called *openjas*, or jacket, derived from the Dutch, and the other a loincloth (B. *gom*)—were offered a copy of the Qu'ran.[13] As if religious difference issued directly from distinctions of dress, the Dutch openjas of the former, being graced with a pocket, immediately accommodated a fit between the man and the new faith. By the same token, the other Aruese, with no place to put even a pocket-size Qu'ran, remained pagan by default of his dress.

Importantly, this story is always told as that of the arrival to Aru of religion in general rather than of Islam specifically. Indeed, this point is already implied insofar as the pivotal contrast on which the story turns is that of pagans and converts, or, in former New Order discourse, between those who "already have a religion" (I. *sudah beragama*) and those who "as yet do not" (I. *belum beragama*). Beyond, therefore, any other kinds of generalizations that the story might seem to invite regarding, for instance, a fit between fashion and faith or the interiorized selves that are commonly held to characterize modern forms of subjectivity, it says instead something highly specific about agama under the New Order, about the materiality of its introduction to Aru, and about the spaces religion carves out for recently pagan peoples like those of Barakai. In this respect and in its marked alterity, Aru's pocket diverges dramatically from the role that pockets historically have assumed in Europe. In Europe, it can be argued, the intimate juxtaposition of persons and pockets, the privacy that pockets conjure through the personal effects they withdraw from scrutiny, and in general the obstacles they present to sight link the purview of pockets to the production of interiorized forms of modern subjection—and ones that are closely connected to the history of religion (Foucault 1988; 1990). Here, instead, the pocket will serve as a figure that flashingly disturbs these kinds of connections, unsettles the stark oppositions between enlightenment and darkness, progress and paganism, and any of the other contrasts called forth by Barakai women and men in their conversations about clothing or the befores and afters of their religious conversion.

Telltale rather than trivial, Aru's pocket is not easily domesticated or glossed over. The tale, in other words, that this pocket might more plausibly tell has to do with a highly specific politics of religion. As expressed in the pocket's tale, this politics is apprehended for what it is by Barakai islanders, namely, not in terms of interiority but as the quite material folding up of their everyday reality. The decisive turnabout in the tale also exposes the dynamics of a religious politics that draws hard and fast lines between those Indonesians who already, as it is put, have a religion and those who as yet do not, and that separates Muslim, Protestant, Catholic, Hindu, and Buddhist national citizens, or those with one of the five religions recognized by the government, out from a residual, recalcitrant, and undifferentiated pagan body. Since the mass conversion of Aruese pagans orchestrated by the archipelago's civil and military officialdom in 1976–77 and motivated by the determination to ensure the participation of all islanders in the 1977 national elections—with participation in turn contingent on the possession of a citizen's identity card on which the category of agama had to be declared—all Backshore peoples with, in my experience, only one exception "already have a religion." (Spyer 1996b). The implications of this double conversion to agama and citizenship, of crossing the gap between the "not yet" and the "already," are far-reaching: "Beginning in elementary classrooms, texts and lectures convey the idea that *agama* is progressive (*maju*) and a requisite of good citizenship. By an implicit logic of opposites, the official endorsements of *agama* make those persons without *agama* appear to be disloyal national citizens, uncommitted to the values of Pancasila, not to mention intellectually and morally backward" (Kipp and Rodgers 1987, 23). Informed by this "implicit logic of opposites," the pivotal position of Aru's pocket between a world alight with agama and one enveloped in paganism reiterates the late Suharto government's own sharp demarcations. Yet insofar as the pocket and the Qu'ran it comes to contain also hint at a hidden theme in the recent history of religion in Aru, it is a repetition that makes all the difference.

Storied, as I said, as the arrival of all religion to Aru and thus pertaining to religion generally rather than more specifically to Islam, the Qu'ran speaks less here to the link made by the Suharto government between agama and a few select "world" religions or to other aspects of a globalized modernity that one might be tempted to read into the book—reference to a larger world of letters, to print capitalism, or other such weighty matters—than to knowledge of a more covert kind. Like the pocket in which it finds a quasi-hidden home, the Qu'ran in the eastern extremes of the archipelago, if to a greater or lesser degree recognized for its connection to Islam, was usually more compellingly linked by Barakai women and men to another kind of power and knowledge. More directly associated with the Muslim traders who have long frequented the Backshore than with Islam per se, the Qu'ran was more conventionally apprehended in relation to the knowledge known as *ilmu*, where it sometimes figured as a prop. Insofar as its practice is clandestine and its objective usually suspect, ilmu may be glossed as "black magic."[14] Doubled by its Qu'ranic content, the hidden dimension of the pocket that elsewhere has enabled part of its private significance appears in this fashion overdetermined. In pocketing a book emblematic here of religion in general as well as commonly singled out for its connection to the covert, the ancestral gesture invoked by islanders in their accounts of religion seems then to imply that the arrival of "religion" to Aru and the designation of its quasi-concealed place are part and parcel of the same thing, that agama and hiding places are cut, as it were, from much the same cloth.

The theme of the hidden forms a connecting thread between Abu Sabuan's sejara of the ship and the figure of the telltale pocket that provides religion with the material means of its introduction and assigns it a proper place. At the same time the pocket outlines on one ancestor's openjas some of the predicaments that Suharto's religious politics, with its decided emphasis on progress, development, and loyal citizenship, produced for those classified until recently as pagans. In the story of the ship, exposure to Malay dress compels those still clad in bits of bark—at least initially—to hide, thereby suggesting that Malay stands for enlightenment and a world opened out to progress, as Aru stands for a pagan primordialism wrapped in darkness, turned in on itself, and embarrassed and fearful in the face of change. These are indeed precisely the terms that Barakai women and men commonly relied on in their tellings of the past as something profoundly different from and set off from their current everyday lives. Yet the striking salience of the pocket fixated on by many of these same people—if taken seriously—begs for a different interpretation insofar as it hints at how on Barakai Island these recently pagan women and men fashion alternative places, or even "pockets," for themselves within religion and until recently under Suharto's New Order.

Dramatic in its abrupt decisiveness, the tale of agama's arrival turns entirely on the having or not having of a pocket. But the predicament of the pagan ancestor here is less that of having to hide, as with those marked by primitivism in the ship's story, than of being totally exposed and left without resources. Unlike the Dutch-derived *openjas*—open yet comprising its own interior space—the pagan loincloth is pure surface. Without folds or creases it is bereft of any place behind which or within which a pagan might conceal a "religion," a pocket-size Qu'ran, not to mention some sort of Foucauldian interiorized "self." Abu Sabuan's sejara and the synoptic tale of agama's arrival suggest, then, respectively somewhat different strategies for negotiating with Malay alterity whether such reveals itself in clothes or as religion. The alternative to hiding in the former means usurping the master's clothes rather than disappearing into the darkness of a primordial paganism. In the latter it is rather paganism that is bereft of any space of retreat, while religion introduces a place of concealment.

While somewhat different, however, these stories should not be seen as opposites. Rather their very existence indexes a fractured social landscape fraught with ambiguity where none of the available alternatives offers a permanent solution or stable resting place to Barakai women and men. In this regard, the relatively unhierarchical coexistence of alternative versions of events and strategies is itself an expression of the indeterminacy and rent nature of the social world that Backshore Aruese are constantly forced to navigate. At the same time, both stories powerfully suggest how Barakai islanders have internalized the gaze of the Malay "outside," how they have taken in the look of Aru as it has been historically documented by outsiders. In Abu Sabuan's account, the Bemunese view of their neighbors is a displaced look at themselves through the eyes of the foreign master that they adopt along with his clothes. This is why the sentiments in her sejara always emerge at those points where "inside" and "outside" converge: the newly usurped "outside" perspective of Bemun's ancestors on Longgar's primitive "inside" provokes pity, while the latter's "inside" paganism in the face of the other's modernity compels intense shame. In the much more succinct tale of Aru's conversion, the discursivity of Abu Sabuan's history telescopes into the immediate lack of a fit between a pagan body and foreign agamacized clothes. Whichever way one looks at it, not having clothes condemns Aruese to vulnerability, hiding, and deprivation, while being a convert often means being a pagan body masquerading in the master's clothes. When worn by the Aruese in these stories, Malay clothing is therefore always tainted by an air of illegitimacy whether the reason implied is the questionable means through which the clothes were obtained or a more internalized dimension that indexes "black magic."

The explicit materiality with which violence is dressed in these different tellings warrants further attention. In the conversion tale the coercive dimension that Barakai islanders commonly identify with the Malay reveals itself in the violence with which the pagan is deprived of any alternatives or space of appeal. In that of the ship, the frantic desire to inhabit and lay claim to the master's clothes predominates. The violence of the Malay "outside" emerges here already embodied by Aruese as the fantasy projected back onto ancestral times of a dramatic reversal: the complete subjugation of the Malay "outside" by the Aru "inside" through the capture and plunder of the great foreign ship. Violence and the radical rift between those with modernity and those without is fully collapsed into clothes, thereby betraying the brutal materiality of those practices that forced Aruese to convert and that continue to make them into agama-minded citizens.

Following the Foucauldian argument regarding the making of modern subjects, a set of exterior, disciplinary practices—such as the panoptical and confessional technologies of state and church, and the regimes of crime, sexuality, and medicine or biopolitics—collaborate in producing the space of interiority that would especially distinguish the "modern" subject (Foucault 1973, 1977, 1990). By extension, the production of the ensuing unified, confessional, and autobiographical persons would, in turn, be contingent on the reproduction of these same external practices—the disciplinary regimes through which subjugated bodies and their concomitant interiorized selves are renewedly and ongoingly brought about. Albeit by a "circuitous imperial route" subsequently followed by more direct postcolonial power politics, especially of Suharto, this modernizing process does to some extent hold for Aru (Stoler 1995, 7). The kinds of Foucauldian selves that modern forms of subjection would commonly produce are absent, however, in these islands. Whereas in Foucault's analysis, modern subjects are, as it were, folded inwards as the effect of disciplinary practices, in these islands such pockets of interiority are instead thoroughly turned out. Thereby they expose, as in the tale of agama's arrival, the materiality and externality that has always gone into the making of modern subjects.

Evident on Aru's Backshore are the clear effects of a state discipline that seems to have brought about—especially with respect to the 1976–77 conversions—through its system of stringently enforced identity cards, fraught religious competition, and physical coercion, the need on the part of the recently pagan to create protective, concealing mantles for themselves. While the sheer materiality of the resulting pragmatic places or "pockets" may seem strange, they are actually no more or less concrete than the disciplinary practices that effected Aru's conversion and that in different ways are perpetuated by local state and church representatives. Nor are they more or less concrete than the practices that preceded them and that came by way of the "circuitous imperial route" that at this far end of the Netherlands East Indies must have been even more tortured and twisted than it was near the colonial capital of Batavia on the island of Java.

This route brought to Aru, especially from the mid-nineteenth century on, those colonial officials who mapped Aru's different "landscapes" and stabilized its more fluctuating forms of settlement (frequently involving the relocation of communities from the interior to the coast);[15] who violently suppressed the uprisings that periodically shook the Backshore between the 1880s and 1917; who in the first decades of this century introduced a head tax, registered Aruese for vaccination campaigns against polio and other diseases, and took censuses; who imposed forms of attire and authority; and who encouraged the schooling of the islands' natives where all of the above were in various ways reinforced. The fact that on Barakai what looks like interiority depends, as it were, on surface—in the same way that a pocket only becomes a place to hide once sewn onto or into an openjas—suggests, moreover, that the kinds of external and concrete disciplinary practices that tend to produce one or another version of a "modern" subject are here neither ideologically suppressed nor rendered invisible as, for instance, in most European countries today, but on the contrary are something these Aruese continually confront in their full materiality.

At the periphery, the power and magicality of interiorizing practices or places such as "pockets" can, not surprisingly, be more apparent than among those who by now take them for granted and thus easily overlook them. In a reality formed, as it were, increasingly of folds, agama appears to provide Barakai women and men with one or more "pockets" within which to hide. It is, however, only one possibility within a larger shifting field—thus another "pocket," albeit a more tenuous one, might be thought of as a pagan elsewhere, as elusive cassowary country within a somewhat more stabilized landscape made up of Catholics, Protestants, and Muslims. A "pagan elsewhere" is then one possible description of the Aru space into which Bemunese annually retreat when they celebrate the flighty cassowary as the emblem of the Aru in antagonistic opposition to the Malay.

Yet another possibility—less a "pocket" than something that underscores how Aruese continually face the disciplinary practices of state and mission in their unavoidable materiality—is what I have elsewhere called serial conversion (Spyer 1996b). A phenomenon that was especially prevalent during the years immediately preceding and following the 1976–77 conversions, serial conversion refers to the pattern according to which both women and men would switch from one religion to another, in some cases moving through all three local options—Islam, the Protestant Christianity of the GPM, and MSC Catholicism—before settling on one. For some, the mobility of such multiple conversions seems to have been an attempt to negotiate alternatives within agama, while for others it may have involved a more direct refusal of the straitjacket exemplified by the choice of a single religion on the Indonesian citizen's identity card (cf. Steedly 1993, 207–8). At the same time, serial conversion can also be understood as a larger conversion to seriality—brought to the archipelago through, especially and most powerfully, the enumerative practices of state and church—writ small. Like the pocket singled out by islanders for a pivotal role in Aru's religious history, serial conversion is just one example among other practices on Barakai built out of repetition and number that enhance and extract the power and magicality of very concrete technologies that on this periphery appear more salient than among those for whom they are already normalized.

Barakai islanders have developed several strategies through which they variously negotiate the alterity both of the Malay and of Aru's "pagan elsewhere," which in recent years has increasingly come to stand for an ambivalently valued past. While the latter is the topic of later chapters of this book, the strategies deployed with respect to the former include the rising concealment and even casting off of suspect practices, the retailoring of agama into a place of protection and surface accommodation, and the occasional elusion of the disciplinary grids imposed by state and church. Thus, before returning to Abu Sabuan's history of the great ship, I consider the concrete technologies and materiality of agama's arrival to the Backshore.

Parcels, Packages, and Cargo

In the memoirs of his service as a colonial officer in the Indies, J. van Baal recalls an incident from around 1937 in which he placed a Catholic schoolteacher under three weeks' arrest in what is today the Indonesian province of Irian Jaya after the parents of some school children complained about the punishment their children had received for playing hookey. "In his zeal" the teacher had tied the eight children to a single length of rope, using the infamous "Atjeh knot" to fasten each individually to it, and then, in a potentially "life-endangering" situation, slipped the end of the rope over his horse's neck and "rode them in this manner triumphantly around the village in order to demonstrate what happens with school children who play hookey" (van Baal 1985, 114).[16] To dispel any potential doubts that he might harbor antipapist feelings, van Baal includes for the record an equally egregious example of Protestant "zeal" to show that "with respect to violence" these missionaries were no different from their competitors.[17] Several years after the incident involving the Atjeh knot, van Baal told the story to an old friend. "That you can get worked up about that. I even saw Manokwari hookey players nailed by the ear to the school bench," the friend remarked on hearing it. Van Baal notes that his friend neglected to mention that the ears of the victims were already pierced under the assumption that this aspect of his story would be understood. But whether or not there had been holes in the school children's ears would not—van Baal astutely observes—have diminished the fundamental actuality of this colonial situation in which "the stupid Papoea, the 'Papoea bodoh,' had to be compelled to civilization by the teacher." This fact, concludes van Baal, has had its political consequences up to the present day—a point that I have been intent on demonstrating in this chapter (van Baal, 1985, 115).

Conjoining the material and the spiritual closely in their all-around civilizing mission, Protestant schoolteachers from Ambon active on the Backshore from the 1920s on intervened energetically in the refashioning of Aruese.[18] As elsewhere, some of the most violent assaults on local appearance were aimed at restructuring male and female attire along proper Christian and gendered lines (Comaroff and Comaroff 1991, 1997). Beyond the usual covering over of especially female bodies, some older men in Bemun recalled, for instance, the violence with which their Ambonese schoolteacher ripped the earrings right out of their lobes. Evidence again from the Sacred Heart mission field of Merauke underscores the importance invested, in this case by the Catholics, in clothing the Papuans—how, for instance, a "good teacher" would make copra with the older school children in order to purchase clothing for them and the others from the profit they made, and how these Sunday bests would then be stored in the teacher's house to be distributed and then recollected once a week on this holiday (van Baal, 1985, 282). "Good teachers" thus introduced, along with clothes, Christian notions of work, money, and time. In the early 1960s, when Dutch Catholic missionaries began their own proselytization on Aru's Backshore, they too set about refiguring—albeit more subtly in post-Independence Indonesia than their Protestant predecessors—some of the material grounds on which the more dramatic conversions of the mid-1970s would subsequently be played out (see also Scheurs 1992).

Clothing together with schooling and medicine figured high on the list of the various materializations that the Catholics aimed to introduce into the lives of pagan Aruese. In 1955 in a report of one of the first service trips to Aru before the establishment of a Sacred Heart station in these islands, a missionary wrote to his bishop about the surplus of clothing he had seen in the context of Aruese adat feasts. Yet once the mission set up a permanent post in the island capital, such surplus seems to have been forgotten or at least displaced—the cast-off clothing of Catholic families in the Netherlands being one of the main material things repeatedly called for in the correspondence from Dobo to Ambon. Initially, the distribution of Catholic clothing in the islands appears to have been limited to single articles or to outfits construed as a return on gifts presented to the bishop by relatively well placed Aruese. "Herewith a package," writes the Bishop to the Aru missionary Father van Lith in 1971,

> in which I have placed various costly things (D. *kostbaarheden*), collected over time. Make sure no quarrels or jealousy come of them. The cross is

for Andreas, former headman of Benjuring. For Maimete of Marlasi, a sweater. There is also a Maria statue for the Feruni church. I promised that to Daantje for the Feruni church. You should give something extra to the former headman of Kabalsiang (I received some pearls from him and promised a cross). . . . At any rate, give as much as possible to the officials (D. *grootheden*) of the different villages, especially those who have been dismissed because of agama, like those of Kalar-Kalar and Longgar.[19] I also promised Klara of Kabalsiang something for her casuary eggs. To the former headman of Kaibolafin I also promised something, at any rate he asked for one pair of trousers, one shirt, one sweater, but there are no trousers. You might also think of the people in Papakula regarding the jewelry that still remains. I heard that the parrots came from there. Perhaps not for nothing.[20]

As in earlier colonial times when cloth of different colors was given to Muslims and Christians, religiosity rubs off easily onto clothing (de Hollander 1898). Here, one shirt, two sweaters, and potentially one pair of trousers commingle promiscuously with Maria statues and Christian crosses in the same package sent to Aru. Today, some twenty years later and postconversion, the connection between Catholicism and clothing continues to be made, for example, in the two church rites with which Bemunese are most familiar, namely, baptism and marriage. The new outfit that in the 1970s came to many villagers with conversion comes today with the baptism of their babies, while the lone white wedding gown present in Bemun in the mid-1980s cycled back and forth between its Chinese owner and those young women who rented it from the tradestore for the sanctified moment of their official church union.

But it was in the 1970s, as the drive for the conversion of Aru's pagans assumed momentum to meet the goal of a fully agamacized archipelago for the 1977 elections, that the connection between clothing and conversion, and especially Catholicism, was most concretely and consistently made. This was a dramatic epoch, of which Barakai people more readily recalled being plied with commodities or intimidated and coerced than being coaxed into conversion by theological argument and instruction. In retrospect, at least regarding the Catholicism to which Bemun ulti-mately—as one of the last communities of the archipelago to succumb to agama—converted, things loomed large in the memories of many of

Women and children heading for their baptism. From the collection of
Pater van Lith MSC.

Barakai's Catholics. A man named Abu Magar recalled the confusion he
felt at the time from being beset on all sides by the proponents of different faiths: "Islam said come join us, the Protestants said come join us,
they tried all kinds of things, but only with van Lith [the Dutch Catholic
missionary at the time] did it become possible—he captured people's
hearts, he would arrive with chest after chest of clothing, he would inject
people free of charge—trousers, skirts, shirts, sweaters he distributed,
cans of oil he also distributed." With sacks of clothing dealt out in Backshore villages by numbered lottery, with rosaries, religious pictures, and
eventually church paraphernalia like candelabras, crosses, ciboria for
communion wafers, and so on bestowed on deserving communities, the
Catholics rivaled the Protestants and Muslims, many of whom were
members of Aru's civil and military officialdom.

The Dutch Catholic missionaries were not unconcerned about the
ways in which their own work was swept up within a larger bureaucratic,
national, and coercive project about which they had serious misgiv-

ings.[21] Yet notwithstanding the at times equally strong misgivings they expressed about the unsubtle material means with which they met and countered their opponents,[22] the missionary van Lith, who in 1968 had already voiced discomfort about his increasing affinity to St. Nicholas,[23] felt the need to complain at the height of the conversion drive about his dire shortage of "rosaries, medallions, and pictures, and little images for which the teachers and new Catholics continue to ask. I hope to receive a veritable cargo of such." "Best regards," he concludes this letter to Ambon's bishop, "I have to go out now to baptize around 500 people. . . . I go around with buckets of baptismal water but have nothing more in the way of religious articles. Please do something about it, signed A. van Lith."[24] While for the mission trousers and sweaters have little in common with "religious articles," such fine material distinctions were undoubtedly lost on most Aruese and even more so during the frantic times of their own conversion.

What does seem to have registered and erupted compulsively as rumors from time to time into the Backshore everyday of diving and trade is the impulse on the part of Malay others to inundate Aruese with their own clothes. A family resemblance ties the sporadic rumors of boxes of clothing sent to the village by far-flung relatives in portugis to those dramatic times when the Catholic mission showered the islanders— along with rosaries, medallions, pictures, and little images—with chest after chest of hand-me-down and leftover Dutch clothes. Yet, although a faint echo of these charged times resonates through the rumors, the one is not reducible to the other. Rather than a deluge, the rumors always report the same basic failure: the shipped boxes in fact never arrive. As women and men would patiently explain, the packages sent to them thus far must have been either lost in a maze of regional bureaucratic red tape, waylaid by greedy Dobo officials or other Aruese covetous of foreign goods, or, according to what may be the most frequent speculation, forwarded to the wrong address under the assumption that the descendants of the people who previously lived in the Village of the East— Wanusumor or, in Malay, Seltimor—would still live in the same place. Packages from portugis and destined by right of affinity for Bemunese may, in other words, owing to a simple linguistic mixup, have been diverted to other Aru villages with names similar to that of their own former site of habitation—maybe to Selmona or Selilau, or even to Kobaseltimor. Yet, amidst all the rumors of presents gone astray, there was never any mention of action undertaken to retrieve them. When things wandered off in the wrong direction, Bemunese were helpless in the face of the failings of the state bureaucracy and what passes in these islands for a postal service, or, indeed, when confronted with the misdeeds of others who, like themselves, have a weakness for foreign clothes. Instead of taking action, what they did was speculate how things arrived elsewhere and never quite happened their way, and in so doing they voiced all the doubts, delays, and indeterminacies that on Barakai, along with coercion, make up the Malay.

A last thread in Abu Sabuan's story hints at why—as it was sometimes rumored—their *portugis* relations might have felt compelled from time to time to put together packages and dispatch them, destination Aru, across the sea. The same thing that would have driven the shipmaster's son with his bride away from these islands long ago explains, this *sejara* teller intimated, the imagined impulse on the part of this couple's presumed descendants to send their Bemunese affines the occasional box of clothes. In the story the shipmaster's son leaves "in order to find a way for those things, those pearl oysters," and Abu Sabuan's *sejara* is therefore also the tale of how trade as Barakai islanders knew it in the mid-1980s—with the diving and the debt that comes with it—first began. "It would be better if we left," he said to his bride. "And that was good," Abu Sabuan explained, "because the village had paid for the wife." Recall in her account that not only had "all of the villagers" acted as wife-taker to the shipmaster's son by paying for the wife, but they had also simultaneously assumed the role of wife-giver by selecting a woman for him from the *fam* held to be among the first on the island and thus, here, capable of standing for the sum total of *fam* in the village.

Not surprisingly, on Barakai Island as in other parts of the Moluccas and the Lesser Sundas, wifegivers and wifetakers normally sit on opposite sides of a marriage exchange (Fox 1980; McKinnon 1991). Put simply, a woman goes one way, while the bridewealth paid for her, or "the woman's price" (B. *kodarne ken wil*), goes the other. Then, on Barakai, the group that receives the woman, in turn, reciprocates this payment with the so-called woman's things (B. *kodarne ken len*). Although the latter consists of a range of household necessities intended to help the young couple set up its own home, the content of the "woman's things" for any given marriage are negotiated, argued about, and spoken of as a return made by the wifegivers for the bridewealth they in part would have already received. Abu Sabuan's insistence on the double role of wifegiver and wifetaker assumed by the ancestors may have been an attempt to suggest that, having given so much, something in return remains owed to Bemun by Malay outsiders. Seen in this light, it is probably not trivial that she told the story especially for me. Yet, in the rumors of packages sent by relatives from portugis, there was little sense of a vast gift unremitted but rather the airing of a suspicion that things never quite come their way.

There are also other, more disturbing implications to be gleaned from Abu Sabuan's story. It could be argued, for instance, that by sending off to portugis an Aruese wife with her bridewealth fully paid and a cargo load of oysters, the ancestors alienated the means of their own reproduction and forged therewith their dependency on the whims of the Malay world. In giving up, morever, any means of ensuring a return on what they already had given away, the ancestors of the sejara created not only dependency but also expectancy vis-à-vis a beyond of trade. At any rate, the collapse of the difference between wifegiver and wifetaker short-circuits the possibility of any balanced reciprocity between an "inside" Aru and an "outside" Malay, while clearly demarcating these positions as sharply opposed. The same could also be said of the seizure of the ship insofar as it is based on violent usurpation rather than trade. From this perspective, the legacy of the ancestors would be the lack of any hold on the Malay rather than a legitimate claim to its modernity and civilization. The sejara establishes a gap between the Aru and the Malay along with the exclusion of the possibility of any real reciprocity between them. This gap is therefore also the one that separates the strategies that people devise to fulfill their expectations and the desires that on Barakai infuse the Malay. Together with trade, pencarian, and the arguments and strategies with which Aruese would bridge this gap, what fills this space is especially ambivalence, deferral, and indeterminacy. The misgivings with which this space is riddled surface in the authority wielded through a misplaced staff, in the insistence that the long lost portugis relatives must be there—betraying simultaneously the desire to reestablish the circuit of communication and the doubt of this possibility—in the rumors of packages that never arrive, and in the lingering sense that the clothing one wears as an Aruese is not quite right.

4   Mothers of Pearl

I take a shell in my hand
new to itself and to me
I feel the thinness the warmth and the cold
I listen to the water
which is the story welling up
I remember the colors and their lives
everything takes me by surprise
it is all awake in the darkness
—W. S. Merwin, "The Blind Seer of Ambon"

The Scent of the West Wind

A song sung to me one evening in Bemun tells of two young men who, having left Aru for the big city, are overcome by feelings of longing and homesickness when they catch the scent of the west monsoon.

Gwe rua dam tobaba	[Two young men only recently
derko il janjamor	traveling
dalis dal kud	they ride horses
kudne alalau wi je mair	those horses on the move night and day
awar gamamau	the fragrant scent of the west wind
koleng siring kowel jornom	I remember, I remember diving]

The singer, a man in his late forties, told me that the two men of the song originated from the neighboring village of Apara and that they had traveled with Chinese merchants to the metropolis and trade entrepôt of Makassar in what is today south Sulawesi. There, it seems, they led the good life—gallivanting and touring the city day after day and night after night. But one day, the scent of the west season, riding the sea breezes from the far end of the archipelago, brought these men to their senses, as it were, stirring memories of diving and—the singer added—of their former companions on the boats critical to this form of livelihood. In so doing, the fragrant wind introduced an element of complexity into a life that, up until this moment, had been wholly carefree.

This is, indeed, the sort of song that Barakai islanders are wont to say "touches" or "strikes" (B. *artome*), capturing its subject matter and thereby also its audience to the point of an almost physical identification with it. The pull of the "livelihood" known locally as pencarian comprises the complex of diving, the trade in sea products, the undersea that opens up to men when they dive (and somewhat differently to women), and the structures of indebtedness with which all of these are enmeshed. If in the song the appeal of diving has the power to traverse vast geographical distance, the discourse on pencarian, of which diving forms a part, often acts in other ways that can unsettle the conventional distinctions among things on Barakai. What men and women call pencarian tends to provoke sentiments that by their very excess potentially disrupt the already relatively fluid boundaries between persons and objects (and their spirit providers) that transgress ethnic lines and, more generally, may set into motion desires and attitudes that do not necessarily allow things to be kept in their proper places.

For most islanders, though certainly not all, the pull of pencarian shapes dramatically their evelution of the difference between the year's east off-season and the west season devoted to diving and trade. In so doing, it hints at the preeminence assigned to trade over other activities, of the marked tendency to privilege a livelihood obtained from the sea versus one carried out on land, and of a Malay as opposed to an Aru coloring of the everyday. There is much to suggest, however, that this preeminence is hardly consolidated but rather in a tentative flux. Thus, while the relation between the Malay and the Aru is not only shifting but comprises crossings and mutual reallocations as well as contrasts, the fact that the latter coexists at all as a complexly posed alternative to the former underscores what at times emerges in the form of an unsettling détente. Once a year, as well—and for whatever this kind of momentary performative assessment is worth—the preeminence of the Malay and of pencarian as perhaps its most compelling manifestation is critically assessed in the context of Bemun's annual celebration. Here, however, my main focus will be the complex ways in which pencarian, as both a livelihood and the discourse through which this livelihood is imagined and produced, delineates a space for the gendering of subjectivities and the figuring of interethnic relations on the Backshore. My discussion is thus necessarily concerned with suggesting how pencarian opens certain possibilities to the imagination while foreclosing others and with respect to both has far-reaching implications for the women and men who live and trade on Aru's Backshore.

The Bemunese woman's warning with which I opened the previous chapter—"save your old clothes and make a garden, because we won't be going to the store and we won't be buying new clothes"—conjures the setting in which a sense of pencarian's appeal can be most readily ascertained. The attraction of the west season and the ambiance of excitement and possibility that it generates in good times is nowhere better felt than in Backshore stores in the early evening at the height of the diving season. During my fieldwork of 1986–88, after the evening meal the men and adolescent boys of the village would flock to one of the two trade-stores in Bemun to hand over their pearl oyster catch of the day, as they also did in the neighboring villages on Barakai. Often accompanied by one or more of their younger children, who anticipated a treat like a sugar cookie or candy if their father's catch had been good, the men would crowd into the front room of the store, where they stood or squatted, smoking and talking among themselves. The large front room of the usually raised building where the men would await their turns with the tradeswoman or, less frequently, her husband, is the store prop-erly speaking. Behind the store, the back portions of the house divide loosely into living quarters and storage room for merchandise and trade produce, although when the latter are plentiful, the two spaces merge easily into each other. The kitchen and washroom are always located at the rear of the house and where possible, as in the capital, are built overhanging the sea to allow for a convenient disposal of waste. On the Backshore, as in Dobo, Aruese refer to the entire trade station by either the Indonesian word for "store," *toko*, or more specifically by the name of the tradesman who is its owner.

In addition to their basic layout, one Backshore tradestore much re-sembles another with its broad-beamed wooden floors, a desk at one end of the room piled high with notebooks documenting the debts of islanders as well as, more recently, those of the divers brought in from Kei and south Sulawesi (deba-deba), and other books containing records of stock and orders placed in Dobo, Surabaya, or Ujung Pandang. A large scale suspended from the ceiling on which much of the produce brought in by men and women is weighed and its value assessed usually dominates this front room. Shelves lining the walls display a range of goods behind glass; others may hang from the ceiling, while more bulky merchandise like brooms, plastic buckets, and cast-iron woks are stacked and ranged in corners. Burlap and net bags holding produce like trepang and copra lean against the store walls.

In contrast to the east season, the stores are plentifully stocked during the west season, especially at its onset and height from approximately early October through December. In the off-season, from approximately April through September, when traders do the bulk of their wholesale buying, they may close their stores, abandoning the village (as it is, indeed, often seen by the store's clients) for its duration, as was the case with both of Bemun's trading couples in the 1990s.[1] Alternatively, a trading couple may choose to remain on the Backshore but maintain a low profile, keeping trade—and credit—at a minimum and often closing the store for a day or an afternoon to visit relatives in neighboring villages. In 1986 and 1987, one of Bemun's two stores boarded its windows and doors for the entire off-season, appointing a man to watch over it and to collect the eggs laid by the tradeswoman's chickens, while the other trading couple stayed behind. At least in part, the latter's decision to stay seems to have been motivated by the favorable market price of eucheuma seaweed, a product that unlike pearl oysters can be harvested during the east as well as the west season.

Along with extra articles that the traders stock in the west season, like more and better quality varieties of clothing or expensive items like diving goggles or flippers that Aruese divers do not commonly wear, a tradesman, or occasionally a tradeswoman, will, in reasonable anticipation of a good season, usually return from a buying trip to Dobo with special luxury items with which to tempt their customers. After one such trip in mid-September 1987, a Barakai tradeswoman took me aside to show me some "gold" and bejeweled bangles and earrings that she planned to display in her store once the diving season was under way a few weeks later. Ever since their first appearance in Backshore villages in 1987–88, tape decks have been another item in great demand during the diving season. By 1994 most traders would put in a good supply of these before the season began. Besides these larger, more expensive luxury goods, Backshore tradeswomen often—and only at this time of year— made special treats for sale like sugar cookies and, during one season, even popsicles. During the west season as well, divers themselves occasionally put in special orders with a trader for such things as mattresses and bed frames that can only be obtained in the capital. In addition to offering a greater quantity and more luxurious goods in Backshore stores during the diving season, some tradeswomen deliberately deploy a commodity aesthetics in their stores to augment their visual appeal. Thus, one Barakai store boasted a menagerie of stuffed animals and other toys dangling from its ceiling, which the tradeswoman said she had hung there as "decorations" to attract people to her store, although she was not expecting anyone to buy them.

By the time the divers reached the particular store at which they traded, talk of the day's diving would usually have had enough time to make the round of the village and their catch would therefore already have been known by many in the community, especially if it had been very good or, inversely, if a diver had returned from a day at sea empty-handed or "empty" (B. *alé*). Between October and December in particular, during the optimal time for diving, a great deal of talk concerning the divers and their relative successes and failures circulated in the village. Suspicions and private accusations of sorcery often accompanied this talk and revealed the hidden underside to pencarian's male camaraderie. While the luckier among the divers awaited a turn in the tradestore to have their accounts tallied up, some of the less fortunate among their companions on the trader's motorboat might have been consulting those among their close kin known for their divining skills.[2] When the possibilities entailed in pencarian were thwarted and success in the form of oysters was diverted to others, diffuse feelings based on envy, bitterness, or a history of conflict with other islanders often became codified within attributions of sorcery. Especially on occasions when a man had come home "empty" for several days in a row or if his take diverged dramatically from that of his diving companions—suggesting perhaps that one or more of these had been diverting oysters destined for him to themselves—the apprehension animating the small group gathered for a divination could be almost as tangible as the pearl oysters around which all of these activities coalesce.

In the communal pile of oysters building slowly at the center of the tradestore floor following a day of diving, it is possible to discern a figuration of community as a delicately fraught interplay of presences and absences constructed around the telos of trade. Pencarian's pull, its power to make the community present, takes visible shape in the growing stack of pearl oysters formed out of the contributions of those men who add their shells to the pile after their accounting with the trader. Yet such presencing is immediately haunted by a series of absences—those of some of the diving companions of the day—along with the speculations that such absences often give rise to regarding why the divers returned home "empty" and the divinations that they may provoke in the households of those divers whose shells are lacking in the growing pile at the center of the store. Additionally, this particular figuring of community is at best partial. Whatever sense of wholeness the pile at a particular store may conjure, in 1986–88 it was inevitably fissured by the rift that ran between Bemun's two tradestores whose owners had not been on speaking terms since the early 1980s and who each respectively claimed the loyalties of different villagers. In turn, the villagers themselves often followed fam lines in their adherence to one or the other store, so that, for instance, most Jonjonlers tended to trade at one store while the Gomarirs went to the other.

As a crucial dimension to pencarian, the inscription of the pearl shells with the initials of the trader is the final act that certifies trade as the telos and meaning of this accumulating pile and along with it of the larger complex of diving. The tendency of many of the most important fissures of the community to follow tradestore lines and to be articulated vis-à-vis trade suggests that this certification is at least partially successful. If the trader's inscription of his oysters is practically intended to safeguard them against theft by islanders during their temporary storage in undersea caches as well as against their potential purchase by competitor traders should they indeed be stolen, the initials scratched into the shells also graphically convey all the power and authority that is invested in the signature. Throughout this chapter I will return to these shells and the distinct powers and desires that these focalize as they inscribe the telos of trade within a range of activities, while also complicating and diverting pencarian from its normative channels. The fraught dynamic of the commodity allure of pearl shells, always in excess of their value and absorption within trade, is well captured in the remark of a women who, while referring to shells as "produce" (I. *hasil*), indulges in their excessive, seductive pull: "It makes our hearts swell," she explained to me, "when we see one of those shells with its mouth open. The inside is very pretty with some reddish and blackish flecks."

If the sense of possibility and celebration associated with pencarian along with the undercurrents of rivalry that run through it peak at the height of the diving season, when Barakai families have the most to either gain or lose, the men continue to dive until approximately mid-April, when climatic conditions make it impossible. Although usually by January pencarian is not as lucrative as before the New Year, the activities enabled by the relative wealth of the diving season occupy women and men across Barakai Island until approximately April as well. Among the most important of the costly occasions that bring large gatherings of people from the different Barakai communities together are marriage negotiations comprising the payment of bridewealth by the man's to the woman's people (especially bronze gongs and cash), the large-scale hospitality extended by these groups to their supporters and opponents, and the return by the woman's people to the man's of a substantial payment of household goods; the different stages corresponding to the construction of a house, with the hospitality provided to workers and guests when its cement foundation is laid or its wooden frame raised, and the feasting and gift-giving that occurs when the house owners take up residence in their new home; and, finally, the festivities that welcome a newly purchased boat (belan) into the community and celebrate subsequently its maiden voyage. In other words, the sense of possibility that animates the west season is realized in multiple ways—in the creation and recreation of marriage ties among different Bemun fam or among these and the fam of (primarily) neighboring Barakai villages, in the founding of new households and the construction of new homes, and with the purchase of boats as significant economic and social investments.

By late April or early May, the flow of persons and produce to the tradestores, already reduced to a mere trickle during the previous month or so, ceases almost altogether. After school lets out around the begin-

ning of June, entire households desert the village for greater or lesser
periods of time, which they spend in their gardens, on the islands off the
eastern coast of Barakai where some families have coconut plantations,
or in the forest where groups of kinsmen engage in sago processing. If
between 1986 and 1988 engagement in these activities remained largely
restricted to the east season, since the late 1980s and early 1990s they
have increasingly come to the fore as alternatives to pencarian itself. By
my return to Aru in 1994, these markedly nonpencarian activities had
made important inroads in the pencarian season as strategies that Barakai families could turn to in the face of the rapid depletion of their oyster
beds and the less favorable credit conditions extended to them by the
traders.

It is important to insist, however, that in the context of the west season
these activities remain for most islanders—and especially those from the
pearl-diving communities of Bemun, Longgar, and Apara—strategies of
last resort that enjoy only a secondary appeal that pales before the attractions of pencarian. Nonetheless, in 1994 voices of dissent were beginning
to criticize the life associated with this livelihood by—for the first time in
my experience—positing a direct link between diving and the accumula-
tion of a substantial debt. If on my previous visits the traders had themselves often come in for sharp criticism, in particular for the demanding
terms they set on credit, pencarian itself and its entanglement within the
debt relations of Backshore trade had always remained out of the picture
and thus beyond critique. While acknowledging pencarian's temptations, some of these critics lamented their own acquaintance with its
possibilities—in short, as one woman put it, that they had ever heard
about pencarian at all. On the whole, people who voiced such criticism
differed little, if at all, from those who did not. Several of them were
among the more outspoken women and men on Barakai, while some
had suffered slightly more than their fellow islanders in the recent hard
times. Others occasionally offered more optimistically their opinion that
beyond shells there were many other sources of pencarian to turn to,
notably trepang, the product toward which increasing numbers of islanders were directing their energies in 1994, as they had done even more
intensively in the past. Most of these hastened to add, however, that the
advantage of oysters over trepang is the immediate credit the former
bring with them. By contrast, "trepang's food is far," people often noted,

invoking the pat phrase that summarizes the direct implications for themselves of the extensive processing this trade product undergoes before it can be sold (Spyer 1992, 93–94; see also Osseweijer 1997). Still other villagers, citing a range of reasons, claimed that the large-scale "disappearance" of shells off of Barakai—and indeed, as they knew, throughout Aru—was a temporary affair and even something that they had experienced before, if less dramatically. "One year," explained an older man recalling his own pleasured encounter with the resurfaced shells, "there are almost none but then another year—hey, these things are here again!" Still others, confronted with the massive devastation in the early 1990s of their oyster beds ensuing from a deadly combination of disease, overfishing, and the incursions into Barakai community diving areas especially by the deba-deba teams employed by their own traders, denied the shells' "disappearance" altogether. Introducing some local initiative into this dismal process, many of these women and men saw the oyster depletion as disappearing *acts* or willed protests on the part of undersea spirits against the reckless trespasses into their territory by unauthorized persons who ventured there without heed to the etiquette and claims that regulate its entrance and use.

If the above discussion intimates how the shifting place of pencarian is creatively construed in differing fashions by Barakai men and women, it also alludes to some of the limits that this particular discourse runs up against. Crucially, one of the possibilities that the pencarian discourse itself forecloses is that of the permanent depletion of Aru's pearl oyster beds. "How could these pearl oysters disappear," a diver insisted vehemently when I suggested things might be otherwise, "if it is from this that we live?" As in other statements that while voicing criticism end by reaffirming the privileged status of pencarian to a greater or lesser extent, this man spoke poignantly of his charged investment in a familiar way of life. However problematic this life in certain respects and at times might be for many islanders, the discursive field associated with pencarian has enabled Barakai women and men to insert themselves into the workings of trade and debt and, in so doing, to assert influence over their erratic rhythms. And thus far, it seems, and to the extent that I can know, they have managed to do so without having to confront the possibilities foreclosed by pencarian discourse. For the moment, suffice it to say that pencarian, the west season in which this livelihood embeds itself, and the pearl oysters that form its material pivot continue to enjoy a preeminence on Barakai, albeit one that is under increasing pressure from a variety of forces, whether ecological, political-economic, or phantasmatic.

It is, for instance, telling that the Indonesian word for "livelihood" applies in Backshore parlance exclusively to those activities concerned with the collection of sea products and subsumed—through the mediation of trade and its system of debt—within a transnational political economy. Following this understanding it is almost as if the women and men of Aru's pearl-diving communities claim that they enjoy a "livelihood" for only one season out of two. Although the off-season for some has its own limited attractions, when the east wind blows, many islanders complain of its chill, of the difficulty of obtaining fish, and as the season progresses of the increasing dryness that periodically causes severe drought. Especially when the water resources dry up, the vulnerability that many associate with the east season gives free reign to wild rumors about sightings of headhunters and encounters with less tangible "bad things" that roam about restlessly, themselves driven from their hideouts by the scarcity of water.

The comparative disregard in which the east monsoon is generally held derives additional negative force from the activities with which this season on Barakai is commonly linked—especially gardening. Since for the most part the men and women of the three pearl-diving communities located on Barakai Island's southeastern point tend only seasonally to their gardens, many of these suffer from such neglect that much of the east season is spent resurrecting and mending fences damaged by the incursions of wild boar and deer. In contrast to other south Moluccan peoples, Aruese have a widespread reputation in the region as poor gardeners, while historical sources often insist on the same. This is a stereotype that many of the archipelago's divers themselves seem to perpetuate with their adamant celebration of a pencarian-centered life and their often strongly voiced disinterest in gardening and to some extent even vegetable foods. This attitude cannot, however, be explained as simply a natural extension of their sea-oriented existence. The issue is rather the preeminence of pencarian, its as yet largely unchallenged status as the "livelihood" of the majority of peoples living on the Backshore, and the further reinforcement of pencarian's position by the predominance of trade in the archipelago.[3]

Pencarian Time

Pencarian's preeminence presumably also accounts for why the temporality of pearl diving structures the organization of activities on Barakai throughout the entire year. Despite the difference in ambiance between the east and west seasons and the disparate socioeconomic possibilities they represent and enable, the cycle of the tides together with related marked fluctuations of the sea provide an ongoing pattern for everyday life across the five island communities. Other calendrical criteria operate as well and, woven within the rhythm of diving, highlight the annual cycle's important moments. Probably significantly, many of the crucial markers of seasonal and sea changes that women and men on Barakai commonly attend to are consistently made to correspond to holidays derived from the Chinese calendar and celebrated by their own traders. In passing people will, for instance, casually remark that the west wind gusts most fiercely and is at its most dangerously unpredictable immediately following the Chinese New Year, while others will tell you that the east season begins around Cebeng, or the Chinese Day of the Dead. Insofar as all Barakai traders today are Chinese Indonesian and all Chinese Indonesians on Barakai are traders, the singling out of this group's holidays to punctuate pencarian's rhythms suggests, once again, how trade's telos becomes inscribed within the ordering of—in this case—Backshore time.

Yet, as with other aspects of the preeminence of trade on the Backshore, the extension of pearl diving's temporality across the entire year is neither complete nor uncontested. Importantly, the opening of the diving season is itself staged as an interruption that is purposely set against pencarian's pervasive rhythm. If the annual celebration held to honor Barakai Island's proclaimed autochton, the cassowary, thus constructs a crucial rift between the Malay and the Aru, the sea patterns that islanders weave into their daily activities also enable, though less dramatically, the assertion of a difference between that which properly belongs to Aru and that which derives from elsewhere. An inflection of the larger malayu-gwerka pair, this distinction sets "the work of Aru" (B. *kerja gwerka*) off from something else that islanders call "the work of the sea" (B. *kerja lalau*).

On first reflection, it would make sense to assume that the rhythm of sea changes and expanding and contracting tidal flats would be more intimately caught up within "the work of the sea" and more firmly entwined with the activities that occupy Barakai women and men during the west season, and especially when it is in full force. After all, it is during times when most islanders orient their lives around the collection of sea products for sale that the conditions set by tides, shallows, and sea currents bear most directly on their lives and structure their daily existence. Yet, besides its obvious relevance to pencarian, the tidal cycle serves as the main reference for the timing of sago processing expeditions; of trips to the small islands east of Barakai to collect coconuts, make copra, and fish; and for the other activitities that women and men engage in during the east season—the majority of which have nothing whatsoever to do with the sea. Above and beyond its immediate, seasonal entailment within pencarian, the tidal cycle lends its rhythm to a wide range of social practices influencing, for instance, when to hold the feast that commemorates the laying of a house foundation or celebrates the completion of the new residence, when to begin plaiting the mats that will be given by wifegivers in return for the bridewealth they receive, when to begin baking the sweets to be consumed during bridewealth negotiations, when to stage the negotiations themselves, when to pay visits to kin residing in other parts of Aru, when to make a trip on the trader's motorboat to the capital, and so on.

Besides the oscillating movements of ascending and descending tides, Barakai islanders distinguish two conditions of the sea that also correspond to the presence or absence of extensive shallows at low tide. Approximately every seven to ten days the two differentiated seas alternate with each other. A "drifting sea" on Barakai describes the state of the sea when the high tide is not too high and the low tide rises and ebbs gradually, making for a relatively weak current and optimal calm, clear conditions for diving. Islanders contrast this sea with one they call a "ripe" or "full" sea, marked by a strong current and turbulent, murky waters.[4] Although traders will occasionally take their divers out during these "ripe" intervals, the men are unlikely to harvest many oysters. Along with incoming and outgoing tides, drifting and ripe seas, women and men also pay close heed to the timing and extent of the lowest tide of the day, since the large expanses of tidal flats offer an ideal occasion for the collection of trepang and other sea products. With regard to these flats, islanders distinguish "large" and even more extensive "great" ones—the difference also being a gendered one, with the former identified as "male" and the latter as "female."[5] When the tidal flats stretch as far as the eye can see "to the place where the sea licks the sky," then this phenomenon again has its own designation.

During the periods of "drifting seas" and extensive tidal flats, life revolves around "the work of the sea," which in a marked sense refers only to those objects produced by and associated with the traders. In common Barakai usage, however, and in distinction to "the work of Aru," this category also embraces all trade activities, including the islanders' own engagement within it through pencarian. By contrast, "the work of Aru" comprises objects produced locally by Barakai women and men like plaited mats, sago sieves, baskets, and carved wooden drums as well as gardening and other activities that islanders engage in when they are not about the business of pencarian.

In considering these issues of time reckoning and more generally the marking of the west versus the east season, it is crucial to recognize that such reckoning is realized not merely by a conceptual reference point such as a "ripe" sea or a codified system of gendered shallows, but in the practice of persons "attending to" such reference points as parts of projects that engage a larger temporality within their present circumstances and goal-oriented actions. Such persons are not, in other words, passively positioned "in" time but rather construct it and their own time in the relations they form between themselves, their activities, and a given spatiotemporal reference (Munn 1992, 104). On Barakai the construction of a wider frame by islanders for their activities ends by extending the rhythm of pencarian to the patterning of the year as a whole, thereby reiterating the significant marking of the west season and its characteristic engagements versus those of the east.

Once again, everything subtly conspires to create and preserve pencarian's privileged place. Time and "livelihood," the seasons and their respectively ascribed subsistence forms have been made to seem inseparable to such extent that only recently and under considerable duress have some people cautiously begun to sever the posited links that—to the virtual exclusion of other possibilities—dictate for them one acceptable way of life. It is no wonder then that Barakai men at times may sing of how two adventurers from Apara could momentarily be arrested in their carefree carousing in a far-flung metropole and, rustled by the west wind, swept away by the memories of pencarian riding its powerful, sweet scent. And while women, excluded as nondivers from the exploits and amorous encounters associated with Aru's undersea, often speak somewhat differently than men of pencarian's appeal, many of them still insist that "great things" come from the sea, while only "smaller things" can be sought on land. In so doing, these women conspire in construct-ing their own, at least superficially, subordinate position vis-à-vis pen-carian. Yet, if one delves a little deeper into Backshore figurings of its undersea, a different, more complex and shifting, set of positionings emerges.

Behind the Sheen of Pearls

Since the nineteenth century, trade and the debt system through which it is implemented in the islands has been one of the most salient and remarked upon features of everyday life in Aru. Today, on those rare occasions when Aru makes it into the national news, chances are the report pertains not only to trade but, more specifically, to its local ex-cesses. In 1987, for instance, an article on the southeast Moluccas that appeared in one of the nation's leading newspapers singled out the Aru debt system as exploitative and tenacious by any standard.[6] And in the fall of 1993 Indonesia's prominent weekly *Tempo* featured a lengthy piece on pearl diving in Aru that focused not on the diving of Aruese but instead on that of the deba-deba divers who, since the early 1990s, have been displacing the former from their central position in this Backshore trade. Taken together, the two articles document an important shift in pearl-diving practices in the archipelago and one that my own fieldwork, from the first trip in 1984 to the most recent in 1994, also spans. In the case of Aru, however, it is crucial to recall that the fact that this ten-year period happened to witness such a shift is not unusual (chapter 1).

At least as far as most Backshore Aruese are concerned, any disappear-ances that they take note of—such as that of pearl oysters—are only of passing concern, however problematic they in practice might be. More crucially, and notwithstanding the common privileging of oysters on

Barakai, both historical sources and the memories of women and men invoke a host of products toward which on different past occasions and for a variety of reasons they have shifted their attentions. In recent memory, these include alligator skins, copra, and shark fins, while even pearl oysters are no longer collected on Barakai for the same reason they were in the past—that is, for the mother-of-pearl shell with which the oysters are lined as opposed to the breeding grounds they represent today for the archipelago's pearl cultivation industry. Although Backshore Aruese tend to speak as if things have never been otherwise, they are in fact quite accustomed, historically speaking, to redirecting their energies from one product to another, to accommodating themselves to the reverberations that these changes mean in the trade and debt relationships that they construct with the traders, and to riding, as best as they can, the quirky rhythms of the bust-boom cycles that have for long characterized this transnational luxury trade. It is certainly plausible that this time around Aru's pearl oysters, already on the brink of ecological exhaustion, will truly disappear and, contrary to islanders' all-around expectations, fail to resurface as they have before. If with respect to certain trade products it becomes possible within the foreseeable future to speak ecologically of an ending, in political-economic terms the shift in pearl-diving practices between 1984 and 1994 should not be seen as a before and an after but rather as part of the recurring, erratic momentum to Aru's trade. Culturally speaking, as it were, the pencarian discourse, as it attends to and constructs these same rhythms, excludes altogether, as I will later detail, the possibility of a disappearance that would be anything more than a passing, voluntary occurrence.

Although the newspaper and magazine articles mentioned above focus on two different moments in trade and diving in Aru, in other respects they are remarkably similar. Much like the 1987 piece titled "The Southeast Moluccas, the Miserable Moluccas," the 1993 article "Behind the Sheen of Pearls" has the character of an exposé and documents in detail the many abuses of the diving-debt complex in Aru.[7] A companion article to the latter that appeared in the same *Tempo* issue carried on in the same vein, focusing on the tumultuous "ups and downs" in the lives of the deba-deba divers, on the dubious and dishonest labor practices to which they are often subject, on the formidable health risks of diving, on the lack of insurance, and so on. While the 1987 article deals with Aruese

involvement in trade, the 1993 piece describes a more recent development in the islands—the recruitment by Aru traders of labor for pearl
diving from elsewhere, especially the neighboring Kei Islands and south
Sulawesi. Yet notwithstanding their differences and the important shift
in local trade practices that the articles taken together record, the tale
told in all three is a familiar one of the good guys versus the bad guys (see
Young 1990, 5).

Rehearsing a time-worn theme in the history of Southeast Asia as well
as in that of Indonesia, the "Chinese" are cast in the national and regional media in the stereotypical "bad guy" role of "outside" exploit-
ers of indigenous peoples. And whether the latter are Aruese or divers
brought in from Kei and south Sulawesi, they nevertheless are always
seen as more "native" than the archipelago's traders, even when the
traders come from families that have been in Aru for several generations.
Yet if sinophobia has a much longer history throughout Southeast Asia
from the early pogroms against the Chinese in Manila and Batavia to the
Dutch colonial turn-of-the-century discourse about the "Yellow Peril"
(D. *Het Gele Gevaar*), the good guy–bad guy, inside-outside, native-
foreigner scenario continued through Suharto's New Order, erupting
most recently in the violent attacks on Chinese Indonesians accompanying this same order's downfall.

Admittedly, only rarely did the violence of 1965–66 that inaugurated
the Suharto regime cast a direct shadow on evaluations made in Aru of
the archipelago's "Chinese." Only once or twice did I hear someone make
a connection between the islands' traders and the PKI, the former Indonesian communist party that had maintained close links with China and
whose members—along with many ethnic Chinese—were the target of
mass killings in 1965–66. It was instead at a much more diffuse level that
the stereotypes pervasive in Indonesia regarding persons of Chinese descent and the idea that they, nationally speaking, posed a "problem"
permeated conversations and cropped up in attitudes toward the traders
in Aru. In the articles at issue here, the descriptions of the traders—even
when not explicitly identified as Chinese—are clearly meant to index this
ethnic group. In the singling out of a "Chinese" ethnicity identified with
specific characteristics, the dichotomy these articles set up between good
"natives" and bad "outsiders" draws, at least in part, on an older discourse that was widespread in the nineteenth and early twentieth cen-

turies and that blamed the Chinese and their role as intermediaries for the backward state of indigenous communities in the Indies. With respect to the southeast Moluccas, marked within the national program of development as a region largely "left behind," and regarding contemporary trade in Aru in which Chinese act as middle persons, this older discourse receives some new life—even in such critically engaged media sources as *Tempo* magazine.

From the foreshortened perspective of the trader-diver duo, there are a number of things that one can say, and Backshore women and men themselves often complain of the burdens placed on them by the traders. One could mention the exclusive ownership by the traders of the motorboats that convey male divers to pearling grounds. Although Barakai islanders themselves use a type of plank-built sailing boat, these boats had become, by the mid-1980s, increasingly inefficient for diving: the combination of overexploitation and the disruption of the oyster beds by shrimp trawlers and the so-called Taiwan nets used in this industry and in shark fishing had largely depleted those areas easily accessible by local craft. To gain access to the most highly valued articles of trade, Barakai divers had come to depend more and more on the motor-powered boats of traders. Indeed, it was only as a result of the boom in shark fins in the late 1980s that led the traders increasingly to deploy their motorboats in shark fishing as opposed to pearling—leaving Aruese divers stranded— that the indigenous boat industry itself briefly took off. More recently, the marginalization of Barakai divers by the import of the deba-debas in the context of the recent pearl oyster boom has meant that Aruese men, usually a father and his sons, will do their utmost to finance the construction of their own small motor-powered boat. Frequently a man's trader will front much of the money for this kind of investment and in this way attempt to ensure that whatever produce the boat takes in will still be brought to his store. Yet if the former situation had certain disadvantages for divers especially because of the growing dependency on the traders resulting from the oyster depletion, these more recent developments potentially spell real disaster for Barakai men and their families with the demise of their pencarian-centered life.

In the 1980s, when a Bemunese diver decided—and there were always various reasons for doing so—to dive off the boat of one or the other trader in the village, he placed himself under the obligation to surrender

Launching a trader's motorboat

all the pearl oysters he collected to the boat owner. In the late afternoon, when the boats would come in to the harbor after a long day of diving, it was commonly the wives of the traders who would board with note-books and pencils in hand to ensure that this obligation would not be disregarded. Before the divers disembarked, these tradeswomen—who share the responsibility of running the store and family business—would record each diver's catch carefully. Often, at the height of the diving season, the chalk cliff overlooking Bemun's harbor would also be crowded with other women—the wives, mothers, and sisters of the divers together with their children—who would wait to greet their husbands and sons and to hear how the divers had fared. Once at the store, several hours later, the oysters of the day were incised with the trader's initials and tallied against the goods that the men selected from the storeroom shelves. One important consequence of the practice of obliging divers to surrender their shells on the day collected was that it denied these men and their families, to a considerable extent, the ability to negotiate when, how, under what conditions, and to what extent they paid off and en-tered into debt.

The fact that there are two traders in Bemun alone—as well as a good many more in neighboring Longgar, Apara, and, more distantly, Dobo—offered divers and their families some room for negotiation and deception. Sometimes divers managed to hold shells back and conceal them from the tradeswoman when she boarded the motorboat. Holding back one or more oysters meant that a diver could turn during the off-season if not to his own trader—since he would thereby expose his deception—to another for cash or supplies in exchange for his shells. Sometimes divers kept shells aside to speculate on the market, as it were, with the plan to sell them when prices rose. Indeed, the savvy attitude of Aruese regarding the workings of the marketplace has long been noted by European observers (van Hoëvell 1890, 33). Today a range of strategies are deployed. Where possible, some villagers even try to bypass the mediation of the traders altogether, transacting the oysters they concealed directly against supplies, cash, or credit from the pearl farm boats that stop periodically in Barakai during the diving season to buy up the oysters required for pearl cultivation.

Two men who over several years consistently saved some of their oysters—some siphoned off from the trader's share and many others obtained from diving off of their own sailboat—in undersea caches to sell directly to the pearl farms explained in 1987 why. They said that the boats sent around Aru by the "Japanese" pearl farms offered better prices for basic commodities like coffee and tobacco than Barakai stores, that they were more willing to give cash rather than goods in payment, and that they offered the opportunity to accumulate credit with the idea of eventually, after several seasons, converting it into something big like a boat motor. Reiterating an ethnic stereotype found throughout Indonesia (see Tan 1991, 123), the men further claimed that, unlike "the Chinese who trick us," the "Japanese" observed the proper measurements of oysters when calculating prices. When I asked my friends—a father and son—why so few of their fellow divers had followed their example, the father remarked with a certain pride that he, along with one of his brothers, had taught his sons to manage their debts well, implying that since they had only insignificant debts, they also had more room to maneuver.[8] Another, perhaps more important, deterrent lies in the following. Somewhat disparagingly, the men also offered that most villagers were afraid that were they to engage in similar practices, then, if and when some "need" on their part should arise, the traders would no longer feel obliged to assist them.

As Barakai islanders well know, credit is predicated on the sense of the relation's futurity and especially on the constancy of their own contributions to it. But it is also predicated, for instance, on the accountability toward their clients of the traders, themselves residents of the community. More diffusely, it also rests on the density of the connections that—notwithstanding crucial differences—pertain between them. By contrast, such accountability appears almost entirely lacking in the exchanges between divers and the crews of the pearl farm boats. Thus, such exchanges can easily backfire—at least for Aruese when the exchanges are modeled after the relations that islanders maintain with their traders. When I returned to Barakai in 1994, the son in the above conversation had lost a large fortune to the pearl farm, as much as Rp 800,000, he claimed, that he had built up in credit during the oyster boom of the early 1990s. He had been told that the pearl farm representative with whom he had cultivated a connection over several years had suddenly died, allegedly leaving no record of his transactions with Backshore Aruese. Lacking any evidence of his accumulated credit and without the know-how, linguistic skills, contacts, and material means to appeal his loss in court, the man could do nothing more than mourn his bad luck, consoling himself somewhat with the idea that throughout Backshore Aru, or so it was said, the pearl farm representative had left scores of people bereft.

On the traders' end, the presence of a competitor in their own village and a good deal more a mere twenty-minute walk away meant in the mid-1980s that those resident in Bemun would extend at least some credit to their clients during the off-season, which villagers would expend on basic necessities like kerosene, tea, and tobacco. The degree to which a trader was willing to extend credit to his divers and their families varied not only according to his relationship with each diver and his assessment of their individual ability to bring in shells and pay off debts, but also seasonally for everyone—if trade has a season, so, by extension, does credit. Even during the diving season, credit could be relatively more or less generous depending on the trader's overall expectations for the season, the pearl oyster catch as it unfolded over time, at what point in the season a request for credit or a more costly commodity like a tape deck was made, the amount of stock the trader needed to unload on villagers to pay off bills in Dobo and elsewhere, as well as broader market considerations.

Generally in the 1980s, traders felt obliged to extend at least some credit to their regular clients, even during the season when they did not bring produce into the store or they did so only in insignificant amounts. By the 1990s, when the traders had themselves become much less dependent on the labor and produce of Aruese, this sense of obligation had clearly begun to wane. If previously islanders were wont to compare one trader to another in terms of relative tightfistedness regarding credit, talk in the 1990s focused more on the "fear" traders were allegedly beginning to feel regarding debt. One tradeswoman would reportedly even hide in the back of her store when she saw people already indebted to her coming to purchase more things. It was also clear from conversations with the traders themselves and from the openness with which they complained about the outstanding debts of their clients—much more than in my previous experience—that they had become more discriminating in their evaluation of different divers and more differential when it came to offering credit. In their own situation of uncertain finances in the wake of the devastation of the oyster beds by disease the previous year and the losses they had thereby suffered, even the sounds of a tape deck playing somewhere in the village could trigger a conversation about how its owner had not even made a dent in his substantial debt. Almost as frequently, this kind of conversation would turn to how the indebted party had also been deceiving them by turning his oysters in at the competitor store.

The peak of "generosity" or the moment when Barakai women and men could expect their traders to be most forthcoming with credit occurred in the 1990s, as it had in the previous decade, at the onset of the west season during diving's prime time. Also at this time the stores are fully stocked with new goods, some of Barakai's tradeswomen deploy the aesthetics of the commodity in their stores, and the traders are themselves perhaps occasionally swept away by the prospects of a potentially good season. Summing up his own observations built up over the years of the seasonal fluctuations in the traders' attitude, one Bemunese man claimed: "I've been sitting and hanging around stores for years and I've figured them out. . . . They try to flatter you at the beginning of the season so that you will bring in your produce." In addition to the onset of the diving season, credit is also freely extended immediately before renewed diving, when the traders are busy restocking their stores for the season and Bemunese preparing themselves for their annual cassowary performance.

By extending ample credit at this time of year, the traders ensure a sumptuous adat feast and a source of products and, previously, labor for themselves (in the early 1990s largely supplied by the deba-deba teams) during the diving season that the feast inaugurates (cf. Hugh-Jones 1992, 64). Yet in contrast to the divers, who commit themselves to surrendering their shells to the trader when they dive off of his boat, the trader himself was never under any explicit obligation to extend credit during the off-season when shells are not collected. In practice, when traders remained on the island during the off-season, they also more or less committed themselves to extending some credit to their clients during this time, albeit of a limited nature that they could easily keep in hand. Seen in this light, spending the east season elsewhere can be understood as a strategy by traders to avoid precisely this disadvantageous situation for themselves. To a considerable extent, then, the traders determine both the timing and terms of credit and in the 1990s even more than in the decade before. As the sole record holders of transactions, through their superior education and bookkeeping abilities, and because of the means of enforcement that they, in extreme cases, can resort to in order to ensure that outstanding debts will be paid, the traders largely control debt accounts.[9] Within a certain range, they also establish the prices according to which goods are bought and sold, and these prices are inevitably higher than in the archipelago capital.

On luxury items like clothing or alcohol there is sometimes as much as a 100 percent markup that is more or less consistent across the different island stores that stock essentially the same goods and demand the same or only slightly different prices than their competitors.[10] One man recalled how a trader whose store he used to look after during the east season, when the trader was off in Surabaya, had once shown him a list of the wholesale prices he paid in that city for some of his goods. Especially the price of maleleuca oil (I. *minyak kayu putih*)—popular throughout Indonesia as a smelling salt and an ointment for sore limbs and throats—seemed to stand out in his memory: one dozen bottles could be purchased for Rp 2,500 in Surabaya. "But, here, he sells one bottle for Rp 500 or Rp 1,000—how many times increase is that?" the man inquired rhetorically, knowing well what the answer would be. He then went on to say how on seeing the list he had rebuked the trader—"That's a sin," he had told him. He recalled how the trader had laughingly accepted the accusation: "I keep cutting away at your throats!" Laughing himself at the recollection, the Bemunese drew his finger across his throat in imitation of the trader, and, shaking his head, he added by way of explanation, "You know so-and-so, he likes to joke around a lot." In so doing, this man also defused the passing sense of injustice that a good guy–bad guy scenario sets up, relying instead on a macabre sense of humor to somehow bridge the gap that had opened up between himself and his trader—without, at the same time, dissolving their difference.

Grievances about credit, prices, and the increasing reticence of the traders toward debt are regularly voiced, while the general attitude of traders regarding payments in cash comes in for special complaint. "Last year," a man named Magar recalled, "when one shell was worth Rp 30,000, some would bring in more than Rp 100,000 a day, but in one night it would all be finished." "What would people buy?" I asked. "Clothes?" "Clothes would be all right, but, no, they bought cartons of palm wine. I told Njong-Njong [his youngest son] one or two bottles is all right, but don't buy by the carton. They [the traders] like to sell like this, because then they can subtract a large sum all at once from the produce [that a diver brings in]." Especially in the 1980s the traders had an active hand in maintaining the virtual demonetarization that then characterized the island economy. Although prices mediate the transactions of produce for goods in island stores, and islanders have other, albeit limited, means of obtaining cash, the traders would rarely give out money in payment except in special circumstances when villagers required at least some, for instance, for an upcoming marriage or the purchase of a sailing boat.[11] In other more everyday circumstances, when asked for cash, the traders commonly claimed they had none. Their deliberate efforts to restrict the access of their customers to cash is not surprising. If a diver has no oysters to trade but can pay for goods with cash, he is also free to establish relationships with other store owners on the island and even relationships of a different kind. Although Barakai islanders are deeply involved in a cash economy—not the least because the Indonesian rupiah serves as the standard of reckoning in tradestore transactions—the limited circulation of money across the island abets the dependency of Aruese on the traders.

With the recent partial redefinition of the debt ties between Barakai divers, their families, and the traders, and the shift in the latter's attention to the deba-debas, increasingly cash as opposed to credit is being given out to islanders by the traders. By the same token, Barakai children, who are commonly sent to the store on small errands, are more likely to show up today with a request and a pink one hundred rupiah note clutched in the fist than with an egg or a trepang as they would have several years before. At the same time, traders still prefer to unload merchandise onto their clients than to pay money for the produce people bring in. To a selected few among their customers, the traders continue to extend credit, but more to cover the costs of large investments like a motorboat that have direct advantages for themselves than on an ongoing, everyday basis. Rather than the islanders, it is now the deba-debas who seem to accumulate large debts with the island stores, a development that is not lost on Barakai women and men, who in 1994 would occasionally taunt their competitors with a ditty composed locally about them and their debts.[12] The pleasure islanders derived from the song and from the deba-debas' annoyance at its singing probably had as much to do with seeing others succumb to the burdens of debt as with the displacement of their own habitual indebtedness vis-à-vis the traders.

Seen from the foreshortened perspective that the Indonesian media characteristically adopts when it speaks of trade in Aru, there do appear to be a number of practices that considerably favor the traders and ensure the systemic indebtedness to them of the large majority of islanders, that limit the economic autonomy of divers and their families, and that discourage the development of viable alternatives to pencarian on Barakai. Yet, once this perspective is broadened to encompass a wider field that extends beyond the narrow trader-diver bond—which in isolation facilitates the reproduction of pervasive sinophobic stereotypes—a quite different picture emerges. In the larger scale of things, the traders appear then as the middle persons that they in fact are. Seen in this light, they are themselves usually indebted to wholesale stores in Surabaya and Ujung Pandang as well as dependent on the Japanese-Indonesian joint ventures or Indonesian-owned pearl cultivation industries that, among other things, set the prices of pearl oysters for all of Aru. At least until the recent successive booms in shark fins and oysters, some of these Backshore trading families were not that much better off than the people with whom they traded. Accounts of trade and debt in Aru that home in on the exploitation "behind the sheen of the pearl" necessarily privilege the dyadic tie between a diver and his trader, and in so doing dissolve the larger picture within which such ties are realized. A larger picture would, for instance, include the interests and implications of regional and state governments in Aruese pearl cultivation, the knowledge and technology provided by Japanese experts, the significance of such transnational connections, and so on. It would reveal that those who trespass into the pearling grounds of Backshore Aruese are themselves often responsible for enforcing order on the island, while a look at labor conditions throughout Indonesia would show that the objections raised in, for instance, the aforementioned *Tempo* articles concerning the lack of appropriate health standards or insurance and the generally exploitative conditions of diving in Aru are far from specifically Chinese but rather endemic throughout the country.

Indeed, the bond between the traders and Aruese—though to a lesser extent the deba-debas—militates in certain respects against real exploitation. Several Barakai divers told me that, when asked, they had in fact opted not to become deba-debas, while those that had been deba-debas never pursued this form of pencarian for very long. Not only does this kind of diving entail leaving the village for several weeks on end, it also, as one old diver wryly observed, means that "the Chinese rule" and "when it's still dark they already have you diving." Many Barakai islanders also mistrust the oxygen tanks that deba-debas use. They also point out that oysters acquired by a man on his own or even during a daily excursion on a trader's motorboat where "diving naked" prevails and tanks are not used are priced higher and differently than the shells collected by deba-debas.

If, as I suggest, the picture of trade and indebtedness in Aru needs to be expanded to encompass a larger field of commercial and sociopolitical relations, it also demands a certain localization. For crucial as abstract determinations such as demonetarization, debt and credit terms, debt system, and the like are, their local significance and, hence, reality are always necessarily realized within a complex of meanings, memories, and practices capable of investing the compulsion to trade with the movements of agency and desire. In refiguring their tradestore debts for themselves, Barakai pearl divers and their families simultaneously make and unmake their ongoing indebtedness to the traders in ways that fracture and complicate the workings of trade and debt. One crucial question that will be developed in the following section concerns agency construction—specifically, not whether "local agency" is this or that, but how out of conflict, contradiction, and ambivalence the obligatory is made desirable.[13]

As Taussig warns, writing about a particularly brutal system of debt operative in the Amazon rain forest during the first decades of this century, such a system can only be deceptively transparent (1987, 63). The asymmetry that infuses the debt ties between Barakai islanders and the traders exists within a highly intricate interplay of personal relations that is shaped in the ongoing face-to-face interaction between them, in the need on the part of the traders to maintain a measure of goodwill and trust toward themselves over extended periods of time, and in the loyal-ties and historical involvement that link Backshore communities to par-ticular trading families and different fam to certain traders. It is, for instance, not arbitrary that both trading families in Bemun and the vil-lagers themselves are all Catholic (Spyer 1996b). Shot through with the fantasies, ethnic stereotypes, and specific perceptions on either side of an exchange with an important other (Humphrey and Hugh-Jones 1992, 13)—involving roughly, and among other things, pervasive notions among the traders of Aruese as backward, primitive, and dark-skinned, and among the latter of "Chinese" as inevitably rich (or well on their way to becoming so), white, and money-minded as well as superior in lan-guage, education, and especially etiquette[14]—this interplay of personal relations engenders simultaneously the subordination of the islanders to the traders as well as the often warm and genuinely friendly exchanges between them.

As much as many Barakai islanders complain about the "Chinese," many of them are only too willing to place their children, and especially daughters, in the care of the traders as (I.) *anak piara*—literally "foster children"—who work and live in the stores. Although teenage boys also work for the traders, they rarely reside in their homes except when they accompany the traders to the capital. Nor does the physical work boys do like chopping wood and fetching water teach them any particular skills. Girls, by contrast, live as servants in the stores, where they learn how to cook a range of relatively elaborate fare as well as to bake. The latter skill is especially valued as essential on Barakai to the extensive hospitality that is offered by the islanders in the context of bridewealth negotiations and other large-scale public events. The few women who in Bemun oversaw the baking of the dozens of cookies and cakes consumed in these settings often commented with pride on their special expertise.

A recurrent assumption made by many Backshore parents is that, by entrusting their children to the stores, they are helping them to "become someone" (B. *desewa mansia*) through, for instance, the trips they will make in the employ of the traders to the island capital, gaining thereby important experience of the "city," and the various skills they will learn— again, notably in the case of girls. Young women who work and live in traders' homes often enjoy close, familiar relationships with the trades- women with whom they work at domestic tasks and, in many instances, chat and gossip as friends.[15] Above and beyond this kind of intimacy with the traders, the practical experience to be gained by working for them, or the monthly remuneration that is often paid in cash rather than credit,[16] there also seems to be the notion that the traders and especially their wives exert a "civilizing" influence on their anak piara. In part, this prevalent view probably is related to the role of the traders as the primary channel through which such influences regularly reach the island from Dobo, while, inversely, the traders' motorboats were until quite recently the only means of transportation that connected Barakai women and men to the capital. The small celebration that is sponsored in a child's or young person's name to commemorate her return to Barakai after a first trip to Dobo underscores the overriding importance attributed to these cosmopolitan links by many islanders.

Not even, for the most part, local schoolteachers or church and gov- ernment officials who visit Barakai from time to time enjoy the same kind of status. In Bemun, as in most other Backshore villages, the school- teachers are also the main catechists and religious officiants. Whether through kinship ties, regional identifications, or simply a shared sense of relative superiority vis-à-vis Backshore Aruese, these persons can draw situationally on their various connections to the archipelago's civil and military officialdom. At the same time, although they usually command considerable respect, the majority of Aru's teachers originate from the neighboring south Moluccan islands, predominantly Kei, and, being often almost as impoverished as the islanders themselves as well as in other respects akin to them, cannot conjure the same kind of metropolitan aura as the Chinese. Even the Catholic brothers and Dobo priest who stop on Barakai several times a year and have occasion enough to invoke their ties to other parts of Indonesia—especially the bishopric capital Ambon, the site of the Sacred Heart seminary in Menado, north Sulawesi, and Java—or even Rome find their "civilizing" influence, while of course far-reaching, does not seem to stand out in the same way for the islanders as does that of the Chinese. Much the same although negatively applies to the archipelago's government officials, who are generally regarded with suspicion and dealt with carefully when they appear on the Backshore.

Although the Chinese traders emanate for many islanders the allure of a larger, metropolitan, malayu world and their etiquette, clothing, and jewelry tend to be closely observed, at least by women, neither the value they embody nor the mimicry they frequently incite is without ambivalence. Often the same people who will tell you that the adolescents employed by one or another of the island or Dobo stores will "become someone" will also comment that the Chinese abuse and overwork their anak piara. Perhaps because they see no contradiction between "becoming someone" and becoming part of a world in which exploitation (for lack of a better word) is part and parcel of the same thing, these views often surface side by side in the same conversation. Over the same glass of tea one afternoon in 1994, a woman explained how she had replicated the symmetrical serving arrangement she had observed at a trader's party in Dobo—two women and two men catered to the guests—during the housewarming feast she had held the previous year. Only slightly later she assented when her neighbor and the latter's daughter relentlessly mocked the growing quantities of gold worn by Aru's tradeswomen in the wake of the archipelago's latest booms. The daughter, a recent first in Bemun to attend high school in the island capital, where she had lived and worked in a tradestore, exaggerated what she saw as already an excess—"anklets and even a ring for their toes!" "This is really too much," her mother chimed in, adding in disbelief, "They say they buy gold for their old age."

If the island's Chinese and perhaps especially its tradeswomen serve in certain respects as ambivalent exemplars of a Malay world for Barakai women and men, the shifting instability of the position they occupy comes sharply to the fore in the figures of the undersea consorts of male divers to which the traders are complexly related. In refracting aspects of interethnic trade through the fetishized figures of these spirit women, Aruese pearl divers at the same time generate the social hierarchies and differences that make for their own subordination and open up novel spaces for the construction of agencies where the value of debt and men's powers over it become partially, if only fleetingly, transformed. If one risk run by an approach that would treat Aru's debt system as transparent would be that of underwriting pernicious stereotypes of Indonesia's Chinese, another would be that of obscuring how the performance of commercial transactions on Barakai also opens up for men—and somewhat differently for women—a space of gendered imaginings where they reestablish, refigure, and dispute the everyday order of things. Coextensive with trade through circulation but at the same time at a remove from it, this space is both the physical actuality of an unbounded undersea and an open-ended realm of possibility suffused with the differentiated desires and problems that inform interpretations of experience by Bemunese as well as the formation of this "experience" itself.[17] As crucial performative reevaluations of the meaning of trade and debt, the bonds divers construct with these undersea spirit women occupy a privileged place within this watery domain and have everything to do, as it were, with "the sheen of pearls" and their glamorous fetishized appeal.

Mothers of Pearl

The pull exerted by the undersea is enacted, for instance, in diving songs such as the one that opened this chapter, in which the scent of the west wind precipitates memories of diving, or one that begins with the pleasing sound of a gong wafting over the waves and announcing the arrival of a trader's junk to the island and subsequently focuses on the fine figure cut by a Chinese trader—one big status umbrella—as he strides into the village to trade,[18] or even the one that homes in on a monkey's gaze as the animal, perched on a rock overlooking the harbor, stares at the spectacle of a man who, drunk and talking fast, boasts of an impossible bounty in oysters. Besides the songs, sung annually by groups of men during the feasts that open the diving season as well as informally on other occasions,[19] the tales of undersea storehouses of treasure and death with wide-open doors that overflow with pearl shell and into which divers can disappear and the rumors that circulate throughout Aru of the persons made filthy rich in the "booms" that periodically overtake these islands—the shark fin boom of the early 1990s, the boom in feathers provoked by fin de siècle French fashions, or "the moment of booming" in pearl oysters announced by the *Tempo* article above—produce a particularly tantalizing topography. Other figures that trace the contours of this space and infuse the undersea with shifting expectations include that of the great sunken ship of limitless cargo, which in its excess at the origins of trade marks the utopic horizon of a debt-riddled economy (Shell 1982) or simply the kind of *imaginaire* of boundless possibilities that often animates boom situations, as well as the figure of the erotically ornamented female undersea partners of male pearl divers.

In their overriding ambiguity these female figures, or "sea wives" (B. *kodar ta*), tend to fuse what can also appear as two alternative possibilities in the diving-debt complex—the seduction of wealth and its draining, death-dealing aspects. This capacity for fusing itself underscores the problematic character of wealth within the debt bond that links a man to his trader—not to mention the bearing these "sea wives" also have on the figuring of interethnic encounters and gendered subjectivities. Diving is a paradigmatic activity where the productivity and virility of men is continually constituted and put to the test and in relation to which women act as both enabling and as an important audience. Diving is also suffused with multiple dangers that derive from the activity itself as well as from the structures of indebtedness with which diving is inextricably entwined.

To say that women are an audience for the feats of men performed in diving is not to assign them a subsidiary role, nor is it meant to associate them with passivity. If men—especially when they are drunk—may boast about their diving exploits, their wives are usually the ones to taunt and humiliate them when their catch has been low, often with recourse to a language laced with sexual innuendo and put-downs—such being the flip side of the erotic appeal with which diving is otherwise invested. On one memorable public occasion, for instance, a woman elaborated in song on the theme of the sole miserable trepang procured the previous day by her husband's boat as a metonym for his recent meager pencarian as well as, quite explicitly, his penis. Or, using a more conciliatory strategy often deployed in the same situation, a woman may remind her husband to set out a plate of offerings for her undersea counterpart, hinting thereby at an almost gendered collegiality between human and spirit women. Such a parallelism bordering on collaboration is often perceived by men, who claim that if things are not well at home, that is between husband and wife, a man's relationship with his sea woman will also suffer. Most men recognize that women on land, like those under the sea, have their own particular needs and desires that in both cases are subsumed by the stories they tell under a strict reciprocity logic: "If a sea wife is pleased, then she'll be good; but if she's deprived of her share, then she'll be bad. My wife [on land] will eat her heart out if I dive and don't give her clothes. She's killing herself cooking [and not getting anything in return]. . . . That's really bad. . . . If things are not happy within the home and you go out diving, you won't get any shells." In the most extreme instance, a man's wife may even, or so men sometimes say, curse her husband's pencarian leaving it barren or "empty": "Your wife will put an oath on you. She'll say, 'If he goes out diving, I hope he doesn't get a single shell'—not *one* shell—and it's true, this is what happens."

If one way or another, a woman keeps a close watch on her husband's pencarian, intervening when necessary in the management of what is commonly her family's primary source of income, a man's sisters and to a lesser extent his father's sisters mediate the critical moments in their brother's or brother's son's life that allow him to engage in and potentially profit from the livelihood he obtains through trade. For instance, a man's sisters prepare the meal that is served on behalf of their brother when as an adolescent he takes his first pearl oyster—a coup that some take as the sign of the boy's successful creation of a bond with a female sea spirit, henceforth his "sea wife."[20] Later in life, if a man invests in a boat, his sisters are the ones especially charged with welcoming it with ululations and gifts when the boat sails into the village harbor after being purchased elsewhere in Aru.[21] And when it comes to pass that prolonged lack of success in a man's pencarian suggests that his boat's soul may be languishing, it is, again, left to his sisters and father's sisters to assume the

Women return after feeding an ailing belan

task of preparing the boat's special food in its own miniature clay pot and of wading into the cool waters of a Backshore daybreak to carry out the ailing vessel's "feeding."

If sisters, then, facilitate and, where necessary, smooth the path of their brother's participation in pencarian, wives, on land and at sea, more directly control the supply of its products. This division of labor parallels that of marriage, where a man's sisters and father's sisters are a crucial and highly visible source of support for their brothers. Balancing a large bronze gong on her head, a man's married sister will often lead a long procession of members of her husband's fam bearing bridewealth contributions to the place of negotiation. Wives for whom such bridewealth has been paid are expected to bear children for the new fam to which they belong (Spyer 1992).

In addition to the active if different involvement of wives and sisters in the pencarian of Barakai men, a Chinese tradeswoman and a sea wife commonly frame a pearl-diving expedition—receiving a man at either end of the journey that takes him out to the undersea space of diving, where he obtains pearl oysters from his female spirit partner, and back to the harbor, where he presents these "products" to the tradeswoman for an initial accounting. At the height of the diving season, this latter transaction often takes place under the watchful gaze of the gathering of women—including often a man's wife and sisters—who congregate on the rocky point overlooking the harbor when they hear their trader's motorboat come in. The fact that only men accompany the boats heading for the community pearling grounds—an observation that applies equally to the traders' motorboats and to the less powerful vessels of the islanders—and that diving songs often underscore the male camaraderie of the activity they are sung to celebrate adds another dimension that, I believe, fosters the pervasive imagining of Backshore trade as a gendered exchange.[22]

Beyond the male camaraderie that accounts for some of diving's appeal, the undersea realm is itself repeatedly aestheticized by men as a place apart—wondrously beautiful and compelling, if not always easy to fathom. It is possible that some of this space's attraction is that it solely selects for men. Seen thus, the undersea is a space apart produced by a double exclusion—that of women, who do not dive in Aru although they often venture out onto the tidal flats, and of traders, who dive only to ensure that the oysters surrendered to them by Aruese remain alive and intact in their undersea caches. In the immediate sense, then, the undersea is reserved for men alone although the specter of "woman" in the guise of the sea wife as well as the shadow of trade loom large in this space located at a once remove from the Barakai everyday.

For some men at least, the undersea is also a place where in other respects their authority appears less compromised than on land: "On land we follow the way of the government, but the undersea is different— if you announce yourself well [to the spirits], then even if a shark comes around to look at you, he will go away and not come back. Because you already have permission, right, so he can't do anything to you." In a space where even the government has no say, if you adhere to the undersea's etiquette and rules of courtesy, the outcome remains predictable. This in contrast to "those sharks that travel on land"— the political incumbents in a language of statecraft prevalent elsewhere (Sahlins 1985, 79)—who are much less amenable to being contained and mollified by local pleasantries.

When women speak of the undersea, which they do less frequently than men and often more circumstantially, they sometimes invest it with a female solidarity that takes the authority over this place entirely out of the hands of their husbands. A telling argument broke out one day between a husband and a wife when I asked whether the sea wives had children. Clearly feeling beleaguered by recent demands on both sides—land and sea—from his two wives, the diver flatly asserted that, of course, they did not. "Are you crazy?" his wife demanded. "On *land* they do." This remark, in turn, provoked a curt reponse from her husband to the effect that if he was already "half dead" as it was, how much worse it would be if the sea wife also came with a slew of sea children. When he left shortly thereafter to bail out his boat, Abu Matagwa availed herself of the opportunity to explain to me why sea wives necessarily produce offspring—they have *daughters*, she insisted, whom the sea women train to succeed them when they themselves step down from their functions in old age.

If both Barakai women and men continually need to negotiate and accommodate themselves to prevailing power arrangements—from island traders to the Indonesian state—this woman's vision of maritime matriliny takes this process a step further. Posed in opposition to men's predominance in pencarian, this claim wrests the undersea from men as an exclusive province in which they assert their authority and define its contours. It is through such claims and counterclaims that the undersea is staked out as a space of criticism from which both women and men, albeit often differently, can unsettle, contest, and imagine alternatives to the parameters of their everyday existence on Barakai.

Descriptions given by men of what diving actually involves for them underscore the seriousness of its dangers as well as its alien appeal—at best, some describe it as venturing into foreign territory analogous to a village that is not one's own, where a range of restrictions therefore apply, such as announcing one's arrival and asking for permission to take things like oysters and trepang. Or, in an analogy to the official letter that the New Order government required all its citizens to carry when they traveled beyond their immediate home—for Aruese, outside of their own archipelago—one man spoke of a kind of *pas jalan* for the undersea. In contrast to the diver above who envisioned a space of a different order beyond state intervention, this man simply added another "amulet"—

modeled after one through which the Suharto government controlled its subjects' movements—to the bundle of protective measures with which divers surround themselves when they embark on their trips undersea.[23] At worst, other men characterized diving as waging war (cf. Volkman 1994, 565)—although one might infer here the potential trophies to be gained with victory—or even entering a coffin, an image that makes unequivocally poignant the overlap between diving and death. Yet notwithstanding the precautions and possible perils surrounding an entry into the undersea, men also insist on its special beauty, most frequently dwelling on the fine and delicate covering of the sea floor and on the red and white coral "flowers" that grace their undersea travels and that one diver—drawing on a familiar trope of the foreign in Indonesia—claimed follow seasons in which they either flourish or "fall."

If such descriptions capture somewhat diffusely some of the dangers and desires that permeate the undersea, the female spirit consorts of divers crystallize with an uncanny and insistent corporality both the seduction of things and the tyranny they potentially wield over persons. In so doing, they simultaneously abet and speak to the specific dangers of indebtedness on Barakai while refracting and reformulating other facets of Backshore trade—specifically its interethnic and gendered components. It is the ambiguously seductive and formidable figures of men's sea wives who provide divers with their trade products and in particular with the most highly priced article commonly transacted in island stores: the valued pearl oyster that once engraved with a trader's signature becomes a major counter of a man's debt. In return for shells, sea wives demand sacrifices from their diver husbands: betel, bits of tobacco, sometimes an egg—"for what if she were to exchange it for a pearl?"—and especially store-bought white plates. In a sense that is performatively reinforced again and again, pearl oysters and plates can be seen as payments for each other. The (ideally) pure white plates deposited by divers under the sea or in the weatherworn niches that dot the sandstone cliffs on which many Backshore villages are built are obtained at the island stores and, at least indirectly, tallied against the oysters that the divers turn in to their traders. If by stocking a steady supply of such plates the traders demonstrate their own more distant involvement in producing the undersea, the islanders themselves speak of the plates cast into the ocean by divers for their spirit consorts as a "payment" (B. *dawair*) or a

Offering to a sea wife

"return" (B. *detebeen*) on oysters. The invocation of a language of reciprocal payments drawn from bridewealth exchange—like the etiquette that patterns the divers' undersea excursions—is an attempt to bring a more predictable, mutually accountable, and productive form of interaction to the trade the islanders conduct with the Chinese.

Theoretically, this argument is predicated on the blurring—if not suspension altogether—of the boundaries classically drawn in anthropology between a realm of gift exchange imbued with the sacred and another regarded as the site for more matter-of-fact everyday transactions. It involves methodologically a fetishism (Appadurai 1986, 5; Pels 1998) that entails highlighting things and tracking them throughout the range of their *own*, as it were, social encounters, as they accumulate and relinquish "fame" and other forms of culturally constituted value on their travels (McKinnon 1991; Munn 1986; Tambiah 1984), as they build biographies (Kopytoff 1986), and as they become enmeshed in novel political-economic regimes (Parry and Block 1989; Taussig 1980, 1995; Thomas 1991). From these theoretical and methodological adjustments the trajectories of things made to cycle between the island tradestores and its undersea come sharply to the fore, thereby also allowing the overlap of the debt bond between a diver and his trader, on the one hand, and that between him and his sea wife, on the other, to surface. Seen in this light, the ambiguous interpenetration of pearl oysters and plates as quasi-payments for each other and the striking resemblance of shape and color often insisted on by islanders become all-important. Viewed as a life cycle, plates return as pearl oysters—they undergo the proverbial "sea change." Concretely, these emphases and convergences suggest that if the pearl oysters surrendered by divers to the traders implicate—by virtue, at the very least, of their circulation—the bond between a diver and his sea wife, then so, by extension, do the plates demanded by these female spirits involve the debt relation between a man and his trader through which these objects (the plates) were first obtained.

By demanding sacrifices of store-bought rather than locally produced goods, the sea wives aid in perpetuating the debts of their diver husbands and show themselves as covertly complicitous with the traders who own the motorboats and stores. Yet at the same time that a sea wife can be seen as deepening the debt of her diver husband, she can also be seen as sharing its burden as the source of the trade products (the pearl oysters) through which debt is diminished and credit obtained. Being themselves a potent blend of female spirit and trade product, the double agency of these "mothers of pearl" as figures that both alleviate and perpetuate debt, provide and drain off wealth in the related transactions of pearl oysters and plates, captures some of the ambiguities that animate the relations between the traders and Barakai men and women. At the same time, the kinds of interactions that characterize the diver–sea wife bond are caught within the dynamics of the debt-ridden cycles of commodity circulation in Aru and allude to the pervasive ambivalence of islanders toward what they, in certain contexts, construe as a Malay configuration of trade, missionization, and the nation-state. Analytically, the sea wife personifies what might be called a paradox of trade in Aru—the fact that in the context of debt relations wealth is inevitably drained in the same move that it is gained. But if the undersea spirit woman subsumes or even collapses what in actuality are often moments in a more drawn-out process, she also embodies the promise of a surplus that transcends the double bind that debt commonly describes.

The seductive side of things surfaces prominently in divers' descriptions of their undersea consorts when they linger over their alien richness, getting caught up in the excess that, like the bottomless bounty of the great Malay ship in the previous chapter, constitutes in Aru the origin of trade itself. Not surprisingly, while Barakai men and women speak in many ways alike in general terms of these figures as "female," as "wives," and as coupled with a diver in what more often than not is construed as a monogamous relation analogous to a man's marriage on land (but see below), conversations with Barakai men about their sightings and transactions with sea wives summon forth a more diverse gallery of women. Across a variety of settings and situations, men's talk about "sea wives" ranges from highly eroticized fixations on the oyster itself in which the trade product assumes an active, seductive role—its opening move, as it were, read as an invitation extended by a woman to a man—"when pearl oysters open up like that, men go crazy for them, because these oysters are women, women with reddish hair"[24]—to somewhat more fleshed out portraits that tend to focus on the flowing coppery red hair with which these figures cloak themselves as they float about the undersea on their pearl oyster perches,[25] to—less frequently—more sober fishwives who only, and then rarely, appear to their diver husbands in the guise of a

fish—usually something a bit out of the ordinary (not to mention potentially dangerous) like a stingray.[26] But whatever specific form their apparition assumes for individual Barakai divers, sea wives, at least in good
times, provision their men with the most prized of trade products destined to pay off debts in island stores. By the same token, these spirit
women are themselves credited with a desire for things of the "splendid
and trifling" kind (van Leur 1955): in addition to generic white plates, the
sea wives covet "gold" jewelry. If, then, sea wives can be seen as entangled
in the networks productive of debt on Backshore Aru, they are also
(in)vested—at times quite literally—with an aura of alluring wealth.

The varying investments of islanders in the figures of the undersea
spirit women, the tantalizing, often eroticized influence that sea wives
exert sporadically on land as they enter the homes of divers and into the
relations between Barakai women and men with a range of repercussions, and the promise of surplus they embody make these figures much
more than a sanction that serves to enforce a certain system of debt or
simply a form of false consciousness reproductive of exploitation. That
more is both at stake and imagined with regard to undersea transactions
by women as well as men was, for instance, suggested by the diverse
reactions of a group of women when a man with a wife and daughter
found three pearls—one quite large—in his shells within the space of two
weeks. If a kinswoman of the diver said she feared the "heat" emitted by
so much "produce," as she termed the pearls in tradestore lingo, another
joked, "He has three wives!" To judge from the looks and laughter of the
other women present, this comment implied a connection between the
diver's virility and his pencarian that made him far from vulnerable. And
when talk turns to sea wives on Aru's Backshore, one story frequently
heard tells of an undersea spirit woman who was so smitten by her diver
husband that she not only showered him with an abundance of things
but one day, out of the blue, followed him home in the back of his canoe.
Men whose pencarian is especially bountiful are also often suspected of
practicing black magic (I. *ilmu*). Owing to the skill said to be required to
deploy this knowledge in such a way that it yields benefits rather than
danger, this suspicion can serve to enhance further the prowess attributed to the alleged diver-practitioner—albeit as something more ambivalently valued. If a diver can then turn the temptations of pencarian to
his own advantage in such a way that his seduction of the sea wife

translates into his broader appeal among women on land—with the double possibility of eliciting a transgression not only of the watery boundary between land and sea but also of monogamy on land—women themselves are not oblivious to the more direct pull of pencarian. In a conversation in which one woman spoke to me of her attempts to ensure an alternative career to diving for her son, she explained:

> Boys are more tempted by those oysters than they are by going to school, and the teachers don't force them to go to school. Usually they want to get oysters as much as they want to get girls, it's as if the oysters tempt their hearts. . . . When I go out on the shallows and see one of those oysters with its mouth gaping open [and she placed her hands flat against each other and then opened her palms toward me in imitation of the live oyster], I enjoy seeing them so much that I say, no wonder those kids like them so much. . . . Sijor [her son] got one once, and I forbid him [to go out looking for more] because if he went out on the shallows again, he would stop going to school. . . . Those things, pencarian, its temptations are great. . . . I see those kids who get oysters and they don't go to school, they're lazy about going to school.

Sea wives are crucial figures through which islanders—including perhaps even school children—negotiate and reposition the transactions they engage in on the motorboats and in the stores within a discourse that endows their own interventions with a forceful appeal and that is punctuated by the destinations that they themselves determine for pearl oysters and plates. Yet sea wives are also much more than that, being identified not only, as I have tried to suggest, with a critical imaginative surplus but also because they recede and reemerge in the lives of divers and their families, triggering as they do a variety of scenarios and counteractions. The deeds attributed to the sea women are themselves reflexive of and refract a range of happenings on land that are subsequently ascribed to the spirits' initiative. Sea women are sensitive to certain things and often brought to bear on alterations that occur in the homes of their diver husbands, such as shifts and dissatisfactions in the relations between husbands and wives or setbacks in the health of household members, especially children. Most recently, the sea women have also been implicated by some in the dramatic fluctuations in the supply and catch of oysters. Much of the stuff of everyday intimacy within Barakai homes

is somehow registered in the delicate balance of reciprocity that pertains between divers and the undersea spirit women. Sea wives, in other
words, are "floating signifiers" of a sort insofar as they do not refer to a
baseline of stable relations but instead are situated within a field of
tension with other discursive and social possibilities, among which marriage is the most prominent (Lévi-Strauss 1950, xlix).

Marriage and Trade

In evoking the context of marriage, which on Barakai brings together the
largest numbers of people, motivates the circulation of vast quantities of
wealth, and also is contracted with an eye toward producing offspring,
the transactions between divers and spirit women seem to suggest the
multiple riches these undersea ties might produce for individual men.
Given the exchange on the occasion of marriage of important powers
and possessions among participating social groups, it is—as so often has
been pointed out—not surprising that interpretations of marriage and
commerce should so easily overlap. If marriage is frequently sensitive to
values of a commercial kind, trade in Aru appears imbued with the
intimacy and mutual obligations of a Barakai marriage. It is as if, in
forging ties with female sea spirits, Barakai men would resolve some of
the ambiguity that inheres in the debt relations binding them to the local
traders. Cast as a "marriage" and thus not only as a kind of trade but also
as a relation of male to female, ties with such mothers of pearl may for
many Barakai men seem more manageable, more negotiable, and potentially more fruitful than the ones they enter into with traders in the
island stores.

Yet, women under the sea like those on land are not so easily kept in
place. For the most part, women on Barakai, whether spirit or human,
only stand by their men when they are satisfied. They thus unwittingly
defied the Suharto government's designation of Indonesia's women as
"wives" and "mothers" exclusively, to be viewed only relationally or as
derivatives of their husbands—a conflation and position called "State
Ibus" in the felicitous phrasing of one feminist scholar of the region
(Djajadiningrat-Nieuwenhuis 1987; cf. Sears 1996; Suryakusuma 1996).
In this crucial respect, the identification of undersea female spirits as

Women with bridewealth contributions

"wives" and more complexly as "mothers"—who occasionally produce pearls, which in dreams designate children—is of a different order than that propagated by the country's former president. Although vis-à-vis the state, Barakai's undersea women and, by extension, their counterparts on land might seem to incorporate some emancipatory potential, the suffusing of the diver–sea wife bond with the ambiguity that pertains between a man and his trader suggests that such possibilities are not so straightforward. Beyond the immediate transactions of trade, the ambiguities inherent in the exchanges with sea wives emerge within a wider condition of repression, marginality, and disempowerment that involves state policies such as the requirement of a pas jalan and a citizen's identity card for all Indonesians as much as the more intimate interactions in stores.

The extent to which a pervasive ambiguity is inscribed in the "marriages" that bind divers to their sea wives is apparent in the discourse concerning the wealth of pencarian—a discourse in which women and men often draw explicit comparisons between the round gongs that figure as the most important article of bridewealth payments and pearl oysters as the marked articles of wealth in trade transactions. Within this discourse concerning pencarian, gongs and oysters trace parallel movements and are one way that islanders construct analogies about the ambiguous role of wealth in different kinds of relations. Most strikingly, both women and men have occasion enough to point out that a highly productive pencarian, as measured in both the quantity and quality of pearl oysters collected, is bound to have the same consequences for the reproductive family life of a man as an excessive bridewealth payment would for that of a woman. In excess, pearl oysters like gongs emit a dangerous and seering "heat" (B. *ken rara*) that causes infertility and the death of offspring.

This kind of argument is most often heard as a post hoc rationalization when things go wrong in families or as precautionary advice in the context of marriage deliberations. In such circumstances, islanders may claim that if the bridewealth demanded by a woman's people from their wifetakers is too high, the heat generated by the excessive quantities of gongs will cause the bridewealth—rather than being consumed by wifegivers—to turn back on the bride to "eat" her.[27] In bringing barrenness to the young couple or death to its offspring, the gongs' heat destroys precisely what the movement of bridewealth from the man's to the woman's people was supposed to bring about: the reproduction over time of the bond established between these two groups through the birth of children in relation to whom both the man's and the woman's people exercise distinct, ongoing obligations.

Similarly, as islanders will often say, if a diver gathers a great many oysters or discovers one or more pearls in the shells he collects, his sea wife may even venture onto land to extract the price he must pay for her products. Draped in seaweed, the spirit woman is said to hide in the cramped space under the diver's house and to bring illness and death to its inhabitants. Villagers may find pools of seawater and damp footprints where she has been. The diver's children are the choice victims of her attacks; when they die, both women and men will often claim that their father's sea wife has eaten them. Note that the threat represented by the spirit woman venturing ashore to demand her payment serves to enforce debt relations both on land and at sea insofar as the fear of one form of consumption provokes the other. One could argue that it is above all this threat that motivates the diver's return to her of (especially) white plates obtained from his trader at the village store. For sure, most divers take care to prevent such visitations, and many people, especially small children, wear protective cords with talismans around their necks and waists. If such precautions together with the repetition of plate payments to the sea wife safeguard the lives of a diver's children, they also, indeed, abet the production of the doubly determined debt that binds a man to his trader and to a female sea spirit.

Given everything that has already been said, however, it should be clear that it would be a mistake to see the figure of the sea wife as simply a sanction enforcing a certain system of debt. At the same time, the foregoing suggests that the discourse of a compelling surplus embodied in the enticing figures of undersea consorts is not the only discourse available regarding divers' sea women but in fact operates in tension with another that would restrict the imagination of excess to the parameters of a deep-rooted egalitarianism. This tension emerges, for instance, quite explicitly in the contrast between the male camaraderie that is emphasized in diving songs and casual conversation with men, and the fact that men who dive together are each other's main competitors as well as those most likely to suspect each other of acts of sorcery directed against themselves. It may also offer another way of understanding the close link between the seductive and treacherous sides of undersea spirit women— a connection that Barakai divers and their families themselves negotiate when they set plates and pearl oysters in circulation as payments for each other and thereby combat the less compelling aspect of the sea wife with their own kind of commerce and commodity aesthetics.

Aluli's Blue Pearl

The most elaborate set of transactions linked to pencarian that I either witnessed or heard about took place in early March of 1988. They were triggered by the discovery in an oyster of a large and highly unusual pearl. Even before I saw it, the pearl had already been described to me more than once within a mere hour or two after the motorboat carrying the divers had returned from its day at sea. Invariably, accounts of those who had seen and handled the pearl focused on its large size, its perfect shape, its curious translucence, and its odd bluish hue.

A number of divers speculated that someone had played a trick on the man in whose oyster the pearl had been found. Trickery among divers is not uncommon. Often enough a man will place some small object in the pearl oyster of a friend in jest. Yet others who had seen the pearl, especially when it was discovered, argued that there could be no prank. First, it would already have gone on too long, especially since Aluli, the young diver in whose shell the pearl had been found, was already apprehensive of its consequences.[28] Second, and more important, those who had witnessed the pearl's discovery on the motorboat claimed that, when it was found, the pearl—like any other pearl—was encased in what divers call its *sarong*, or the fold of epithelial material that protects the pearl during its maturation.[29] On seeing the pearl, some Bemunese probably still had reservations, especially since the trader off of whose boat Aluli dove rejected it on the grounds that the so-called pearl was in fact glass.[30] What must once have been its original blue color was weathered down to a faint bluish tinge, presumably both from age and from its time under the sea.

To settle the issue of the object's status, a divination was held by Aluli's immediate fam members that confirmed that the diver had, indeed, found a pearl that day and one of the finest quality. The kinsman of Aluli who performed the divination also recommended the articles that the diver should sacrifice to his sea wife: a dozen pure white plates and a full set of (imitation) gold jewelry, including a pair of earrings, a necklace, a bracelet or two, and a ring. Together with the meal of sweetened rice that Aluli's wife would prepare for the other divers who accompanied the motorboat and the gifts of sugar that he would make to the women classified as his sisters, the objects cast into the sea by Aluli for his undersea consort were meant also to "cast off" (B. *detebeen*) the immense heat emitted by his blue pearl.

Unlike Ben Franklin's pig—kept and cared for so that it might continually reproduce itself for the owner's benefit (Weber 1930, 49)—wealth in Aru is only generating, potentially prolific, and bereft of danger when it is set into circulation. When the discovery of a pearl is known, it is al-

ways sold shortly after it is found, and a portion of the credit obtained
from the sale should go toward covering the costs of the food given to sisters and fellow divers as well as the requisite objects for the man's sea
wife.[31] A pearl's heat is then diffused when the double debt that entangles
a diver, a trading couple, and an undersea spirit is disentangled and the
benefits a diver receives from the pearl's sale are distributed across a
dispersed network of social relations. Briefly, this distribution means
compensating those women—a man's sisters and his father's sisters—
who through their various interventions with respect to their brother's
or brother's son's pencarian fulfill an enabling role in his "marriage" to a
sea wife—just as, incidentally, they do for his marriage on land. It also
means entertaining his fellow divers, those with whom a man shares
camaraderie on the trader's motorboat and in his quest for shells as well
as his main competitors therein and those most likely to be envious of
his success in pencarian. On Barakai, these men would be either kin—
members of his own fam—or his affines or potential affines. A man's
affines especially would be suspected of trying to divert oysters destined
for him to themselves by deploying ilmu or would see him as doing so to
them.[32] With the aim of transforming competition into the camaraderie
of more or less equals, a man shares his catch with his fellow divers in the
act of collectively consuming "the pearl's food." Like the sugar for sisters,
the sweetened rice enjoyed by the divers evokes smooth, friendly, and
mutually pleasing exchanges.[33]

Intertwined with debt and inscribed again and again with the marks of
a larger Malay world, the seductive side of such wealth, while it may yield
a profit, can also have a high price. What I earlier called a paradox of
trade as well as the more diffuse ambivalence of many Barakai islanders
toward what they see as the Malay are succinctly and poetically conveyed
in the various things given by the diver Aluli to the sea wife who provided
him with the blue pearl. Being store-bought and measured in trade
quantities, the dozen white plates metonymically recall the tradestore,
perpetuate the debt relation between a diver and his trader, and iconically evoke the signed pearl oysters as both measures of wealth and
counters of debt. As a return on the debt incurred by the receipt of the
pearl, the plates together with the sugar for sisters and the meal shared by
companion divers cast off the pearl's heat and diffuse the dangers entailed in the immense wealth it represents. At the same time, the other

Men sharing a meal after diving

gifts that were deposited under the sea by Aluli for his sea wife acknowledge precisely that other seductive side of wealth that makes it both so
productive and so problematic.

Through the imitation gold jewelry—objects simultaneously of beauty,
of (false) wealth, and of excess—bestowed by the diver on his sea wife, the
spirit woman who represents the source of a man's riches comes to
embody their deceptive seduction and surplus appeal. Crucially, this
beautification occurs at the very moment when, having provided her
diver with considerable wealth, the spirit woman is also at her most
demanding, dangerous, and insistently corporeal. It should perhaps at
this point go without saying that the gold that so boldly inscribes the
paradox of trade on the sea wife's body is store-bought. As a "payment"
the beautification of the sea woman is at the same time an erotic investment that diffuses the spirit's demands, deflects her danger, perpetuates
the doubly determined debt of her diver husband, and reinstates a crucial imaginative surplus. In short, the seductive beauty of the undersea
spirit woman powerfully conveys not only the fetishization on Barakai of
the pearl oysters the sea wives provide but also the fetishization of the

debt bonds that largely describe Barakai islanders' most immediate access to the Malay and that itself is inscribed over and over again on oysters in the form of one or another trader's signature. This fetishization, which relies on the repeated generation of a sense of deferred surplus, a promise held out to them by the Malay, is one crucial factor that motivates the ongoing engagement of Backshore women and men in the debt ties that bind them—often ambivalently—to their local Chinese traders. Perhaps more than anywhere else, such engagement achieves a most compelling realization in the image of an undersea spirit woman decorated and beautified by her diver husband with a full set of imitation gold jewelry—earrings, a necklace, a ring, and an armful of glittery bracelets—which this man obtains for her from the Chinese trading couple who own the motorboat off of which he dives, run the store at which he trades, and keep and control his debt account.

Sea Changes

I have attempted in the foregoing to flesh out the covert complicity between Barakai traders and the undersea consorts of divers by focusing on how the fetishized figure of the sea wife motivates—in certain important respects—the participation of the islanders in trade and, by extension, their entanglement in the relations of debt that trade transactions necessarily trace out in Aru. Rather than simply making trade meaningful or mirroring in an unproblematic fashion given social realities, these figures have a practical efficacy; they are part and parcel of the workings of trade and thus also—and equally importantly—of its continual refashioning in the context of islanders' negotiations of a range of crucial happenings in their lives—from some of the most intimate alterations that occur in Barakai homes to the staccato swings that mark the making of advanced transnational capitalism on this periphery, to the policies and pressures of the state in a place like Aru and, most recently, the effects of dramatic ecological devastation.

Even the aesthetic appeal of the sea woman has little to do with detached contemplative appraisal; as an imaginative surplus it continually compels actions that transform the obligations of debt into an intrinsic component of the expression of desire. Exercising force, the figure of the sea woman demands the practical involvement of the diver as he, for instance, shops around for those things he imagines will most please—selecting one pair of earrings and rejecting another—or, in the words of one man, "If we like something in the store we can give it to her. . . . like that necklace you're wearing, a ring would also be all right—things a woman would wear she likes." The need for embellishment entailed in the practical realization of divers' *imaginaire* of the relations they entertain with their sea wives is a common feature of the fetish object. Always under-elaborated and incomplete, the fetish continually compels renewed articulations of the desires that supplement it, whether through narrative or by other discursive means (S. Stewart 1984, 136). A drifting strand of coppery red "hair," the receding glitter of a gold chain as it disappears under the waves, the glistening interior of a gaping oyster, or the sound of an undersea treasure trove as it whishes by are those fragmentary realizations that in Backshore Aru powerfully evoke the Malay and thereby the imagined possibilities of a world that simultaneously abuts and lies beyond the Barakai everyday.

As a thoroughly historical space, the undersea has inevitably witnessed its own succession of sea changes. Regarding the historicity of the undersea and, by extension, the shifting content of the Malay—with which the former, at least for some time, has been associated—there is, not surprisingly, only scanty evidence to go by. Nonetheless, I would like to venture here into what can only remain at the level of speculation. It is clear that for the last one hundred years or so an undersea realm of sorts has already been in place. Several nineteenth-century sources mention sea spirits or offerings of gongs and other wealth cast into the sea, while a colonial map from the end of the last century indicates the location of "sacrificial posts" (D. *offerpaal*) in the coastal waters of a number of prominent Aruese pearl-diving areas (de Hollander 1898, 524, 527; Riedel 1886, 266; Sperling 1936, 151).[34] The latter may be the forerunners of similar posts placed in pearling grounds today, which often boast the white flag of divers and are sometimes said to anchor an undersea storehouse of wealth (Riedel 1886, 266).[35] Seen in this light, the claim made by the leaders of the resistance movements that swept Aru's Backshore at the turn of the century of holding special powers over the sea—including the ability to lay it dry should the Dutch attempt an attack—is also suggestive. If, indeed, the undersea had already been granted a place of sorts in the negotiation of commerce and debt, then the obliteration of this place in the context of a wider move to expel from the islands all colonial trade would only be appropriate.

Talking to older divers and especially elder men who no longer dive reveals some pervasive differences in descriptions of the undersea that they recall from the past, specifically with respect to its ethnic and gender composition. Unlike the Chinese today, some of these men told me, the Buginese and especially the (B.) *Abibi*, or Arab, traders had an in-depth knowledge of this space and could recite, for instance, the names of the different *nabi*, or prophets, who ruled over each layer of the undersea that a diver traversed in his descent to the sea floor.[36] A similar familiarity seems to have characterized the interactions between the Muslim traders and the islanders in the early part of this century, when the former still predominated in this southeastern part of Aru's Backshore. When the traders arrived on Barakai at the onset of the west monsoon, they commonly took up residence with an Aruese family and usually the one in whose home they had dwelt the season before (a fact that may account for the "mistreatment" of local women by Islamic traders that is so often cited in colonial sources). To this day, the offspring of Bemunese in whose homes the traders formerly lived maintain casual visiting relations with the descendants of these traders, that is, if the latter continue to reside in Dobo, which is often the case.

The intimacy of the knowledge and the religious identification ascribed by Barakai islanders to the relations between Muslim traders and the undersea as well as the relaxed sociability of the continued if infrequent encounters between the descendants of these traders and those of Bemunese contrast with the relatively distant and sometimes guarded exchanges between the latter and the Chinese.[37] Nor is any knowledge of the undersea attributed by Barakai men and women to the Chinese at whose stores they trade. Together with this shift in knowledge assigned to traders and the relative de-Islamicization of the undersea, the available information hints at a refiguring of its gendered makeup. Men's entry into the undersea once presumed a passage along a succession of male prophets—as the guardians of descending sea levels who were themselves emblematic of a powerful knowledge. Presumably this passage also took place within a wider setting, in which one might suppose that knowledge in the form of ilmu practiced by divers was also important in articulating differences among these men. While still recognized, covertly applied, and commonly held to originate with Muslim traders today, the knowledge that is ilmu seems largely to have made way for another set of skills—the "arts of seduction" and the exercise of an allure over female undersea spirits. Might one then see the sea wife's more distant foreignness, the ambivalence and value with which this figure is simultaneously invested, and her complicity with the Chinese vis-à-vis the islanders as—in part—a commentary on the ethnic divide between Chinese and Aruese as well as a move that transgresses this divide in imagining a land-sea "marriage" with all the possibilities and complexities that such might imply? In other words, could one not see the seductive sea lady with her pale skin, coppery hair, and promise of plenty as a kind of border fetish (Spyer 1998a), oscillating as she does between celebration and critique, and constituting thereby a very concrete reevaluation in social practice of the meaning of value itself?[38]

Yet just as wives, sisters, and tradeswomen, or for that matter pinups of Asian bathing beauties—prevalent as elsewhere in Indonesia also on Aru's Backshore (Tsing 1993, 217)—do not provide the model for sea wives, so too should the bond between traders and divers not be seen as the original of which that between divers and their undersea consorts would then be the copy. Although in this chapter I have emphasized the convergence between divers' debts with traders and those with sea wives, they are not entirely the same, just as pearl oysters and plates—however much alike—are not identical either. Instead of seeing the sea woman as a mirror of one or another thing, it is perhaps better to imagine an open-ended kaleidoscope that refracts, fragments, reassembles, and illuminates aspects of commercial, gendered, and interethnic exchanges.

If these figures attest to a fierce investment in the Malay, they also in their overriding ambivalence potentially critique the main components of which the Malay for Backshore women and men is characteristically made up—beyond trade also missionization and the nation-state. With regard to trade, sea women convey the hope held out by things as well as the tyranny these things might impose. As for missionization, the intimate link posited between men's success in pencarian and the potential promiscuity of spirit women (not to mention that of their counterparts on land) might be seen as compromising mission efforts to promote ideas of marriage in which the monogamous couple stands central in a sacred church union. At the same time, the elevation of the husband-wife bond to the pivot around which pencarian turns appears to testify precisely to the power of these same ideas. And if the forcefulness and self-assertiveness associated with undersea spirit women is a far cry from the domesticated guise in which the Indonesian state would dress its female citizens, in the undersea—for which some now say an official pas jalan is needed—these spirits may still refract some of the state's insistent demands. If, then, no single model exists for these female spirits, the inverse is also true—the spirits themselves are not a model that women in any way emulate. While Barakai's sea women do not enjoin the construction of any particular fully specified forms of agency, they can nonetheless analytically be seen as both complicitous with and complicating productively Aruese entanglements within a wider, largely Malay world.

Vanishing Acts

At the same time, the shifting designs described by the actions of sea wives and the changing contours of Barakai's undersea suggest that this imaginative field, as any other, has its own limitations. The same reason that allows the figures of divers' undersea consorts to subsume and do so much symbolic work in the lives of Barakai men and women—namely, that they are crucial embodiments of surplus—also forecloses for the islanders any idea of ecological exhaustion insofar as the sea wives stand in the way of admitting that "surplus" can sometimes end. Thus, although talk regarding the rapidly diminishing and diseased supply of oysters was rampant on Barakai in 1994, discussions remained without exception caught within a certain understanding of the undersea. The assumptions and imaginations regarding this space's essential makeup and potentialities appeared entirely untouched, uncontaminated, and in no way limited by what islanders and traders on Barakai and all across Aru otherwise experienced as an overwhelming disaster. What women and men talked about on Barakai was not anything akin to what environmental specialists and the media refer to as ecological devastation. Instead—for they could not see it otherwise—they spoke of how shells were being "hidden," "withheld" by disgruntled spirits, or willfully and temporarily "disappeared" by their undersea guardians (although some divers claimed that the "signs" and "traces" of oysters could sometimes still be detected in the sandy surface of the ocean floor).

In one of the most striking descriptions to which an ad hoc gathering of divers assentingly contributed, a man explained how at the height of the disease the oysters that divers brought up were in fact always in good condition when they were found on the ocean floor. Once deposited on the deck of a belan or motorboat, however, the oysters were by then already "weak" (B. *zwak*),[39] their mouths only lightly shut or gaping open without force. Finally, after the shells were surrendered in the stores, they subsequently died by the hundreds and even thousands in the undersea caches of Barakai's traders. Some men and women tended to invest this disease trajectory with a certain morality, with one diver putting it bluntly as follows: "You [Chinese] are too rich, so God is getting back at you." Others in early 1994 linked the above to a story that was doing the rounds concerning one of the local tradeswomen, who allegedly had flung an undersized oyster in the face of the young diver who had offered it to her. When it landed on the floor between them, she then ground it to a powder with the heel of her sandal. When the story was told, which it often was, this act tended to assume sacrilegious overtones.

True "weapons of the weak," the fetishized oysters of Backshore fantasies exemplify in their remarkable disease trajectory the silent struggle and evasive techniques that are held to mark the most everyday forms of resistance among marginal and subordinated peoples (Scott 1985). And what better place could there be on Barakai, as I have tried to suggest throughout this chapter, for registering dissent, counterclaims, and a protest against the parameters of the everyday than in the island's undersea? The women and men of Bemun who along with their traders were victims of the diminishing oyster population circumscribed local agency to either the vanishing acts of undersea spirits or the dissent that many saw registered in the well-orchestrated deaths of the oysters. Once the traders caught on that the oysters—even if healthy on purchase—were probably already diseased and refused to buy them, then the islanders themselves were fully confronted with the oyster crisis. The reaction of the Bemunese community to this crisis suggests that if an alternative to imagining the complex of diving, sea women, and pencarian as a surplus was not readily available, there was nonetheless a widespread feeling on Barakai that a familiar way of life was beginning to falter.

So much so that at the height of the oyster disease the Bemunese decided that their community needed a "propping up" to be achieved through the staging of the life-affirming "feeding of the village" performance. Recalled only in the memories of the oldest of villagers, who remembered the last "feeding" from their youth, the performance involves the ceremonial construction of mounds of festively decorated yellow rice, simmered in coconut milk and perfumed with flowers, all along the pathways that traverse Bemun as well as at other strategic points in the village. If the display and dissemination of such surplus is itself productive (Pemberton 1994, 210–16), the impression I have that many on Barakai in the mid-1990s were beset by a sense of fragility regarding their way of life—and not just with respect to pencarian—comes especially from the specific "propping up" part of the performance. I was told that, armed with long and sturdy poles, the community split into two equal groups, with each positioning itself on one of the two beaches flanking on either side the cliff on which the village is built. Analogous to the most dangerous and ritually charged moment of a house raising, when a group of men erects the frame in a single concerted effort, a similar procedure was carried out for the community as a whole in the context of the "feeding": all men, women, and children propped up and erected a "new" village with their poles, thereby stabilizing and, above all, affirming their familiar way of life in the face of an uncertain future. A similar situation in which the instability of a "mooring post," held to mark the spot of an undersea storehouse, becomes metonymic of the increasingly shaky foundations of Barakai existence presents itself in the following chapter.

5 Prow and Stern

When I returned to Barakai in 1994 for the first time in almost six years, one of the most pressing concerns among my Bemunese friends was to bring me up to date regarding the cassowary performances that had been held in my absence. The understanding more generally shared by Bemunese that my project was intimately linked with their own passions for this privileged and elusive bird accounted, in part, for their concern. Another reason may have been that my return to Aru triggered a recollection of the community's performance, itself the paradigmatic annual occasion for recalling persons who are far away, long gone, or otherwise absent. Indeed, in the context of the 1987 performance that everyone knew was my last for any foreseeable time and again six months later, when I left Barakai to return to Chicago, both my daily companions and Bemunese to whom I was less close had already predicted that my presence would be most vividly remembered during their community's subsequent performances. Yet with respect to the dynamics of the cassowary celebration more generally, it is important to realize that these annual events are themselves decidedly historical—not merely because they form part of larger, shifting circumstances but because Bemunese themselves situate and evaluate many of the changes that occur in their communal life with reference to these annual celebrations. In contrast to the periodic repetitions of traditional truths or essentialized rituals that a canonical perspective might prefer to make of them (Asad 1993, 55–79), these men and women are not misled about the sense in which their own performances should be taken.

According to the national calendar of Indonesia, which follows the Gregorian one introduced by the Dutch colonizers,[1] a year begins with a new date that thereafter serves as the basic reference for the meaningful ordering of events falling within the time span demarcated by a given numerically identified year. A person might easily say, for example, that

1987 was the year in which Suharto was (once again) elected president of the Republic of Indonesia, or that May 1998 was the month in which he was deposed. Along with other Indonesians, women and men across Barakai observe the new year designated by the national calendar and celebrate January 1 as a day to drink, eat special treats, and visit relatives and friends in new clothes. Additionally, four of the five Barakai communities sponsor annual performances that usher in another new year, which opens the trade season and to a much greater extent than the national calendar structures their daily activities.

For Bemunese, the arrival and ensuing exile of the cassowary, as opposed to numbered years or, for that matter, dates that are rarely and unsystematically used, sets the broad framework for positioning various community happenings in relation to each other—for instance, such and such was the year when the hunters pursued some wild boar right into the village, an occurrence that once named can become a point of departure for the ordering of other events that fall between this performance and the next. Except with respect to momentous interventions associated with state power, such as the mass conversions of 1976–77 preceding the 1977 elections, and elections themselves, years as numbered entities are seldom invoked. In Indonesia, where, as a rule, elections under Suharto's New Order government were styled as a "national ritual" (I. *upacara nasional*) and always won by the government party Golkar "with striking statistical precision" (Pemberton 1994, 4),[2] one could even argue that such periodic displays of government "success" accorded more closely with the canonical model of "ritual" than Bemun's cassowary performances.[3]

Almost two years after I left Barakai, I received a letter from Gita, one of my closest companions and my main assistant in Bemun, who between the usual greetings and expressions of thanks for things received and an enumeration of marriages and deaths (Berlinda married Hengki, Gwara married in Longgar, Alisa married a Keiese . . . Asamjawa's older sister Sidokol/Meri's wife died, Sondo's father also died . . . Yana's mother also died, date 25 January 1989. . . .) writes:[4]

Furthermore:

That Patcy actually I already sent news to America about *doing momosim* [same as Indonesian *adat*] this year. Because very many things were not carried out or not done well. So that *there were many transgressions* so that this year again *they did the great [cassowary] performance again. Because the mooring post fell again. The problem is that Apa Z. [Bemun's headman] goes about momosim the same way he goes about dinas [his official duties as a bureaucrat] and so the ancestors are angry.*[5] *So then they went to bring the white plates, and they set up a new mooring post, but it fell down again.* Patcy, we villagers were surprised. The problem was that one day we set up the post and the following day it fell again. So finally the old people sat adat for two nights in the pemali house ["sacred" house, here the adat official the Prow's home] consulting together for those two nights. So that they could ask people who know [about these things] to go flatter the guardians of adat. So if possible *they could bring white plates once again.* Finally they could be flattered. *Patcy, if you had been here during this you would have loved it,* because they gathered in the pemali house and then each and every person began giving his opinion. *There were some who said they had once heard stories telling how it was possible for the mooring post to fall after one or two days and then to collect white plates and bring them to set up the mooring post again.* And there were some that didn't agree. There were some who said from the time they were born until they were old nothing had ever happened like this. It would have been great if Patcy had been here. Because they talked about the history [sejara] of the cassowary as it happened long ago. All the elders congregated in Batola's house, so we were afraid of going there. Only my father told us in broad strokes about it.

The problem with this particular performance in 1989, the second one after my departure from Barakai, is clearly spelled out in Gita's letter. The tottering, unstable mooring post—a simple twigged branch of the *sir* tree that stands about two hundred meters off the Barakai coast and is held to secure the imaginary "Sea House of the Land" (B. *Gwalar Ta Re Kanien*) at its undersea site—signals the anger of the community's adat or, in Barakai, momosim guardians and specifically those whose task it is to safeguard the status of the annual performance.[6] The cause of the spirits' annoyance is also spelled out in the letter, namely, that Bemun's headman, Apa Z., engages in momosim activities—here the annual performance—in the same way that he attends to his official duties as a government bureaucrat (I. *dinas*). To my knowledge, although first articulated in this setting, the conflict between adat or momosim and dinas had been building for years. At least since the 1970s it had already been played out in a range of conflicts, negotiations, and rumors that tended to crystallize around the timing of Bemun's annual performance and had as their main protagonists the village headman, on the one hand, and the paired adat officials, the Prow and the Stern, on the other. What was at stake in the battle between adat and dinas, while not actually named as such, had already surfaced in the Stern's account to me of a performance that he claims took place sometime in the 1970s and that he characterized intriguingly as "a ritual without an ending."

Before turning to the Stern's story of this truncated performance—severed, he and others maintained, almost unnaturally before reaching its proper end—a brief excursion to a theme park in the national capital of Jakarta is in order. A tour of Beautiful Indonesia in Miniature Park (Taman Mini Indonesia Indah) powerfully suggests how the battle between adat and dinas waged over the past twenty years on a small scale on Aru's Backshore cannot be seen as simply a localized conflict between men vying for authority over Bemun's adat affairs. Nor should it be understood as a confrontation between the Indonesian state, deploying its understandings of dinas across the archipelago, and a pristine Aruese community that somehow—or at least regarding its adat rituals—has remained untouched by this or other "outside" realities. Everything I have written thus far suggests otherwise. Instead, what was at issue was the changing status under the former Suharto regime of the place and definition of adat as a select means through which this state attempted to realize its aim of producing a unity within the diversity of this nation's two hundred or more million people.

Unity in Diversity

Unity in diversity (*bhinneka tunggal ika*), the national motto of the Republic of Indonesia, is a representation of statehood that explicitly and succinctly spells out the ideal relationship between the state as a set of rituals and routines (Corrigan and Sayer 1985) and the people for whom, by whom, and through whom these are deployed. Throughout Indonesia the motto is on display everywhere: under photos of the republic's

leaders and heroes, on plaques in offices, inscribed on public monuments, and on posters depicting the "customary clothing" of the country's twenty-seven provinces (including the annexed former Portuguese
colony of East Timor). Commonly conjoined to the national emblem of
the Garuda bird, the motto also circulates on money, stamps, and other
national tokens. So familiar to Indonesians, and rapidly to visitors as
well, "unity in diversity" is often taken at face value, as a mere epithet
describing a certain congruence held to underlie the astonishing variety
of peoples and cultures within the nation's borders.

However, the assumption of "unity in diversity" as a fait accompli,
established once and for all with the Declaration of Independence (Pro-
klamasi Kemerdekaan) by the nationalist leaders Sukarno and Hatta and
the founding of the nation-state on August 17, 1945, can be questioned.
Rather than describing a given state of affairs, the motto targets the
diversity of Indonesian peoples as an affair of the state. In the simplest of
terms, it captures the dynamics of a process that took place in Indonesia
under Suharto rule and, set in motion, is presumably still ongoing, a
process that, like the national motto itself, is twofold. First, it implies the
fostering and even enhancement of certain aspects of diversity that have
come to stand in a *pars pro toto* fashion for culture (I. *kebudayaan*),
tradition (*tradisi*), custom (*adat*), or art (*kesenian*). And second, if such
diversity is indeed destined to bear the mark of unity, then this process
necessarily also entails the creation of a common measure that can be
identified simultaneously within each particular codified token of difference as well as across all of the nation's differences. Selected cultural
forms and practices of diverse peoples throughout Indonesia have come
to be set apart from other aspects of their daily lives as "culture," "tradition," "custom," and "art" (cf. Bowen 1991; Hoskins 1993; Keane 1995;
Kipp and Rodgers 1987; Pemberton 1994). The selection of specific practices and dimensions of social life over others already imposes a standard
on difference. The correlate expectation that every group has its characteristic adat dress, dance, or marriage ceremony turns this assumption
into a prescription, one that is given currency in the national television
(Televisi Republik Indonesia, TVRI) programs on "culture,"[7] devoted one
week to Minangkabau dance, the next to Ambonese dance, and so on (cf.
Bowen 1991, 126–27).[8]

What might loosely be termed the aesthetics of this double process that dominated the politics of culture under Suharto—the codification of diversity in costume, performance, house styles, ethnic markers, tourist objects, kitsch, and so on—has in recent years been an increasing focus of scholars working throughout Indonesia (Adams 1998; Ellen 1988; Geertz 1990; Hatley 1993; Kartomi 1993; Kenji and Siegel 1990; Volkman 1990). In this regard it has become almost perfunctory to invoke the image of the Beautiful Indonesia in Miniature Park, which is laid out at the heart of the nation in its capital Jakarta on the island of Java.[9] Built by the former first lady Ibu Tien Suharto's Our Hope Foundation (Yayasan Harapan Kita) and dedicated on April 20, 1975, the park boasts as one of its main features a vast artificial pond with miniature islands that replicate those of the archipelago and display houses constructed according to the alleged "genuine customary architectural style" of each of the nation's provinces (Pemberton 1994, 152). These houses, in turn, often contain costumes and artifacts held to represent the standardized inhabitants of each province, who are themselves, as Anderson points out, notably absent (1990, 182).

A space of the state in which all diversities become exchangeable, the pond captures on its shimmering surface the varied reflections of the Mini houses, which thereby are cast as manifestations of the same underlying unity. If the Mini archipelago conjures the formal aesthetics of a certain image of diversity that was actively propagated by the former Suharto regime, the cement boundary that outlines and contains the pond demonstrates more effectively how such diversity was possible only within the framework generated by the unifying agency of the state. Indeed, what one author terms the "concrete ideology" of the Suharto regime—the definition of public space through official monuments and architecture that conveyed New Order aesthetics and promoted certain understandings of the Javanese past as the past of the entire nation—can also be taken quite literally (Lindsay 1993). Seen in this light, the cement boundary that encompasses the nation's miniature archipelago makes a powerful material statement about the characteristic conjoining under the former New Order of this government's program of economic development with one of national cultural development (Foulcher 1990; Pemberton 1994, 154).

Just as in Aru "development" commonly enters Backshore communities as, first and foremost, specified quantities of sacks of cement granted to villagers for the construction of government-preferred types of housing, the central pavilion of the last addition to Taman Mini while Suharto was still in power, representing East Timor, is, unlike the majority of the other adat houses in the park, made of concrete. It is as if the surplus of New Order intentions vis-à-vis this highly contested site—"the one pavilion which inevitably keeps its Indonesian flag flying throughout the entire day and maintains a security guard at its entrance" (Acciaioli 1996, 32)—compels this unmediated materialization of the state's unifying agency, as if the aims regarding the illegally annexed province, where a government priority has been a TV in every village, could only be expressed this "concretely." In contrast to the other houses in the park, which wear their diversity superficially on their sleeves, as it were, the "cement suit" in which East Timor has been cast makes absolutely transparent the violence that underlies the "calm and complete" vision trapped in Mini's pool. Rather than self-evidently given then the unifying framework of the New Order was actively constructed through radical transformations that aimed to convert local differences into state-sponsored diversity. Yet even within the confines of the Mini park itself or in its clones like Taman Miniatur Jawa Tengah (Tamjateng) or Taman Miniatur Sulawesi (Tamsul) that were more recently spun out—by government decree—at the provincial level, and perhaps even more at such a far remove from the national center as Aru, such transformations (once Indonesians form part of the picture) can also upset state constructions, become charged sites of confrontation, or unwittingly spawn quirky, offbeat forms like rituals without endings.[10]

In considering the Stern's account of how a performance of his community's cassowary ritual "never reached its end" (B. *nang awan ken jurun*), I will attempt to avoid the pitfalls of positing either a pure beyond—an essentialized native identity celebrated for its resistance to the incursions of outside powers or its capacity to authorize absolutely its own cultural productions—or the complete loss of self in which cultural alterity would be thoroughly subsumed, dominated, and erased within the power grid of the state, late-twentieth-century capitalism, or any other such colonizing force. I suggest instead a third possibility, in which the inescapable insertion within a wider world is infused and, at times, unsettled by the sense of coming from a "different" place (de Certeau 1986). By beginning to trace here the parameters of this third possibility, I prefigure my discussion of other aspects of Bemun's annual performances in the following two chapters.

In reference precisely to these issues of entanglement and difference, it is not arbitrary that the conflict between Bemun's headman and one of the community's most important adat officials erupted over the issue of timing. Ostensibly, the conflict between the Stern and the village headman revolved around whether the performance should have been set to last four or five days. Yet to restrict one's understanding of the conflict to this matter of a day, more or less, would be to misconstrue it fundamentally. Among other things, such an interpretation would give an impression of orthodoxy that is unwarranted in this context. While the colonization of time by the Indonesian state and the relationships between authority and temporality in this Backshore community are crucial, to see their difference as a clash between two fully constituted calendars at odds and out of sync with each other would entail a reification of a customary domain of adat, on the one hand, and an essentialized understanding of the state, on the other. Such a view would also deny the adjustments and entanglements out of which Bemun's annual performance itself emerges: the very dynamics of the annual celebration depend on reifying and thereby problematizing something that otherwise does not exist, namely, the two distinct domains of malayu and gwerka, the Malay and the Aru.

Beginnings and Endings

Once a year at the transition from the east to the west monsoon and immediately before the opening of the trade season, the inhabitants of the small south Moluccan community of Bemun sift and sort out what they regard as belonging to the Malay world of trade, missionization, and the nation-state from that which they associate with an autochthonous and ancestral Aru past. Although the Malay always reasserts its hegemonic preeminence at the end of the annual performance, for a brief moment in the year these islanders carve out a space that is elsewhere, other, and forgotten in relation to it. A space of the past, it appears significantly set off from the everyday conditions of commodification, trade debts, and domination by the mercurial demands of the inter-

national market that suffuse their daily lives. It is in this context that
Bemunese men, women, and children celebrate an autochthonous cassowary spirit whose material presence in the village and subsequent exile
effect the seasonal change, propitiate an abundance of trade products,
and open the season in which these are collected, processed, and traded
to the ethnic Chinese who operate stores on the island, the pearl farm
representatives who before the oyster disease of the early 1990s would
regularly pass by Barakai during the west season, or, more rarely, to
merchants in Dobo.

Put simply, Bemun's annual performance falls into three parts. These
parts, which are distinguished by the islanders themselves and bear different names, will be discussed in detail in subsequent chapters. The first
part, "following the river" (B. *dajur mar*) consists of a fish poisoning,
which initiates the process by which the villagers separate the Malay
from the quintessentially Aru. This process of separation draws the cassowary spirit—as the emblem of the unadulterated Aru—from his reclu-
sive home deep in the forested Barakai interior to the immediate outskirts of Bemun. The second part of the performance, termed simply
"doing the cassowary" (B. *dai koder*) centers on the cassowary in his
two related and interconnected manifestations. During the daytime, for
however long this part of the performance lasts (three to five days), the
cassowary is pursued in his animal guise by the able-bodied men of the
community during a hunt that takes place in the forest; subsequently at
night he is celebrated in palm frond effigy form by all the villagers. The
cassowary's killing and exile from the community until the following
year makes way for the commodity circulation and trade that Bemunese
identify, above all, with the Malay and that they themselves set into
motion in the third part of their annual performance. In this final part
called "casting white plates" (B. *detebeen kujur*), the community organizes a mass distribution of store-bought white plates (regarded as "payments" for the pearl oyster harvest of the upcoming trade season), which
are deposited at various named land and sea places where guardian
spirits of Bemun's momosim practices reside. Just as Bemunese in their
performance annually aim to produce themselves as Aru for a larger
Malay world, so too do they firmly embed these overdetermined tokens
of the Malay—the same kind of plates also demanded by men's undersea
spirit wives—within the Barakai landscape immediately before resuming

trade. In the context of the plate distribution, the men also fortify, re-new, or resurrect—as the case may be—the mooring post marking the undersea site of the "Sea House of the Land," as, among other things, that place where Bemun's ancestors would have long ago first touched base on Barakai.

With regards to the cassowary—the first representative of Barakai sighted by the ancestors after touching shore—the islanders are them-selves relatively Malay, suggesting that the relation between the Malay and the Aru, autochthonous and foreign, past and present is itself a shifting one. Throughout their annual performance, Bemunese actively represent their community as a boat committed to a single voyage held to recapitulate the arrival from elsewhere of their ancestors to Barakai in the distant past and their establishment of settlement rights on the island through the hunt, capture, and killing of the cassowary indigenous to its landscape. Even in the context of the cassowary performance, the rela-tionship of the Aru and the Malay is never resolved in the same way from one year to the next. If Bemunese men kill a real cassowary in Barakai forests during the hunt held at this time, the community has successfully created itself in the image of its ancestral founders by strictly observing the various prohibitions through which they create themselves as non-Malay. Inversely in years when a cassowary is not taken, the reason always given is that members of the community—and more often than not its women and children—have lapsed into speaking Aru Malay, have ne-glected to remove sandals or conceal Western-style clothing, or in one or another fashion have been guilty of transgressions thereby constituting themselves as malayu. Beyond all this, Bemun's annual performance serves to substantiate the community's claims to the village site and pearl-diving grounds as well as their relative autochthony vis-à-vis the other four Barakai communities.

At other times of the year and in contrast to some of the neighboring south Moluccan islands where stone boat platforms, sometimes includ-ing a carved set of prow- and sternboards or even an anchor salvaged from a shipwreck, formerly graced village centers (Drabbe 1940, 50; McKinnon 1991), Bemun's boat is simply anchored in the house altars of the community's two most important adat officials and in the titles of these men.[11] The major responsibilities of the paired officials collectively known on Barakai as Belamon and Belamur, or the Prow and the Stern, are activated when the community "sets sail," as it were, pursuing the cassowary in boat formation in the context of its annual celebration.[12] Whenever the need arises throughout the rest of the year, the Prow and Stern may be called upon—separately or as a pair—by Bemunese villagers, members of neighboring communities, or even the local traders to present requests and offerings to guardian spirits and ancestors at their respective altars.

Within the course of Bemun's performance, the pairing of the officials Prow and Stern is transformed into an active duality that guides the community on its annual voyage. Stated somewhat differently, the organizational strategies of the performance disclose and actualize the temporality presupposed by the beached boat at the center of village space. The transformation from a primarily spatial and immobile representation of the boat to a temporalized, mobile one hinges on the embodiment through ritual action by the Prow and the Stern of the beginning and end of a process, which thereby establishes a continuity between the past of the ancestors and the present of their Aruese descendants. This temporalization of the Prow and Stern relation within an unfolding performance is what gives significance to and authorizes the spatial juxtaposition of the two officials' houses at Bemun's center as a conjunction that frames certain claims about the community's locality and position within the wider sociopolitical setting of Barakai Island as well as increasingly within the larger context of the Indonesian nation-state. Thus temporalized and made explicitly political, Bemun's boat—one made up of two halves (B. *ken wien ru*)—may effectively bridge the gap that exists in the present between the authorizing actions of the ancestors who settled the island long ago and the occupation of the village site by their contemporary Bemunese descendants. On Barakai, at least, this kind of legitimizing link cannot be taken for granted but needs to be created in performance.

Significantly, the potential for this transformation is already prefigured in the Barakai language titles of the officials Belamon and Belamur, or the Prow and the Stern, which allow either a more spatial or a more temporal reading. *Bela-*, the first part of the title, derives from *belan*, a variety of plank-built sailing boat produced locally in Aru today. Perhaps appropriately, given their status as the onetime vessel of diasporic ancestors, belan are modeled after a prototype originating in the Kei Islands,[13] while some incorporate stylistic elements inspired by colonial ships. In 1893 a Dutch writer described a Kei boat type that he claimed was produced only for local consumption but that clearly provides the model for the belan still used in Aru today: "The largest type, the *belan waho tetear*, that is only built for indigenous use . . . has at the front as well as at the back a tapering board, usually beautifully carved à jour and painted, that terminates in a sharp point. A knob, of which the model is borrowed from that of ships' lanterns of the last century, is placed at the top of this point, in which triangular flags with long pennons are affixed at the top" (Pleyte 1893, 115). The second part of the titles, *mon* in Belamon and *mur* in Belamur, function by virtue of the opposition between them as both spatial and temporal markers in daily speech. *Mon* and *mur* describe, respectively, the front and backside of basic material forms such as the human body, a house, or a boat. Combined with the prefix *sel-*, they produce the contrasting terms for the front of the village, *selmon*, and its rear, *selmur*. Or they are employed as simple temporal markers in conversation: *mol mon*, "you go first," or *ir dal mur*, "they will come later." A more formalized version of this temporal difference is exemplified by the pair *monen*, "elder," and *murin*, "younger," which distinguishes between same-sex siblings on the basis of relative birth order. It may be understood as "senior" and "junior" when age is the main focus or as "first" and "last" if a more general sense of precedence is desired. The high generality and varied linguistic deployment of *mon* and *mur* is important to bear in mind; this symbolic underdetermination accounts for the wide range of layered associations that these words are capable of evoking. Importantly, it suggests how the everyday spatial opposition of Prow and Stern, as the front and back of a belan, can easily be imagined temporally in the course of ritual action as a correspondence between the beginning and the ending of a process.

Similarly, a look at the house altars corresponding to the respective positions of these two men suggests that here, too, a set of spatial differences also embeds a distinction in temporalities. Relatively speaking, a contrast between before and after, past and present, ancestral powers and contemporary projects—only potentially made continuous through the conjoined actions of Prow and Stern in the annual performance—crystallizes in the objects and altar layout of each official. Besides the spatial distance between the two houses themselves, the Prow's altar is accessible only by ladder and the objects with which it is associated are therefore invisible from below, while those identified with the Stern's altar are displayed on pandanus mats in the front room of his home. Apart from the Prow, only men climb the ladder to his altar and then only once a year to mark for themselves the beginning of the cassowary hunt with a personal offering of betel—something that underscores not only the difference between the two altars but the privileged access of Barakai men versus women to ancestral sources of power (chapter 7).

In contrast the four large gongs—aged and gray like old stones propped up against the wall—and the stacks of dusty plates and glasses containing desiccated offerings that make up the Stern's altar are in full view of anyone who enters his house. Even if I had not been told by this official and other Bemunese that the community traces the acquisition of these gongs to an intervillage friendship feast with an alliance partner (bela) in central eastern Aru, the prominent visibility of these objects as well as their status as goods pertaining to Bemun as a whole already implies that they derive from a time more recent than that of ancestral beginnings on Barakai.[14] Yet notwithstanding their relative historical traceability, these objects are still overdetermined as indexical of the ancestral agency through which they were first obtained. Members of the Stern's household and visitors to his home make obvious efforts to keep dogs and children away from the altar when necessary. Disrespectful behavior like drunkenness is to be avoided in the presence of the gongs, which are referred to with the Barakai term for both ancestors and living elders, kajinembu.

Again, relatively speaking, the objects that the Prow takes down from his elevated altar once a year to be deployed in the context of his community's annual celebration are, if only for this rarity, more powerfully charged. The bow and matching three arrows that the Prow carries at the head of the procession of hunters when they depart in boat formation for the forest underscore his decisive role as "the one who pierces first" (B. asin nal mon). Iconically motivating the division of labor in the manning of a belan that the Prow and Stern index as a pair, "the one who pierces first" evokes for Barakai men and women a range of intersecting images: the pilot poised above the waves guiding the vessel past dangerous coral reefs and treacherous shallows, the prototype of the harpooner ready to send a missile at the dark, fleeting shapes that occasionally surround the boat, or the prow itself as it cuts a straight path across the mobile, undulating surface of the sea. According to the same imagery, the Stern at the boat's rear "holds the rudder" (B. *asual gwilen*) with which he steers and controls the belan's course.

Yet notwithstanding the operative ambivalence between Prow and Stern and the precedence of sorts that the former enjoys (Bemunese sometimes call his altar the "center" [I. *pusat*] or "source" [B. *ken un*] of their community's momosim practices, and it was here, after all, that the adat meeting described in Gita's letter took place), both officials represent adat affairs in Bemun and, as such, have equal access to and association with ancestral powers and agency. Seen in this light, the following confidence on the part of the Stern's wife, told to me one afternoon, makes perfect sense. Since, as she put it, she and her husband had "held" Bemun's momosim affairs (B. *dasual momosim*), they had, she complained, rapidly aged. Although she and her husband were the same age as other villagers whose hair was still black, theirs, by contrast, had gone prematurely white. This was so, she explained, because the kajinembu (both the ancestral spirits and their stony representatives in the Stern's altar) with whom her husband communicates on behalf of his fellow Bemunese were ancient and wished to make the Stern and his wife, as their representatives, conform to their own image.

In the context of Bemun's annual celebration, such an identification between living women and men and their ancestors cannot be assumed but has to be brought about actively. To achieve both continuity with what Bemunese regard as ancestral and Aru, and difference from all things Malay, the actions of the officials Prow and Stern are balanced and played off against each other as beginnings and endings throughout the performance. Ideally, this play demarcates a space and a time that, having a sharply articulated beginning and ending, is decidedly Aru and other. At the level of the performance as a whole, the forging of a link between past and present, between ancestral authority and contemporary claims, is at the same time the move that establishes the otherness of the Bemun community and its difference within a larger Malay world and especially vis-à-vis trade, missionization, and the nation-state. In other words, Bemun's annual celebration, with the cassowary as its emblem, is a performance through which the community organizes not only its relation to itself, to its ancestors and guardian spirits, and to its

Barakai neighbors but just as crucially, its relation to what, following Bemunese, can be glossed as a Malay preeminence.

Performatively, the demarcation of the difference of an Aru suspended at the margins of a much larger Malay world implies a sort of tacking back and forth between the assertion by the Prow of beginnings as origins and foci of ancestral power, on the one hand, and, on the other, the appropriation by the Stern of these forces for contemporary projects through the transformation of beginnings into endings. Identified with beginnings, the Prow opens the annual ritual performance as well as all subrites within it and also initiates communication with the ancestral spirits of Bemun. Sociologically as well, the fam that holds the office of Prow is said to have been the first to have settled the land, while that of the Stern is held to have arrived later. When the Stern does something first, the act therefore acquires the character of a kind of desacralization, since it always occurs in contradistinction to a prior action of the Prow and thereby entails a distancing or differentiation from ancestral origins or a translation of beginnings into endings. For instance, "he eats first" (B. *aga nal mon*) refers to the lifting of the prohibition on women touching game killed during the male hunt by the Stern's biting the tip of a wallaby's tail. This named action, repeated at the conclusion of each day's hunt, offsets the Prow's offering made to the ancestors at the day's beginning. In thus transforming a beginning into an ending, the Stern also appropriates the game killed by the men to be cooked by the women and consumed by the wider community. In analogous fashion, the Stern lifts the prohibitions imposed at the outset of the performance by the Prow and does so again by acting first. For instance, to lift the prohibition on physical contact with water (except for drinking) in force during the performance, the Stern washes his hands first ("he washes his hands first," B.*aur lim nal mon*), a named action that may then be replicated by all the male members of the village. Later that same day when the Stern's wife washes her hands, she lifts the prohibition for female villagers on contact with water for this body part. Again, the Stern's full bathing the following morning ("he bathes first," B.*artur nal mon*) means that men and boys may bathe fully, while his wife's bath shortly thereafter signals the same for the women and girls of Bemun.

In the same way, at the level of the ritual as a whole, what matters is that the performance be completed with the transformation of a culturally privileged beginning into an authorized ending—a transformation that is itself contingent upon the reciprocal actions of the officials Prow and Stern, and upon the correspondences and differences with which they engage each other in performance. More specifically, this transformation also hinges on the particular authority constructed over the course of ritual action that each man can lay claim to in his respective role as beginning or ending at the conclusion of a given performance and thus for the new year that the performance inaugurates. In turn, the authority of these men emerges, at least partially, out of a complicated series of mirrorings and deflections through which the interactions among ancestral spirits, Bemunese women, men, and children, and even the game pursued in the forest are refracted, caught up, and deployed in the organizational tactics and moves of the Prow and the Stern. To say therefore that the two adat officials orchestrate the performance is not at all the same thing as saying that they run the show.

It should be clear, then, that ancestral powers can only be activated, set into circulation, and brought to bear on the projects of living Bemunese when the two men act as a pair by repeatedly prefiguring, retroactively engaging, and entailing each other for the duration of the performance. While in theory both stand to gain or lose somewhat in the eyes of their fellow villagers in terms of their own individual performance, together the Prow and the Stern assume and conjointly construct the authority, responsibility, ancestral potency and, hence, agency that pertains to and ensues from Bemun's annual performance. Following Ortner (1985) and Strathern (1988), Keane challenges the "common Western inclination to locate agency . . . in biologically distinct individuals" (1997a, 7). Rather than being absolutely localized in particular persons and positions or even readily locatable, participants in the highly ritualized settings characteristic of public life on the island of Sumba, "*interactively* define themselves and each other" (ibid., emphasis in the original). Such, indeed, is also the case here.

The Sense of an Ending

On Barakai, the authority that the Prow and the Stern conjointly produce with their fellow Bemunese and ancestors in the context of the community's performance can be reduced neither to its originating source nor to its ending—that is, to neither of these officials as allegedly more important or primary than his paired other. Important in the paired interactions with which the Prow and the Stern engage each other is not simply the determination of a beginning as an absolute locus of value in relation to which all else would allegedly be reckoned, but also "the sense of an ending" that creates a consonance between the present and something seen as its source (Kermode 1966).[15] Following Kermode, the positing of an end humanizes process by giving it a particular form and by bestowing organization onto mere duration. When speaking for instance, of the ticking of a clock, "we ask what it *says*: and we agree that it says *tick-tock*. By this fiction we humanize it, make it talk our language" (ibid., 44). The problem then becomes that of defeating "the tendency of the interval between *tick* and *tock* to empty itself; to maintain within that interval following *tick* a lively expectation of *tock*, a sense that however remote *tock* may be, all that happens happens as if *tock* were certainly following" (p. 46). In this way, social action becomes charged with a meaning and efficacy that ultimately derives from its relation to this end. Or, put somewhat differently, in a manner that directly addresses the problem of origins while still preserving the notion of precedence, "the second is not that which merely arrives, like a latecomer, *after* the first, but that which permits the first to be the first. The first cannot be the first unaided, by its own properties alone: the second, with all the force of its delay, must come to the assistance of the first. It is through the second that the first is first. The 'second time' thus has priority of a kind over the 'first time': it is present from the first time onwards as the prerequisite of the first's priority without itself being a more primitive 'first time'" (Descombes 1980, 145). These insights offer a way of understanding the dynamic and productive interaction of the Prow and the Stern in Bemun's performance without reifying "origins" or, thereby, glossing over the question of why the constitution of ancestral origins itself presumes an interactive pair.

Insofar as any given end defines its own origin or site of value in the same move through which it establishes a concord among action in the present, a beginning, and an end—in the same way that the Stern continually indexes a prior action of the Prow—the above discussion also suggests how the anthropomorphization of origins in the form of the ancestors can emerge in the performance as a generative source of value. Bemun's boat, consisting of its "two halves," the Prow and the Stern, and linked in the performance to the past of diasporic ancestors and their settlement on Barakai, represents such a site of value: a constellation of rights, obligations, privileges, and powers in which a more diffuse discourse concerning locality, precedence, and origins crystallizes into a political construction. The possibility of this crystallization as, to some extent, not only "official" but also male is always contingent upon the reciprocal actions of the Prow and the Stern, on the engagements and interventions of their fellow Bemunese in the performance, and on the willingness of the latter to participate in their community's most collective cultural production. As with any other "foundational fiction," Bemun's boat is not only historically constructed but also contingent and, at times, subject to contestation (Sommer 1991).

The efficacy of Bemun's ritual and its recollection of the mythic diaspora of Bemunese ancestors from elsewhere to Barakai is contingent upon its staging from "beginning" to "end," as these positions are defined from within the performance itself. The import and practical inscription of the entire ritual process is revealed at and as its conclusion: as the territorial occupation of the village site by a community that constructs itself as internally related and empowered by its continued, reiterated adherence to postulated beginnings on Barakai as these are held to be embodied in Bemun's distinctive adat practices. By the same token, the auspiciousness that participants in the annual performance hope to bring about is not obvious or given beforehand but hinges precisely on the assertion of closure and the sense of an ending.

As one might expect, however, the determination of completeness—the illusion of closure that, in this context, is regarded as efficacious—and the authority claims of the ritual both within the regional setting of Barakai Island and within the more global one of the former New Order could never be settled in the abstract. It was always a political matter that brought to bear on any given adat performance the concerns, conflicts, fears, and aspirations at any given time of Bemunese men and women. In light of the definitive importance of the beginning and ending of the performance, it is not surprising that the colonization of adat under the New Order played itself out in this Backshore community through conflicts that were focused on the performance's beginning, ending, and timing as well as in relation to those persons who ideally embody the authority bestowed by beginnings and endings, namely, the Prow and the Stern.

Time and Trade

At least since the 1970s, repeated conflicts have broken out between the Prow and the Stern, on the one hand, and the government-appointed headman, on the other, over the timing of Bemun's annual performance. Undoubtedly, the timing of this performance (for however long it has been held) has always been a complicated and politically charged matter. Yet, while the two officials—and especially the Prow, as the one who alone opens the entire ritual sequence—have always had to take into account numerous different and often conflicting criteria when determining the beginning of Bemun's performance, such criteria have multiplied with the increasing presence in Aru of the nation-state, the introduction of schooling to Barakai, and the mass conversions of the 1970s. A sense of the different criteria is necessary to understand how a conflict about ritual authority could so easily crystallize around the issue of time.

Given the seasonal nature of pencarian on Backshore Aru and the kinds of trade products historically collected by Barakai islanders, climatic and seasonal criteria have necessarily always been critical to determining the opening of a performance that is itself directly related to trade. As mentioned earlier, climatic conditions associated with the west monsoon need to be met before the collection and trade of sea products off of Barakai can begin. Specifically, the strong winds of the east season should already have subsided and the seas should have begun to regain the calm that permits diving. Given as well that, at least today, the opening rite of Bemun's performance is a fish poisoning held at an estuary in which the participants stand knee-deep for several hours, the performance must also begin on a day on which the low tide falls in the morning—the time of the day when this rite is held—and is at its most shallow and extensive. Taken alone, these climatic factors give those who determine the ritual's precise timing several weeks' play between approximately late September and mid-October when the fish poisoning can be held.

In the past the performance also had to be timed so that the conclusion of the island-wide sequence of performances that runs in succession through Mesiang, Bemun, Longgar, and Apara would have more or less coincided with the seasonal arrival of traders to the Backshore. In other words, the islanders had to have some system of time reckoning in place that would have enabled them to predict fairly accurately this arrival, among other things. It is my belief that the island-wide ceremonial cycle once provided Barakai women and men with a calendrical organization that had such predictive value. Based on lunar months,[16] such a calendar would necessarily have comprised a method allowing for the insertion of intercalary months at irregular intervals in such a way that the lunar and solar years would never get more than one month out of step with each other.[17] It is my suspicion that the current composition of the sequence beginning with two performances each having a hunt at its core—in Mesiang's case, until recently, that of the wild boar (B. *dai weov*) and in Bemun's, the cassowary—and followed by two more performances focused on the sea, with the last, Apara's, culminating every two years in the construction of a miniature "sea house," has long inscribed Barakai trade relations together with its related temporal scheme onto island space. Seen in this light, the ceremonial cycle hints at a much older topography of island-wide commercial relations: one in which former settlements in the Barakai interior provided those on the coast with forest and horticultural products in exchange for trade goods like cloth, alcohol, and ceramicware (chapter 1). Finally, I suspect that this calendrical structuring of trade-related labor and politics and the intimate articulation of commerce and ceremony on the island ended up ceremonializing trade in certain respects while also commercializing ceremony. Regarding the latter, one of the explicit aims of the annual performances held to open diving and commerce is the propitiation of an abundance of products that can subsequently be collected for trade. One could also wonder about the kinds of predicaments that may have followed from this double role of the regional ceremonial calendar as a general form of time reckoning, on the one hand, and a commercially motivated timepiece, on the other—whether, for instance, the occasional tension that must have arisen between them did not itself abet the erosion of the calendar through its displacement by other imported forms of temporal calculation.

Yet even as several Barakai communities have, in the last fifteen years

Apara's sea house under construction

or so, opted to "cast off" those parts of their annual performances that were deemed "backward" or otherwise reprehensible by the New Order government, the regional ceremonial cycle as it unfolds across the four participating Barakai communities continues to influence the timing of Bemun's contribution to the island-wide cycle. Being the second of four, Bemunese should wait to hold their cassowary celebration until the Mesiangese have concluded their abbreviated performance, consisting since the 1970s only of sea-oriented rites. During the two performances of 1986 and 1987 that fell during my residence in Bemun, this sequence was never raised as an issue affecting the timing of its performance;

Mesiang had always held its performance at least several weeks before Bemunese began to think of holding their own. What was sometimes raised as an issue was that Longgar, which follows Bemun in the cycle, had on several occasions in the recent past begun its performance before Bemunese ended theirs. The upshot of this affront not only to their neighbors but to the order laid down by adat itself was, according to those Bemunese who complained about the Longgarese lack of compliance, a poor diving season for the latter troubled by clouded seas and sharks.

Today a plethora of calendrical criteria as well as others having nothing to do with calendars operate simultaneously in Bemun as in the other four Barakai communities. Almost all Barakai homes boast at least one calendar and sometimes even more in the front room of the house where visitors are received. All of these calendars, whether issued by the Catholic or Protestant churches or, more commonly, by commercial enterprises like the national *kretek* (I. clove cigarette) company Gudang Garam Inc. or the locally important Abadi Nylon Rope and Fishing Net Manufacturing, Ltd., follow the Gregorian calendar and are marked with important national holidays—and, in the case of the Catholics, religious ones as well. Because of the Indonesian law, adopted in 1967, that prohibits the use and display of Chinese characters, it is not surprising that I never saw a Chinese calendar in Aru (Blussé 1991; Tan 1991). Nonetheless, the approximate timing of a number of holidays that are celebrated by the traders figure as important reference points for Barakai islanders during the year (chapter 4).[18]

Given the patterning of everyday activities on Barakai, more salient for islanders than an abstract numerical system that is attended to on a daily basis are certain dates that are singled out for special behavior and attention (Munn 1992). The most important for Bemun are the national Day of Independence on August 17, the Day of the Indonesian Armed Forces on October 5, Christmas, New Year's, Ash Wednesday, Palm Sunday, Easter, Sundays in general, the beginning and ending of the school term (not fixed dates but determined by the schoolteacher's arrival and departure from the village), and, as noted above, holidays observed by the traders, especially the Chinese New Year and Cebeng, the Day of the Dead. Only Hari ABRI (ABRI being the acronym for Angkatan Bersenjata Républik Indonésia, the Indonesian Armed Forces), because of

its timing in early October, poses a potential problem for Bemun's annual performance.

Timing was inevitably the main topic of conversation in the several
weeks before the performances of 1986 and 1987, when Bemunese women
and men returned to the village from their gardens and sago processing
sites, where they had spent the greater part of the off-season, and began to
prepare themselves for the arrival of the cassowary. Broadly, what concerned them most was whether they had accumulated an adequate food
supply for the feast in view of the overflowing hospitality with which it is
identified and whether they had cleared away the brush from their gardens and from around the bases of their sago and coconut palms to
protect them somewhat from the fires that Bemunese hunters set in the
forest during the cassowary celebration. By the performance's opening,
Bemunese households need also to have stocked up on store-bought
goods like coffee, sugar, and flour, as well as on articles of personal
adornment, such as hair cream and cologne, that women and men use in
abundance during the feast. Before the performance begins, they should
have gathered firewood, filled their water urns, and cleaned their houses.
Naturally, different Bemunese households will differ in the extent to
which they have completed these various tasks and, consequently, in their
opinions regarding the timing of the performance's beginning.

The two trading families resident in Bemun also have a stake in and an
indirect influence on the timing of the performance. First, their stores
should be well supplied to meet the demands of their Bemunese clients
immediately before and during the celebration, lest they take their business to stores in the neighboring villages. Ideally, they are also fully
stocked with new wares in preparation for the active trading of the
diving season that the performance inaugurates. The traders also need to
have laid up a supply of palm wine to offer to the dancing villagers when
they congregate by turn in front of Bemun's two stores on the final night
of the cassowary celebration. With these requirements in mind, one
trading couple returned both years to Bemun after spending the east
monsoon in the capital with a stock of new wares with which to re-
open its store, while the other made a quick extra buying trip to the
capital—and even a second run in 1987—once the community's celebration seemed imminent.

With varying emphases for any given performance, all the above conditions, calendars, and considerations figure jointly as a loose frame within which the Prow ideally makes the final decision alone—although he may first choose to consult with his counterpart the Stern—regarding when to begin Bemun's annual performance. Year after year, as far as I could gather from talking to Bemunese, this collective framework scales down the possibilities almost, but not quite, to the day. Within these parameters, an element of surprise is expected and even relished. Indeed, the surprise occasioned in both years when, after much speculation regarding the performance's precise timing, the Prow decided to "walk" and set the performance in motion on a given evening is clearly an important aspect of the efficacy of the performance's beginning. Since "the Prow's walk" (B. *Belamon amor*) or round of the village should occur unseen and uninterrupted by encounters with his fellow villagers—"invisibly," as it were—and since he is escorted by ancestral spirits, the surprise of this opening has a slightly unsettling side to it, a feeling that significantly contributes to its power. Because the beginning is "invisible" to start with, the opening act of the ritual season is never entirely predictable and usually seemed to take the majority of Bemunese somewhat aback (and sometimes even the Stern). Ideally, with the suddenness with which the night overcomes the day in the equatorial tropics, the Prow emerges in ancestral dress and begins his round. In this way, his entry has the effect of a minor coup that transgresses and disrupts the space in which he moves, thus making way for something radically different (de Certeau 1984, 79). In de Certeau's terms, this kind of artful ploy "*makes* a hit ('*coup*')" far more than it simply describes one; its force lies in the effect it has of seeming to elude present circumstances through the creation of a fictional space—a space, as it were, of "once upon a time there was. . . ." (ibid.). The fact that the beginning of the performance occurs as a disruption in which the past, as it were, overtakes the present also accounts for its perceived danger and the association of this danger with the ancestral spirits who escort the Prow.

As I said at the outset of this discussion of time and trade on Barakai, the timing of Bemun's annual performance has in recent years become a point of considerable conflict between the village's headman and its two adat officials, the Prow and the Stern. One aspect of the headman's pressures aimed specifically at the Prow that seemed to bother Bemunese women and men most is that the act of fixing an opening date, as the

headman for the past several years had attempted to do—though unsuccessfully—would deprive the performance of its initial and somewhat
startling force. Before turning to a particular example of such conflict—
the aforementioned "ritual without an ending"—I turn first to some of
the sources of difference that have brought Bemun's headman into repeated confrontation with the Prow and the Stern.

The Prow, the Stern, and the Headman

Much of the village headman's efforts—as someone acting for the most
part as an unwitting accomplice of the nation-state—to extend his control to encompass adat affairs has to do with the dilemma that his position as *kepala desa* (village headman) sometimes, and perhaps increasingly, puts him in. Within an administrative hierarchy that assigns full
responsibility for the state of the village to its headman, there are a
number of issues that burden him more than other Bemunese. For
instance, it was the headman and no one else who expressed to me his
concern that government bureaucrats in Dobo should be kept unaware
of certain aspects of Bemun's ritual that he feared they would find backward and, hence, objectionable. Since the ostensible purpose of the annual ritual is to open the diving and trade season and since, moreover, it
should finish before the national holiday of the Armed Forces on October 5, it is in the headman's interest to ensure that the performance gets
under way and out of the way as soon as possible. By timing the performance properly, Bemunese can both avoid the contradictions entailed in
the mixing of adat and government affairs that would follow from an
overlap between their ritual and Armed Forces Day, and profit from the
most favorable climatic conditions for pearl diving.

Yet for Bemun's headman, who implements and executes government
plans for his community and also has followed specialized "refresher"
courses for village headman (I. *Penataran Kepala Desa*), his position is
increasingly fraught with ambiguities.[19] Aiming for a delicate balance,
the headman must play off the "modernizing" ambitions and demands
of the government against the villagers' own often contrasted sense of
their obligations within a complex process about which they have restricted knowledge. More and more, the headman has been forced to

adopt, assimilate, and represent ideas of authority that depart from and challenge those articulated, for instance, by the adat official the Stern in the account that follows. By the same token, the chief has increasingly come to stand for these ideas in the eyes of many of his fellow villagers. Thus, in the process of carrying out the rationalizing projects of the Indonesian nation-state—fence-building being the main one during my 1986–88 stay on Barakai and also the one most brutally enforced—the headman has himself been forced into an ever more rationalizing position that detracts from and complicates his other social obligations in the community.[20]

Because Bemun's headman at the time belonged to the fam that traditionally holds the office of Stern and is himself directly in the line of succession,[21] opinions differed among Bemunese as to whether he exceeded his rightful authority in trying to coerce the adat officials (especially the Prow) to begin the performance at a time established by him. On the whole, villagers sympathized with the headman's predicament when one year, owing to the shortsightedness of these same officials, Armed Forces Day fell during the hunt of the cassowary. Given the prohibition at this time on contact with all things Malay such as the Western-style clothing introduced to Aru by Dutch missionaries,[22] imported white rice, and the Indonesian language, the government order to hoist the red and white national flag in observance of the holiday placed the headman in an unenviable position. He was forced to choose between honoring the day and facing the repercussions of angry ancestral spirits, on the one hand, and refusing to honor it and exposing himself to the equally formidable power of the Indonesian government, on the other. In the end, the village headman seems to have settled on a compromise that mollified both the ancestors and his own perception of his administrative and ceremonial duties as a member of the Indonesian state bureaucracy. Shortly after dawn on October 5, the headman, wearing the men's loincloth of the ritual season rather than the militaristic garb more usual on such occasions, walked alone to the schoolyard and hoisted the flag. Later in the afternoon of the same day, after the men returned from the hunt, he again went alone to the schoolyard to lower the flag.

More often than not, however, Bemunese have found themselves uneasy with their headman's repeated attempts to intervene in adat affairs.

In 1987, for instance, many villagers were indignant when the headman threatened to impose a fine on the Prow in the form of community labor if he refused to open the ritual on the day selected by the headman. The most disastrous intervention so far, however, in which even members of the headman's own household felt that he had overstepped his jurisdiction, seems to have occurred during a performance in the early 1970s that was characterized to me by the Stern as having never reached its end.

The Ritual without an Ending

I first heard about this ritual without an ending from the Stern when he was trying to lay out the procedures that distinguish a short, three-day cassowary celebration from a longer, five-day one. At the core of the ritual sequence lasting approximately three weeks, the cassowary celebration usually lasts three days. Once every four or five years and sometimes longer, as it was explained to me in the mid-1980s, the mooring post securing the submerged Sea House of the Land topples over, thereby triggering a longer ritual. If it topples, Bemun's cassowary celebration should last five days. Instead of the shorter sequence called "doing it small" (B. *dai ken titia*), the community stages a longer and somewhat different performance described as "doing it great" (B. *dai ken jinjin*).

One year, probably around the early 1970s, the mooring post of the Sea House of the Land fell over. All Bemunese I questioned claimed that the connection between the falling of the post and the staging of a more elaborate ritual is automatic. Indeed, when the post fell in early 1988, many of those Bemunese I was most close to lamented the fact that I would have to miss the great performance that they now knew lay ahead of them. Even if the post falls only a month or so after Bemun's annual ritual, villagers know that the following year a great performance will have to be held. The falling of the post a mere day after its resurrection, as described in Gita's letter, and immediately following a great performance shocked Bemunese. This event was apparently so unsettling that, rather than relying on the customary practice of deferral in which the falling of the post commits the community to holding a great performance when the ritual season again comes around, the Prow and the Stern convened an adat conference in 1989. In the early 1970s, however, the problems and issues at stake in the community's celebration were much more inchoate than they now appear to be. What happened in the year that, according to the Stern, began with a ritual that never reached its end was that instead of observing the cassowary ritual with a five-day hunt corresponding to the "great" performance required that year, the headman reportedly pressured Bemun's adat officials into holding a shorter performance only lasting four days.

It is not clear to me how the shorter version of the great performance was pushed through or, for that matter, if the difference between a four- and a five-day performance was truly an issue at the time. According to the Stern, his opposition in the early 1970s to a four-day performance was vehement. In emphasizing to me his strong objections, the Stern also implied that he already foresaw at the time the grave consequences that a temporally truncated version of the great ritual would have not only for his younger brother, the headman, but for the Bemunese community at large. His remarks seem to suggest that, for any given performance, a duration of either three or five days is dogmatically fixed beforehand, according to whether or not the mooring post has fallen.

Yet the impression of orthodoxy conveyed by the reported dispute over length is misleading for a number of reasons. First, at least with regard to the duration of a regular, "small" version of the annual performance, there is evidence of great flexibility. A small performance may last either three or four days without any qualitative difference made by Bemunese between the two versions. Perhaps even more important, the decision-making process that sets the length of a given small performance at either three or four days appears to be structured precisely to avoid the kind of struggle over ritual precedence that arose between the Stern and the village headman. In brief, at the outset of the performance, after being summoned by the Prow's round of the village, the men and adolescent boys of Bemun who plan to participate in the cassowary hunt gather around a fire at the center of the village to "speak" (B. *dalwaler*). Among other things, the men address the length of the impending hunt. Commonly, when this particular issue is raised, it is settled by the teenage boys present. In 1987, for instance, it was their role to voice a preference for either a three- or a four-day cassowary hunt, in the case of the small performance to be held that year. I was told, moreover, that the issue had always been decided in this way. In leaving the issue of length to what villagers regard as the whims of adolescents, an element of deus ex machina is introduced. Although in this instance the *deus* is powerless rather than all-powerful, the decision is placed beyond the influence of those adult men who might have a stake in determining the immediate shape of adat affairs and exercising their authority in relation to the community's annual celebration.

I have no direct evidence suggesting analogous flexibility with regard to the length of a great version of the cassowary hunt and celebration. I do have the insistence by Bemunese women and men alike that, if the Sea House of the Land's mooring post falls, a great performance must be held as well as two examples of this injunction indeed being carried out, namely, in the performances of 1988 and 1989. Some of the women and men I spoke to also volunteered that such a performance lasts five days, which is presumably how long it often, or at least recently, has lasted. Yet the deliberate allocation of the decision regarding a small performance's length to Bemun's teenage boys makes it unlikely that community members would allow the same issue to become a factor of overwhelming importance in the case of a great performance. Given prevailing understandings of beginnings and endings as mutually constituted through performance, it is also unlikely that length as an abstract variable could have become the object of contestation. If such indeed is at odds with notions of ritual process as generally understood by Barakai women and men regarding when and how to begin and end a given performance, then why did the Stern in his account give the issue of length, the matter of a four- or a five-day ritual, such prominence!

Beyond its literal meaning, I believe that this insistence on a prescribed duration powerfully suggests the extent to which authority on Barakai is inextricably implicated in the patterning of time and, more specifically, draws its very force and legitimacy from its connection through performance to a temporal diacritics or a specific mode of marking time. The focus on temporality discloses the critical performative dimension of authority with respect to adat affairs: who has the authority to impose ritual closure and to decide when it should be imposed, how this authority should be constituted, and wherein it should reside. Of overriding importance is not simply who can rightfully occupy the position of the end and thereby define a given length and performance as normative, but rather the authorizing process itself through which a particular person comes to be identified as an ending. From this perspective it is of utmost importance that the person who told me of this ritual without an ending was none other than the Stern, who himself, when all goes as it should, comes to embody the end.

Besides the string of disasters that befell the village headman and his family, the Stern's account consisted of a listing of a series of displaced and misplaced endings that he maintained had had an effect on the community as a whole. I begin with the disasters. Following the Stern, ancestral retaliation for the truncated ritual of four days took place in some cases immediately during the performance itself and in others shortly after it had ended. The anger of the ancestors and the guardian spirits of the village had direct consequences for a number of people. Two of the headman's children died before the following year's performance was held. A woman who played a critical part when a great version of the Bemun's annual ritual was held—and who had played such a part in the truncated great performance—died suddenly not long after the performance had ended. While the hunt was still in progress, Bemun's headman also received a special sign of his transgression—as the Stern rather dryly put it, "the headman got his sign" (B. *orang ka artom ken tanda*). In the heat of the action of one of the days' hunts, a wild boar—fleeing the fires that the hunters set in the forest to drive the game out into the open—ran so close by the headman that it almost knocked him over. The headman made an attempt to spear the boar but succeeded only in cutting off its tail, which remained dangling from the end of his spear point as the animal disappeared into the smoky haze ahead.

As endings, boars' tails play a crucial role in the cassowary portion of Bemun's ritual. The final act of the cassowary hunt involves a boar's tail that must be shot westward by the Stern to rid the island of any "heaviness" (B. *ken didiëne*) or generalized inauspiciousness that may still linger after the performance. As the most vicious animal inhabiting the Barakai forests, the wild boar evokes in this context not only all the dangers threatening mankind but also the potential for danger that resides in man himself—for reasons that will become clear in chapter 7, I do mean *man*. Under normal circumstances, the ritual send-off of the tails presented to the Stern during the course of the hunt—as the terminal body part dispatched by an official who in the context of the performance ideally comes to embody all endings—constitutes at the same time an auspicious beginning for things to come.

But what happens when the boar's tail is identified with someone who,

not signifying an ending, cannot be its rightful recipient or even temporary safekeeper? In the Stern's telling, the headman's transgression in
attempting to establish his authority arbitrarily over the length of the
hunt becomes transformed into something more than a displaced ending. As a boar's tail indexical of danger to humans, it can also be read
as an externalized sign of the headman's own misplaced ambitions or of
the inauspiciousness that necessarily ensues when an ending is asserted
through the wrong person. From the long list of disasters that befell the
headman and his family, it is also clear that by cutting the ritual off
before its "natural" end, the headman brought the inauspiciousness condensed in the tail upon himself.

Without a foundation in a complete and great rendering of Bemun's
annual ritual, the mooring post of the Sea House of the Land lacked
stability and fell within a week or so after the performance had ended.
This meant that the following year a great performance had to be staged
again and, by implication, that the four-day performance had somehow
fallen short of its objective. According to the Stern, the consequences of
this ritual without an ending were so drastic that they continued to be
felt in the community for several years after and became concretized in
the failure of Bemunese hunters to kill a wild boar in the performances
of the following two or three years. As a result, there were no tails for the
Stern to shoot westward; "heaviness" could therefore not be fully dispatched from the village but hung over the community, instilling a general sense of malaise and misfortune. For several years as well, Bemun's
ancestral spirits begrudgingly had to make do with the simple betel quid
with which the Stern informed them that the ritual had reached its end.

Reading the conflict between Bemun's headman and the Stern as one
about the performance's length defined in abstraction from all else di-
verts attention from the more important confrontation over authority:
not simply who has it, but how it should be created, realized, and articulated with respect to adat affairs. To understand this distinction means
focusing not on normative generalizations but on the practice of the
Stern's account, on why he couched his disagreement with the headman
in terms that demand a certain understanding of completeness or why
completeness for the majority of Bemunese hinges, in this context, on
the performative relationship between a beginning and an end. For instance, if the four-day performance is considered exclusively in terms of
what the participants did, then the curious link between a certain idea of

completeness and the missing fifth day is more sharply posed. That completeness is not contingent on the actual length of the performance and that it is not numerically defined is borne out by the fact that, except for the missing day in and of itself, the four- and five-day renderings of Bemun's great ritual were, as far as I could ascertain, otherwise equivalent. A purely descriptive enumeration of the persons, objects, and actions involved in the four-day hunt would therefore fail to reveal anything amiss with this particular performance. As in any other annual cassowary celebration recently put on by the Bemun community, a fish poisoning was held, loincloths were donned, the hunters left in boat formation for the forest, and a coconut frond cassowary effigy was fabricated, paraded around the village, and at the end of the night's festivities, killed. In other words, since everything ritually demanded was accomplished within the space of four days, the value of the missing fifth day cannot lie in the extra time it would have given to Bemun's performance. And even if it could be argued that the Stern objected to the headman's show of authority merely because it compromised his own, this assertion would still not explain the particular form in which he couched his objections.

What, then, was the value of the fifth day? The Stern's insistence on the fifth day had in actuality little to do with a rigid adherence to one or another predetermined temporal length or numerical specification defined in abstraction from any particularities of time and space. Rather, it was only in retrospect that the fifth day became a signifier for the crucial significance that the temporality intrinsic to the ritual process had for the constitution and definition of local authority. In dislocating the fifth day, the headman inadvertently undermined the crucial performative link between a beginning and an end, between his community and its postulated origins, between the particular shifting constellation of rights, obligations, privileges, and powers that are held to comprise local adat and their embeddedness within everyday circumstances.

Boats and Bureaucracy

The lengthy briefing I received from the Stern on my last visit to Aru, in which he attempted to bring me up to date regarding the previous years' cassowary performances, suggests that up until that time the ending of Bemun's annual performance and, by extension, a given person's authorizing link to it could not simply be posited outside of the ritual process as if by a bureaucratic stamp (I. *cap*) or signature. In the 1970s, by merely fixing the end of the performance at four rather than five days and, in so doing, opposing himself to the Stern, the headman asserted his authority over the ritual in the only way available to him, through an isolated act of power. By defining the great ritual's structure—its organizational strategies and tactics—in terms of his own administrative position, the headman also located the meaning and legitimacy of the performance within the bureaucratic chain of command that emanates from Jakarta and extends to the far corners of the Indonesian nation-state. Seen in this light, it becomes possible to interpret the missing fifth day or what amounted to the same, the displaced boar's tail, as an objectification of authority out of place or of authority obeying a different and, in this context, threatening order of time and space. Externally derived rather than internally constituted and embodied through ritual action, the headman's authority ultimately failed to connect with the adat practices at stake in the annual cassowary celebration. Rather than emerging out of the moves and momentum produced in performance, the village headman's position with respect to adat affairs in Bemun stood out like a tail out of place or a rudder without a boat to steer.

Sometimes the headman's interventions left their marks less perceptibly on the performance. In 1987, this time in confrontation with the Prow, the headman again used his administrative office to push through his preferred timing for the annual performance. Thus, while the headman favored a speedy beginning, the adat official wanted to postpone the ritual's opening to the next occasion when tidal flats would again stretch out in front of the village in the morning (approximately seven to ten days later), setting thereby the appropriate circumstances for the community's fish poisoning. Most Bemunese with whom I spoke tended to side with the headman in wanting the performance to begin, while a number also voiced their suspicion that the Prow's desire for deferral had more to do with the personal plans of his family to finish rebuilding their kitchen than with the demands of adat itself.

The Prow, however, argued that many households had not yet completed their preparations for the performance. Those Bemunese who were ready complained that if the ritual was postponed another week or more, they would be forced to consume the food that they had already set aside for the feast. To force the decision, the headman dispatched a member of his governmental staff, the village crier, to the Prow's house with the message that he wanted him to "walk" either that evening or the following one. When the "walk" failed to materialize, the headman again sent the *marinyo* to the Prow, warning him that if he were to abstain from "walking" again, the headman would fine him a month's worth of community labor. That night the Prow relented, setting his community's performance in motion with his "walk" and avoiding the fine that he otherwise would have had to pay. As they also allegedly had in the 1970s, many women and men—including some who had insisted that the performance should begin—grumbled about the headman or in other ways manifested their disapproval about what they saw as the abuse of his office vis-à-vis a domain, adat, to which it did not properly apply.

Yet by the time that Gita, the Stern's daughter, wrote her letter to me some two and a half years later, the attributed source of the problems troubling Bemun's annual performance seemed to have shifted somewhat. From the previous widespread perception that Bemun's headman had over the years increasingly overstepped the bounds of his legitimate jurisdiction, intruding repeatedly and ill-advisedly in adat affairs, a sense now seemed to be emerging that the annual performance might itself be in danger of being marred or even undone by more generalized attitudes and actions alien to it. Compelling evidence in local terms for this shift is the substitution in Gita's letter for her father's earlier emphasis on the personal afflictions the headman suffered as a result of his transgression with a much more generalized shock that "we villagers" experienced when the mooring post set up one day collapsed immediately the next. In the Stern's 1987 account of the "ritual without an ending," the headman's misdeed of the 1970s occupies center stage with the repetitive theme of displaced tails and misplaced endings lending rhetorical force to the gravity of his error, while iconically evoking it over and over again. No misdeed is, however, specified in Gita's 1989 letter; instead adat stands off against dinas in an explicit and uncompromising fashion. And if the mooring post fell in the 1970s as just one among many other tangible aftershocks ensuing from the headman's wrongheaded intervention, in the 1980s the post's refusal to stand had itself become the source of shock and consternation in the community—unsettling enough to provoke an extraordinary adat sitting. What kind of protest does the tottering post of Bemun's adat traditions register?[23] What does its instability signal? And what, inversely, is at stake when the post stands secure or, for that matter, in the boat of the Prow and the Stern with its foundational value for this Backshore community?

Set side by side in the emergency meeting summoned in Bemun in 1989 were different ways of going about things or styles of action productive of distinct capabilities and forms of authority. An *art* of saying in de Certeau's terms, Bemun's boat and the mooring post to which it is performatively linked form part of a discourse of narration that is characterized more by a way of asserting and exercising itself than by any object or aim that it might define (de Certeau 1984, 77–80)—as opposed to, for instance, adat in its serially produced and scaled-down Taman Mini style. In convening a conference to address the objections of their guardian spirits, these Backshore men and women explicitly acknowledged that beyond the surface appearance of an adat performance, beyond the Beautiful Indonesia in Miniature signs of diversity, and beyond a mere "going through the motions" lie the attitudes, motivations, and aptitudes that make such practices not only meaningful but, as such, necessarily embodied in persons and historically inscribed in time and space. Through the pressures brought to bear by Bemun's headman on his community and its annual celebration, the notion of Malay—still opposed to adat but here recast as dinas—had become more fine-grained, more bureaucratic, more decidedly New Order, and more in service of the state. By the same token, the protest perceived by many in the community's wavering post seemed to conjure for them the increasing contingency of certain kinds of practices—hitherto identified as especially Bemunese—under the former Suharto regime.

If the boat at Bemun's center has been a privileged means through which this community has manifested and maintained itself in time and space—with respect, for example, to its rights of settlement on Barakai— it has also been the vehicle through which the community annually charts, in the actual topography of the village, the limits and contradictions of its own receding authority. While the boat asserts the powers of the community's ancestors and guardian spirits over its inhabitants, it marks simultaneously the shifting threshold and vanishing point of these same powers. Between 1986 and 1988, when I lived on Barakai, the authority of the Prow and the Stern was highly circumscribed insofar as the two adat officials mutually referred to each other and, it seemed at times, to precious little else beyond the annual performance. Once the performance was completed, the cassowary celebrated and exiled until the following year, and the annual requirements of adat met, Bemunese women and men appeared tacitly free to devote themselves to the mundane matters and demands of a predominantly Malay existence. In short, following the performances of 1986 and 1987, everything happened as if, for either year, issues of adat had been settled once and for all, as if the boat at Bemun's center consisted merely of its "two halves" and nothing more.

Yet the confrontations described here, the insistently prone mooring post, and the voiced opposition to dinas all suggest that while the field of adat's application may be more and more circumscribed and beset from different sides—for instance, along with the state by the villagers' newly acquired religion—the boat itself remains a site of possible political articulations insofar as it grounds a style of action that can still authorize certain things while also foreclosing others. The third possibility alluded to earlier in this chapter regarding what might be at stake in Bemun's annual performance lies not, then, in some sort of alterity defined as a given—whether understood as the particularities of a Barakai past, the intricacies of a "local" system of representations, or even marginality as a kind of steady state. At stake, rather, is the practical realization through performance of coming from a "different" and, in many respects, impossible place (de Certeau 1986, 229). Such difference articulated in the form of a quintessentially Aru style of action is, crucially, not only destined to be deployed at the edge of a Malay world but, even more, is meant precisely for such an insertion—one that at the same time registers a fleeting form of protest. This difference, the topic of the following chapters, has little in common with the propagated diversity of the former New Order and in quirky ways eludes its serializing grid. Given, moreover, that the "difference" annually instated in Bemun's performance is meant explicitly for insertion in the Malay, it increasingly runs up against predicaments, such as those discussed here, that were additionally aggravated by the Suharto regime's own cultural designs regarding adat and "cultural" difference. The kinds of problems posed in Aru by these clashing modalities of constructing "difference" are nowhere better conveyed than in the solitary figure of Bemun's headman, barefooted and clad only in the loincloth of an Aru past, hoisting the national flag in a performance of some twenty years ago. This early Backshore version of the nation's "unity in diversity" doctrine poignantly captures not only the headman's own personal dilemma at the time but also the more general one that the many diverse peoples of Indonesia all too frequently were forced to confront under Suharto's New Order.

6 The Cassowary's Play

Like those birds that lay their eggs only in other species' nests, memory produces in a place that does not belong to it. It receives its form and its implantation from external circumstances, even if it furnishes the content (the missing detail). Its mobilization is inseparable from an *alteration*. More than that, memory derives its interventionary force from its very capacity to be altered—unmoored, mobile, lacking any fixed position.
—M. de Certeau, *The Practice of Everyday Life*

Another Species's Nest

What would it mean to reverse the terms in which performances such as Bemun's annual cassowary celebration are often approached in the anthropological literature? What might the implications be of an epistemological shift that would depart from an emphasis on performance as commemorative rite in which a traditional past—however invented and imagined such might be held to be—is somehow brought to bear on the present? And what would it mean to insist instead that in Bemun, as presumably in other similarly peripheral places, a ritual may perform and enjoin a forgetfulness of the past as much as or in the same move that it celebrates and fleetingly calls it into existence?

Somewhat retooled, the canonical position resurfaces today in a politics of identity in which remembering reflexively reproduces community and a proud sense of belonging. Insofar as both the point of departure and the telos of such reproduction is always the self, the outcome of such an approach is necessarily normative and essentially known from the start. As opposed to this seamless view in which ritual enacts what is already in place and the "Aru" inevitably produces once again the "Aru," the alternative possibility can only be gleaned obliquely. Lest I be misunderstood, the point here is not the positivistic one in which memory is always selective, only fragments taken from some past out there to be mined, worked over, and subsequently deployed for present purposes. Nor is the point simply that memory and forgetting are mutually constituted. Instead, I propose a shift in understanding the structure of performance itself as such pertains to the past: from a view that might be characterized by a process of presence-performance-presence to another in which performance is rather suspended between two absences. As opposed to a politics of identity, the latter view from the margins discloses forcefully a "memory politics" in which identity and its undoings engage each other in the always unfinished, fraught, and shifting process of community production on the Backshore.

As with many other marginal collectivities positioned in the frontier spaces of modern nation-states and marked by these states as backward and traditional, the price of a sense of belonging to the present order is often a forgetfulness of one's past. In Aru this more or less explicit injunction complicates and confuses the process that an identity politics exclusively attends to—the reproduction of a proud sense of belonging to one's own group. If other communities in contemporary Indonesia have managed to retailor their performances as tourist attractions (Volkman 1990), recast reviled histories as anticolonial protonationalisms (Hoskins 1993, 306–32), or otherwise retrace their genealogies and origins, the solution in Aru has been neither to deny nor to revise the past radically but instead to inhabit fully the predicament that their past often presents for them—as it most recently has under the former New Order government of Suharto. This solution entails a simultaneous straddling and sidestepping of ambiguity and an attempt to make out of all the different dilemmas and possibilities the past presents today one official custom-made "memory."[1]

A number of things are involved here that are important to note from the start. As I suggested above, memory is not the means for staging a return to origins in the sense of an identity or essence "prior to" or "behind" the performance. It is rather a memory that comes from elsewhere and as such an effect of the very modernity that in Aru as much as in, say, Jakarta or Amsterdam institutes a radical rupture through the introduction of a "new" time. This temporally marked rift opens the place for a discourse regarding the past from which the present is set off and in relation to which a selection occurs between "what can be *under-stood* and what must be *forgotten* in order to obtain the representation of a present intelligibility" (de Certeau 1988, 4). In contrast to the workings of "the structure of repression and displacement called modernity" in the metropole (Seremetakis 1994, 33), in peripheral places like Aru's Backshore what must be forgotten commonly gains the upper hand over that which can be understood and is acceptable within the present situation. This predicament in turn makes for a much more fraught, uneven, and wavering relationship vis-à-vis modernity. In Freud's terms one might characterize Bemun's annual performance as a "return of the repressed" or, to a considerable extent, "a return of what, at any given moment, has had to *become* unthinkable in order for a new identity to *become* thinkable" (de Certeau 1988, 4).

At the same time, as I have argued thus far, the Backshore's relationship to the economic and discursive forces of trade, the colonial *mission civilisatrice*, and the more recent postcolonial Indonesian nation-state has been incomplete and discontinuous, marked by a staccato rhythm of engagement and oscillating forms of entanglement. This fact also implies that what in present conditions becomes unthinkable and hence must be forgotten by Backshore peoples is never clear-cut or certain but rather ambivalent. The vaguely delineated domain of the unthinkable and of things that must be forgotten comprises a wide range of practices from the specific detail of those aspects of adat performances that have already—within living memory, as it were—been "cast off" (as this decision is called on Barakai), to others that while performed are considered somewhat shameful and better unmentioned, as well as, in Bemun, the explicit injunction post-performance to erase and forget the cassowary that frames the annual ritual as a whole.

Forgetting also happens the other way around. Elsewhere in Indonesia among the members of a minority religion in highland Sulawesi, stalking a headhunting victim—which at times even involves the omission of the surrogate head (a coconut)—demands, understandably, a certain forgetting of the present where, among other things, headhunting is forbidden (George 1996, 103). While this kind of forgetting necessarily also occurs on Barakai, notably in the context of the cassowary performance, where the Malay "present" must be forgotten in order for the Aru "past" to emerge, the politics of the former New Order state toward "backward" communities greatly overdetermined the forgetting of the Aru as opposed to the Malay. Sometimes, as in the case of practices that on Aru's Backshore have been "cast off," this kind of forgetting is irreversible—in contrast, again, to the performative temporary lapses in memory regarding what Bemunese call the Malay.

The play of attention and amnesia that annually stakes out the recalled domain of past "custom" in Bemun and pulls its performance in one direction or another has not only to do with the history of these performances—what, for instance, has been included and excluded in the past—or with present circumstances in an immediate sense, that is to say, not only with the permanency and the shifting contingencies of its annual stagings. Crucially, the drama staged between memory and its forgetting has to do with the way the performance is framed and specifically with how from the very start it is destined, however ambivalently, for insertion within what women and men on Barakai regard as the Malay.

I was, I must admit, initially taken in by the status of Bemun's annual performance as a space apart and am still taken by, as most Bemunese themselves claim to be, the compelling quality of their performance and by the cassowary's evocative and moving power. I was therefore initially perplexed by some of the codified statements that both men and women tended to conjure whenever they spoke of their community's performance, specifically by remarks asserting an ancient link between cassowaries and pearl oysters. When trying to explain their performance to me, women and men would often insist that, when the world came into being, it did so with cassowaries and oysters. A sequitur to this kind of statement was usually that the cassowary spirit (koder) as the "source" or "root" of pencarian, "holds"—or controls and has authority over—trade products, in particular the pearl oyster harvest, which, up through the recent crisis has been the most marked medium of Barakai's characteristic form of livelihood.

To a certain extent, these unquestioned assumptions were obvious even to me. After all, the timing of the annual performance already implied that its objective was to open the diving and trade season. It was also the cassowary's concrete presence in the village and subsequent dramatic exile that marked for Bemunese the transition from the east to the west season and assured the calm seas necessary for diving. Inversely, the spirit's displeasure during his celebration might provoke him to flap his diminutive wings in protest and, in so doing, cause high winds that would force the islanders to avoid the sea. This in fact was the explanation when in 1986 strong winds prevailed immediately following the performance. Some said that the cassowary had become irritated when both the Prow and the Stern had returned to Bemun before the other hunters on the hunt's final day. It was rumored that a young boy had spotted the cassowary at the outskirts of the village performing a spirited dance and beating his wings energetically. Both officials made offerings at their respective altars to appease the spirit so that he would allow diving to begin.

Yet, while in varying circumstances pertaining to the annual performance, Bemunese had occasion either to allude to or to insist vehemently on an originary link between cassowaries and oysters or, more generally, between the spirit and pencarian, the entire organization of their celebration appeared to belie precisely such a connection. As I have argued in the previous chapter, the performance's very possibility turns on a process of selection that extracts what is held to be Malay and thus belongs to trade, missionization, and the nation-state from that which is associated with ancestral beginnings in Aru. Out of this process the cassowary emerges as the concrete embodiment of an allegedly pure, unadulterated, and seamless "Aru" past, and as a spirit pursued by islanders who aim to refashion themselves in the guise of forebears who did not engage in trade. It was this stark contrast that made the constant pairing of cassowaries and oysters initially confusing to me.

It took moving beyond the charmed circle of the cassowary's performance, away from an "Aru" that merely reproduces an "Aru," toward a consideration of how its quality of a space apart is practically effected or how, in de Certeau's terms, this "memory" is deposited, as it were, by external circumstances to glean the connection between cassowaries and oysters that this shift in perspective allows to surface. To establish the space apart of the cassowary's annual play means, at the same time, to produce a frame that demarcates the difference between what is Malay and what is Aru, between an 'exterior' and an 'interior,' between "external circumstances" and the "memory" from which these are set off.

Samuel Weber's discussion of Derrida's essay on the parergon has been helpful to me in thinking through the ritual work of framing in Bemun's performance—of how the frame or, in Kant's analysis, form serves as the enabling limit and, indeed, the precondition for the emergence of the work itself (Weber 1996, 223). In this view, it is the *parergon* or the *hors-d'oeuvre*, as something not itself properly internal to the work and with a certain materiality of its own, that in fact allows the oeuvre to assume form and quite literally to take place. The frame operates, in other words, as the other that delineates precisely where form or, in Kant's terminology, the object of aesthetic judgement stops and thus also at the same time where it begins (ibid.). In order to carry out this function of other, there must, following Weber, be a nonaesthetic quality to the frame, a distinctive materiality that makes absolutely clear the difference between the frame and the oeuvre that it marks off (ibid.).[2]

All of the initial effort in Bemun's annual performance is devoted to the production of a malayu frame that thereby gives Aru "custom" a recognizable contour and shores the process of selection and criticism out of which the current cassowary performance emerges. In contrast to this memory space that has no existence apart from its performative creation, the Malay, understood as comprising commercial relations, Bemun's conversion to Catholicism and related mission activities, and the demands and more diffuse presence of the state on the Backshore, has a decided, persistent, and authoritative materiality. It is the aim of the first part of the performance, the period from its inception to the rite called "following the river," leading up to the cassowary's arrival in Bemun, to radically displace the material presence of the Malay through essentially three moves—first by confronting the authority of *mala lir*, the Malay language, with *gwerka lir*, or Aru speech, second, by reversing the direction of the force of violence that in everyday circumstances runs from malayu to gwerka, and third by erecting a defensive rampart against malayu contamination through the institution of bans and prohibitions as well as through more informal conversations and rumors that in agonizing detail depict the fate of persons who would "try out" or put Bemun's performance to the test.

In the following sections, concluding with "Bans and Prohibitions," I consider the materialization of the Malay frame by Bemunese men and women during the first part of their performance. The emergence of this frame, in turn, allows an Aru-marked space-time to take place as the site of the so-called "cassowary's play" (B. *koder ken main*) with which it is identified. Throughout I intimate how the Malay frame is constantly threatened to be "unhinged"—as Derrida might put it (Weber 1996, 24)—through fusion with the Aru. And how the ability of the Aru to itself take place uncompromised by Malay intrusions is also repeatedly called into question by the unwitting actions of the participants.

Piling up the Words of Momosim

Recall that the very first act of the ritual season takes place as a "coup," as a dramatic fracturing blow in which the past in the form of the Prow, or "the one who pierces first" (B. *asin nal mon*), rends asunder the ongoing continuum of the present. Like a coup, moreover, the power of this beginning is highly focused and charged. It presupposes, or so I was told by those with whom I awaited one evening in late September 1987 in the Stern's house the Prow's possible appearance, an enormous effort of concentration on this official's part. Before the Prow descends from his house and hangs the lantern that serves as the sign that he "walks" and that villagers should therefore keep to their houses and await his arrival, he must think of all things pertaining to the performance—"the words or discourse of momosim" (B. *momosim ken bijar*)—and "pile" or arrange them accordingly (B. *nam susun aukurane*).

These first words that inaugurate the ritual season are immediately followed by a marked occasion on which the men and adolescent boys of the community "speak" for the first out of three times. When the Prow descends from his home, his walk always follows the same route— taking him from his own house to the Stern's, where he stops briefly for a smoke and some coffee, to the houses located at the "front" of the village, then to those at its "rear," pausing outside of each to tell the men inside that they should soon gather at the so-called momosim fire to "speak." The Prow's round takes him full circle back to the Stern's house, where he receives embers from this official's hearth with which to build the momosim fire. Like the "coup" of the Prow's first walk, the words that he piles up immediately before his round, and the concentrated force of the loincloth that he alone of all villagers wears at this opening moment and that immediately identifies him with the ancestors and guardian spirits who imbue this walk with their presence, the momosim fire marks a highly charged site.

Some said that the glow emanating from the fire would be sufficient in itself to draw the men of Bemun to the center of the village, from where it beckons them. Long after it dies out, this power lingers in its ashes and is said to be capable of burning anyone negligent enough to step there. Importantly as well, the group of men and older boys that gradually forms around the fire evokes an image for many Bemunese of the ancestors warming themselves by the light of fires built long ago. As an initial gesture toward the Aru refashioning that marks the performance, the men remove their T-shirts before they come to the fire, lest the ancestors and guardian spirits who join them there would otherwise fail to recognize "their people" and become "startled." Since women are excluded from this as well as some other aspects of the annual performance and children are kept inside, the village remains dark and silent except for the men who emerge in small groups out of the shadows and seat themselves in the fire's glow. This quietude adds to the impression that something special is at hand and identifies its source in the pool of light and life that at the village center is hemmed in by a sea of darkness.

Taken together, the three occasions on which the men of Bemun "speak" punctuate and organize the double process through which the Malay is objectified as separate from the Aru, and the gradual rapprochement that characterizes the involuted space apart of the latter is also brought into effect: on the one hand, the Bemunese community increasingly refashions itself as Aru, and, on the other, the cassowary gradually approaches the village from the western and densely forested far side of the island, where he otherwise resides. When the men gather around the momosim fire for the third and last time on the night before the hunt begins, the cassowary is said to conceal himself on the immediate outskirts of Bemun. Once the spirit is in their midst, the need to "speak" becomes superfluous and the cassowary's "play" can begin in earnest.

More than "magical" speech as a performative that brings into existence that which it names (Tambiah 1968), each time the men gather at the momosim fire to "speak," a number of important decisions are made that serve to coordinate the action of the first part of the performance. The first time the men "speak," they "speak of the root" (B. *dalwaler ka gwagor*) that provides the stupefying sap used to poison fish during the river performance that imposes the ban of the sea and, in so doing, severs the community from the Malay-infused space of pencarian.[3] I was told that the talk on this first occasion concerns the selection of the various locations deep in the Barakai forest where the root will be gathered and the formation of the groups that will set off to these different places. Similarly, on the second occasion, when the men come together "to speak of following the river" (B. *dalwaler dajur mar*) two days later,[4] the group chooses three men from among those present to bring three out-rigger canoes to the head of the big river early the following morning before the fish poisoning begins. The task of building a dam of twigs and leaves at the extreme mouth of the estuary where the performance is held also falls to these men. In the context of the performance, they will punt their canoes from the head of the river deep in the forest to the sea and then back and forth many times at the river's mouth, as the canoes' occupants beat on the bundled roots and release their poison into the river. Depending on the amount of fish caught during the fish poisoning, on how prepared different households are for the hospitality that reigns during the time that the cassowary is in the village, or on other contingencies, the Prow will summon the men and adolescent boys of Bemun for the third and last time after a one- or two-day interval "to speak of taking to the land" (B. *dalwaler dawa re*). The talk on this occasion concerns the length of the cassowary hunt as well as the day on which this part of the performance will begin.

In 1987, immediately after "speaking of following the river," several men chatted about how the sea is often stormy when they take the canoes along the Barakai coast to the estuary as if restless in anticipation of the performance that imposes the ban of the sea. One man grumbled that since the current "chief of the river," the adat officiant of this ritual, had been in office, this had hardly been the case, evoking thereby the perception at the time among many Bemunese of this person's inappropriateness for the position. If a new person is to be selected as "chief," for this hereditary office then selection should also take place when the men gather "to speak of following the river." When the following day the catch from the fish poisoning proved even more meager than that of the previous year, bitter criticism of the "chief of the river" was on the lips of many, especially as it was also rumored that a number of men had asked him to step down before the performance. When the "chief" refused, one man is said to have remained at home "to gather palm fronds" (B.

nal karau)—as nonparticipation is called throughout the performance—
out of protest. Long before late afternoon, men and women complained,
the participants had already returned to the village more or less empty-
handed. If the fish had been plentiful, they would have remained in the
river until the sun sank in the sky, and even the canoes would have been
low in the water, filled to the brim with fish. This, I was told, was the way
things used to be. In that case, a day or so would have passed to give the
men, women, and children of Bemun time to gorge themselves on fish
before the Prow "walked" again to summon the men for the third and
last time "to speak of taking to the land."[5]

Beyond the frustrated appetites that in 1987 provoked the condem-
nation by many of Bemun's "chief of the river," two other criteria of
evaluation should be mentioned. A direct causal linkage articulates and
positions the three different "portions" of the cassowary celebration
distinguished by Bemunese—following the river, taking to the land, and
casting white plates—in relation to each other and ultimately in relation
to the pencarian for which the performance is supposed to ensure success. If the yield of the fish poisoning is considerable, then Bemunese can
also expect the men to bring in an abundance of game during the cassowary hunt and this abundance, in turn, to prefigure a bountiful harvest of
trade products, especially oysters.[6] While this causality is more subtle
than such a brief consideration makes clear, the basic point is that in
principle the momentum of the performance is capable of being assessed
at certain marked and recurring moments—if, that is, people for one or
another reason choose to do so and make thereby an issue of either the
fish poisoning, some aspect of the hunt, or the distribution of plates.

The various motivations people might have for doing so are political
and, consequently, most likely to be directed at persons who officiate
during the performance's different parts. Given that the performance is
itself the context in which such persons are commonly selected through
more or less informal means to occupy different offices, the charged
politics that at times imbues and embitters the ambiance of the performance is hardly surprising. Along with the specific politics of ritual
positions, prevailing tensions in the community often well up and disturb the annual performance (especially when there has been much
drinking). Although during the entire ritual season an explicit injunction against bickering and quarrels is in force and, indeed, often reiter-

ated, the fact that such is necessary at all only confirms that Bemunese are themselves aware of how social divisions and conflict in their community can erupt and mar their performance. To accept at face value the official story line, as it were, of this or, for that matter, any other performance, in which a group memory (or forgetting) invariably emphasizes group solidarity, amounts to a depoliticization of social processes going on within the collectivity and of the inevitable differences that pertain in any community. Such a totalizing position thereby also entails a deindividuation of the persons who participate and glosses over the important exclusions out of which any performance emerges—in Bemun's case that of not only the Malay but also to a large extent of the community's women. It is important to keep this fact in mind while reading the present chapter, which focuses especially on the larger dynamics of the relation between the Malay and the Aru. While the specific exclusions on which this contrast rests are touched on here, they receive fuller attention in the following chapter.

As I began to argue above, the words piled up by the Prow, which according to some Bemunese provide their performance's opening with its initial punch, and the three marked male contexts of "speaking" abet the production of an Aru capable of standing off against the Malay. Especially telling, in the context of the explicit reign of Aru speech that applies during the entire performance are therefore those words and phrases that resist translation (see also Rafael 1993). Since these expressions are neither casual nor uncodified, they help to expose the authority of the Malay frame that provides the contour, or parergon, and to a certain extent contains the focused force of an Aru backed by an army of ancestors and a past that in the specific form of sejara can, in certain circumstances, strike back (chapter 3). It is precisely when the Aru appears most in place that the Malay framing of this space apart or elsewhere emerges, betrayed by language. The two codified mala lir phrases crucial in the performance—*pikiran panjang*, or "long thoughts," and *kapal kenangan*, "the ship of memory"—both have to do with memory and remembrance. As such, they hedge the forgotten space of the Aru, perhaps thereby suggesting that what is remembered and what must be forgotten is largely set by the forces and authority that imbue a larger Malay world. If the first, the "long thoughts," overtake and overwhelm Bemunese on the evening before the cassowary hunt begins, the second, the "ship of memory," is the vehicle through which a return to the everyday space of the Malay is effected at the end of the performance. Between the "long thoughts" and the "ship of memory," marked in Indonesian as distinct, the Aru elsewhere takes place as the space-time where the cassowary once a year comes to "play." For the remainder of the year this space along with its Aru emblem and other material signs is supposed to be forgotten.

Long Thoughts

Once the men "speak of taking to the land" and especially after they visit the graves of their dead relatives in the late afternoon before the first day of the hunt, the mood that has prevailed in Bemun during the previous several weeks shifts and takes on a different cast. Generally, throughout the initial preparations for the performance, when what is called the "Cassowary's Song" begins to be sung or hummed by men and women as they work, and during the opening rite of the fish poisoning, an attitude of expectation and excitement predominates in Bemun. Even the sense of diminished prospects occasioned by the subdued river performance in 1987 did not significantly dampen the enthusiasm with which men, women, and children awaited the cassowary's arrival. Yet as the spirit's presence in the village was felt to be imminent, many Bemunese became pensive, introspective, and often sad. Invariably, they claimed to be troubled by what both women and men described in Indonesian as "long" or "far-reaching thoughts" (I. *pikiran panjang*) that concretized themselves as memories and longings for persons either long gone, dead, or otherwise absent.

Surprisingly, the "far-reaching thoughts" that most commonly took hold of Bemunese on the evening preceding the hunt in both 1986 and 1987 seemed only in part to have been provoked by their visits to the graves earlier that same day in the late afternoon. To be sure, this day is the marked annual occasion on which Bemunese visit the graves of their deceased relatives, clear the simple cement borders that outline these sites of the weeds and debris that have collected there since the previous year, and share a repast at the grave with their dead. The dead person receives her "share" (B. *ken gwang*) of the meal, buried in a shallow hole at the head of the grave, and is also "informed" with an offering of betel and tobacco that her relatives are about to begin celebrating the cassowary. This informing is necessary, a man named Abu Magar explained, because the ancestors themselves preceded their living descendants in holding this celebration. Beyond the respect demanded by precedence, any process of "informing" on Barakai, such as that preceding bridewealth negotiations, also extends an invitation—in this case to the community's dead to join their relatives in the performance. The multiple invitations extended at this time represent a recognition of the bonds that conjoin the living to their dead and thus also Bemunese to those who lived before them.

In the case of persons who have died since the previous year's performance, the cassowary celebration is the context in which the final act of public mourning takes place on the last evening of the spirit's celebration and shortly before he is exiled once again to the far west side of Barakai. "Long thoughts" and sorrow are expected on the part of the relatives of these recent dead; their absence would elicit gossip and criticism of those men and women who seem oblivious to their losses. By the same token, any sign of sorrow or withdrawal at this time of year is taken at face value. When in 1986 a woman whose husband had died several months before began to sob loudly the night before the hunt began, her weeping was ignored by others present in the Stern's house, for whom its source was so obvious as to be undeserving of comment. Their failure to comment was somewhat surprising to me, given that this same woman had been widely condemned by other villagers, especially women, for her apparent nonchalance over the death of her husband and for the affairs that subsequent to his death she had soon embarked on. Yet no one questioned her grief at the time, since presumably it was then only a more extreme and understandable manifestation of the general mood taking hold of the community.

Expressions of grief over the recent death of loved ones and memories of those lost for longer are hardly noteworthy during a performance that commemorates all Bemunese ancestors, officially closes mourning for those persons who have died within the year, and is itself a kind of mortuary ground. Yet the "long thoughts" that trouble women and men at this time are also promiscuous and indiscriminate, traveling indeed "far" and wide, well beyond the recollections of their dead relatives. Nor are these memories limited to Bemunese, to persons who participated in some past performance, or to those who in one or another fashion can be considered gwerka. Recall that my Bemunese friends claimed that I myself would be most remembered and missed at the time of their performance (chapter 5). In the early evening of 1987, after Bemunese had returned from visiting the graves of their kin, it was striking and moving to listen to the Stern as he quite spontaneously began to reminisce about a Buginese friend who had died some thirty years before. With a quiet and measured voice, he spoke wistfully of how the two young men had hunted deer and crocodile together, of how the Buginese had used ilmu to assist him in trapping and killing the animals, and of how he had made sacrifices of gold to his spirit helpers. As he recalled this long-gone friendship, the Stern became increasingly thoughtful and sad, even as he recounted proudly the many crocodiles they had snared and skinned, and the deer whose meat they had shared and sold to traders for a profit. Nostalgically the Stern elaborated on the intimacy of the bond between the two men, on how the Buginese had offered to teach his friend the secrets of his ilmu, and on how he had refused out of fear for the lives of his wife and young children.[7]

Notably, while the importance of this friendship and its impact on the Stern clearly emerged and underlay his recollections, it was only within the circumscribed context of the cassowary celebration that I ever heard the Stern reminisce or even mention this old friend. Itself the effect of a summoning into existence of something that is otherwise absent, the cassowary's concrete presence in the community gives life and form to losses of a highly personal and intimate kind and conjures them as "long thoughts" or memories. It is also the cassowary, in his palm frond effigy form, who on the performance's concluding night is made to incorporate and carry off the dead, while his expulsion to Barakai's west side keeps the "long thoughts" that plague villagers during his performance otherwise at bay. If Bemunese are sad, thoughtful, quiet, or miss faraway loved ones at other times of the year—which, of course, they sometimes do—it is never described as "long thoughts." It is worth noting that, because of their promiscuity, the "long thoughts" of Bemunese women and men continually undermine the very difference between the Aru and the Malay that their explicit focus on memory, loss, and the past also calls into being. Already the "untranslatable" form such "long thoughts" take, formulated in Malay as pikiran panjang, rubs against the space defined as the province of Aru speech (gwerka lir). The tendency of "long thoughts" to travel well beyond the Aru inevitably also betrays again and again the entangled conditions out of which and against which the Aru emerges as well as its ongoing unraveling into the Malay in the context of the performance.

Beyond the performance, mentioning the cassowary or speaking of his celebration is actively discouraged and regarded by most Bemunese as potentially dangerous. Singing or even humming the "Cassowary's Song"—held to enumerate all things pertaining to his celebration—is strictly forbidden at other times of the year, while the objects with which the spirit is associated (loincloths, bells, the Prow's bow and arrows) are also hidden away. I was told that any questions that I might have about the performance had to be asked while it was still in progress, specifically before the scattering of white plates that closes the ritual cycle and preferably before the cassowary's exile to his far-off home. Nor was I permitted to carry around my usual pocket-size batik notebook and pen, which otherwise marked my identity as a "student" in Aru. Only after an offering of one white plate was made at the altars of both the Prow and the Stern was I allowed to take notes on the performance—but then only out of sight in my own room behind closed windows and door, and only in the Barakai language. Given that the cassowary and all he conjures is supposed to be obliterated after the performance, that vis-à-vis his figure an explicit refusal of inscription is in force, it was perhaps fitting that the limited recording permitted to me should have taken place in an "unwritten" language. Regarding the other two forms of "mechanical reproduction" (Benjamin 1969) that I wielded as an anthropologist—photography and a tape recorder—I was only permitted to photograph and record his song immediately before daybreak on the performance's concluding night. The most obvious reason for the timing of this window of opportunity made available to me was that the bans on the Malay had already, by this time, been lifted to some extent.[8]

Everything is done, in other words, to restrict the Aru to the Aru and the Malay to the Malay. This radical difference is articulated in many different ways throughout the performance, from codified statements such as the one enunciated by Abu Jepang immediately before the 1986 performance—"What belongs to the sea truly belongs to the sea; what

belongs to the land truly belongs to the land; and [the two] don't mix"
—to more circumstantial remarks triggered by transgressions during the
performance itself. In 1986, for instance, a man named Pendek had
already begun his "walk" to gather poisonous roots for the fish poisoning
but decided to climb a coconut palm near his house to cut some coconuts to take along as refreshment during the trip. When his wife's father
unwittingly asked him whether he planned to take the family canoe to
Mesiang later that afternoon, Pendek did not respond. Since his "walk"
was already in progress, it was forbidden for him to speak with persons
who were not taking part in the expedition. But when his wife's father
insisted, still unaware that Pendek "walked," the young man replied, yes,
he would take the canoe to Mesiang later. I was told that at this point the
machete that Pendek had stuck in the trunk above him suddenly fell
from its place and struck him in the neck, causing a small wound from
which blood flowed. What was surprising was that most Bemunese with
whom I spoke about the event later that day emphasized not so much the
transgression of Pendek's speech but that what he had spoken about—a
canoe—was incompatible with the task that Pendek had set in motion
when he began his "walk" to gather roots. The Stern's wife, who first
mentioned the incident to me, explained the contradiction as follows:
"When they go to collect the root, they don't go by canoe; when they go
to follow the river, they go by canoe."

Yet the kinds of oppositions insisted on in these statements, inflections
of the stark opposition that pertains in the performance between the
Malay and the Aru, are in part already undone by the "long thoughts" of
women and men as these thoughts travel beyond and exceed the tightly
circumscribed arena of the cassowary's performance, extending even to
such unlikely figures as Buginese crocodile hunters and Dutch-American
anthropologists. Put somewhat differently, the "far-reaching thoughts"
that trouble Bemunese at this time (some more than others) and only
surface once a year in the gap that opens up between a Malay present and
an Aru past undermine the very distinctiveness with which they are
endowed in the performance. Despite the all-around efforts exerted in
different registers to extract the Malay from the Aru, the "long thoughts"
that, on the one hand, propel men and women into the inward- and
backward-looking space of the performance, forcefully locate them, on
the other, in the entangled, hybrid, and shifting spatiotemporal frames

of their day-to-day lives on the Backshore as well as in relation to their individual biographies.[9]

If the performance privileges processes of bereavement and gives free reign to particular kinds of personal losses suffered over the years by different Bemunese, this space out of time also appears to highlight an acute awareness of the passing of time and of the absences that go with it. In part, I suspect, this sense of absence and change is enforced by the routine, repetitive character of the performance: its annual recurrence marks what is not repeated and both formally and informally foregrounds the absence of friends and loved ones who were once present. As Munn observes, "So-called 'circular' (repetitive) time does not logically exclude 'linear' sequencing, because each repetition of a given 'event' necessarily occurs later than the previous ones" (1992, 101). Regarding ritual this insight has important implications insofar as it suggests how what might seem repetitive and predictable to an outsider is quite varied and different for those who participate year after year in an annual performance, both personally for individual men, women, and children and more collectively with respect to the larger social processes that are played out in any given year. The need to bring me up to date in 1994 on the cassowary celebrations that had been held during my absence from Aru confirms this view (chapter 5). Under the rubric of routine ceremony are the scores of individual persons with varied lives who participate in and undergo the effects of a performance and are altered by its possibilities, promises, and demands. Rather than a sense of routine ceremony, participation in a given ritual over the years can make those who partake on repeated occasions acutely aware of their own varying personal and family circumstances as well as of historical transformations that make for variations in the performance itself (such as a persistently prone mooring post). Looking at ritual participation over the long run as opposed to the limited terrain of one or two performances may also in part help to explain what a number of Bemunese meant when they told me that the sadness that permeates their annual celebration remains largely inaccessible to outsiders—not because of any assumption of a collective past abstractly conceived to which a non-Bemunese would not be privy, but because the sadness that is part of the ritual's force as it highlights absence and loss is itself built over the years.

The Ban of the Sea

If the aim of the first part of Bemun's annual performance is to produce a malayu frame for the gwerka—an "outside" Malay distinct and set off from an "inside" and self-enclosed Aru—the Aru itself admits no "outside." It is only at the very last moment of the entire ritual cycle that the internal "outside" within the cassowary celebration—the exclusion of women from the performance's most valued and crucial dimensions—is dramatically staged and ambivalently if partially reversed. It is a move that briefly and fleetingly puts Bemun's men to shame and forces them to hide (and change out of their loincloths into everyday clothes) and that dramatizes thereby the quasi-illegitimate, ephemeral, and impossible status of the Aru as it has just been produced in performance. But all of this is left to a final revelatory moment that discloses in fact that which has been the case all along—that women are excluded from the celebration's central activities—notably, the three marked occasions of "speaking" that set the performance in motion, wearing the cassowary's effigy, and, less remarkably, the hunt (chapter 7). I should add that I never heard women complain of these exclusions and that they seem to enjoy the annual performance just as much as the men.

Before this final moment, however, the Aru admits no "outside" insofar as nonparticipation in any part of the performance is recast as an alternative form of participation—in effect, making nonparticipation symbolically impossible. "To gather palm fronds" (B. *dal karau*) describes the action that is attributed by others or by nonparticipants to themselves when for one or another reason they opt out of participating in the entire performance or some part of it.[10] Whatever the specific reason for opting out might be, the explanatory "he/she gathers palm fronds" credits equally the man or woman who decides not to go on the fish poisoning, is too old to keep up with the hunters, or has small children to care for during the nightly dancing of the cassowary as engaging in this activity. Nor is it just any activity that is intended here. Concretely evoked in the expression are the glistening new white fronds harvested from the tops of coconut palms for plaiting together the cassowary effigies that are made anew each evening and paraded around the village during the three, four, or five successive nights of the spirit's celebration. Throughout the entire performance then, nonparticipants are characterized not only as contributing to the ongoing work of the performance but as actively engaged in the production of its central emblem. In turn, this characterization implies that all members of Bemun— without exception—"participate" in their community's celebration.[11]

One portion of the performance that women by choice increasingly do not participate in is the fish poisoning. The number of older women who in their youth participated in this rite and the enthusiasm with which most spoke of it makes clear that the fish poisoning was much more popular with women in the past than it is today. This is indeed what Bemunese themselves say. Young women today, often backed by their parents, are reluctant to participate, although occasionally a prepubescent girl may decide to accompany an older brother or her father on the fish poisoning. The reason that young Bemunese women inevitably give is the prohibition in force during this part of the performance on concealing their loincloths under sarongs and the "embarrassment" (B. *demta*) they would feel at the exposure of their breasts. Women in their mid-thirties and forties recalled the time before the mid-1960s when women wore only loincloths throughout the annual performance; some remember covering their breasts with palm frond shawls and dancing in the shadows of the trees and bushes that border Bemun's central pathways. In retrospect at least, they thereby suggested that, already at the time as teenage girls and young women, they had begun to feel the "embarrassment" that young women claim overwhelms them today.

The consequences of missionization and the Catholic mission's distribution of Western-style clothes for women and men (and especially the former) is an obvious influence here, as is, more diffusely, the sense that comes from the archipelago capital, from the limited exposure Bemunese have to the national media, and from the tradeswomen who set some of the trends in dress on the Backshore that women who bare their breasts are backward and primitive (if not something worse). Another more inchoate and subtle effect may also play a part. If my speculations regarding the de-Islamicization of the undersea and the heightened gendering of transactions pertaining to trade—most notably through the figure of the sea wife (chapter 4)—are not off the mark, then the explicit feminization and exclusion of the Malay that occurs during the fish poisoning may be a further deterrent today to women's participation. At the same time, several Bemunese told me that participation by women in the fish poisoning means a greater yield of fish, suggesting perhaps a mimetic relationship between the fertility of women and the harvest of fish.

In order to prefigure the effect of the radical rift between the Malay and the Aru that is the aim of the fish poisoning, the set of procedures that make up the ritual and the dramatic setting of the estuary where it takes place—on the shifting border between land and sea where the opaque density of Barakai's forest gives way to the wide expanses of the tidal flats—posit as the performance's point of departure a state of relative undifferentiation. This state is characterized by the blurred commingling and flow of what will subsequently separate as Malay versus Aru and by an avoidance vocabulary that draws on the language of bridewealth exchange. In addition to the estuary itself, which conjoins the forest and the sea, the performance draws the cassowary spirit from his habitat on Barakai's farside to the head of the river at the same time that it cuts off the sea together with pencarian and the Malay world of commerce and circulation. Some two hundred meters in the sea immediately in front of the estuary stands the "mooring post" marking the undersea site of the Sea House of the Land, which is itself a hybrid place where a female ancestress resides who figures implicitly in the opening of the annual performance and prominently at its conclusion in the context of the plate distribution. Much like the Malay that she exemplifies, this female spirit frames the markedly male cassowary celebration that lies at the core of Bemun's performance and is herself "excluded" with the ban of the sea that the fish poisoning imposes.

Another procedure that fosters the impression of a lack of differentiation and sets the scene for the fish poisoning is the prohibition on the use of personal names. Instead of the usual kin terms, teknonyms, and personal names with which Bemunese commonly address each other, those who participate call each other *jol*, *jojol*, or *joli*, all of which are variations on the Barakai term for a bond that is spontaneously established between persons of the same sex who reside in different villages and take a special liking to each other or one of a more formal nature that links persons by virtue of their marriage to same-sex siblings. Unusual in this setting is that the term *jol* applies not only to persons of the same sex but to those of the opposite sex as well. In the context of a performance that is structured around the exclusion of the female and the malayu, I can only speculate that this degendering of persons may appear especially contradictory to many of Bemun's young women in light of the markedness of their identity as female that baring their breasts in this day and age brings to the fore.

As with the "coup" through which the Prow effects the performance's beginning, the creation of a rupture between the Malay and the Aru rests on an act of implicit violence. The necessary violence and the supremacy of land over sea, gwerka over malayu, that the fish poisoning institutes for the duration of the performance assumes the form of an assault by the land on the sea or, perhaps more precisely, by the forest on the commingling of land and sea that is the estuary. Visually, the effects of this assault can be assessed by participants in the performance when the estuary turns cloudy from the effects of the poisonous roots—which the men who collect them insist grow far and deep in the Barakai forest—or, in good years, shining white with the upturned bellies of the fish that have become "drunk" on the poison. The onslaught is also felt by those who stand knee-deep in the river; as the poison takes effect, it stings and burns their feet and calves. Although some cannot resist shifting cautiously from foot to foot, they should refrain from rubbing their legs or for that matter from scratching themselves if stung by the sandflies that at times are a plague at the estuary. Even the mention of these pests is prohibited at this time, suggesting that the bodily discomfort that those in the river are subject to during the performance is also part of its effect.[12] Put very simply, a product identified with the densest and most distant parts of the island's interior overwhelms a product specific to the confluence of land and sea and hence in this setting, the Aru and the Malay: the varieties of fish that are particular to the estuaries of the archipelago. Another way of putting this is to suggest that to institute the ban of the sea the fish poisoning must begin as a performance from a banless situation or one in which such a ban is suspended. This is so because the demarcation of "what belongs to the sea truly belongs to the sea. What belongs to the land truly belongs to the land; and [the two] never mix" only achieves the prescriptive force of a ban when enunciated against the backdrop of a situation in which such distinction does not apply.

Another aspect of the workings of the performance that may help to establish the impression that the land overwhelms the sea is the emergent effect created by the appearance of the canoes and the sound of the "drummers" they carry down the river. In 1986, when I participated with Gita, the fish poisoning began when the Prow stepped into the river and everyone else followed his example, aligning themselves in two parallel lines opposite each other immediately within the river's banks. The Stern, who should be the last to enter the river, positioned himself opposite the Prow. Beginning about twenty feet within the twig and leaf boundary that sets the river off from the sea and was erected earlier that morning, the double line of men (primarily) followed the bends of the river into the interior of the island. Those making up the two lines remained silently facing each other across the river, holding their fishing spears erect with the prongs pointing skywards. The sun, at its highest, burnt strongly on our backs, and bodies began to glisten with sweat. Occasionally a slight breeze relieved the scorching heat, causing the colorful tails of the men's loincloths to dance in and out of the line of glinting spears. After what appeared an eternity but was probably no more than a quarter of an hour, a faint drumming could be heard coming from what seemed the deepest recesses of the Barakai interior. Gradually the drumming grew louder and closer, as if traversing an immense distance, until finally its source could be identified as the three canoes shot around the bend of the river, as if out of the forest, and made their way down the double line of spears. Important to the effect of the performance, this emergent quality is the result both of the slow crescendo of the drumming—the canoe occupants beating the roots with mallets to release their poisonous juices—and the dramatic setting of the estuary itself (see Schieffelin 1976, 177). Until the roots are fully depleted of their contents and the chief of the river takes hold of the first fish, those waiting along the river banks maintain their hot vigil.

I have enumerated some of the procedures and operations that make up Bemun's fish poisoning and that have the effect of establishing the relative undifferentiation out of which the Malay and the Aru subsequently emerge as a stark contrast and of creating the impression that the forest overwhelms and engulfs the sea. I turn now to consider more closely what precisely is excluded with the ban of the sea. During the fish poisoning, several terms that in everyday parlance apply to bridewealth refer here to fish or other sea creatures that are found in estuaries, potentially pose a threat to humans, and are therefore considered "hot" (rara). "Elephant tusk" (B. *siaan*), for instance, replaces garfish, a type of fish credited with shattering the island of Luang in the southwest Moluccas that some Bemunese claim as their original home; a small variety of gong called *bungbung* provides the avoidance term for a large type of stingray, while *kalimlim*, a kind of bracelet that women claimed formerly figured in marriage, lends its name to the poisonous stonefish, which are, indeed, quite common in the Mamar estuary.

Abu Meme, an older woman in the household in which I lived during my first year in Bemun, told me that taken together this "hot" wealth made up the "things of the woman"—things, that is, belonging to the female spirit guardian and occupant of the Sea House of the Land. The link between this female spirit and wealth comes to the fore when the "mooring post" marking her residence topples over and compels the staging of a "great" version of the cassowary celebration. In this context a living woman—the eldest or one of the oldest from the fam from which the Prow is also chosen—provides the spirit with a tangible, visible form as "the women's shadow" (B. *kajing kodarne ken ko*). Since a "great" version of Bemun's performance was never staged when I resided in the village, my sense of its difference from a "small" performance and especially the role of "the woman's shadow" (which besides the additional day or two added onto the cassowary hunt seems to be the main difference) is limited. What stood out, however, in the comments of both women and men regarding a "great" version of their annual performance was the emphasis that many placed on the resplendence of this female "shadow": the fiery redness of her attire and the brilliance and abundance of the gold jewelry adorning her hair, chest, ears, and arms. Collectively summarized as "the decoration of the woman" (B. *kajing kodarne ken jurtain*), such objects of adornment were formerly worn by Barakai brides. While young women are still nicely arrayed for marriage today, I was told that in the past this wealth made up part of the payment owed by wifetakers to their wifegivers.

It would be a mistake to take the figure of this female shadow or the prevalence of terms relating to bridewealth in the context of the fish poisoning too literally. A representation of a "marriage" that would pertain between the cassowary and the inhabitant of the Sea House of the Land is not at issue. Rather, the effect produced is, I believe, more diffuse. The proliferation of references to the "hot" bridewealth brings to the fore only one among the many possible aspects of marriage and the negotiations that on Barakai bring it about—specifically, the dangers and potential threats that a female "outsider" may represent for the fam into which a woman marries. While this kind of thing does not much preoccupy islanders during their daily lives, it may be foregrounded here in order to establish performatively the effect of a female "outside"—as, indeed, does talk of bridewealth itself, since it not only establishes a connection but also demarcates the two parties between which this wealth flows. Inversely, the resplendence attributed to the "woman's shadow" and the detail with which Bemunese tended to embellish their descriptions of her also suggest that this beautiful and enticing Malay "outside" is not so easily distanced or cut off.

One other aspect of the avoidance vocabulary deserves mention here. Besides the rhetoric of bridewealth and riches that describes the flow of the river and the threats it may contain, the language used for the action of the participants in the river performance prefigures the small uprooted tree "from which meat hangs" that the Prow plants early in the morning of the first day of the hunt. Subsumed under a single avoidance term, the different varieties of fish caught at the estuary are "leaves," while the two-pronged instruments with which they are speared are "branches." As already mentioned, the catch of the fish poisoning is seen as having a predictive value with respect to the hunt that immediately follows it and more generally the pencarian of the upcoming year. What the avoidance vocabulary suggests, however, is that this predictive value is not a passively assessed measurement but one that also depends on the actions and abilities of Bemunese themselves, on the enthusiasm with which they throw themselves into the fish poisoning and subsequently into the hunt, and on the scrupulousness with which men, women, and children observe their performance's many bans and prohibitions. It also depends on the interventions of Bemun's guardian spirits and ancestors and, having been "informed" that the performance will take place, their willingness to engage with the living in its activities.

Close communication with these spirits is therefore an integral part of the fish poisoning, as it is throughout the annual performance. As those in the river dashed and leaped through the water calling out to each other, "Hé joli!" as they speared the "drunken" fish, they paused from time to time to scoop up handfuls of sand from the river bottom, presumably to assist the poison in further taking its effect. Spraying water and scattering sand, they called out to the spirits as they did so, "Replace our palm wine!"—a favored substance, like betel, of communication with the ancestors. Given that the catch is the product of a collaboration between Bemunese and spirits, the tumpline baskets in which the participants carry their fish back to the village are not surprisingly called *gar*, the term for the miniature betel basket that the Prow at this time of the year carries concealed in the folds of his loincloth, which contains the betel and the little bells with which he invokes the ancestors.[13]

In Dialogue with Dissidence

On the evening before the cassowary celebration begins, advisory tales are told throughout Bemun to children and adolescents, to kin from the neighboring communities of Longgar, Apara, Mesiang, or less commonly elsewhere, who have decided to participate in the performance, and more generally for the legitimizing and bolstering effect these tellings have on the range of practices that come to Bemun with the cassowary. Those who recount the transgressions of the past and thereby also depict the terrible fates that await present-day trangressors apparently feel the need to engage with potentially dissident discourses and images, and to appropriate them to reenforce the power of the performance that is about to take place. At the same time such tales and the need to tell them amount to a de facto recognition of the power of the opposition to performances like that of Bemun's cassowary in late-twentieth-century postcolonial Indonesia and of the instability that permeates adat as it is played out in a specifically "Aru" register today. Hence the widespread consternation in the Bemunese community over the insistently prone "mooring post" and the obligation to hold several "great" performances in succession to secure it. This attitude and the actions undertaken to dispel concern suggest that Bemunese may see this crucial marker of the community's adat as succumbing to new and larger forces and may themselves be quite aware of how what they regard as their own way of doing things is increasingly under threat of being unmoored.

While those who transgress the serious bans of the annual performance may also suffer violent deaths, in the mid-1980s the talk of the evening before the hunt focused on persons who in the past had "tried out" or put to the test the power of Bemun's cassowary celebration. Occasionally in 1986 and 1987 these persons were named—such and such Chinese who had died suddenly ten years before or you know that man in Longgar who limps and walks with a stick, well, one year . . .—but more often than not they were simply generic examples in which the emphasis was on the fate of anonymous individuals or anyone who dared to behave as they allegedly had, rather than on named subjects. When I returned to Barakai in 1994 and was "briefed" by the Stern regarding the performances that had been held in my absence, this briefing took the form of a long lament in which the stories of the "sins" committed by different named Bemunese were loosely strung together with a "now I'll tell you about so and so" or "that's one, now here's another." The details of their individual transgressions were spelled out in rapid succession in what seemed an account of ritual errors without ending:

> If it was just one person, it would be all right, but this was lots of people, lots of people fooling around, saying things they shouldn't have said. . . . Hé, *setengah mati*, I was really *setengah mati* [literally half dead]. . . . If it had been children, it would have been all right, but it was adults, so I got it, it's my responsibility . . . before you knew it someone else would appear [to say he or she had committed some transgression and to ask the Stern to make an offering on his or her behalf] . . . if it had been children. After the celebration was over, then they would come and say, "When I was in the forest I touched water," and then I would make an offering and it would be all right. . . . [At this point the Stern paused, only to begin again with a gesture toward the altar in the front room of his house.] Look at all those plates . . . people's wrongdoings, these past years . . . the Prow's house is the same—an excess of plates.

If the language of "sins" and, to a lesser extent, the easy slippage between adat and agama was new to me,[14] so too was the relocation of the main source of threats to the ongoing successful performance of the cassowary celebration: from more or less generic "outsiders" and the larger context of the Malay in relation to which the Aru should remain fenced off and "forgotten" to mounting challenges from within the Bemunese community itself by adult men and women who, following the Stern, had begun to take their annual performance less seriously than before. Rather than or—perhaps more likely—in addition to a sense among Bemunese that their performance was besieged from without, at least some in the community and certainly adat's most important officials felt engaged in a battle within the circumscribed circle marked off annually for the cassowary's play.

Whereas in 1994 the Stern's story revolved around his own fatigue occasioned by the accumulating and seemingly never-ending task of righting the wrongs of his fellow villagers, in the mid-1980s the performance itself appeared to have had enough power to deal effectively with its transgressors. Tales told back then posited a mimetic relationship between those who had "tried out" or put the performance to the test and the gruesome aspect of the game as it is roasted on an assemblage of wooden stakes at the conclusion of each day's hunt. Described in graphic and lurid detail by both women and men, the consequences of dissidence were literally burnt into the bodies of transgressors, whose limbs, they claimed, would contort like those of the game engulfed in the flames; their hair would sizzle and smoke, their eyes bulge, and disease and death would overwhelm them as an unabating burning sensation and an immense heat.

While the cassowary effigy that is fabricated each evening of the hunt together with the fronds from which it is made are already considered "hot"—albeit with varying degrees of intensity depending on the age and sex of the person with whom they come into contact, that is, the least for adult men, who take turns wearing the effigy—additional precautions were taken in the 1980s and 1990s to augment this heat on the final evening of the celebration, when spectators from neighboring villages are allowed to enter Bemun. To ensure that this heat will have its full effect on those who would "grab" (B. *dasual*) the cassowary whether casually (*dai sembarang*), in jest (*dai gené*), or to test his potency (*dam coba*), an official called the cassowary's master (see below) blows masticated ginger root, a "hot" substance, onto three select places on the effigy. These places are the effigy's teats, the upper back between the miniature wings, and especially the top of the anus. As if this were not enough, the cassowary's master calls on the guardian spirits of the village momosim, asking them to "sit on the [effigy's] tail, so that people won't act irreverently toward it."

Beyond the stories of violence and agonizing death, Bemunese reminisce more generally about their previous cassowary celebrations on the evening before the hunt begins. A rehearsal of some of the highlights of these performances over the years is also part of the informal instruction given to an outsider when he or she participates for the first time. Such stories focus on the abundance of game killed in past years, the number of cassowaries taken during a given performance, and the excess and exuberance of the feasting that occurs, or they single out especially memorable events, such as the time that wild boar fled the hunters right into the village and gave women and children an immediate taste of the dangers and thrills of this part of their annual performance. While these stories may further buttress the power of Bemun's spirit and his annual celebration, they also convey a sense of the excitement, the boisterous festivity, and the all-around enthusiasm that prevails once the cassowary is installed in the community's midst.

Finally, the performative strategies that effect the turning inward and backward or the Aruization of the community—the bans and prohibitions in force during the cassowary hunt—are repeatedly enumerated for first-time participants, such as myself in 1986, and for children. All of these prohibitions, which make up a large portion of the exegetical knowledge associated with the performance, can be clearly articulated by both men and women, and even to an astonishing degree by children, to whom their importance is continually stressed. Although relatives and visitors from the neighboring communities, having attended the performance as spectators in previous years, are often well aware of most of Bemun's bans and prohibitions, the persons with whom they reside during the performance usually give them a cursory socialization in its routines and rules. Since either the Prow, the Stern, or both also make an offering on behalf of every novice to "inform" the spirits that an "outsider" plans to participate, these officials usually reiterate or add to any instruction that this person may have already received.

First and foremost among such instruction is a simple listing of dos and, especially, do nots. While often glossed as "the bans of the momosim [performance]" (B. *momosime ken lul*), this general category subdivides into relatively more serious observances termed *lul* and somewhat less stringent ones that are "prohibited," or momosim. The critical distinction between them lies in the severity of the repercussions that follow from transgressing a lul, which may be as serious as death (and even as bad as the kind of death discussed above). To a certain extent, this difference also has to do with the degree of intentionality involved in either case or, put differently, with how, for the most part, with regard to things designated momosim, inadvertent slip-ups occur more easily than in the case of lul. For instance, it is easy to spill water on oneself accidentally, but it takes a certain desire to transgress the prohibition on sexual relations during the performance. What is more, most momosim oversights can immediately be rectified. If a person, for instance, slips into Aru Malay or "touches water," then she or others in her presence can excuse her with the simple claim stated out loud that "I/she drank palm wine" (B. *kon/nen tuak*). Nor is this claim altogether unlikely in the context of a performance in which spirits flow liberally and the main emblem of which is himself credited with a taste for alcohol. Throughout the performance one hears men, women, and children excusing themselves and others for minor transgressions, especially physical contact with water (except for drinking) and speaking Aru Malay. Children especially "drink" astonishing amounts of palm wine during the annual celebration, though adults inadvertently or unavoidably do so as well, as, for instance, when a hundred or more hunters "drank palm wine" in 1987 when they were caught in a downpour in the forest.

While momosim serves purely as a negative injunction against certain Malay objects and actions that are "prohibited" during the performance, observances designated as lul demand special attitudes and behavior beyond that of mere avoidance. Although Bemunese tend to speak of the difference between these two sets of prohibitions as one of degree, they are in fact qualitatively distinct. To reiterate, while the only action demanded by momosim is avoidance, lul lay out specific forms of behavior that are markedly contrasted with those of everyday life.[15] The bans in force during the cassowary hunt are intended to organize the behavior of community members in such a way that the hunt proceeds safely and efficaciously and the men bring in a multitude of game. Furthermore, the new year that follows immediately upon the performance is meant to benefit and prosper as a direct consequence of the procedures—including the bans and prohibitions—that Bemunese set into motion in the context of their annual celebration.

Bemunese list a total of five bans that are operative during their performance: (1) The ban of the sea (*dai lul dawa ta*), according to which villagers avoid all contact with the sea and its products. Ensuing from the fish poisoning, this ban temporally precedes the others, although it, too, is only in full operation on the morning the hunt begins.[16] (2) The ban of men observed by women (*dai lul dawa ilbu*) and, inversely, the ban of women observed by men (*dai lul dawa kodarbu*). Following this ban, men and women should refrain not only from sexual intercourse but from all physical contact with each other, including the use of items of personal adornment and cleanliness such as eau de cologne, powder, combs, mirrors, or soap—otherwise for the most part ungendered—that belong to members of the opposite sex. (3) The ban of dogs (*dai lul dawa tarau*), following which cooking vessels containing meat from the hunt must remain uncovered lest the dogs fail to bring in more game. Additionally, Bemunese should treat their dogs with special kindness and attentiveness during the performance, feed them treats like cake or scraps from the hunt, and also refrain from the curses and kicks that otherwise tend to characterize villagers' interactions with dogs. (4) The ban of game (*dai lul dawa tabol*), following which women should not sweep the floor in their houses while the men are in the forest, since this action is held to disperse the animals. This is just one example of the mirroring mimicry that pertains between village and forest and between the actions of women and children, on the one hand, and the hunters, on the other, and that explains why the former and their alleged transgressions are so often blamed for mishaps that take place during the hunt.[17] (5) The ban of sharp objects (*dai lul dawa langgar*) only applies to women and most stringently to the wives of the Prow and the Stern, who observe extra precautions throughout the performance. This ban concerns specifically the hunting spears of the men, which may not be touched by women or brought into the house. More diffusely, the quiet, peaceful demeanor adopted by the wives of the Prow and the Stern to protect the men while they are on the hunt also falls under this ban.

If the bans enumerated above pertain directly to the hunt of the cassowary and the larger space of the performance as, for instance, set off from the sea and characterized by a marked male-female separation, those objects and actions grouped under the rubric of momosim are intended to ensure that this space will not be contaminated by what Bemunese regard as the Malay. What is selected as worthy of representing the residual category of Aru adat that remains once the Malay is extracted is the result of the play in present-day circumstances between current foci of attention, on the one hand, and the need to condemn to oblivion certain memories, experiences, desires, and forms of action, on the other, as well as the specific history of the celebration's past inclusions and exclusions. It follows that this space of adat comprises things that should be forgotten or, alternatively, that provide an inverse Aru reflection of issues demanding attention on the Backshore and causing concern in the context of the more everyday, more Malay lives of Bemunese—things like language, clothing, religion, and trade. At least one of these, religion, is clearly new, while the others have assumed varying contours in changing historical circumstances. An inventory of the objects, artifacts, activities, and spatiotemporal arrangements of the performance suggests that these are already preselected and configured according to the standards of perception, the politics of memory, and the prevailing concerns that govern the present on Aru's Backshore.

What does an inventory of the malayu as it is objectified under the rubric of the "prohibited" in the performance reveal? Given, that the first onslaught of the Aru on the Malay is an effect of language—the words of the momosim piled up by the Prow immediately before he launches the performance and the three marked contexts of "speaking" that convene the men of Bemun in its initial planning—it is not surprising that the mala lir is momosim during the celebration and targeted for special attention. Besides the prohibition on speaking Aru Malay, the written signs and vehicles of the national language Bahasa Indonesia (also simply mala lir) like books, notebooks, paper, pencils, and pens are all momosim. So, too, are the artifacts of print capitalism (Anderson 1991) in the primarily popular form these take on the Backshore; in preparation for their celebration, Bemunese clear their houses of all the wall hangings with which Moluccans throughout the province prefer to decorate their homes—calendars of bikinied Asian beauties advertising stores in Dobo, Tual, Ambon, and Surabaya; posters of film and rock stars; and calendars, crosses, and colored prints depicting religious scenes that Bemunese obtain from church officials. Not all of the above fall exclusively under the category of mala lir; the calendars advertising stores also overlap with the prohibition on any association with traders or stores (not to forget pencarian itself), while crosses and the like obtained through the church are also prohibited through their link to adat's sometime rival agama.

Cloth and malayu forms and styles of dress are another site of erasure during the cassowary celebration. Clothing and cloth are artifacts that recurrently—at the turn of the century and thereafter, during the Japanese occupation of Aru, and more recently in the context of Backshore missionization and conversion—have been primary loci of identity in Aru. Today clothing serves especially to mark a past from a present and a time of the ancestors from the larger *moderen*, or "modern," context of the Indonesian nation-state, although one could argue that similar distinctions were also more or less operative from the beginning of the century on. From early on the morning that the hunt begins, malayu clothing, including any shoes, sandals, or thongs, must be stored out of sight.[18] All curtains and cloth coverings that serve as doorways in homes are taken down and put away for the duration of the performance. At the request of Bemunese, the traders who live in the village also remove all curtains from their windows, since they are visible from outside.

All interaction with traders, commercial transactions, and visits to the stores are also malayu and thus off-limits during the performance. The traders themselves, including their children, remain almost entirely confined within their homes throughout the celebration, only emerging to use their outhouses or to leave the village to visit relatives or friends in the neighboring communities. If, on such a trip, they obtain or purchase some fish for their dinner, then it must be hidden out of sight as it is carried into Bemun. One of Bemun's tradeswomen claimed that they should not bring fish into the village at all and that if Bemunese knew that she and her husband did so, they would be angry. On the final night of the cassowary celebration, when the prohibitions are somewhat relaxed and spectators, especially from Longgar and Apara crowd the sides of Bemun's pathways, the traders come out to serve palm wine and cakes to the revelers who congregate singing and dancing in front of their stores.

Nothwithstanding the prohibition on contact with the stores, Bemunese sometimes run out of basic supplies like coffee once the performance is under way. When such things happen, they can turn to one of several persons who have decided to "gather palm fronds" for the duration of the performance. Such persons are inevitably Bemunese women married to men from Kei or their husbands, who may also be asked to check and bail out villagers' boats. Like the traders, all these palm frond gatherers stay close to home, while the women usually wear sarongs until the performance is over. Sometimes women who participate in the performance ask a female palm frond gatherer to prepare the coconut milk that enhances the porridge of taro and sweet potato that is served to the hunters when they return from the forest; the prohibition on "touching water" means that they are unable to do so themselves.

Incidentally, this latter prohibition may, I believe, in part be an extension of the ban of the sea insofar as the prohibition on "touching water" may have the effect of highlighting for villagers the erasure of the sea from their lives or the obliteration of the large body of water with which in pencarian men and women enjoy intimate contact. The sensory effects, at any rate, of this prohibition make for one of the most thoroughly felt aspects of the general embodiment by Bemunese of their annual celebration (Comaroff and Comaroff 1992, 72): the general "heat" that characterizes the performance as a whole directly permeates their bodies, while its effects are immediately apparent in the perspiring, shiny faces and bodies of men, women, and children. It also ensures that the ceremonial washing of hands and the first bath of the Barakai new year will have an easily perceptible efficacy.

Along with the malayu language, clothing, tradestores and commercial exchanges, signs of religion—which are relatively few and far between in Bemun—are also momosim and set for erasure. Besides churchgoing, which is suspended if the hunt happens to fall on a Sunday, agama's main signs are the church calendars and other graphic material that is removed from the walls of Bemunese homes. Finally, "government" (I. pemerintah) is also excluded from the space of the performance, with the only possible conflict being that of Armed Forces Day. Bemunese claimed that if officials from the capital or church representatives were to arrive while the performance was in full swing, they would not be received and would have either to wait until the hunt was over or to come back later.

Beyond the transgressions of Bemunese, which over and over again throughout the performance betray their easy slippage into the Malay and constantly reaffirm its presence in the face of the Aru, other aspects of the performance suggest how the Malay in the late twentieth century necessarily and unavoidably permeates the Aru in ways that Bemunese themselves do not choose to focus on. For instance, it is only at this time of year that Bemunese string light bulbs along the village pathways and hold a collection to pay for the oil that will keep the village generator running throughout the night. While electricity on the Backshore is associated with "development," government, and, by implication, one would think, the Malay, the latter connection is one that Bemunese themselves do not make. Notwithstanding appearances, clothing, the sea, and trade are considerably more Malay than other things and, as such, become the pivotal sites of ritual attention and reworking. The more important point, however, is that such "inconsistency" is inevitable in a performance that, however much its dynamics insist on a separation of Malay and Aru, could not be more situated and shaped within the entanglements that make up Barakai Island's and with it Bemun's history. Certain conditions resulting from this history will be demanded by the performance and take precedence over a more literal reading of the difference between malayu and gwerka. Thus, if the performance may once have been held to coincide with a full moon, electricity can take the place of the moon today. Although Bemunese waxed poetic over the soft light cast on the cassowary's play when his celebration happened to coincide with a full moon, other factors of timing associated with the larger world in which they live today may make such a coincidence impossible. Today as well, where hospitality and generosity on the Backshore have come to mean the offering to guests of luxury consumables like coffee, cigarettes, and cakes prepared with flour and sugar (according to recipes first taught to Backshore women by Chinese traders), such meanings will necessarily carry over into the annual performance. The impression of luxurious abundance and overflowing hospitality that is so crucial in this context would be entirely lost if the dancers who cluster nightly around the cassowary were served sago cakes instead of fancy flour ones and, to a somewhat lesser extent, tea in place of the more expensive coffee.

The above "inconsistencies" aside, the space of Bemun's performance is carefully hedged off by the whole range of procedures and operations, by the institution of bans and prohibitions, by the advisory tales and the recitation of past exploits and excitement that fill the evening before the hunt begins, as well as by the specific instruction and more diffuse socialization that takes place in the context of the celebration. Yet not only is the performance not free from contamination by the Malay, its very dynamics and drama betray even more the pressures on their celebration that most Bemunese feel from without. And notwithstanding the great defense thrown up against all the attempts that might be out there to undermine the cassowary, this spirit lurks somewhat shamefacedly on the margins of the Malay and is himself a weave of contradiction, ambivalence, and equivocation. In other words, the cassowary's presence during the performance very much embodies and magnifies the history of the Aru's own exclusion.

Taking to the Land

My focus thus far has been on how what is normally elsewhere, other, and forgotten in relation to the space of the everyday is recalled and remembered, precipitated and released in the long thoughts that plague Bemunese women and men, by the violence with which the Aru interrupts the Malay, and by the gradual emergence of the cassowary on the performative scene. In what follows I consider how the further action of the performance inscribes what is otherwise absent and excluded—thereby making it present—as the community aims to bring about a seamless fit between itself and the time of its ancestors. This construction relies to a large extent on the fabrication of the plaited palm frond effigy of the cassowary. A semantically dense artifact, this spirit's "image" or "shadow" (B. *ken ko*) allows those absences to materialize that are among the most painful and wrenching for Bemunese—only to banish them once again shortly after they are made present. Both the plastic form that this community has selected to image the cassowary and the song with which they annually praise him are critical to this process.

Yet even when the spirit materializes in the elusive, "shadowy" form of his effigy, his presence is always already haunted by absence: the cassowary's play, much like the hunt after which it is modeled, enacts a drama of presence and absence as the spirit plays hide and seek with the villagers who pursue, track, and taunt him with their coconut frond spears and, finally, at the conclusion of each night's pursuit, "kill" the effigy. In this way, the cassowary's presence also hints at the larger forces and strategies that would erase, marginalize, and banish all that he is emblematic of. Although Bemunese, as the relatively Malay occupants of the ancestral belan that figures as the cassowary's opponent in the performance themselves stage the annual erasure of the Aru, they also at the same time, complexly recall and reestablish their attachments and affinities to it through the medium of its emblem—the palm frond effigy they plait of the autochthonous spirit. Crucial to this drama and indicative of the fissuring of the community in relation to the two elsewheres of the Aru and the Malay is that the same men who hunt the (real) cassowary during the day become themselves this Aru emblem at night, when they don and dance with the effigy by turn. Women, by contrast, in this male-dominated performance hover on the boundaries of the Aru and the Malay with important implications for both their possibilities and their limitations in this context (chapter 7).

It is worth noting that several hunters insisted that the already difficult to track and elusive cassowary had, in recent years, become even more flighty than before. Since several cassowaries were killed in the "great" performances of 1988 and 1989, and perhaps in later ones as well, I believe these statements say more about the growing uneasiness among Bemunese concerning the acceptability of their adat performance than about any actual decrease in Barakai's cassowary population. Put somewhat differently, the increasing reluctance of the cassowary to allow himself to be taken and the mounting flightiness of the spirit registered by some Bemunese suggest that those powers that aim to do away with such performances or transfigure them into something fit for display in Jakarta's "miniature park" can claim a certain success.

Before the cassowary spirit enters the village with the hunters on the first day of the performance to take part in the nightly dancing of which he is the central focus, the community undertakes the final preparations for this arrival. On the morning of the first day of the hunt, the village begins to stir somewhat earlier than usual. Men chop firewood, women sweep around their houses and in the pathways in front of their homes, and everyone fetches water. Since the procession of men, women, and children trails the spirit's dancing "shadow" up and down Bemun's central pathways every night of the performance, the village must be clean throughout; the cassowary will be angry, several people mumbled to me as they cleaned, if during the nightly feasting he happens "to cast an eye" (B. *etebe mes*) on any stray debris that has not been cleared away.

The Prow and the Stern are also busy—the former having left well before dawn to obtain a sapling that more than one Bemunese described to me as the "center" or "navel" of their celebration. This sapling is planted by the Prow in the fenced-off enclosure called the "Front of the Path," where the hunters gather before and after their return from the forest and which is off-limits to women. Rootless, the sapling withers and dies shortly after the performance ends, and as such this "center" of the annual celebration seems perfectly emblematic of the sterile, timeless space that remains once the Malay, women, and much that is "female" has been excluded. Before the Prow plants the sapling, he clears the enclosure of the weeds and brush that have taken hold there since the previous year, dismantles the arrangement of stakes on which last year's game was singed, and discards them at the rear of the enclosure (which opens out onto the forest) together with the three or more bleached and withered "cassowary skins" (B. *koder kalin*) or effigies from the preceding year. The Stern is also busy and, assisted by his wife, clears the large bronze gongs and the piles of plates that compose his altar of the dust and cobwebs that have settled on them during the year.

In addition to the Prow and the Stern, who fulfill by far the most important tasks during the performance, a number of women and men who trace themselves to the first fam said to have settled on Barakai enjoy a privileged relationship to the cassowary and are said to "hold" his celebration (B. *dasual koder*). Collectively known as the Sister's Children, this group has specific obligations and duties vis-à-vis the spirit and his performance just as the children of a man's sister have in relation to their mother's brother, whom they in certain respects regard as the fount of their life and well-being (Spyer 1992; see also Fox 1971, 1980). From within this group, which acts solely in the context of the annual celebration, one man is selected—usually by his immediate predecessor—to occupy the position of the cassowary's master.[19]

After they clean their houses and the village, the men, women, and children who participate in the performance bathe for the last time until the celebration ends. Everyone should don a loincloth before the men set off on the hunt. Today all women conceal these under sarongs, with the only exception being the wives of the Prow and the Stern, who may not cover their silvery "ancient" barkcloth loinwraps or even come into contact with cloth for as long as the celebration lasts.[20] The men and boys especially devote considerable time to their appearance before the hunt—they shave, trim each other's hair, and apply scented oil to their beards and scalps. Some wear bead necklaces with pearl-shell pendants,

often carved in the form of birds.[21] After making a personal request for
safety and success to the spirits with an offering of betel at the Prow's or
the Stern's altar, most often at both,[22] the men return to their houses to
await the Prow, who "passes by the houses" (B. *awa gwalar*) to summon
them to the Front of the Path. By contrast, the Stern waits in his house
until he is sure that all the hunters have had time to convene there before
he joins them.

Women and children stand across the pathway from the enclosure,
watching the men and dogs gather from the acceptable distance offered
by the verandas, yards, and doorways of the houses that face onto this
space. Already the sight of the hundred or more hunters arrayed in
loincloths with colorful waving tails and armed with spears is impressive
in this otherwise relatively quiet community of some three-hundred-odd
people. But it is the dogs who really express the tense expectancy that
pervades the group of men and boys; unlike the men they cannot contain
their excitement, and the air fills with their whines, collective howling,
and snarls that accompany the occasional fights that break out among
them. Once the Stern joins the group, the Prow makes the first offering of
the day at the foot of the sapling that he planted earlier in the morning.
Thereafter, the men quickly fall in line between the Prow and the Stern,
assuming a place in the belan that will set off and return from the forest
for the duration of the performance.[23] As soon as the order of the lineup
is established on this first morning, the boat formation may not be
altered for the duration of the hunt. The men shoulder their spears and
call out to their dogs "fiol, fiol!" or by name. Amidst the uproar of the
barking and the cries of the men to their dogs, the line of hunters winds
out of the enclosure and slowly disappears into the forest.

The sudden quiet that descends on the village once the men depart is
remarkable. For the most part, the women stick close to their houses to
tend their hearths, which may not die out, and keep a close eye on their
children, who are scolded if they play near the Front of the Path. Much of
the day is spent in subdued visiting, especially after the women finish
preparing the sweet porridge of taro, cassava, and bananas (I. *kolak*) that
they will serve to their men when they return from the forest in the late
afternoon. As the celebration progresses and villagers become increasingly tired from the nightly dancing, the women and girls catnap during
the day. The hushed silence that—when all goes as it should—tends to

reign in the village when the men are off on the hunt is only broken from time to time by the measured sound of dried sago palm stalks being clapped together in a game played by women and girls (B. *daitar gabar*), together with the laughter that accompanies it, and by the occasional outbreak of ululation among them when hunters emerge out of the forest to deposit game in the enclosure.

Directly linked to the general festivity that surrounds the cassowary hunt, the women's palm stalk game, a man's game that uses a rattan jump rope (B. *daitar gogor*),[24] and others recalled by some of Bemun's older women are only engaged in at this time of year.[25] The games described by some of the older women include that of the "breadfruit," in which a woman by turn would hop down a double line of women while clapping her hands; that of running in snake formation (B. *dala jel*), in which a single line of ululating women would snake twisting and turning up and down the village pathways; and that of "running [up and down] termite mounds" (B. *dala buser*).[26] Through the energetic and lively games played by women and girls back in the village—games that index the flora and fauna of the landscape that lies between the village and the forest and is off-limits to them at this time—a bond rooted in "the pleasure of play" seems to be evoked between themselves and the hunters off in the forest (Valeri 1985, 219). In this manner, I believe, the women's play complicates the marked contrast that is otherwise drawn between themselves and the men, and between the village and the forest. In so doing, the games intimate a continuity that is in all other respects denied and thereby prefigure and lay the ground for the mediating role that will subsequently be assumed by the betwixt and between landscape of elephant grass and bush during the so-called "women's share" of the hunt on its concluding day.

Apart from the diversions offered by these games and by the more subdued visiting that goes on among the women, the suspenseful hush that hangs over the village while the hunt is in progress is from time to time throughout the day suddenly rent asunder by a burst of high-pitched ululation. The ululation begins in the homes of women whose houses overlook the Front of the Path and who keep a steady watch over this space; it then reverberates through the village and is echoed and taken up by other women, who rush to see the game being carried into the enclosure by the hunters' envoys. Not all game receives an applause of ululation, however. Women only ululate when large (B. *koal jinjinen*) as opposed to small game (B. *koal titikin*) is brought back to Bemun.[27] While the cassowary is a category unto itself, large game comprises deer and wild boar, with small made up primarily of the wallaby and the bandicoot.

The main objective of the hunt and that which gives shape and lends its name to the entire performance is the pursuit and killing of the cassowary. Indeed, the movements of the spirit trace the progress of the performance as it unfolds—the journey of the spirit to Bemun, his brief, emotionally charged stay in the villagers' midst, and his final exile—and weave a connecting thread through its distinct portions. The spirit's rapprochement with Bemunese begins with the imposition of the ban of the sea in the fish poisoning, when this performance has already drawn the cassowary from deep in the forest to the head of the river. A day or so later, when the men speak of "taking to the land," the cassowary is said to be on the edge of the village in the enclosure at the Front of the Path, where he conceals himself in the "cassowary skins" or effigies still hanging there from the previous year. The following day the cassowary returns with the hunters from the forest to animate the effigy that is fabricated as his "image." During the day, the cassowary is also hunted in the forest, where, if his celebration's bans and prohibitions are strictly followed by women, men, and children, he may be captured and killed by the hunters. In the case of a "small" performance such as those of 1986 and 1987, on the final night of feasting the cassowary is "killed" for the third and last time right before dawn and banished into oblivion until he is summoned again the following year.

Although related, the cassowary's effigy and the living animal in the forest are hardly the same, with the former, after all, being the "shadow" or the "image" of the latter. The terms used respectively to refer to each make this distinction clear, as do the overlapping though divergent procedures that apply when a real cassowary as opposed to the effigy is killed by the hunters in the forest. Nonetheless, it would be a mistake to see the effigy as a mere "shadow" or as some representation of the real animal. If the effigy itself is termed the "skin of the cassowary" (B. *koder ken kala*), once it is animated by the men who don it by turn, the dancing cassowary's "shadow" partakes of the spirit's heat, power, and energy. In other words, the effigy is never entirely separate from the cassowary himself; as a materially dense artifact that makes things that are otherwise absent concretely present, its force is neither distinct from the plastic form through which it realizes itself nor from the procedures or the persons who produce and wear it. Describing a similar process for archaic Greek idols known as *xoanan*, Vernant argues that the power of these idols was inseparable from the processes through which they were made visible and present. Following this "presentification," the representation of the idol could never be wholly separated from the ritual actions directed at it: "embedded within the ritual, the idol in its plastic form has not reached full autonomy" (Vernant 1991, 155). On the one hand, then, the cassowary effigy is not entirely separate from the animal tracked in the forest—indeed, how could it be given that the spirit returns with the hunters to animate the effigy they produce?—on the other, he also partly fuses with the men who take turns bringing the spirit to life when they dance with the effigy. In Bemun, however, differently than in ancient Greece, the presence of the spirit is itself haunted by its imminent absence in such a way that the process of "presentification" is always flawed from the start. The cassowary's tentative and elusive presence also extends beyond the fabrication of the palm frond effigy itself to the entire game of hide and seek that characterizes the cassowary's interaction with Bemunese—whether in the forest or back in the village.

If the effigy is called simply by the everyday Barakai term for "cassowary," or *koder*, the animal pursued in the forest is designated at this time of year by an honorific formerly used to address an elder, *kajinwaten*. Indeed, this term is itself a conjunction of *kajin*—the root of *kajinembu*, or the collective body of elders held to embody the knowledge of adat and sejara, and also the root of *selkajinen*, which places the third person plural possessive *sel* in front of *kajinen* to describe a marked set of ancestors called emphatically "*our* ancestors"—and *waten*, or "body."[28] The seamless fit in disposition that Bemunese attribute to their ancestors, on the one hand, and the ability of the hunters to down a cassowary, on the other, lends support to my view that, in this setting, the living cassowary is an ancestral body and therewith also a vehicle of the dead. Besides the final mourning that takes place via the medium of the cassowary's "shadow," tales told by the hunters of their sightings in the forest of spirits who transfigure from human to animal and back or of dead game blocking their path, already killed and laid out for them by the ancestors, further substantiate the porous interchangeability among spirits, animals, and, to a certain extent, hunters. Men claim that they sometimes mistake a fellow hunter for game in circumstances in which this would otherwise be impossible and attempt to spear him rather than the animal, subsequently to be appalled by their mistake.[29]

While easily provoked and volatile, the spirit lords' evaluation is, however, by no means capricious. Rather, the agency they unleash is always an inflection and a derivation of the actions and the attitudes of the villagers during the performance. What really lies between the hunters' prowess and the ancestors' willingness to allow themselves to be taken in cassowary guise is the behavior of Bemunese men, women, and children and, specifically, their observance of the bans and prohibitions that are in force at this time. Rather than itself being some representation of an Aru past, the cassowary could be more aptly described as the concrete embodiment of the villagers' shifting relationship to this past. It is important to recall that, as the occupants of an ancestral belan that both at night and during the day sets off in pursuit of the cassowary, Bemunese are themselves relatively Malay vis-à-vis this Aru spirit. A ready explanation is therefore always at hand in those years when a cassowary is not taken (as in 1986 and 1987), namely, that members of the community—and more often than not its women and children, "people in the village"—have lapsed into Aru Malay, neglected to remove sandals or conceal malayu clothing, or in one or another way been guilty of transgressions and thereby revealed themselves as Malay. "The observance of bans [in the village] is poor and therefore the ancestors are dissatisfied" (B. *lul [dem wanu] kalager ja kajinembu demlam*), or, put otherwise, transgression opens up a rift between the community and its ancestors, between the present and the past, and between the malayu and the gwerka. When, inversely, the hunters do kill one or more cassowaries, then it would seem that Bemunese have succeeded in their rapprochement with the ancestors by strictly observing the various bans that, being embodied acts, allow them to transfigure themselves, however temporarily, into persons that are relatively non-Malay. Indeed, this success makes of the space of the performance an entire mortuary ground that conjoins the community in a commemoration of all its dead rather than the specific named dead of the past year. At the same time, although Bemunese spoke in glowing terms of the festivities that would take place if a real cassowary was taken, they only seemed mildly perturbed by the failure of hunters to bring in one in 1986 and 1987, and claimed that it does not matter whether a kajinwaten is killed or not. The above discussion brings to the fore the fact that the performance is never the same from one year to the next: each year Bemunese honor and mourn different dead, and each year the relationship between the Malay and the Aru, already a shifting one, realizes itself in a subtly different way.

Some of the hunters told me that when they kill a cassowary during the hunt, their hair stands on end, a physical reaction that marks encounters with spirits of all kinds. Just as in the song, they claimed, they throw down their spears, break out in the "Cassowary's Song," and begin to dance. A messenger is sent back to the village to inform the women and children of the spirit's killing, so that they can prepare themselves for his arrival by arraying themselves in their best Aru finery. In the forest, the hunters also ready themselves for their entry and decorate their spear points with tufts of white palm frond and round "lanterns" shaped from the same. When the line of singing and dancing hunters enters Bemun, trailing the cassowary, which is supported on a pole between two men, the feasting that usually takes place around the effigy at night begins while the sun is still high in the sky.

At every house the procession pauses—all the while dancing and singing—to allow people to refresh themselves with the palm wine, coffee, and cakes that the women of the household bear ululating out of their homes as offerings to the bird and to their fellow Bemunese. At every house as well, members of the household sprinkle the dead cassowary with cologne and pour libations of palm oil out on the ground before his dancing bearers. The same kind of libations are poured out shortly before dawn on the final night of the festivities to honor the dead of the past year and to finalize publicly the process of mourning for them. In ending the mourning for particular persons, the libations of palm oil also confer on the recent dead the status of ancestors. Importantly, this process is accomplished through the medium of a substance that derives from the same fruit-bearing tree that also provides the material from which the cassowary effigy is itself entirely made. The transfiguration of the recent dead into ancestral spirits thus rests on a procedure that posits a link of shared substance between the effigy and the ancestors by manipulating human artifacts derived from the palm tree.

More generally, the relationship between cassowaries and palms in this setting is overdetermined.[30] Only splinters of coconut palm stalk—the "cassowary's bones" (B. *koder ken tul*)—as opposed to other woods or materials, should be used to pick out bits of meat that get stuck between Bemunese teeth. According to the village schoolteacher and catechist, the close connection between cassowaries and palms also meant that the celebration of the first Palm Sunday held in Bemun posed serious problems. Many Bemunese today still recall their fear of ancestral repercussions on this first Palm Sunday in the late 1970s, with the main trouble being the prominent display in the procession planned around the village of the same "white" palm fronds used in the annual making of the cassowary and paraded in his performance down the very same pathways.

The Cassowary's Play

If a cassowary is not killed, then the spirit's presence restricts itself to the effigy as a kind of stand-in and "shadow" of the animal in the forest, and its "play" animates the village for the three successive nights of the performance—or even longer in the case of a "great" version. Usually the same men gather at the side of the Stern's house to make the effigy, although theoretically any man may take part in its fabrication.[31] Apart from the main body of the cassowary, consisting of the conjoined spines of two large coconut fronds that rest on the shoulders of the dancer and serve the effigy as a frame, a number of different parts have to be made. A small head crowned by some frond feathers is carved from palm wood and then attached to the effigy's long, plaited neck and breast. In addition to the head and breast, the men plait a pair of diminutive wings, which are attached to the conjoined palm spines. The palm leaf streamers that flow from the effigy's breast are left untied to swirl about the legs of the dancer and give an impression of bountiful feathers. The flamboyant splendor of the cassowary's tail is a critical feature, and much attention is devoted to it. To achieve the necessary effect, the men attach additional streamers at the tail end of the frame. A site of special potency, the knot at the top of the effigy's tail where the streamers shoot up and then fall away to the ground in a grand sweep is called "the top of the buttocks." Finally, the last feature of the effigy, a pair of small teats—one long and one short, which, according to the hunters, are an exact replica of those of the animal in the forest—is attached to the effigy's breast only when the effigy is already worn by the first dancer. In marking the completion of the image, this final detail also brings it to life.[32]

The cassowary's "play," or his concrete and animated presence at the head of a procession of dancing and singing Bemunese, always begins with a game of hide and seek. After the teats are affixed to the effigy's breasts, the cassowary crouches for an instant, then leaps up and flees from the men who made him, with his great tail rustling and swaying behind. The hunt has begun: the spirit must be tracked and located before he can be regaled and finally killed. Bemun's children especially delight in this part of the evening festivities. They scramble in the underbrush and dark foliage at the "front of the village," where they know the cassowary hides, "barking" and "tracking" him like hunting dogs. Once discovered, the cassowary rises out of the bush and begins to dance.

A mere handful of Bemunese fall into step with the cassowary when he appears out of the dark and begins to dance (B. *ato*, *ken joto*) in the illuminated pathway at the front of the village. Indeed, many of those who dance behind him are the children who "tracked" him down. With his small following in tow, the cassowary proceeds first to the house of the Prow and subsequently to that of the Stern. In effect, the concrete presence of the cassowary dancing in turn in front of Bemun's two adat houses calls the community's ancestral belan—and thereby his own Malay adversary—into existence. Villagers fall into place—the men first and then the women and children—and the procession that forms behind the dancing spirit grows rapidly in size. On the first two nights out of three (in the case of a "small" performance), the festivities continue until well after midnight, and the procession makes two or more rounds of the entire village. The cassowary pauses to dance in front of each house in the village, and at least on one night out of three refreshments of coffee, tea, palm wine, cakes, and cigarettes are brought out on trays by ululating women and served to the dancers. At the end of the night's dancing—a moment ultimately determined by the cassowary's master, who is always the last man to wear the effigy—the cassowary is led to the center of the village, where he dies in a cloud of palm frond spears.[33] On the third and final night of the performance, this "killing" (B. *dawunen*) does not occur until dawn or sometimes even after daybreak if the villagers insist on prolonging the feasting.[34]

Majestically imaged in a towering cascade of glistening white fronds, the spirit hovers and sways above the crowd of singing Bemunese that throngs around him. For the most part, his movements are graceful and measured, in tune with those of the procession he leads.[35] The cassowary's dance, like that of the men, consists of a simple bouncing back and forth from foot to foot, rhythmically bending the knees in time with the music. At times, his "play" becomes more animated and the spirit leaps and whirls, sweeping his great tail in the faces of the dancers that press around him and rushing headlong into the crowd that pursues him. Except when one or more of the men decides to close in on the effigy, challenging and menacing it with their coconut frond spears and reminding their fellow performers what lies ahead for the Aru spirit, the men bob up and down with their arms crossed over their chests. The women, by contrast, carry sprays of white fronds in each hand and use these or palm frond "shawls" to accentuate the use of their arms. Theirs is a delicate, light step from side to side and a loose swaying of the arms that echoes the undulating, flowing motion of the cassowary's tail. When the singing crescendoes, women ululate. Some, especially the younger ones, may throw up their arms and wave the fronds above the heads of the dancers in an arched movement that reminds villagers of birds of prey suspended with spread wings over the sea. Regarded by islanders as especially lovely, the movement is called "to [dance] like great sea hawks" (B. *dai nawa*).[36]

Bemunese see their celebration, renowned and respected across Barakai for its special power, as beautiful, exciting, deeply moving, and especially sad. Starkly set off and hedged by the forgetfulness and exile that throughout most of the year ensure the absence of the cassowary and, along with him, of much that women and men regard as making up the Aru, the single, annual visitation by the spirit is an event in the lives of both men and women that for many seems unsurpassed in its emotional power. Just as those things that are most markedly singled out for forgetting tend to perdure obsessively in memory, so too the dramatic and violent banishment of the cassowary at his celebration's conclusion and the spirit's prolonged inaccessibility throughout the year create a carefully balanced tension between distance and proximity, absence and presence regarding his "image." It is this marked contrast especially that,

The cassowary at play

I believe, ensures that the concrete presence of the spirit in the village, in either animal or effigy form, is singled out by many Bemunese for the immense impression it leaves them with. And it is, I believe, one way that this Backshore community, in the face of an encroaching Malay predominance, briefly, fleetingly, and imaginatively weaves a fragile, if ultimately impossible, world around itself.

The tangible materiality of the cassowary's presence is made all the more efficacious by the respectful attitudes that pertain toward it. Although in the excitement of the dance, Bemunese cannot always prevent themselves from brushing up against the cassowary as they press in on him or from being caught by the sweep of his tail when he spins in their midst, they take pains to avoid physical contact with the effigy's "hot" plumes. I have mentioned the extra steps undertaken to ensure that the cassowary's power will have its full effect, especially on those outsiders who would question it—a precautionary lesson that undoubtedly is not lost on Bemunese, for whom it is largely meant. Other aspects of the performance touched on earlier further enhance the solidity of the cassowary in villagers' imaginations as well as the strong identification not only of men but also of women with their annual celebration. Or at least they are meant to do so and, I believe, largely have their intended effect. Recall that although men have a more active role in the performance, all Bemunese are credited with participating in the practices that draw the cassowary to themselves and allow him to materialize in their midst. By the same token, the simple generalization "gathering palm fronds" that men and women use to describe themselves or others when they opt out of participation potentially allows each of them to see an aspect of himself or herself as concretely incorporated in the spirit's image. A number of events that take place on the final day of the hunt also bring the women of Bemun in closer relation to the cassowary so that they too will ideally identify intimately with the Aru spirit and more fully partake of the mourning and death that exiles him into oblivion.

Beyond the living, the figure of the cassowary is made to embrace and embody the entire, undivided Bemun community, which comprises not only all its women, men, and children—excluding no one due to the generalization of "gathering palm fronds—but their ancestors as well. This aim at an all-encompassing and totalizing effect is most apparent on the concluding night of the celebration, when the effigy is made to incorporate the final act of public mourning, in which the community participates as a whole, that is observed for every deceased member of the village. Such an effect is enabled, for instance, by the contemporization of all the deaths that happened throughout the year (George 1996, 110), which glosses over their distinct timing and circumstances along with the identities of the different deceased themselves. At the same time, the incorporation of these differences by the cassowary suggests that his own composition and identity is ever transforming and in flux. Even as the cassowary glosses over the differences between individual deaths in the community in this final public mourning, he is brought into association with the necessarily varying sentiments and memories that link living Bemunese to different dead persons. At least potentially, the cassowary's presence will assume a heightened poignancy for those Bemunese women and men who have most recently lost a loved one. As acts of incorporation, these last commemorations, punctuated by the high-pitched wails and keening of female mourners, only augment the layers of associations that already cluster around the figure of the cassowary. It seems as if with every palm oil ablution poured out at the feet of the dancing spirit immediately before his exile, the memories and emotionality associated with the deceased for whom it flowed would hence-forth be powerfully evoked in the concrete presence of the cassowary or that behind every tear shed before the exuberant mass of quivering fronds would lie a revivified and deeply felt absence for a loved one. Shot through with the multiple shadings of their varied imaginations, memories, and desires, the presence of the cassowary places Bemunese once a year in poignant intimacy with their "long thoughts" that touch on and conjure up dead loved ones, friends long gone, and, more generally, the absences, sorrows, and losses of their personal and collective lives. By extension, the Aru, with the cassowary as its privileged emblem, itself becomes a site of loss, desire, and imminent absence.

The "Cassowary's Song"

Beyond the annual presence of the cassowary in their midst, Bemunese commonly make special note of the "Cassowary's Song" (B. Koder ken Sab) when they speak of the sadness inherent in their performance. Said to "touch" on all aspects of the cassowary and his celebration—even the spirit's excrement—the song seems somehow to condense for them its experiential force. It is singled out by the majority of Bemunese, and equally by women and men, as the part of their performance most likely to move a person to tears, as indeed it often does.

1.   E la koder a wol ka, wol ka
        asuarnal ken sa, eno ele sin wowoleru
        [The cassowary has bamboo (stakes), wood (stakes)
        he grabs his excrement, the (cassowary's) anus is open]

2.   Etale mutabe butale, le koder a mutabe
        le koder a butal, butal a mutabe
        [You throw down your spear(s), the cassowary, you throw
        the cassowary's spear(s), spear(s), you throw]

3.   La koder nen tua, nen a gwiyer
        nen, la koder a nen
        [The cassowary drinks palm wine, he drinks water
        he drinks, the cassowary drinks]

4.   La koder a teh, teh, ile yo wowo
        la koder a wowo
        [The cassowary has tea, tea, he has bells
        the cassowary has bells]

5.   E la koder a teh, teh, il yo wowo
        la koder a sin woler
        [The cassowary has tea, tea, he has bells
        the cassowary's anus is open]

6.   E la koder a wol kai kai, yo emloiloi
        emle tarau emloiloi
        [The cassowary has bamboo (stakes), wood (stakes), it hangs
        it hangs, the dog hangs]

7.   Le tarau emloiloi ele al wol kai kai
        el koder a wol kai kai
        [The dog hangs on the bamboo (stakes), the wood (stakes)
        the cassowary's bamboo, wood (stakes)]

8.   El koder a wol ka, wol ka
        asuarnal ken sa, eno ele sin woler
        [The cassowary has bamboo (stakes), wood (stakes)
        he grabs his excrement, his anus is open]

Only the position of the first and last stanzas, which are identical and serve the song as a frame, are fixed. Hunters claim that they begin the song with this stanza after successfully killing a cassowary in the forest. This stanza also opens the nightly feasting when the effigy steps out of the bush and accompanies his death at its conclusion. Yet notwithstanding the stanza's privileged position, both men and women were at a loss to provide any explanation for it. The most that they could make of it was to observe that the fact that the cassowary's anus is open indicates that he defecates, as does the mention of his excrement. While these words struck most Bemunese as amusing, they could only reiterate that the song necessarily "touched" on every last thing relating to the spirit and his celebration—down to his very excrement.

Stanzas 2 through 7 do not follow a set order, although some stanzas lead more easily into each other, such as 6 and 7 or 7 and 8, and therefore tend to be sung in sequence. It is up to whichever man happens to be singing the lead to establish the sequence of the stanzas that are repeated in slightly varying order throughout the night.[37] The interpretations of the song's eight stanzas given by different persons were remarkably consistent. Invariably, the second stanza "you throw down your spears" was held to summarize the exuberant behavior that takes hold of the hunters when they kill a cassowary in the forest and begin to sing and dance on the site of his death. Stanzas 3, 4, and 5 "touch" (B. *dam kena*) on objects that Bemunese regard as emblematic of the cassowary and the celebration held in his honor: the palm wine and tea (coffee and cakes) that are served at each house to the dancing villagers, and the bells that jingle on the arm and leg bands worn by some villagers and provide the sole instrumental accompaniment to the singing.[38] Some suggested that the "bamboo" and "wood" mentioned in four different stanzas evoke the arrangement of stakes on which the game is singed at the conclusion of each day's hunt. Others suggested that "bamboo" and "wood" are the trees of the forest themselves that the hunting dogs leap up against or "hang from" in pursuit of the game. Already "touched on" in the song, dogs are crucial to the annual performance; their importance is foregrounded during the nightly feasting when men interrupt their singing to call out "fiol, fiol" as if summoning their dogs and, occasionally, when villagers "bark."

To attempt somehow to extricate the compelling sadness the song holds for most Bemunese from the above text would bear little fruit and would, I believe, be fundamentally misguided. It is crucial not only to consider the song as performed and sung but also, in so doing, to reflect on the circumstances in which that singing exclusively takes place.[39] As noted above, once the cassowary begins his nightly two-step the procession that trails him does not pause, even once, in singing his song. Sung over and over again in slightly varying combinations and over the course of the three or more nights of the annual celebration, the song only ceases—and then abruptly—when the cassowary is dispatched once and for all until the following year. The compelling and moving effect of the song on Bemunese lies in a crucial sense beyond the text transcribed above—in the unifying rhythm the singing lends to the nightly feasting; in the steady, repetitive backdrop it provides for the thin wails of mourning villagers; and in the momentum that slowly builds each evening into an ultimate, final crescendo. In a very real sense, the singing of the song's final stanza four consecutive times—one for each cardinal direction faced by the effigy—triggers the cassowary's killing.

What then remains to say of the song itself? Above and beyond the crucial stanza that marks its beginning and ending, the others merely "touch" on emblematic aspects of the annual performance. Presumably the precise aspects "touched" on are less significant than the codified and often reiterated assertion that the song as a whole "touches" on the entire celebration. Just as in the end the more personal, biographical "long thoughts" and memories of individual Bemunese are subordinated to and (ideally) taken up within an encompassing image of memory writ large,[40] so too the multiple, varied losses of different villagers are transformed into one great loss that is held to afflict the community as a whole: the exile of the cassowary and, with him, the Aru, and the brief charged release of final mourning made in the spirit's name. In other words, the annual performance is a privileged context that registers an ideal moment of concord from which symbolically speaking no Bemunese is excluded, in which the various factions and fam in the village allegedly unite in acclaiming and then banishing the Aru that they have performatively summoned to themselves, and the living and the dead sing and dance side by side on a common mortuary ground. Yet if the precise contours of this official version of the Bemun community are practically and thus historically realized in this setting—in the final public mourning for its recent dead and in the intense gwerka socialization of its younger members—the version that is here performatively construed is in the end both as symbolically central and as ephemeral and fleeting as the cassowary himself.

Because the song "touches" on all things pertaining to the cassowary and because of the way it is framed, it conveys the same sense of all-encompassing closure as the tightly woven effigy itself and, indeed, as the involuted space to which the latter is annually invited to "play." The phrase with which the song begins and ends—initiating the cassowary's play and triggering his death—seems to condense this process of involution and closure. In grabbing his own excrement at that moment when a potential opening is revealed—the gaping anus that as a site singled out for extra protection by "hot" substances and ancestral guardians reveals itself as the spirit's Achilles' heel—the cassowary's body closes back on itself. It is through this transgressive move that the Aru spirit unequivocally identifies himself both with death and as animal-like—and hence as unfit to reside in a "moderen" and "developed" Malay world (see Comaroff and Comaroff 1992, 78). Note that the full association with death as excrement—already prefigured in the cassowary's song—only comes to the spirit at the end of each night's performance and especially on the final one, that is, once he has been made to incorporate the community's recent dead. Reserved for the final hour before the cassowary's last killing and subsequent exile, the incorporation and mourning of the recent dead makes the larger connection between the cassowary and death all the more compelling. Yet it is also at the precise moment in which the cassowary grabs his excrement and closes in on himself that an opening is revealed, one that marks a decisive separation between life and death, between the living Bemunese and their dead relations.

In 1987, as the procession neared the center of the village after completing the mourning for that year's dead, a woman cried out above the singing, "He is leaving" (B. *agai abane*), while slightly later another loud and anguished voice exclaimed, "He is about to die" (B. *agai agwé*). The cassowary's play became increasingly animated as the procession edged toward his place of death. With mounting excitement, the women pierced the air with their long, drawn-out ululations; men menaced the spirit with imaginary and coconut frond spears, while others "barked" furiously. The fine voice of the headman, hoarse from the previous nights' singing, still invigorated the crowd, and the chorus was exuberant as it broke in on the last stanza of the cassowary's song. As the singing swelled, Bemunese pressed in around the spirit and pushed him toward the space of his death, where they rotated in an increasingly tight circle around the effigy—the men forming its inner core, the women a somewhat looser, outer ring, and the younger women hovering at the circle's edge with their arms in the air like great birds of prey (see also Comaroff and Comaroff 1992, 78). It was at this final moment that the last stanza of the cassowary's song was sung exactly four times, once for each cardinal direction faced by the effigy. Just before the dance came full circle as the cassowary turned east, he was brought down by a white hail of palm fronds and died facing the direction of the sea, pencarian, and the Malay amidst an incredible din of ululation, "barking," and, on this last night, wailing.[41]

Aru's Charmed Circle

According to the same logic—that of an inversion of magnitudes—that makes a minute gift from a god great and a great gift from humans to gods relatively minute—the miniature circuit traced by the cassowary at the center of Bemun immediately before his death summarizes the life-giving aim of his celebration (cf. Brown 1981, 96; Valeri 1985, 66). In a circumference described as "taking four" (B. *dai kau*) or "he encompasses the wind directions" (B. *nam ane wawen toon*), the cassowary circles slowly counterclockwise in the direction taken by the dead and faces each of the four wind directions in turn, beginning with the north and ending with the east.[42] As the ring of dancing Bemunese moving around the effigy grows tighter and more focused, the emblematic place of the cassowary as the "source" or "base" of a specific Backshore form of life and livelihood is not simply inscribed in his movements. It exerts a concentric pull on the crowd, is mirrored, and taken up by the throng of men, women, and children who press in around him from all sides, singing the last stanza of his song as he rotates among them.

This miniature circle of the annual celebration reiterates and retraces on a small but potent scale other circles that at repeated moments in the performance have been outlined, inscribed, and branded into the Barakai landscape. First among these are the circles of fire set daily by the Sister's Children in the forest to drive the game out into the open. Since their purpose is to surround and entrap animals as they flee the fires from all cardinal directions, this practice is referred to as "taking four" (dai kau). Preceded by offerings of betel to the cassowary together with requests for an abundance of game, the burning of circles recalls a practice that is performed in the village of Mesiang at the onset of marriage negotiations. Accompanied with a request for the fertility of the young couple and in particular that which "sits on the mother's brother," a round gong is slowly rotated in the center of four betel baskets placed as to evoke the cardinal directions (dai kau). Like the focused circuit traced in his final dance by the cassowary, the gong's rotation is an operation that is intended to draw and concentrate life-affirming forces from all directions.

Yet more than the individual fertility of Bemunese couples and the prosperity of marriages that conjoin community members, the primary articulated aim of the annual celebration is to ensure a successful pencarian, with the number of game killed held to reflect the prospects of the upcoming pearl oyster harvest. One could, however, be easily misled concerning the character of this reflection. Much more at issue than a simple correlation between numbers of game killed and shells collected, in which the first would assume an absolute precedence vis-à-vis the second, is a complex of concerted actions implicating Bemunese and ancestral spirits side by side in a play of reciprocal mimicry. A dream related to me by Abu Sabuan that she had shortly before the onset of the 1987 celebration hints at the complex mirrored interactions that are seen as capable of making or marring a given performance's efficacy.

In her dream, Abu Sabuan walked out on the tidal flats accompanied by two male kinsmen. While the two men walked on ahead, she lingered behind to collect the numerous oysters with "gaping mouths" that were strewn across the exposed sea floor. This was as much as she could recall, but it was evident from her comments that she experienced the dream as meaningful. To her, it suggested that immediately before the onset of the performance, the ancestors were already preparing themselves for the task that would engage them while their human descendants were off hunting the cassowary in the forest and simultaneously avoiding the sea: at this time, she told me, the ancestors would be diligently seeding the sea floor with oysters (B. *kajinembu daur borom*). Much like the circles of fire burnt by the hunters into the land, she explained, the crop of shells is also laid out to describe a circle and to encompass all four wind directions (dai kau). Indeed, following Abu Sabuan, the circular form of each oyster is traced with spectral fingers directly into the sandy floor of the undersea, or as she put it, "After the ancestors draw in the sand, the shadow of the oyster remains behind." And importantly they only do so when the hunters are also branding the Barakai forest and brush with their own fiery rings.

If the prosperity of Barakai's oyster beds rests on ancestral agency as triggered and compelled by human performance, which, in turn, takes the form of a mimicry of an ancestral past in the context of the annual celebration, it follows that the pencarian engaged in by women and men must also be carried out according to the ancestors' terms. To ensure such compliance, the same ancestors who sow the sea floor with oysters intersperse the "images" of shells with those of poisonous stonefish. In the same way that oysters serve as an index of the variety of trade products collected under the rubric of pencarian, so too the stonefish as pencarian's "heat" seem to summarize its dangers. Since encounters with both oysters and stonefish along with other undersea riches and dangers always imply ancestral intercession in human affairs, islanders claim that a "reason"—in the sense of some oversight or insult regarding a spirit or dead relative—can always be divined when a diver or other villager is stung by a stonefish or for that matter attacked by a shark or a poisonous sea snake.

To come full circle, as it were, the miniature Aru circuit traced by the cassowary's dancing feet at the village center looks as if it might describe a perfect fit between Bemunese and the world of their ancestors if it were only allowed to achieve closure. But in collapsing the difference between living Bemunese women and men and their ancestors, this closure would also inscribe a space of death. The cassowary is killed before his circle closes, and he dies facing the sea, the direction of all things Malay and pencarian—and, in this Backshore sense, life itself. Immediately before this killing, the cassowary incorporates the dead of the past year so that he will carry these away with him together with the "long thoughts" of Bemunese women and men that his own imminent presence triggered at the performance's beginning. The violent opening of the Aru out onto the Malay with the cassowary's death is only possible as a result of operations that take place on the last day of the hunt, carried out in the name of Bemun's women. By exposing the inherent fissure on which the performance rests and foregrounding the alterity suppressed in its context, what Bemunese call the "women's share" prefigures the cassowary's exile and therewith a return to the Malay.

7 The Women's Share

While I rarely heard men speak of their dreams, among women dreams were commonly shared and commented on in the casual gatherings that daily filled Barakai kitchens, while washing and bathing at the village well, or when groups of female kin set off together to collect firewood or to work in their gardens. Some dream images have fairly standardized interpretations on Barakai. When pearl oysters appear in dreams, for instance, it is commonly held to index children, thereby confirming once again the parallel that women and men tend to see between marriages on land and those under the sea (chapter 4). Other dreams are striking enough to become caught up in the round of rumors and reported stories that at any given time circulate in Bemun. Many of the dreams, visions, and uncanny happenings that unsettled villagers during the frenzied times preceding and accompanying their forced conversion continue to be recalled today and occasionally crop up in conversation.

The baptism of the cassowary, allegedly the first among Bemunese to convert to Catholicism, figures prominently in such talk. Some villagers invoked the image of a broad and resplendent beam of light sighted by several Bemunese on the evening preceding one of the community's three group conversions. A great shaft splitting the night sky, it is said to have illuminated precisely the spot where once a year, at the conclusion of his celebration, the palm frond cassowary is killed at the center of a throng of circling Bemunese. Others sometimes recalled a dream of Abu Sabuan in which the cassowary appeared as double in the form of a male and female pair, thereby suggesting how an alternative take on the performance's official version can emerge. Both the dream image and its continued reiteration by men and especially women today also intimate how such alternatives may play themselves out in a polyvocality that opens possibilities otherwise largely suppressed in the context of Bemun's celebration. In this case, one woman imaginatively made room for herself alongside and in relation to the most important emblem of her community's male-dominated performance. Once the dream began to circulate, other Bemunese could comment on it as well and perhaps also reflect on the possibility of alternatives to their adat's customary male form.

If Bemun's performance can in certain respects be seen as counter-hegemonic, in the sense that it calls up and celebrates that which under Suharto's rule had increasingly become "unthinkable" (de Certeau 1988, 4), on Barakai Island itself it falls under the "official" forms of communal life (George 1996, 96). Given, moreover, the cassowary's own ambivalent status for Bemunese and the literal expulsion by the community of this Aru emblem at the end of the celebration, it would be a mistake to exaggerate the performance's oppositional possibilities vis-à-vis the nation-state. Being "official," however, the performance can provoke alternatives to itself such as that potentially implied in Abu Sabuan's dream. The fissuring along gender lines that remains implicit throughout much of Bemun's performance, surfacing only on the last day of the cassowary hunt, can become the point of departure for the imagining of alternatives to the normative, "official" form that Bemun's performance customarily takes. On the hunt's last day, the gendered split that traverses the annual performance becomes a crucial operator for transformations that are part of the ritual process when, in the context of the so-called "women's share" (B. *koderbue il gwang*), this split is explicitly brought to the fore. Once the rift between male and female, between the men's hunt and its apportioned "women's share" surfaces, it also opens a space where different, notably gendered, forms of performance might be glimpsed by Bemunese—one in which, for instance, Bemun's women could imagine a female cassowary alongside the male one claimed by their men.

Yet this kind of imaginative possibility already entailed in the performance's operation is, as Abu Sabuan's dream intimates, probably not sufficient in itself to invite the elaboration of alternatives to the community's male-dominated celebration. Instead, Abu Sabuan's dream registers how recent institutional changes in Bemun, namely, the community's conversion to Catholicism and the place opened up for women by the new religion, have allowed what is only hinted at in the performance to start to emerge. To avoid giving the wrong impression, I should em-

Women setting off to collect firewood

phasize that while Abu Sabuan's dream continued to be mentioned from time to time in Bemun, it has not provoked any gendered forms of resistance, new religious movements, or retooling by Bemunese of their cassowary celebration. Without having had any earth-shattering consequences, this dream nevertheless provides a good starting point for discussing some of the more thorny issues of gender that Bemun's annual performance brings out.

Cassowary Doubles

Like most Backshore dreams, rather than yielding a loosely threaded narrative or even a range of unrelated events, this one crystallized in a single compelling image. In the dream a kinsman of Abu Sabuan sits before the altar of Bemun's church clutching under each arm a cassowary (one male and one female) as these are baptized in what looks like an uncanny fusion of conversion and marriage, those Catholic rites most familiar to Bemunese. Although the prevailing idea in Bemun seems to be a strict avoidance of any overlap between or even convergence of adat and agama, or, somewhat differently, the Aru and the Malay, as the marked contrast onto which the former pair is annually mapped, slippages necessarily occur between the two. A good example is the discourse of sin and redemption that increasingly seems to be intruding within the space marked off as adat (chapter 6)—with, however, an important difference: "sins" of adat as opposed to the church can be redeemed at the altar of either the Prow or the Stern through payment of fixed numbers of store-bought white plates that, in turn, are reckoned in tradestore quantities. A big "sin," in other words, might demand a payment of up to a dozen plates (Spyer 1996b).[1]

If notwithstanding the overt antipathy between adat and agama, a process of mutual borrowing and mimicry is occurring between them, the cassowary himself also, postconversion, appears less scrupulously assigned to a given place. Increasingly, he seems to serve as a kind of shifter, undergoing his own successive conversions across Aru, adat, and agama. The emergence of this pattern is not altogether surprising. With caution, some Bemunese referred to the cassowary celebration as their own agama, while the Aru spirit's annual reception into the community—beckoned forth from the forested interiors of Barakai that are associated with Bemun's past and the backwardness that government propaganda identifies with its former "forest" and nonsedentary existence (see also Tsing 1993)—can easily be construed as a conversion. So, too, the bath taken by Bemunese at the conclusion of their annual performance works much as a baptism back into their ordinary, everyday lives, an association that women and men themselves at times make when recalling their own and especially the cassowary's conversion.[2]

Even more important, however, than these enabling equivalences that construct and define the cassowary's promiscuous religiosity is, I believe, the extent of mission intervention in codifying a particular parallelism and even cooperation between agama and adat. Continually reiterated by schoolteachers, catechists, visiting church personnel, and more and more by Aruese themselves was not only the importance of adat but its equal, albeit different, place alongside agama in community affairs. For instance, the Keiese catechist who was also one of Bemun's schoolteachers always insisted to Backshore women and men as well as in private to me that adat and agama necessarily go hand in hand, that they mutually support each other and fulfill different but complementary functions—invoking, in short, the kind of language that one would more readily apply to a couple. During a conversation on one of my periodic visits to Ambon, the Dutch bishop himself emphasized the critical and beneficial role of adat in maintaining traditional social structures and kin relations. Similarly, several villagers remembered on separate occasions how their all-time favorite priest had assured them that Bemun could never "cast off" its adat, which they, at any rate, took to mean their annual cassowary celebration. If other Bemunese recalled a sermon given by another Dutch priest in which he cast the cassowary as a mere bird that once dead was very much and truly dead, mission correspondence shows evidence of a more generally concerted effort to use adat in the process of evangelization by setting it by agama's side. This strategy is most apparent when a couple is married in succession according to adat (I. *nikah adat*) and agama (I. *nikah agama*) procedures. The parallel between adat and agama is also prefigured in the other church rite with which Bemunese are most familiar and that figured in Abu Sabuan's dream: Once baptized, an Aruese assumes in addition to her "Aru" name (B. *ngaran gwerka*) a "Catholic" one (B. *ngaran katolik*) as well.[3]

In Bemun the relations between adat and agama, cassowary and Catholicism, are very much in flux and subject to intense negotiation. Within this flux, however, what seemed most salient when I was in Aru was less the substitution by which agama comes to replace adat or, more commonly, something construed as the "old" religion,[4] though the demarcation of a "before" and an "after" was certainly effective in some rhetorical contexts, than the construction of a copresence—sometimes amiable, other times uneasy—of agama and adat. Abu Sabuan's dream imaginatively conjures just such a copresence in the church union of a couple, both cassowary and Catholic, under the protective guidance of a kinsman who like herself belongs to the Sister's Children. An implicit marriage of adat and agama, the dream also envisages a cassowary double, a female mate for the community bird, which in marked contrast to the male-centered annual performance puts in an appearance within the novel setting provided by the Catholic church. Bringing in religion, in other words, is a way of introducing women into the picture, although it also means setting agama and adat on intimate terms side by side. If this juxtaposition underwrites the official church position on the relation between the two as well as on marriage, the presence of Abu Sabuan's kinsman rather than herself as ritual officiant in the dream also suggests that the imagination of an alternative to Bemun's performance can only take place within the largely male domain that this performance institutes. While in no way radical, then, the envisioning of a cassowary double besides the one claimed by Bemunese men makes, nevertheless, as any other repetition, a difference (Derrida 1982, 1988).

To be sure, with respect to agama, Bemunese women tend to play a relatively greater role in the new religion than their men, if only because, unlike the majority of their spouses, fathers, and brothers, they, on the whole, more regularly attend church services. Partly, this is pure coincidence insofar as mothers with school-age children commonly accompany them to Sunday services that they are obliged by their teacher to attend. Except for Keiese married to Bemunese women, most men maintain a wary and skeptical attitude toward the church, though many, certainly not all, will attend services on the major holidays or when the priest from Dobo makes a rare appearance to perform baptisms, marriages, and mass. The fact that Abu Sabuan's husband is from Kei and is also a member of Bemun's church council probably helps to explain why she rather than another Bemunese woman had this particular dream. Still, in general, much more than men, though not necessarily out of religious persuasion, Bemunese women appear to have taken a few of the church's lessons to heart, especially those regarding the importance of wearing proper Malay clothes. This perspective, in turn, seems to have had repercussions on how women regard aspects of their community's celebration. Mission influence helps explain, for instance, why the formerly cogendered fish poisoning is today predominantly a male rite, since in its context only loincloths may be worn, which, in turn, discourages women's participation.

As a counter to their relative exclusion from the Aru in the context of the annual celebration, another example of women's positive appropriation of the Malay manifests itself in the striking denouement of the entire performance, when, according to the women—in a final fleeting moment with overtones of a ritual reversal—it is the men's turn to be embarrassed by their clothes (see below). It is also worth noting that, on the concluding night of the cassowary part of the performance, women

encouraged each other (and enjoined me) to change their fancy dress
sarongs no fewer than three times during the course of the all-night
celebration. Following this practice, a new sarong should be donned at
the onset of the evening, another around midnight, and a third several
hours before daybreak. No one could really give me an explanation for
this practice—it was just one of those things that Gita and the other
women who helped me select my three sarongs for the last night of
dancing said had always been that way. I can only therefore speculate that
one important effect of this practice would be to draw attention to the
crucial role of cloth and especially its beauty when worn by fully arrayed
and decorated women. Seen in this light, it is as if, by repeatedly announcing their special claim to cloth and embodying its sensuous appeal, women would counter the men's hold on adat by unsettling it with
the desire that on Barakai imbues the Malay. The fact that the sarong
switching only occurs on the final night of the performance, when—
following the villagers' washing of their hands and the opening of Bemun to spectators from the neighboring villages—the Malay, as it were,
has begun to be invited back in, seems to confirm the special link between women and the Malay that on other occasions is paradigmatically
conveyed by clothes—for instance, in Abu Sabuan's sejara of the great
ship or in the annual preformance's amazing conclusion (to be discussed
below). The repeated changing of new clothes also probably says something about these women's experience of the market, of fashion, and of
the commodity circulation that Barakai islanders commonly identify
with the Malay.

Admittedly, Bemun's male-dominated cassowary portion of the performance does not exclude women altogether. What is more, women
never complained to me or otherwise suggested that they were unhappy
with the part they played in their community's annual celebration. To be
sure, in certain circumstances, the exclusion of women is marked, such
as on the three occasions on which the men gather to "speak" and
thereby organize the activities that summon the cassowary to Bemun.
The hunt of the cassowary itself and the wearing of the spirit's effigy at
night is similarly limited to men. At other times, what is banished from
the space of the performance are not Bemun's women but rather specific
qualities that are identified as female as well as, often in this context,
Malay (Strathern 1984). Women can, for instance, take part in the fish

poisoning, while some Bemunese even claimed that their participation would increase the catch. At the same time, this same performance imposes the ban of the sea, which entails the exclusion of, in this context, a female-marked ocean along with its trade products.

As noted in the previous chapter, a special effort is made on the last day of the cassowary part of the performance to bring women into closer association with the Aru spirit so that they, along with their men, will partake more fully of the grief and killing that sends the cassowary into exile. Although in 1986 as well as 1987 it seemed to occur with little zest and almost as an afterthought on the final afternoon of the hunt, the so-called "women's share" is actually crucial to the reinstatement of regular gender and exchange relations and to the reintegration of the hunters back into the community. Abu Sabuan's dream suggests, however, that the performance's official allotment of a "women's share"—carried out in fact by men in the name of Bemunese women—does not dispel the desire at least some women have of imagining for themselves a more female-friendly spirit, however circumscribed by the official forms of church and custom it might ultimately be.

Beyond the aim of generalizing the procedures and operations that send the Aru spirit into exile more evenly across the community, the ritual requirement of a distinct "women's share" within the otherwise generally unmarked male celebration can be understood as an effect of the fissured space of the performance. From the moment that the ban of the sea implicitly excludes, under the rubric of the Malay, signs of female wealth and power, and even more, once the hunt begins, a radical rift runs as an undercurrent through the performance, marking off separate, differently valued male and female domains that exist in fraught tension with each other. At times this undercurrent surfaces, as when women are blamed for things that go wrong in the hunt or at least are not optimal— often this idea is stated euphemistically, along the lines of "the observations of the performances' bans and prohibitions back in the village [read women] are bad, and therefore the men have killed few game." In addition to its status as a mortuary ground, this radical agonistic gendering is another aspect of the annual performance that hints that the space-time of the cassowary can have no existence beyond the celebration itself insofar as the world that the performance conjures is for all practical purposes an untenable one. More concretely, it is a world where the dead reign supreme and, with the exclusion or suppression of alterity, the very possibility of exchange and therein reproduction is also denied.

Wild Boars and Wallabies

Probably the most striking example of the structural agonism that at a low level permeates the performance is the contrast between qualities identified in its context as respectively male and female—how, specifically, the body parts and traits ascribed by Bemunese to wild boars versus wallabies are manipulated to highlight the alleged differences between distinct forms of gendered existence and, by extension, certain male and female qualities. Elaborated to ultimate extremes, no middle ground conjoins the aggressive and potentially destructive "maleness" of the wild boar with the mild "female" reproductivity associated in this context with the wallaby. Gender becomes a crucial operator for constructing differences throughout the performance—most notably, that between the Aru and the Malay—as well as, importantly, for intimating that a world in which difference is suppressed, exchange obliterated, and alterity denied is necessarily unviable, sterile, and synonymous with death.

If I had not myself already been struck by the strange manner in which the hunters' envoys carried wallabies (a sort of miniature kangaroo) into the enclosure at the Front of the Path, the numerous comments of Bemunese themselves on the unusual mode of the adolescents' carrying and the verb they used to describe it would have alerted me to something out of the ordinary. In marked contrast to all other game, which is transported from the forest on a pole borne on the shoulders of two men, wallabies dangle from rattan headstraps down the backs of the hunters' adolescent envoys. Unlike women, men never carry loads on their heads or in headstrap baskets, and, indeed, women and men alike repeatedly stressed the female manner of bringing the wallabies back to Bemun. Not only did women and men point out the parallel between the envoys with their wallabies (usual several at a time bouncing lightly on the back of the boys) and women bent under the burden of the headstrap baskets (B. *dian*) that they use daily to carry all manner of things from garden produce and firewood to trepang and fish, but many also noted that the word used to describe the hunters' action otherwise applies exclusively to women carrying their baskets. It is worth noting that this particular "female" task is left to adolescent boys, who themselves would not yet wear the cassowary effigy since, being young and unmarried, they are not regarded as fully male. Recall also that these same adolescents first voice a preference regarding the length of the cassowary hunt (in the case of a "small" performance) when the men gather to "speak" for the first out of three times and that in that context, it is precisely their marginal low status that allows them to occupy center stage (chapter 5).

Beyond the productive capacities of women, the overdetermined relationship set up in the performance among women, wallabies, and baskets may also index the transactions mediated by these same female baskets in the context of the bridewealth exchange that on Barakai accompanies marriage. A portion of the bridewealth that is meant specifically for the bride's mother is brought to her by the wifetakers in one of these female baskets. The crockery and cloth that the basket contains are regarded as a compensation for this woman's reproductive and nurturing role and are therefore named for the "mother's milk" with which many years before she had nursed the bride. To elicit a satisfactory payment, a woman will often elaborate on the suffering and many sacrifices that she has made as a mother. Especially if she is dissatisfied with the "mother's milk" or other related payments, a bride's mother, backed by her kin, can dwell at length on the many nights she lay awake breast-feeding her child, on the multiple times she wiped away its feces and urine, and on the many other trials of motherhood (Spyer 1992, 219–50).

If I am not entirely off the mark, the headstrap basket or the carrying of wallabies that in the context of the hunt brings it to mind indexes, therefore, not a generic femaleness but more precisely motherhood and the nurturing, caring qualities associated with it. One could further speculate that the same characteristic is already pronounced in the physiognomy of the wallaby itself—through the striking feature of the pouch in which the female of the species carries and nurtures its offspring—and that this characteristic motivates the animal's selection for symbolic elaboration here. Seen in this light, the wallaby would itself be a kind of female basket as well as a basket meant to contain life. Carrying wallabies in the manner of a female basket suggests, in short, a critical redundancy that compellingly establishes a resonance between these animals and the reproductive powers specific to women.

Poised in obvious tension with the rather innocuous and fertile mildness evoked in the performance by the wallaby, the wild boar suggests all that is potentially threatening and disruptive of it. As the most aggressive animal inhabiting Barakai's forests, the wild boar crystallizes in the performance both the potential wildness that resides in man himself—here exemplified by the hunters—as well as the more diffuse dangers that on Barakai are held to undermine normative human sociality. The Stern's identification of a boar's tail with the headman's transgressive intervention in what the former called a "ritual without an ending" supports this interpretation (chapter 5). When older Barakai men spoke to me of the wild boar and its dangers, several recalled a special type of hunt that was sometimes held in the past at the death of a bachelor. Although never explicitly spelled out, it was clear from the examples given that such a hunt was only held in the case of bachelors who had suffered unexpected and especially violent deaths, as in the example given by Abu Sijor of a young man who was devoured by a crocodile. The purpose of the communal hunt was to divine the cause of the man's death and, having done so, to neutralize its consequences for the wider community. I was told that, following a procedure called "to make [the cause] sit on the wild boar," the men would make an offering of betel, accompanied by the postulation of a cause for the bachelor's death, before embarking on the hunt. Once killed, the wild boar was brought back to the village, where it was mourned as a human in order to expiate the wrongdoing that had been divined as the cause of the young man's brutal death along with its possible consequences for his fellow villagers. When I asked about the kinds of misdeeds that would result in violent deaths, the men singled out the uncontrolled behavior of bachelors and the kinds of aggressive acts some men committed while away from their home village, especially those directed against women like rape.

Juxtaposed with the fertile reproductivity of wallabies, such behavior—insofar as it allows Bemunese to extrapolate from men to wild boars—highlights the opposition at work in the performance between women, whose activity is restricted to the village and, to a certain extent, even their homes, and men, who identify closely with the Barakai forest and are also identified by others with it while the hunt is in progress. If the Stern's nibbling on the tip of a wallaby's tail at the end of each day's hunt releases the men so that they can bring home the singed flesh of game animals to their wives and mothers, who cook them in earthenware vessels named "the cooking pots of male and female loincloths," the final act of the cassowary part of the performance occurs when the Stern shoots those boars' tails accumulated during the hunt in a westward direction away from Barakai (chapter 5). And if the first act highlights the nurturing role of women and is part of the process through which the community refashions itself in the image of ancestors who wore loincloths, the second evokes the link between men and wild boars and is intended to dispatch any remaining "heaviness" far from Bemun. The latter act also intimates that the savage wildness associated with hunters at this time of year is—like that of the cassowary—not without ambivalence. This impression is also supported by what happens on the day immediately following the end of the cassowary hunt, when an opportunity is given to any man who still feels inclined to do so to continue to hunt. The implication of this activity, known as "the remainders" or "carrying away the boar's threats," as it was explained to me, is double: on the one hand, it rids the village of any lingering dangers unleashed by the performance; on the other, it gives especially the younger, more energetic of the hunters a chance to purge themselves of any excessive wildness they may still harbor as a result of their participation in it.

Put otherwise, the salutary effects for the community of the hunters' actions along with the healing powers of the cassowary, as the figure that both incorporates and scatters grief and mourning *and* carries it away, are not without their raw, unpredictable, and animalistic or alien otherness. Drawing on Bernheimer's discussion of the wild men and women of the Middle Ages, Taussig argues that wildness can never be fit fully within the domesticating grids of order but must retain its productive, creative difference. "If wildness per se is not credited with its own force, reality, and autonomy, then it cannot function as a handmaiden to order" (Taussig 1987, 220). Not unlike the cassowary, as Taussig further writes, the wild men of the Middle Ages necessarily "not only bear the burden of society's antiself, they also absorb with their wet, shaggy coats the best that binary oppositions can deliver—order and chaos, civilized and barbaric, Christian and pagan, and emerge on the side of the grotesque and the destructive" (ibid.). Unlike the cassowary, however, who by grabbing his own excrement, as the song reports, reveals the unruly, barbaric, and grotesque dimension of his persona (Comaroff and Comaroff 1992, 78; Stallybrass and White 1986, 108–9), the hunters by way of an implicit, if ambivalent, act of violence against the community's women come down not on the side of the forest but rather on that of order, pencarian, and the Malay.

"They hit and break the women's water jugs," another way of describing "the women's share," identifies the moment of the hunters' final reentry into Bemun at the conclusion of the cassowary part of the annual performance as an act of violence directed against these female womb-like objects (see below). Because it dispels the charged "heat" that hovers over the performance and accounts for some of its creative power, this final women's share in the hunt is also described as a process of "cooling" with overtones of birth. If in the first description the men are the agents who via an act of violence directed against the "female" return to Bemun, in the second this "female" is itself the vehicle for the hunters' reentry in a process analogous to birth.

The Women's Share

Here it is necessary to backtrack a bit in my narrative of Bemun's annual performance and consider more closely what happens on the final day of the hunt. At this time, the last night of the performance and all it involves has still to take place. Recall for the moment that on this last night for the third and last time (in the case of the "small" performances held in 1986 and 1987) a palm frond cassowary is made and paraded around the village, the final rite of mourning is accomplished for all Bemunese who have died during the past year, and the cassowary is killed for the last time and exiled from Bemun until the following year.

On the last day of the hunt, the men of Bemun "walked twice," departing in the morning for the forest in the same way as they had on the preceding days and then in the afternoon returning again to hunt the so-called "women's share." In contrast to the preceding days, the hunters returned to the village shortly after midday as opposed to the late afternoon. Most of them left their spears propped against a tree immediately outside the enclosure at the Front of the Path as they watched the game they had killed that morning being singed on the assemblage of stakes. After a brief rest in their homes, the hunters together with all the remaining men in the community—from newborns cradled in their fathers' arms to the very elderly—crowded into the Stern's house, where this official had already readied a large earthenware vessel filled to the brim with water. In an act that has its analogues throughout the performance, the Stern washed his hands first (B. *Belamur aur lim nal mon*), thereby signaling the end for all male villagers of the prohibition on "touching water" as applied to the hands. Initiating the general cool-down that begins midday on the last day of the hunt and ends after dawn on the following morning, all the men washed, or in the case of infants and small boys had their hands washed, in the Stern's vessel.

While women, following the lead of the Stern's wife, wash their hands later in the day after the "women's share," and all villagers only bathe fully the following morning, the ritual cleansing of hands begins the process of renewal through which the community attempts to ensure itself an abundant pencarian and, more generally, a good, harmonious, and prosperous year ahead. Presumably this process begins with the hands because they are the part of a person's body that in public exchange settings becomes commemorated in the contributions she makes as her "portion/share of the hand" (B. *ken lim gwang*). As such, the hand on Barakai is also metonymic of a particular form of sociality. By the same token, the refusal of the sociality that binds persons and fam to each other and to the neighboring communities in exchange appears to concentrate in the residue of filth and impurities that runs off of Bemunese hands into the Stern's wide-rimmed vessel. That the murky water remaining after the cleansing of multiple hands seems to condense for Bemunese the negation of the sociality that is objectified in exchange as "the hand's share" is clear from the nefarious uses to which it is potentially put. Together with that left from the women's cleansing of their hands, the negatively charged water from the men is poured out by the Stern onto the charcoaled remains of the fire built in the men's enclosure at the Front of the Path. Imbued with the cumulative "heaviness" collected from all these hands, this privileged site of the performance's sanctions and dangers is symbolically speaking "hotter" and more negatively potent than before. As a result, the period beginning with the ablution of this charged water onto this site until the distribution of white plates at named land and sea places is the prime time for engaging in antisocial acts of sorcery at this spot.

Before the men could depart to carry out the "women's share," the hunt held on behalf of the community as a whole had first to be brought to a close. As part of this process, once the men had all washed their hands, the men, women and children of Bemun gathered at the enclosure to rid themselves of the "heaviness"—the entire baggage of sickness, inauspiciousness, as well as what increasingly is glossed by the Indonesian word for "sin"—that had accumulated on their persons and burdened the life of the community over the course of the year. While the hunters retrieved their spears and waited at the outskirts of the enclosure, the women and children—including many palm-frond gatherers and in both 1986 and 1987 one of the tradeswomen with her two small sons—decked out in some of their nicest Aru clothes (with the exception of the tradeswoman and her sons) gathered on top of a small incline at a distance from but with a clear view of the goings-on in the enclosure below. Several women reminded me that we had to take care to stand out of the direction of the wind in order to avoid accidentally catching any cast-off heaviness with our bodies.

To mark an ending—and one that in this setting always already prefigures a beginning—the Stern again acted first, laying his spear at the base of the sapling planted by his counterpart the Prow on the opening morning of the hunt. Silently, all the hunters followed suit, beginning with the Stern and ending with the Prow, one by one and in the reverse order of the boat formation laying their spears on the pile under the tree. After crowning the pile with his bow and arrows, the Prow invoked the spirits with an offering of betel and then, turning again to the pile, retrieved his bow and arrows and assumed position at the head of a new boat formation. Following his example, the hunters once again by turn entered the enclosure, carefully sought out their respective spears, and again took up places in the new boat gradually taking shape behind the Prow. The men took great care to select the right spear, since in the context of the performance this instrument of violence is regarded as the seat of a man's "life breath" (B. *erin gwagorun*). As such, it assumes a significance for men that is analogous to the "cooking pot of men's and women's loincloths" for women.

The preparation of food by women during the annual performance in the "cooking pot of men's and women's loincloths," which takes place when a couple establishes their own household after marriage, is a rite of passage fraught with potential danger. Women must take particular care to prevent the water from boiling over and the meat and sago pudding from sticking to the bottom of the pot. Should these things occur, many Bemunese claimed that death would follow for the cook or members of her family, just as some mishap with a man's spear would represent a disaster for the hunter and his family. Relatedly, young women are warned on Barakai against eating the tasty rice crust that often forms on the bottom of pans, since it is believed that doing so can trigger a miscarriage by causing the placenta to adhere to the side of the womb. When a young woman's cooking pot shattered during an argument of a couple from Longgar who were staying with her while participating in Bemun's performance, many in Bemun claimed that an especially large payment would have to be made on her behalf by both adat officials. When I questioned the Stern about the incident, he seemed unwilling to take on the task—the only time I ever saw him refuse a request—since he believed it was destined to fail. In another example, a woman from Kei married in Bemun readied her earthenware pot for the cassowary celebration. At the last moment she had a change of heart and, opting out of the 1987 performance, left on a trader's boat for Dobo. Abu Meme voiced her concern to me that this women had left Bemun so late, after the fish poisoning had already been held although the hunt had not begun. To make matters worse, the woman had clearly indicated her intention to participate by readying the object most intimately identified at this time with herself and her family. Note that the difference between the male spear as an instrument of violence and aggression and the cooking pot of men's and women's loincloths as a female container associated with reproduction sets up a contrast of male and female qualities similar to those linked to, respectively, the wild boar and the wallaby.

To return now to the hunters and their spears, when the Stern closed in at the end of the line, completing the men's boat formation, Bemun's women and children stood at attention on the hill overlooking the enclosure, awaiting the sign to brush off their "heaviness." After a brief pause, a slight tapping, which rapidly grew louder, began to be heard as it traveled down the formation of hunters. With sticks held in their right hands the men beat rhythmically against the spears shouldered on their left, while the women and children brushed off the "heaviness" that had collected on their bodies throughout the year with rapid, repetitive movements, all the while crying out, "Carry away the heaviness!" Once the drumming had traveled the length of the line and the women and childen had had an opportunity to cast off their heaviness, it ceased abruptly. Without delay, the hunters cast the wooden sticks far to their left, which is also the west, the direction taken by the dead, as well as the space into which the Stern shoots a last arrow bearing the boars' tails of the year's hunt in a final attempt to send any remaining "heaviness" far from Bemun.

In reversing and then reconstituting the formation of hunters composing Bemun's ancestral boat, the community acts to leave suffering, sickness, misfortune, and all-around "heaviness" in its wake as it enters the Barakai new year. It is, significantly, in the name of women that the community charts a new beginning that villagers hope will bring health, abundance, and well-being to Bemun. As both an ending and a beginning, the "women's share" manifests a curious ambiguity. It seemed to occur almost as an afterthought, tacked on at the last moment to the more serious and productive hunt of the men. Since it is held in the immediate vicinity of Bemun, there is little expectation that the "women's share" will bring in much game, which may in part account for why the men seemed to set off on this last hunt with so little enthusiasm. Although both the Prow and the Stern told me that they always request the gift of a specific animal such as a pig from the ancestors to make up the "women's share," they also claimed that they always set aside one or more animals from the morning's hunt to fulfill this function should their request not be granted.

For many of Bemun's women (and children), in contrast to the men, the proximity of the "women's share" lent an immediacy and drama to the hunt held in their name from which they had until this moment been otherwise largely excluded. During the preceding days, the hunt had also been foremost on many women's minds as they watched apprehensively for signs of the proceedings going on in the forest, assessed the amount and variety of game deposited by the hunters' envoys in the enclosure, or scanned the skies for the plumes of smoke created by the men's fires in the Barakai interior. Rising over the forest like a banner waving on a staff, this token of the men's efforts toward pencarian is named for the white flag of the Sea House of the Land and evokes therewith the underwater storehouse of oysters and, by extension, the abundance of trade products that the villagers in celebrating the cassowary hoped to bring about. Sometimes when a woman spotted the smoke, she would exclaim, "There's the flag—its rising!" collapsing with this phrase the creative actions of the ancestors' sowing of the oyster beds under the sea—as graphically described by Abu Sabuan—into those of the hunters on land. Yet notwithstanding the eager attentiveness with which most women tracked the daily progress of the hunt, the part named for them was commonly the only time in which women got a taste of the action, as flames and smoke formed a hazy backdrop behind the village and the blaze of the fire, the barking of dogs, and the smothered cries of stricken animals invaded the quiet that had previously prevailed in Bemun.

Capturing both this violence and the idea of a beginning mediated by women, Bemunese also frequently described this marked portion of the hunt as "they hit and break the women's water jugs," as noted above. Several people claimed that the sharp, crackling sound of burning elephant grass immediately beyond the village echoes the shattering of earthenware pottery, which they said explained this alternative designation for the "women's share." Yet this way of referring to it also brings to mind a common trope in tales of extraordinary Aruese, who are often held to have emerged into the world out of a variety of female-marked containers. One such story, for instance, revolves around the exploits of a woman named Sugarcane Offal, who was born from the combination of an aborted fetus and bits of sugarcane concealed together in a water jug. The image of shattering the women's water jugs also recalls—at the same time that it undoes—the first and only act undertaken by women belonging to the group known as the Sister's Children during the cassowary part of the celebration: that of filling two momosim earthenware water jugs and placing them in front of the Stern's house, where they remain for the duration of the performance. Often, during the nightly dancing, people would deliberately refresh themselves with a draft from this water, because it was felt to have special life-enhancing properties.

It can therefore be argued that the very same action that, as an implicit process of cooling with overtones of birth,[5] serves to reintegrate the hunters into the community also brings the more limited performance of the women full circle. The act of these women in placing their jugs in front of the Stern's home already prefigured this circularity. At the same time, however, since the "women's share" enjoys the ambiguity of both a closure and the beginning to a new year, the hunters' final return to the village is left open-ended. Throughout the afternoon and in no particular order, in groups and singly, the men returned back to Bemun, thus bringing the "women's share" to an ambiguous close. Before confronting the celebration's striking denouement, five days following the cassowary's killing at dawn of the final night of festivities, I turn to the scattering of white plates and the feeding of the mooring post that anchors the Sea House of the Land in the conclusion to Bemun's annual performance.

Of Shares

Early in the morning of the fifth day after the cassowary had been killed, once a requisite of four days had passed, a shiny mass of dozens and dozens of new store-bought white plates spread itself out from the approximate spot where the Prow had first built the momosim fire on the performance's opening night. Recall that this was also the spot where the men and adolescent boys of Bemun had gathered three times to "speak" and, in so doing, had orchestrated the cassowary's arrival. Since the undifferentiated mass of white plates seemed to appear almost magically of its own accord in the center of the village, everything happened as if the actions that the men first set into motion with their speech had had their intended effect—resulting in a surplus of trade products. It was as if the violence of the cassowary's killing and the drama of the Aru's exclusion had allowed these privileged tokens of the Malay to sprout spontaneously in the center of the village, thus concretizing the very telos of trade in the community's midst and confirming the cassowary's role as pencarian's "root." As the stand-in tokens of a bountiful harvest, the plates amassed at the center of Bemun evoke the pearl oysters that their subsequent distribution at named land and sea places are also held to provoke.

This impression is, I believe, not far off the mark. Although the plates represented the contributions of individual men and women from different Bemunese households—as well as of the traders, who also added their contribution to the communal pile—they had ideally been deposited by individual men unseen by others and with as much secrecy as possible in the dead of the previous night. Men claimed that their chances of meeting up with spirits and thereby enhancing their individual luck in pencarian would be greatly augmented if they did not encounter their fellow divers when adding their own household's contribution to the pile. That the Prow should have placed his offering of plates first—accompanied by his usual entourage of spirits—suggests, once again, the fusion and mutual mirroring of actions undertaken by Bemunese and the spirits at this time of year. Another crucial unseen ingredient in these transactions were the traders themselves, who for the explicit purpose of this part of the performance commonly put in an ample supply of preferably pure white plates the sale of which opens for them the new season.

Most Bemunese described the plates as "payments" for the trade products of the upcoming season. Concretizing the surplus of oysters and other produce that, in the upcoming trade season, Bemunese hoped to find and turn in to their traders in Barakai stores, the plates are in effect the image of what they are supposed to bring about. Note, however, that although Bemunese tended to speak of the pile of plates as a down payment for the upcoming harvest of "produce" and aimed through their annual distribution to oblige the spirit providers of oysters to themselves, the plates can also be seen as the material witnesses to the affirmation of the debt bonds with which, through their purchase at the store, most Bemunese had opened the new season for themselves. Between, in other words, the surplus of new, shiny plates at the center of village space and the outlines of potential future oysters traced by spectral fingers in the Barakai sea floor—the first, a retrospective image of things that might be and the second, a shadow of possible "produce" to come—lies the entire complex of pencarian: the claims of Bemun to specific diving grounds and areas of collection; the sejara-riddled landscape of the island that supports and legitimates the ambitions of men and women, fam, and the Bemun community; the figures and imaginings that compel and clothe trade in familiar guises; the gendered structures of debt and transaction; and the stories, gossip, and speculation that shape the shifting and often erratic contours of trade on Aru's Backshore.

Although there seemed to exist a general belief among Bemunese that the more contributions made by individual villagers to the pile, the better the upcoming pencarian of the community as a whole, the contributions of men, like those of women, were made especially with an eye toward their own individual pencarian. At the same time, the point of collectively amassing the canonical tokens of trade was also to redistribute them among the different land and sea places representing important communal and group claims. Again, as in the case of the other performative contexts restricted to men, I was unable to join in the gathering at the center of the village whose task it was to divide the pool of plates into distinct "shares" (B. *ken gwang*) destined for named land and sea places. I was told that the plates were simply divided, more or less evenly, among these various places.

The land and sea places that received offerings appeared to fall into three groups, which also to a certain extent overlapped. The first were places for communal offerings held by either the Prow or the Stern. Several of these offerings were at places pertaining directly to Bemun's annual celebration, for instance, the offerings made by the Prow at the enclosure at the Front of the Path as well as those destined for the named site in the forest "where plates rest," which is also a resting place for the hunters during the annual celebration. The two officials also received new plates for their respective altars and for the two trees in the village that are associated with their offices. The second group of plates comprised those places that, although often of general importance to the community as a whole, were paradigmatically linked to the sejara of different fam in Bemun. These places included the ancestral village of Wanusumor, which is held by the fam Jonjonler and also associated with its renowned ancestral war leader Gwadaur; the former residence site of another fam on the far west side of Barakai, Gwalti; and Kolmes, held by yet another Bemunese fam and the site of a small offering house with a black flag near the estuary where the fish poisoning is held. The third group of plates related more directly to the community's pencarian and to the places with which this activity is associated, such as Gogor, a site on the island of Koltoba to the southeast of Bemun. As a whole, Koltoba evokes Barakai's privileged form of livelihood, and many important diving areas are located in the seas around it. And, finally, the diving ground known as "the mouth of Bemun's deep" (B. *Bemun gwalor weo*) received a quota of plates that were cast into the sea by a man belonging to the Sister's Children. In sum, all of the above sites are claimed by the community or its component social groups and are crucial to Bemun's internal constitution and its political position on Barakai as legitimated and produced in the telling of sejara and through the community's annual performance. As the means through which Bemun periodically renews and marks its claims to different land and sea places, the store-bought white plates materially inscribe the telos of trade onto the Barakai landscape and in principle render the sejara that the community and its members compose for themselves visible to their neighbors, to potential trespassers on their diving grounds, and to others who traffic in the Malay. If the cassowary, as the "source" or "root" of pencarian and thus also of Bemun's ambivalent position vis-à-vis the Malay, remains unseen and hedged by silence once trading begins, the plates as privileged tokens of the desires, hopes, and expectations with which Bemunese invest their pencarian are released at the end of their annual performance to circulate within a larger Malay world.

During the distribution of plates with which the men busied themselves on the fifth morning following the cassowary's violent exile, women belonging to the Sister's Children as well as women married to men of this group gathered in the kitchen at the rear of the Prow's house to prepare the food of the mooring post of the Sea House of the Land.[6] Because the food consumed by men at the post represents a meal offered to them by the female spirit occupant of the Sea House of the Land, its preparation is carried out according to specific procedures, with great care, and by a senior woman from the Sister's Children who holds this special office. Along with this woman, all the other Sister's Children who assisted her with advice on the appearance of the meal and the arrangement of the packets of food that the men would consume at the post wore sarongs and removed their sandals before entering the Prow's house. Donning the dress of their ancestors, they resembled their men, who congregated bare-chested at the center of Bemun to divide the accumulated mass of plates into named "shares." The food prepared for the post in the Prow's home was marked as belonging to an Aru past, while the only cooking implement used—a mold with five slots for baking sago cakes—was earthenware and of a type of considerable date in these islands.[7] Indeed, none other than Wallace himself provides a short description of the baking process as well as a drawing of these "clay ovens" (1962 [1869], 135).

Once the men had divided the communal pool of plates into the "shares" of different places and the women had finished preparing the

Plate distribution

mooring post's food, the cassowary's master and three other men from
the Sister's Children came to the Prow's house to collect the packages the
women had made. In the two years that I took part in the performance,
the cassowary's master always carried the small betel basket belonging
to the Prow, since it was his task to communicate with the female spirit of
the Sea House of the Land during the mooring post's feeding. The other
three men each took up one of the remaining articles—the basket of sago
cakes, the bananas, and the water jug and tin cup—and descended to the
beach to join the group of men awaiting them there with the offerings of
plates and a bolt of white cloth of a single long piece (B. *gom ka ejun*).

The Ship of Memory

In both 1986 and 1987, about forty men crowded into the belan belonging
to one of the fam that is considered a first resident in Bemun and falls
therefore within the group of the Sister's Children, and set off under sail
for the post. Just as the men who embarked on this trip wore the loincloths of their ancestors, so too was the belan itself made to conform to
the requirements of an imagined Aru past. Several features qualified the

belan as distinctively Aruese and therefore in this setting momosim; these included an "Aru sail" woven from pandanus leaves (B. *lar gwerka*), eight "Aru oars" with distinctive round blades (B. *waun gwerka*), and a deck covering of conjoined wooden slats that were meant to evoke the floorboards of a house. Importantly, it is forbidden to refer to the belan as such, that is, by the usual term for this boat type. In the context of the plate distribution, the boat is instead designated by the Indonesian word for "ship," or *kapal*. A number of people insisted that the term *kapal* rather than *belan* applies in this setting because the vessel recalls the houseboat that variously drifted and was rowed to Barakai by some Bemunese ancestors from the faraway island of Luang in the southwest Moluccas.

Most Bemunese commonly distinguished two such houseboats that in the wake of Luang's mythic shattering brought their ancestors to Barakai via the islands of Karang and Enu in southern Aru—one of these, the Sea House of the Land, sank immediately offshore of Barakai, where the ancestors moored it to a post—while the other—simply the Sea House— remained unmoored and continues to move about in the seas around the island, where it is sometimes heard by divers when it whishes by them. While the mooring post of the Sea House of the Land marks for Bemunese a submerged, enabling underside to pencarian as their chosen way of life—hence the community's concern about the post's recent instability—the Sea House proper is a space of death and total disloca- tion. In contrast to the other house, held in place by its mooring post, the latter is known only through its restless circulation and marks a void into which divers can disappear.

While during the performance women and men often referred to the belan that carried the men with their plates to the post simply as "the ship," just as often, it seemed, they called it "memory" (I. *kenangan*) or even "the ship of memory" (I. *kapal kenangan*), using a Barakai deriva- tive of the Indonesian word for memory, *kenangan*.[8] When I asked for an explanation of this name, several people explained that the belan used in the plate scattering had originally been bought with the help of the Dobo tradestore "Kenangan" and that the store's name had somehow stuck for the boat. Most other Bemunese said they had no idea why the vessel bore the name "Memory Ship." Outside of the plate distribution, I always heard this boat referred to by the name of the fam to which it belonged.

Whether or not the belan was purchased at Dobo's "Memory" store,

Decorated belans

what is noteworthy is the obvious concern among Bemunese—already suggested by the substitution of "ship" for belan—with how the boat should most appropriately be referred to during the plate distribution and the fact that "memory" somehow seems right. There must be some compelling reason that would explain why the Indonesian or Malay word for "memory" so insistently attaches itself to the designation "ship." It is also striking that, just like the "long thoughts" that at the opening of the annual performance helped to precipitate women and men into the porous space-time of an Aru past, the "Ship of Memory," which transports them back to a Malay-marked present, similarly resists translation into the Barakai language. Like the codified Indonesian phrase used to describe the "long thoughts" that unsettled Bemunese on the eve of their cassowary celebration, the "Ship of Memory" stands out because none of its composite words derive from the indigenous language. Along with the codified "long thoughts," the Indonesian- or Malay-marked "Ship of Memory" highlights therefore what I characterized as the objectified Malay frame that enables the very emergence or, in Samuel Weber's terms (1996, 223), the taking place of the Aru as a distinct if elusive protagonist vis-à-vis the Malay (chapter 6).

As a "ship," or kapal, the Ship of Memory also recalls another ship, that of Abu Sabuan's history, which for Bemunese women and men is emblematic of everything that the Ship of Memory seems to deny—hence the adamant resistance that met my initial attempts to somehow conflate or find a correspondence between these two imaginary ships. If the great ship's fame on Barakai is especially due to its immense cargo and especially the clothes, the colonial staff of office, and the portugis civilizer it carried on board, that of the Ship of Memory lies in the crucial role it played in populating the island in a mythic, pre-pencarian past. For Bemunese women and men, moving from the world of the one ship to that of the other entails, among other things, the wearing or shedding of the clothes that would have been first obtained by their ancestors from the great sunken ship. By wearing such clothes in their day-to-day lives, Bemunese women and men inhabit a larger Malay world that they distance themselves from once a year by not wearing such clothes, by adopting the loincloths of their ancestors instead, and by bringing about through their annual performance a radical break between an "inside" Aru and an "outside" Malay. In the context of the performance, this difference emerges as an unbridgeable rift between the Aru past with its elusive cassowary emblem and a Malay present that Bemunese associate with the pressures and possibilities represented for them by trade, the Indonesian state, and the church.

If the Bemunese women and men who resisted my efforts to bring the two ships together were therefore merely reinstating a familiar and for them crucial divide, there is nonetheless a subtle and even submerged convergence between the two. Just as the great ship, narrated on Barakai by Abu Sabuan and others, announces the arrival of trade to Aru along with the pencarian that designates the place of Bemunese within it, so too the voyage made by the so-called Ship of Memory pertains to pencarian and, specifically, the propitiation of the "produce" that forms this livelihood's objective. The recognition of an overlap between the two ships discloses something else, namely, how each—memory and modernity, as it were—presupposes the other and how they are therefore inevitably entangled. Under the guise of the "civilizing" instruction of the shipmaster's son in Abu Sabuan's story, the great ship introduces the incentive to dive to Aru and with it the islanders' seasonal collection of pearl oysters. At the same time for Bemunese, every new crop of oysters depends on the annual staging of their performance, with its culmination in the cassowary's killing and the plate distribution as a propitiatory "payment" for the shells of the upcoming season. Once the plates are distributed and the mooring post fed, the difference represented by these ships' two worlds becomes part of the striking denouement to the performance that opens the Barakai new year.

Bringing the Malay Back In

As a woman, I was again not permitted to accompany the Memory Ship on its voyage to the mooring post or to join in the meal consumed by the men at this spot. According to these men, the ship followed a direct course to the mooring post of the Sea House of the Land after leaving Bemun. Once at the post, the oldest man among the Sister's Children, who also carried part of the post's food, reinforced the post together with its small offering shelf. During this reinforcement, all the Sister's Children must steady the post, which suggests that the integrity and negotiation of the distinct powers that converge on this site depend first and foremost on this group or on the qualities that they especially embody. After the cassowary's master propitiates the spirits with offerings of betel and tobacco, the Aru food prepared by women from the Sister's Children is laid out on the post's shelf. At this point, the officiant from the Sister's Children beckons all the men in the ship to gather round and partake of this Aru meal, calling out as he does, "The old woman has finished cooking, let's eat!"

The meal that is symbolically offered to the men by a female spirit, who combines the appearance of a bride with the qualities of a mother (not to mention a cook!) and who lives in a hybrid house where land and sea shade into each other, brings the powers that were exiled at the performance's opening with the ban of the sea back in. All the "female" desirability and "maternal" nurturance that marks the dependency of Barakai men and their families on the Malay converge at the mooring post that—however insecurely—anchors their pencarian and therewith the terms with which Barakai men and women engage the Malay. From this same mooring post, the men depart with the "shares" of white plates that have already been set aside in the village for the different land and sea places destined to receive them. The post therefore also symbolically anchors the circulation of trade produce and commodities that Bemunese in scattering their plates aim to set into motion. Here, too, the men divide the single piece of white cloth that for them evokes the valued mother-of-pearl into three parts: one third for the mooring post's new flag, a second for the Memory Ship's own banner, while the third piece of white cloth is torn into strips that the men tie around their wrists to protect them when they dive. Just as the post is the place where circulation begins, so, too, does the cloth of one piece divided here center and conjoin the undersea storehouse of shells, the men who dive and trade them in island stores, and the Memory Ship of the ancestors at this spot. As all the concern in Bemun about the repeated toppling of the mooring post suggests, it marks for many Bemunese a set of convergences that seem to summarize the life they gloss as pencarian and the entangled, fraught, shifting, and mutually embedded dependency of the Aru and the Malay from which this livelihood issues.

The mooring post's status as a site of convergence, where land and sea, houses and ships, trade products and commodities, divers and female spirits, and the Aru and the Malay come together and where the community's openness to its others and to the alterity excluded during the performance is negotiated and welcomed back in, is overdetermined. This status explains why those persons who officiate here and more generally throughout the annual performance are "the Sister's Children." The name evokes the unique cooperation of brothers and sisters on Barakai as the point of departure for bridewealth transactions and thus also for the circulation of persons and material wealth that marriage on the Backshore sets in motion. When it has its intended results, the deferred effect of this circulation is registered in the reproduction of social relations paradigmatically borne out by the birth of a sister's children, who bear special obligations to their mother's brothers as those who, in turn, exercise certain powers over them—notably those pertaining to their own fertility and reproduction (Spyer 1992). In addition to being physically reinforced by them, the mooring post is steadied during its reinforcement by precisely those persons whose structural position as Sister's Children anchors the relations between different fam who, being joined as wifegivers and wifetakers through marriage, are implicitly "male" and "female" vis-à-vis each other (Fox 1980; Keane 1997b; McKinnon 1991; Valeri 1980). Finally, before the men leave the post to return to Bemun, the post is additionally fortified by having "hot" masticated ginger blown onto it. As with the palm frond cassowary, this "heat" is meant to discourage people from treating the post casually or making fun of it.

Waiting in one of the houses whose rear portions overlooked the sea, I hid with other women and children, having been warned that we should not be seen by the men in the Memory Ship as it approached Bemun. All the men appeared to be standing in the ship with the Prow clearly visible at its center "beckoning" the objects of pencarian to the seas off of Bemun—especially pearl oysters but also different varieties of trepang and anything else collected for trade. Some of the places from which the women said he attempted to draw the valued produce were as close at hand as the waters in front of the other Barakai villages. The Prow's efforts to bring produce from elsewhere to his community therefore also offered a glimpse of the intervillage competition that pervades pencarian on the island and that, along with many other conflicts, triggered in the 1970s the Longgar-Bemun war. Other renowned diving communities farther away like Krei in east Trangan were also, the Stern later told me, the Prow's targets.

As the ship approached the village and headed toward the harbor, I left the house in which I had been on the lookout with other women and crowded with them and others (some fifty in all) into the Stern's home. Having anchored the belan in which they had sailed to the post in Bemun's rear harbor, the men climbed the stone steps leading up to the village in "ship" formation. Lining up for the last time between the Prow and the Stern, they carried the signs of the Memory Ship's mobility—its eight Aru oars and rudder—and jingled the little bells that on Barakai announce and summon the ancestors as they slowly made their way to the Stern's house. With the doors of Bemun's houses tightly closed and their shutters drawn, the village was silent and appeared deserted. Once the "ship" reached the house, the men carrying the rudder and oars leaned them against the front wall of the Stern's home, where they would remain for a requisite four days. Peering again through chinks in the front walls of the Stern's dwelling, we saw how they resumed their positions in the ship lineup. After only a few moments, just enough for the men to catch their breath, they all cried out, at once and exuberantly, "It's dawn!" (B. mairo!). Awaiting this cue in the Stern's house, the women inside flung open its windows and door and, facing the men, burst out laughing, thus greeting the laughs and smiles of those in the "ship." The men then rapidly dispersed.

Women's Laughter

The men's cry of dawn announced the important transition to trade and pencarian, set to begin four days later, and the opening of a brand-new Barakai year. As with other dawns and other transitions, this one also brought to light a number of striking contrasts. Most obvious among these contrasts and the one on which all the others turned was that between women and men; the contrasts drawn in the light of this Backshore "dawn" took on a markedly gendered tone. A "baptismal event" in its own right—in the sense of establishing an existential link between the act of naming and its bearers as opposed to a connection by definition that is thus context-free (Putnam in Keane 1997a, 49)—the men's proclamation of dawn had the power to summon Bemun's women before their men and to release them from the house's dark and shuttered space in which they were concealed. Yet once the women faced the men—and then only for the brief moment that is registered in a smile or a laugh—another power became visible, namely, the one embodied in the startling contrast between the clothing worn by the women and that of the men. Except for a few elderly women who always wore sarongs, all the Sister's Children who earlier that same day had prepared the mooring post's food in sarongs had since then shed the dress of their ancestresses and replaced it with their everyday Malay clothes. Emerging suddenly as the embodiment of the Malay before the men clad only scantily in loincloths and conjuring perhaps therewith the modernizing forces of successive Protestant and Catholic missionaries, of Barakai's schoolteachers, of the Indonesian state, and of many of Aru's traders, the women's very presence exposed the vulnerability that for many Bemunese seems to be especially condensed in their Aru clothes. When I commented on the abruptness with which the ship broke up and the men had scattered in the direction of their homes, several of the women remarked that—embarrassed in their loincloths—they had run off to change their clothes.

Whether the men shared in this opinion is something I never ascertained. Nor was it apparent to me whether most of the women laughed with their men or at them. What was, however, clear is that for some reason Bemunese have chosen to reserve the face-to-face confrontation of the Aru and the Malay or, even, of memory and modernity for this final amazing end to their annual performance. After Bemun's ship was anchored in village space, and memory, as it were, was laid to rest when the signs of its mobility were propped up against the Stern's home, the Aru past and the Malay present stood each other off in an unmediated and somewhat disconcerting, if also amusing, fashion. This occasion was the only time during the entire performance when the Aru and the Malay, productively poised in opposition to each other as agonistic and mutually exclusive forces, were deliberately, if momentarily, allowed to occupy the same time and space. Conjuring a copresence that was amiable if uneasy, alterity emerged here as a slot to be filled by either the Aru or the Malay, depending on any Bemunese woman or man's own—necessarily fluctuating and variable—inclination. This juxtaposition of the Aru and the Malay thus revealed the provisionality and historical contingency of the authority on which they equally rely. At the same time, Bemun's Memory Ship was anchored as an icon at the center of village space, its two halves again divided between the altars of the Prow and the Stern, as the community embarked on a new year. As alterity shaded into a smile, memory dissolved into trade, and "dawn" broke on Barakai, everything happened as if two ships had passed each other by in the night.

What does all of this say, if anything, about gender relations on Barakai? How should the preeminence of men in the context of Bemun's annual performance and the particular hold they have on the community's adat be interpreted? Should the remarkable conclusion to the annual performance with its amusing and its unsettling aspects be understood as what anthropologists call a ritual of reversal, in which women vis-à-vis adat would, however briefly, have the upper hand? And, if so, what would that mean?

Following classic anthropological wisdom, rituals of reversal are periodic and officially sanctioned moments in the life of a community when the world, as it were, is briefly turned upside down—the king becomes a beggar, the slave sits on his throne, women command and invade public space while men stay at home and care for children. The most widespread interpretation of this kind of carnivalesque and transgressive reversal of authority is that it serves as a mechanism for maintaining social control. By airing the social tensions and emotions that threaten social unity, these rituals dramatize and orchestrate conflict in such a way that it is objectified and can be resolved—thereby reinforcing society's normative relations and forms (Bell 1992, 171–81; Gluckman 1963).

Writing of an analogous minireversal in the context of patriarchal domination—which is this kind of ritual's appropriate context—Žižek recalls an anecdote from Adorno's *Minima Moralia* in which a wife who apparently subordinates herself to her husband exchanges ironic, patronizing glances behind his back with other guests while she obediently holds out his coat for him as they leave a party (Žižek 1994, 56). As Žižek argues, the opposition of male and female power here is made to appear as that of semblance versus actual power—the woman's glance seems to say, "Let him think, poor thing, that he is really the master." Exposed as an imposter who only performs empty symbolic gestures, the man in the anecdote appears inferior before woman's exercise of real responsibility.

Crucial though, in all of this, as Žižek points out, is that this specter of woman's power itself only emerges as an after-effect of that of her husband; thoroughly dependent on male domination, it necessarily remains this domination's shadowy double. For that reason, Žižek concludes, "the idea of bringing shadowy woman's power to light and acknowledging its central position publicly is the most subtle way of succumbing to the patriarchal trap" (ibid.).

Does the above offer a way of interpreting the mini-reversal—if that is what it is—at the conclusion of Bemun's annual performance? To be sure, women's ability, at least as they see it, to dismiss their men by confronting them with Malay clothes is a retroactive effect of the men's bringing to light of women's shadowy power. It is also the case that men largely control adat and that women, including myself, are often excluded from the annual performance's most important moments as well as from wearing and embodying its central emblem, the cassowary. And, finally, throughout the Backshore, the most important social groups or fam are organized patrilineally, while the most permanent forms of property—like coconut and sago palm plantations—are exploited jointly by fathers, sons, and brothers with their families.

As feminists have increasingly pointed out, however, it is important not to reify "patriarchy," while the term itself and the intellectual baggage that it carries over from the nineteenth century may even block more productive ways of looking at the actual, often shifting sexual, gender, and kinship relations that apply in a given community (Coward 1983; Scott 1986). The gender inequalities that obtain in specific circumstances for a given group of people do not necessarily speak the larger "truth" of how gender operates among them. Nor do such inequalities in any simple way reflect economic or social structures (Scott 1986, 1058–59). While an ideology of gender equality may gloss over the conditions that allow men versus women to achieve preeminence in certain domains (Tsing 1990), such preeminence along with the differences held to distinguish men and women may also be elaborated, exaggerated, and hierarchicized for specific purposes in well-defined settings. The last, I believe, is the case in Bemun's annual performance.

While often important, ritual tends to be conservative and does not necessarily reflect the day-to-day foci of interactions or the structures of relations in a community. Even less does it hold a mirror to the latter as its clearest and most succinct representation. If Bemun's men emerge as the guardians of adat in the performance their community holds to open pencarian, it is important to recall that many of these same men attribute to their wives the power to curse this same livelihood if they are somehow displeased with their husbands (chapter 4). Recall also that under the sea these same men are further obliged and have to attend to the whims and demands of a female spirit, which as one of "the erotic, fantastic components of human life" on Barakai is also part of its politics—here, specifically, those relating to gender (Benjamin in Scott 1986, 1060).

Rather than speaking the truth about gender on Barakai, Bemun's ritual appropriates gender, because in this context it is especially "good to think" with (Lévi-Strauss 1966). As I have argued in this chapter, things like wild boars' tails and cooking pots of men and women's loincloths are crucial gendered operators that draw out qualities that on Barakai are associated with men and women respectively (Strathern 1988). Developed to extremes, these qualities do not necessarily say anything about the actual attitudes, dispositions, and interactions of women and men on the island. Rather, the sharp demarcation of the Malay and the Aru during the performance seems to demand different sets of operators that can be deployed to effect important transitions from one kind of condition to another, transitions that, for instance, the "women's share" in the hunt or the pronounced wearing and shedding of the ancestors' clothes register and bring about. But if, as I argue, the explicit marking of male and female qualities, the gendering that in different ways structures the performance, or even its privileging of men's over women's actions does not speak the truth about gender on Barakai, any of these things can open the possibility for reflecting and acting on more everyday relations and circumstances. If gender is good to think with during the annual performance, it may also stimulate some thinking beyond it. Abu Sabuan's dream of a female cassowary double, with which I opened this chapter, is perhaps one instance of such thinking.

8 Epilogue: Sweet Memories from Aru

"—but a context, always, remains open, thus fallible and insufficient."
—Jacques Derrida, *Specters of Marx*

"Sweet Memory from Aru" or "Greetings from Pearl Island," the islands' tourist art proclaims in English or in Indonesian, inviting the traveler to take away with her a souvenir of the place. In the backstreets of Dobo, improvised shelves behind dusty windows offer glimpses of some of the archipelago's famous treasures: a bottle cap of tiny pearls, bunches of tortoiseshell tied with string, a pearl-shell ashtray, sea green cassowary eggs almost as large as those of ostriches painted with seascapes of ships under sail framed by mangrove swamps and casuarina trees against the pink smudge of a varnished sunset, or the so-called butterfly mother-of-pearl shells whose sensuous shape and pearly interior make them another fitting canvas for showing off Aru's birds—cockatoos with yellow crests or fully plumed (male) paradise birds hovering between "Sweet memories" and "from Dobo, Aru Islands." Down other back alleys in scruffy shacks suspended above the garbage that the outgoing tide exposes and leaves behind, a visitor might be offered these same birds—live cockatoos, white or even black, green parrots, or dead Legless Paradises. For the official from Ambon, the Japanese pearl farm representative, or the Javanese prostitute, more than the occasional visiting biologist (Quammen 1993), these mementos from Aru might be things to take back home. When I left Barakai in March of 1988 and, again, in late February 1994, I left laden with butterfly shells and freshly blown out, still bright cassowary eggs and the understanding that these would be painted with memories in Dobo. They now sit and hang above my desk as I write the epilogue of this book.

These shells and their lesser cousins are the same ones that their spirit guardians—some Barakai islanders say—were recently dooming to (temporary) disappearance (chapter 4). The now brownish eggs that I dutifully had decorated in the back of one of Dobo's Chinese-owned stores belong to that special bird that the Backshore community of Bemun celebrates once a year and that hunters report has become increasingly furtive and hard to find. That pearl oysters (and perhaps cassowaries in the archipelago's forests) may in fact be permanently disappearing from the seas around Aru is a real and very serious threat. While the surplus that Barakai islanders associate with the undersea spirit women of male divers does not seem to allow the sense of what is known as ecological exhaustion to emerge, the vanishing acts that some of these same islanders attribute to the spirits who control the pearl oysters' supply and flow send nevertheless an ominous signal. Before, however, imagining how these vanishing shells might soon be replaced by their shadows in the capital's souvenirs, with their scenes of a sentimentalized Aru "nature" so imbued with "the beauty of the dead"—de Certeau's phrase for the nostalgic recovery of the "popular" or, by extension, the "ethnographic" as discrete aestheticized objects rising out of a violent extinction (de Certeau 1986; Ivy 1995)—let me first elaborate a bit.

In "The Beach: A Fantasy" (1998), the anthropologist Michael Taussig writes of a disappeared world in which the oceans have been swallowed up and displaced from our imagination. After signaling this situation, he goes on to suggest in this fascinating and beautiful little paper how the sea's disappearance has gone together with its phantasmatic recovery as the beach. Precisely at the moment when, although we in Europe seem not to notice, the world's seas are most heavily plied, marine transport is at its most global and extensive, and sea-borne freight brings "the apples we eat from Tasmania, sun ripened tomatoes from Israel, transistor radios and teevees from Taiwan, cars and computers from the US and Japan, the blue jeans from Medellin, oil from Venezuela and Kuwait" (Taussig 1998, 23), at precisely this moment, the ocean has become invisible. Yet if, indeed, as others in the "Year of the Ocean" also proclaimed, the sea that once so moved our imagination has now retreated from it (*Granta* 1998), for Taussig the phantasmatic recovery of the beach as this vanishing's after-effect bears testimony to the force of the archaic in modernity (see also Ivy 1995) or of what, following Adorno's reading of Benjamin, he also describes as the realization of a "second nature"—a virtual afterlife in which the hollowed out commodities of advanced capitalism, alienated from their former use-values, absorb fetishistically novel secondary meanings into themselves (Taussig 1998, 6). For Taussig, "the beach" rises virtually out of the physical fading away of the sea as its fantastic, secondary filling in and recuperation.

Far from the revamped fishermen's wharves and high-period real estate waterfronts of Sydney, Hong Kong, or Boston, in a peripheral place like Aru, this great sea change seems to have passed people entirely by. Indeed, one of the craziest things one can do anywhere in the south Moluccas is to lie on the beach—which probably just goes to show how much on the edge of things Aruese and their south Moluccan neighbors really are. Sending memory shells to circulate alongside its shark fins, trepang, and pearl oysters, Aru still leaves a physical trace in the world's marine traffic, making a small shuffle in the larger global movement of things, though one that is registered in the "wet" and "dry" markets of Singapore and Hong Kong more than in the remaining ports of Europe and the United States. And while the ocean recedes elsewhere, making way for the beach, some of Aru's peoples carve out a spirited memory place within the space of their larger sea trade.

The men and women whom I have written about in this book claim the prerogative of annually staging the drama of their own erasure. As I argued, this task at least in part has been put upon them and prefigured by forces, expectations, and circumstances larger than and beyond themselves. It is the price that the peoples who live on the backshores and in the frontier spaces of nation-states—or those whom the world's great sea changes occasionally pass by—often pay for a modicum of acceptance and tolerance toward themselves within a larger world. In Bemun the negotiation of this price takes the form of the dramatic exile of the Aru that is annually imposed by the Malay in the context of the community's performance. Yet the men who especially emerge as the guardians of Bemun's adat embody in the same space-time of the performance both the alternatives of the Aru and the Malay—as do, albeit somewhat differently, the community's women.

If I have chosen in this book to focus especially on the negotiation by Barakai islanders of their relationships to the Aru and the Malay and of these two elsewheres to each other, it is because they, indeed, capture so well the kinds of dilemmas, adjustments, and compromises that, demanded by the larger forces and powers dominating and permeating their lives, people at the disempowered fringes of nation-states, as well as more globally, constantly face. At the same time, however, the particular solution that has historically emerged on Barakai in the islanders' oscillating alliances and identifications with, respectively, the Aru and the Malay suggests how "hybridity"—commonly linked to either colonialism's subjects and elite go-betweens (Bhabha 1994) or to the cosmopolitan residents of the world's booming cities—can also be part of the history of those who inhabit some of its more "invisible" and forgotten places. This book locates hybridity in a place where it is least often looked for—among those "indigenous" or "native" peoples that as anthropology's subjects have long been seen as especially localized and territorially as well as culturally rooted. Besides exiling its subjects "out of time" as by now has so often been noted (Thomas 1989), anthropology has characteristically mapped culture, locality, and indigenous peoples seamlessly onto each other (Appadurai 1996, 182).

For women and men like those of Bemun, who make their lives on Aru's Backshore, their ability to ride out the erratic rhythms that rule their engagement in a luxury product trade, to confront and absorb the shocks and interventions of successive colonial and postcolonial regimes, to manage the more regularized asymmetries and abuses of island commerce, and to imagine and introduce their own alternatives into all of this has, I believe, much to do with seeing themselves as simultaneously both Aru and Malay. Indeed, some might even see the facility with which Bemunese and other Backshore Aruese shift, when necessary, from shark fins, to oysters, to trepang, perhaps back again to oysters, and, most recently, I am told, to lobsters as itself the kind of "flexible" attitude most suited and adapted to the late industrial capitalism of a postmodern world (Martin 1992). Maybe.

Against any overhasty celebration of the truly imaginative, creative, and admirable way in which Barakai's women and men largely make and manage their lives, it is essential to recall, as I have insisted throughout this book, the price they also pay as a result of their particular place in the world. If especially suited, strategic, and pliable for the imagining of alternative ways of being, the opening of new possibilities and novel social spaces, as well as indicative of a hospitality toward their others, both the Aru and the Malay are also haunted by a sense of lack, deficit, and depletion. Across many different settings and situations, Bemun's men and women are repeatedly reminded, in ways that are often painful, of the gap that emerges between themselves and their community, on one side, and on the other the two elsewheres to which they are oriented and in so many respects beholden.

If every ritual develops a "theory of context"—or a theory of what the community is produced from, against, in spite of, and in relation to (Appadurai 1996, 184)—beyond this setting such theory remains tacit, as a somewhat distant horizon in the more diffuse day-to-day activities and dealings of Barakai women and men. The stark relief which delineates the Aru against the Malay in Bemun's annual performance gives way to situations where one's standing, as well as the significance of whatever one faces or does, is inflected by the awareness of a world somewhat cast adrift within an often unfathomable beyond. For this locality always already beyond itself the Aru and the Malay are at best approximate glosses—the precarious albeit necessary moorings of runaway topographies. Because the context invoked as the Aru and the Malay unravels, as with any other horizon, the fallibility and insufficiency of context is such that it welcomes a space beyond or an open-ended future as in the striking conclusion to Bemun's annual performance. While I have mapped in this book the shifting contours of a memory of trade, I have also tried to intimate that it is in this uncharted terrain, beyond any mappings, where ultimately Barakai's men and women must find their own ways.

Notes

Preface

1 The Missionarissen van het Heilig Hart form the Dutch province of the MSC, or Société des Missionaires du Sacré Coeur, which was founded in 1854 and extended to the Netherlands in 1894 (Comité 100 jaar MSC 1954; van Weerdenburg MSC n.d.). For a history of the MSC in the Moluccas from the perspective of the mission, see Scheurs 1992.

2 *Fam*, originally from the Dutch *familie*, or "family," is a common term throughout the Moluccas for patrilineally ordered kin groups of various sizes. See, for instance, Platenkamp 1988 and Visser 1989.

1 Introduction: Runaway Topographies

1 For Michel de Certeau, a "library navigation" constitutes the act of making one's own an earlier corpus of literature on voyages, discoveries, travels, and the like. It is not driven by a concern for truth, which would allegedly lie behind such documents. Instead, navigation, is "first of all a labor of displacement, alteration and construction in a space that has been 'invented' by another," while the library "circumscribes the field in which these travels are elaborated and unfold" (1986, 138–40).

2 Beversluis and Gieben report that the taking of Aruese as slaves to work on Banda's nutmeg plantations caused such disturbances that a fort was built at Wokam Island across from Dobo in the 1660s (1929, 17).

3 This can be seen as one possible outcome of the sense of parallelism or simultaneity that Anderson identifies as one of the conditions for the emergence of nationalist imagining in the former European colonies (1991, 187–92).

4 For example, the organizational principle of Sukarno and the so-called Generation of 1928, Indonesia's early nationalist leaders, was that of *sini*, both "us" and "here," versus *sana*, or "them" and "there." As Mrázek explains, "Everything that could make the contrast between the two sides sharper, the dividing line cleaner, the space in between clearer, became policy on which to build the Indonesian struggle" (1997, 138–39).

5 The crews of the loggers were usually Japanese or "Manilans" (Beversluis and Gieben 1929, 195) in addition to some South Sea islanders. Merton, who visited Aru in 1908, mentions the captain of a logger—who was also the diver and along with the tender and five sailors formed the crew—from the Fiji Islands (Merton 1910, 145).

6 During the rationalization and intensification of Dutch rule in the so-called Outer Islands of the colony toward the end of the nineteenth century, two so-called *posthouders* (postholders) were stationed in Aru in 1882. This more permanent Dutch presence replaced the earlier occasional visits made to the islands by colonial representatives to appoint headmen and settle disputes (Riedel 1886, 248). The appointment of a *controleur*—one rank higher than a postholder—meant the continuation of this process undertaken in light of the unrest in the archipelago.

7 The information I have on these movements is based on archival materials from the Algemeen Rijksarchief in the Hague (W. D. van Drunen Littel, Memorie van overgave van het bestuur over de residentie Amboina dd. 15 juli 1918 van den aftredende Resident, ara 314) as well as on the following sources: *De Indische Gids* 1893a, 1893b; *Koloniaal Verslag* 1893; and van Hoëvell 1890.

8 J. G. H. Raedt van Oldenbarneveldt, Memorie van overgave van het bestuur over de residentie Amboina dd. . . . 1916 van den aftredende Resident, ara 312.

9 Trepang, from the Malay *teripang,* is the cover term for a wide range of edible holothurians. Other names include bêche-de-mer, from the Portuguese *bicho da mar* for "sea worm"; also sea slug, sea cucumber, and the obsolete eighteenth-century English term *swallo.* None of these terms quite does justice to the appearance of trepang, being little more than "polite names" for what is seldom an attractive "fish" (MacKnight 1976, 7). In addition to these names, a bewildering array of additional names existed to differentiate trepang more precisely for the market. In the port of Makassar in the early nineteenth century, no fewer than thirty types were distinguished, not only according to species but also by size and by the method and skill used in processing the trepang for sale (ibid., 7). Kolff includes a list of nineteen different trepang varieties in his overview of the "chief productions" of the Aru Islands (1840, 172–74). For additional information on the collection and processing of trepang in Aru, see Spyer 1992 and Osseweijer 1997.

10 The third village, Vree, appears variously as Oeree, Tree, and Vree until its last mention in the sources as Trei in 1865 (von Rosenberg 1867). According to the accounts of Barakai islanders of the settlement history of their island, there were originally three commercially oriented villages clustered at the southernmost tip of the island—Longgar, Apara, and Wire. The three as a whole are designated in the Barakai language as *sellasi,* three [located] on a

cape. The peoples of the three communities are said to have lived in close proximity, but chronic fighting caused the *wiron*, or people of Wire, eventually to move elsewhere. As it is told, the Wiron first relocated to a site between the contemporary villages of Bemun and Mesiang and then, following a devastating epidemic in the early part of this century, relocated again to the small island facing Mesiang that goes by the name of Gomogomo. In the Barakai language the contemporary inhabitants of Gomogomo are called wiron and are linked in narratives of migration on the island to the original site of Wire near Longgar and Apara. For additional historical information on settlement and migration on Barakai Island and on the political organization of Aru in the nineteenth century, see Spyer 1992.

11   Hawksbill shell is more commonly known as tortoiseshell.

12   Aru was certainly known to the Portuguese before 1606, although it is doubtful whether they ever set foot in the archipelago. Galvano, the Portuguese governor of the Moluccas, mentions in his history of the discovery of this region that Antonio d'Abreu and Francisco Serrano sailed by Aru in 1511 (van Rosenberg 1867, xi). Aruese also traded alongside Portuguese in Banda during the sixteenth century (Villiers 1981, 736). Additionally, Jan Huygen van Linschoten's map from 1599 of the Insulae Indiae Orientalis depicts and names "Aru" in its approximate location. This Dutchman lived in Goa and based the information contained in his maps and charts on Portuguese sources (Beekman 1988, 12). I would like to thank Bonnie Urciuoli for bringing this map to my attention.

13   Bandanese who managed to escape this devastation settled on the coasts of the neighboring islands of Seram, Kei, and Aru (Hanna 1978, 55). The peoples of the communities of Banda-Eli and Elat on Kei Besar claim to be descended from Bandanese who fled there in the wake of the 1621 massacre.

14   For an assessment of the historical role of "rarity" in the European imagination, see Pels 1998.

15   These planks allowed divers to hoist themselves back into the boats when they had finished diving (van Hoëvell 1890, 32).

16   The double rudders would indicate the Mesiangese origin of the boat. Today the wide-planked boats from Mesiang locally known as *belan* have two rudders as opposed to those of Longgar, Apara, and Bemun, which have only one that can be switched from right to left to allow flexibility in steering. One Dutchman depicted the seas around Barakai during his visit in 1836 as swarming with the profitable trepang (van Doren 1854, 390). Kolff's description of 1825 is a translation of A. J. Bik's written during his trip to Barakai in 1824 (Bik 1928 [1824]). Kolff's two successive visits to Aru in 1825 and 1826 only took him to the Frontshore (von Rosenberg 1867, xiv).

17   The earliest mention I found of sharks hunted for their fins in Aru is from Wallace in 1857 and the next from 1890 (Wallace 1962 [1869], 329; van Hoëvell 1890, 30, note). Compost devotes a section of his *Pilot Survey of the*

Exploitation of Dugong and Sea Turtles in the Aru Islands to shark fishing, including a comparison of fin and tail prices for different species in Aru as well as in Hong Kong, one of their main destinations (1980, 44–45). Sharks are sought in Aru exclusively for their tails and fins, which are used in some of the most highly appreciated of Chinese dishes, especially the noted soup. Only 10 to 15 percent of the shark is used, since the rest of the fish is thrown back into the sea after its tail and fins are cut off. An attempt by one of Bemun's tradeswomen to conserve the rest of the sharkmeat for sale was declared a failure by herself and her husband, being extremely laborious and relatively unprofitable. After being dried in the sun, the fins are usually sent to exporters in Surabaya and from there to Hong Kong, Singapore, and Japan. A small amount is consumed locally by ethnic Chinese.

18   In late January 1986 the exchange rate was $1 = Rp 1,250; at the end of June, it was $1 = Rp 1,275; and after the September 1986 devaluation, $1 = Rp 1,850.

19   The name *deba-deba* comes from the Indonesian *depa*, or "fathom."

20   Aruese from the Batulay area in central eastern Aru told me in 1984 when I visited there that agar-agar was first collected in Aru in the 1940s. They also claimed that because of its recent introduction, in contrast to the collection of pearl oysters, no adat observances corresponded to the collection of this trade product. Sperling's 1936 article makes no mention of agar-agar although she provides statistics for the oyster exports of 1926, 1928, and 1929 (p. 148).

21   For several photographs—one from as recently as 1957—of Nepalese kings and senior officials wearing elaborate headdresses made from the interwoven flank plumes of the Greater Bird of Paradise, see Swadling 1996, 63.

22   The zoologist Merton writes of the "bordellos" and boarding houses catering to Japanese divers during his visit of 1906 (1910, 144); Tillema, the famous bottler of Hygeia water in the Indies, mentions the one hundred or so prostitutes who previously worked in Dobo at the beginning of the century (1926, 160); Sperling only notes the barracks of Australian and Japanese pearl divers in the capital without any comment on prostitution, although presumably it was not absent (1936, 148).

23   I deliberately choose the term "prostitute" over the increasingly common "sex-worker." Following Benjamin, the prostitute is the incarnation or very enfleshing of the commodity and appears as such in Baudelaire's poetry. Just as the prostitute as a commodity is drawn to worlds in which commodity fetishism reigns supreme—whether the arcades of fin de siècle Paris or Dobo during the boom of the 1990s—so too, commodities tend themselves to cluster around her. As Gilloch observes, one of the main reasons cited by Benjamin for the decline of the commodity palaces of the arcades was the prohibition of prostitutes (Gilloch 1996, 163). By contrast, calling prostitutes "sex-workers" involves a substitution in which the complexities of the commodity as a contradictory site of dreaming and desire are erased

to make way for a normalized world of production in which the platitudes of capitalist globalization find an unthreatening abode. On fin de siècle fetishism and prostitution, see Apter 1991.

24 As at the turn of the century, the prostitutes in Dobo today are foreign to Aru—primarily Javanese women, whereas in the past they were mostly Japanese like the majority of their clients (Post 1991; Tillema 1926)—and will presumably come and go with the busts and booms of the island economy. One legacy of the prostitutes' stay in Aru today is the AIDS virus. Similarly, the spread of venereal disease went hand in hand with the plume boom in New Guinea. Unlike the former case, however, the plume hunters were themselves the source of the disease among various New Guinea peoples (Swadling 1996, 198–99).

25 This is the question with which Stallybrass and White begin their investigation of the struggle over the conceptual separation of popular pleasure and bourgeois economic rationality that was waged in relation to the hybrid site of the fair in eighteenth-century England (1986, 27).

26 For an extended treatment of modernity in Bali, see Vickers 1996; for a compelling analysis of the production of an Indonesian "unmodernity," see Brenner 1998.

2 The Legless Paradise

1 This expression, especially prevalent in the 1930s and 1940s in the debates between Dutch conservatives and progressives concerning the significance of three hundred years of Dutch rule in the Indies, was also the title of a 1941 volume edited by W. H. van Helsdingen and H. Hoogenberk. Today in the Netherlands a similar celebratory tone pervades the nostalgia industry–oriented advertising of such former colonial products as tobacco.

2 Ornithologists refer to these trees as "leks," while the dancing back and forth by males on a lek's branches is termed "lekking behavior." A tree with the right shape—a sparse crown and horizontal limbs that can easily accommodate the displays—might serve many consecutive generations of *P. apoda* (Quammen 1996, 620).

3 A similar inflation of honorifics was extended to the native kings of Java's so-called principalities (D. *Vorstenlanden*). Pemberton writes, for instance, of the "immense ceremonial arsenal of grand-crosses, noble stars, and similar figures of knighthood" that visiting foreign dignitaries bestowed on Javanese kings via colonial officials (1994, 93–94). For photos of Paku Buwono X, the Sunan of Solo, Central Java, who was installed in 1893 in three different guises—religious, as a Javanese ruler, and in a fanciful general's uniform—all of which are encrusted with medals, see Nieuwenhuys 1988, 33–35.

4   The book *Women's Hats* contains many pictures of hats adorned with feathers from different bird species as well as several topped by a whole bird. Page 111 shows a "pagoda of black draped silk velvet" crowned by a bird of paradise "complete with its two lateral tufts of magnificent feathers" (Campione 1989). The same book points out that the nineteenth-century craze for birds and feathers on European women's hats went together with the perfection of taxidermy (ibid., 26–27). From the metropole the feathers and birds from the Indies sometimes made their way—refashioned—back to the colony. For a photo from the early 1880s of the favorite concubine of the Javanese ruler Mangkunegoro V in full riding gear and sporting an "amazon" hat decorated with a paradise bird, see Nieuwenhuys 1988, 44.

5   For the same reasons that velvet or fur, following Freud, evokes the sight of the pubic hair, which, in turn, alludes to the longed-for penis (Freud 1961 [1927], 155). This is presumably why the position of the decorative feather(s) in relation to the wearer is so crucial, and the farther down the body it gravitates, the more erotically charged and socially suspect it becomes (like the cottontails on Playboy bunnies).

6   See Stoler 1992 for an analysis of the highly complex role played by European women in this racism and her illuminating *Race and the Education of Desire* (1995), which via Foucault's *History of Sexuality* links nineteenth-century European sexuality to the practice of imperial racism.

7   There were considerable differences among the European colonial powers regarding the kinds of relations they constructed with their various colonies, as, indeed, there were often important differences in the relations that any single colonizing nation might maintain with its different colonies. Furthermore, differences of class, gender, race, occupation, moment of arrival at the colony, and so on distinguished the various sectors making up the colonizing population itself at any given historical moment—although differently in many respects than at home in the metropole. Nonetheless, for this chapter I have chosen largely to gloss over these differences in order to focus on the "tropical Gothic" imagination that in important respects seems to have been shared by the major European colonial powers at this time. I believe that this approach is not entirely unjustified given that the various colonizing powers carefully watched and learned from each other— the 1857 Indian Mutiny contained, for instance, a lesson that none could ignore. Furthermore, the texts I draw on here are not exclusively those written by Dutch colonial officials, but also include the writings of French and especially English travelers to Aru.

8   There is considerable scholarly debate about how much influence Wallace's own ideas may have had on Darwin, especially regarding the theory of natural selection. For a recent evaluation, see Quammen 1996, 102–114.

9   For a discussion of such "religious habits," see Garber 1992, 210–33.

10 Besides cloth production, processes of hybridization, imitation, and swapping of clothing took place between colonizers and colonized. Telling in this

respect is the prevalence of Dutch loan words in Malay, which suggests the appropriation of an entire semantic field pertaining to dress (Collins 1996). One might recall, in this regard, a minor character in *This Earth of Mankind* by the great Indonesian writer Pramoedya Ananta Toer—the Italian couturier directed by the Assistant Resident to handle the details of the uniforms and clothing worn by the protagonist's father on his installation as regent. Fully regaled in a startling bricolage of Malay, Indies, and European styles, the protagonist Minke wonders: "Why was it a non-Javanese that was making me so dashing? And handsome? Why a European? Perhaps an Italian? Already since Amangkurat I [seventeenth-century ruler of a Javanese polity] the clothes of the kings of Java had been made and designed by Europeans, said Mr. Niccolo Moreno. I'm sorry but your people only wore blankets before we came. Below, above, on the head, only a blanket! It truly hurt!" (Toer 1981, 117–18; see also Taylor 1997).

11 For a wonderful reflection on Marx's coat, see Stallybrass 1998.

12 For information on birds of paradise and the early environmental politics aimed at their protection, see Cribb 1997, 1998; and Swadling 1996, 83–107.

13 For an extensive historical analysis of the plume trade in New Guinea and the nearby islands, including Aru, see Swadling 1996.

14 And they left behind more than that. Besides the "considerable supply" of dead birds left in the traders' hands and the scores of dry-docked motorboats that had once served the feather hunters, the Dutch colonial officer who in 1937 encountered all of this writes that the hunters also spread venereal disease to the New Guinea interior (van Baal 1985, 101). I would like to thank Bonno Thoden van Velzen for bringing this source to my attention.

15 In the case of cultural "specimens," this worked somewhat differently. For sure, as Pratt observes, it was often and indeed until quite recently the case that "the initial ethnographic gesture" was one of total homogenization, "a collective *they*, which distills down further into an iconic *he*" or, again, "the standard adult male specimen" (1992, 64). At the same time it should not be forgotten that descriptions of native women in the downtrodden and exploitative conditions in which they were allegedly found by Europeans and kept by their own men also became an elaborated genre of colonial literature. Whether one wants to call this kind of description ethnographic or not, it meant that women could not always be so easily overlooked as the "female of the species." Importantly, the genre also served the purpose of setting up European men as the liberators of local women, while simultaneously displacing along with the agency of colonized women and men their own exploitative interventions (Mani 1992).

16 For a reading of *The Malay Archipelago*'s backpiece—an engraving of "natives of Aru shooting the Great Bird of Paradise" (see Figure 2)—and the book's more famous frontispiece depicting an "orang utan attacked by Dyaks" in the context of nineteenth-century theories of degeneration, see Boon 1985.

17   Sometimes the fusion between man and bird has been even more complete as, for instance, in those cases when an Aruese dons a headdress fashioned out of bird of paradise plumes (Brumond 1853, 273). Today the so-called bird of paradise dance in which Aruese sport such headdresses is this archipelago's contribution to the regional dance competitions held annually in the south Moluccas. For an extended reflection on similar headdresses in neighboring Irian Jaya, see Rutherford 1996.

18   Aesthetic-psychological notions of caprice, of foolish vanity, and of being swayed by the superficial appearance of things have long been a part of fetish discourse and, more generally, European discourse on the primitive (Pietz 1988, 111). For photos of the Tanimbarese dandies, see *Tanimbar: The Unique Moluccan Photographs of Petrus Drabbe* (Alphen aan den Rijn: Periplus Editions in association with C. Zwartenkot, 1995).

19   This kind of sobriety in male dress was in fact quite recent and ensued from what one historian describes as "a shift in style from peacock male to sombre man of action." She explains: "Every European élite had taken note of the sartorial and political disaster represented by the first procession of the Estates General in Paris in 1789, the prelude to the French Revolution. On that occasion, the representatives of the Third Estate, dressed in sombre black, had been cheered; but the traditionally lavish costumes of the nobility and clergy had met with jeers or silent disgust. 'The magic of ostentation,' as Jean Starobinski puts it, had 'stopped having an effect on spectators who had learned to add up the cost.' From now on, the *habit à la française*, the wigs, powdered hair, brocades, silks, lace, and parrot colours, which had been fashionable from Boston to Berlin, and Moscow to Manchester, was increasingly abandoned in favour of far more subdued and functional male dress" (Colley 1992, 187).

20   As elsewhere in the Indies, the period of the Japanese occupation from 1942 to August 1945 was a time of hardship and deprivation. On Barakai, the islanders largely retreated into the forest, leaving the villages to the Japanese. Everyone was forced to work—many of Barakai's able-bodied men were sent to Trangan in southwest Aru to build an airstrip, women were given other tasks and sexually harassed, and even old people were, for instance, compelled to tend the fires that heated the water under the giant vessel in which the Japanese bathed. Some islanders who were young children at the time recall attending a Japanese school on the island and can still count and sing a few songs in Japanese.

21   A remarkable black rock with bold white stripes located in one of the broad channels that cuts across Aru and known locally as "Flag Rock" (I. Batu Bendera; B. Wa Lulub) is said to have been formed from the loincloth of the mythical ancestor Urlima. For a photo, see Merton 1910, 151. Van Hoëvell mentions men's striped loincloths but fails to note whether they were fabricated from Dutch flags (1890, 29). I believe it is safe to assume that, had Aruese at the time been wearing Dutch flags, this would have been deemed

worth noting (at the very least). I conclude therefore that the loincloths seen by van Hoëvell were not made from Dutch flags and that this fashion probably is of a later, albeit pre–World War II, date.

22   According to Corbin, the period between 1840 and 1860 in France, a kind of golden age for traditional regional costume, was followed by "a period of mimicry" in which "peasant traditions were lost, and regional costumes, no longer worn, were piously collected by folklorists." Even though such a trajectory may seem to record a dislocation of the "past" by the "present," the emergence of "fashion"—in the form of prints and plates that circulated even in rural areas, mail-order purchases, provincial branches of the Printemps department store and so on—as a "modern" phenomenon went hand in hand with the defining of folklore as collectible (Corbin 1990, 490).

23   This is not an absolute contrast. An overlap in this respect between colony and metropole can, for instance, be found in the idea of a "national costume." In late-nineteenth-century writings about Aru, however, this category fulfills the role of yet another reading of allegedly timeless native dress, with the "national costume" none other than "the well-known Tjidako," or man's loincloth, familiar to Europeans as standard male "savage" garb throughout the Moluccas and different from the "aprons" worn by women (van Doren 1854, 396). Notwithstanding the replacement of the prior bark and "leaf" loincloths with ones made of cloth for men or hybrid cloth and mat coverings for women, the "national costume" of Aru in the eyes of Europeans remained, it appears, unchanged (van Hoëvell 1890, 22–23; de Hollander 1898, 522).

24   This meaning of the Dutch word *landschap* refers to a portion of land or a region that may or may not have clearly defined borders. Although the term was common throughout the Netherlands East Indies, where it came to designate administrative territories, historically this particular usage predates the more familiar meaning the term *landscape* enjoys in art history. It is from the latter that the English word *landscape* derives.

25   In actuality, Europeans themselves often had a hand in the production of "mock chiefs," for example, "the wife of a celebrated trader"—who seems to have been quite a tradeswomen herself—who raised several persons in New Guinea to the ranks of *majoor* and *kapitein* (Ellen 1986, 60).

26   Bhabha in his "Of Mimicry and Men" homes in on "the area between mimicry and mockery" as that space "where the reforming, civilizing mission is threatened by the displacing gaze of its disciplinary double . . . so that mimicry is at once resemblance and menace" (1994, 86).

27   The colonizers were out of step with metropolitan mode as well. One colonial author writes that the fashions worn by the colonizer women in the Netherlands East Indies were "a full year" behind those of Europe (Victor Ido in Bronkhorst and Wils 1996, 50). This statement presumably applies to the colonial capital of Batavia, where women would have more easily been able to keep abreast of the fashions in Europe and would have

had more means available to them to do so—either ordering the popular styles from the metropole directly or having local dressmakers imitate and adapt them to life in the Indies—than in the more remote outposts of the empire. Beyond the time lag, there were other important differences between what a recent book on Indies dress refers to as the "tropical authentic" (D. *tropen echt*) style of the colonies and those at home, although the gap between the two narrowed with time (Bronkhorst and Wils 1996).

28   This proposition is supported by the evidence of similar reactions on the part of colonizers elsewhere. "Writing about British attitudes toward Indians wearing European clothes, N. C. Chaudhuri trenchantly sums up the situation: 'They, the British, were violently repelled by English in our mouths and even more violently by English clothes on our backs'" (in Cohn 1989, 333). It is my belief that generally the British were even more stringent in the policing of difference between colonizers and colonized—especially after 1857—than the Dutch. This view resonates with Jean Gelman Taylor's claim that the brief British interregnum of the Dutch East Indies between 1815 and 1819 was an important factor that led the Dutch to draw harder boundaries between themselves and those over whom they ruled in the latter half of the nineteenth century (Taylor 1983).

29   A take-off on Bhabha's "not quite, not white" (Bhabha 1994, 89).

30   In a similar fashion, Cohn notes the impression made on Europeans on the occasion of a visit of the Prince of Wales to India in 1876 by the "military fossils" that were paraded out before them. Owing to the ancient (and heterogeneous) style of the uniforms and arms of the troops, an artist who recorded the scene remarked that the twelfth and the nineteenth century (the latter being the British) stood face to face (Cohn 1989, 326–27).

31   Kracauer observes how fashion details in old photographs "hold the gaze" tightly and how photography and fashion are both timebound in the same way. He also distinguishes between certain traditional forms of attire that, having lost all contact with the present, acquire a timeless status, while other outfits that have been recently worn have a "comical" effect. Finally, Kracauer poetically invokes the class dimensions to such temporally imbued fashion distinctions, "the tightly corseted dress in the photograph protrudes into our time like a mansion from earlier days that is destined for destruction because the city center has been moved to another part of town. Usually members of the lower class move into such buildings. It is only the very old traditional dress, a dress which has lost all contact with the present, that can attain the beauty of a ruin" (1995, 55).

3 The Great Ship

1   See Scheurs MSC 1992 on the mission's concern with the indigenization of its hierarchy in the 1920s and 1930s.

2   As in other parts of Indonesia, the state puts in a seasonal appearance on Aru's Backshore when rumors circulate during the driest months of the year of headhunters set loose in the Barakai bush to collect the heads the government needs for its development projects (cf. Tsing 1993, 85–91). It also comes in the more mundane though equally guarded against form of Dobo bureaucrats, who from time to time travel to Barakai to collect taxes, count its inhabitants, or mobilize them for upcoming elections. The unpredictability of these visits or other potential encounters with state envoys contrasts with the virtually pro forma invocation of the Indonesian phrase "the government decides" (I. *pemerintah putus*) in Barakai dispute settlements. Taken together, the state's unpredictable, somewhat mysterious eruptions and demands and its highly fetishistic all-around presence resonate with the full force of its redoubtable power. Beyond the headman and supporting staff of any given village, beyond the customary adat officials who, in certain circumstances, may locally also qualify as "government," and beyond any state bureaucrats who for whatever reason might make it to the Backshore, the phrase *pemerintah putus* leads a life of its own, demanding respect and deference as a force to be reckoned with and one with which the determination of many things is ultimately held to reside.

3   In other parts of Indonesia, peoples who live at a far remove from the nation's center have refigured this powerful trope of, especially, nationalist history in ways that further their own projects and positionings within the nation-state. For some interesting examples, see Hoskins 1993, 306–32; Tsing 1993, 259–83.

4   On "tips" and "trunks" elsewhere in eastern Indonesia, see Fox 1971, 1980 and Traube 1986.

5   The Portuguese figure in various ways in the imaginations of many Indonesian peoples. Often *portugis* seems to mean simply the first arrivals, that is, before the Dutch, but without any specific nationality attached to them as on Sumba (Keane, personal communication) and in the Tanimbar Islands west of Aru (McKinnon 1991). In the former Portuguese colony of East Timor, where they tend to assume a much more prominent place in popular imagination, they are sometimes seen as the younger clever brother to an older ritually superior indigenous one (Traube 1989).

6   Although this story is my translation of a tape and is in this sense direct discourse, I have broken it up into short segments that follow closely the pauses in Abu Sabuan's speech to facilitate reading.

7   Bronze gongs, elephant tusks, and Chinese porcelain, the main articles of bridewealth in Aru, in particular were stashed away in caves or buried by islanders—sometimes not to be relocated later.

8   Heryanto, who regards "development" as one of the two most important keywords, in Raymond Williams's sense of the term, in use in Indonesia today—the other being Pancasila—provides a detailed, linguistically oriented exploration of the term that considers the various shifts in meaning

(and spelling) and application that the term *pembangunan* has undergone since it first began to be used frequently and publicly in the second half of the 1930s, especially in nationalist circles (Heryanto 1988).

9 When I arrived in Bemun, Abu Sabuan's husband occupied the local office of "Father of Development," because he knew something about construction and could therefore oversee the building of houses using the cement that was distributed in Backshore villages under the rubric of "development."

10 See Kenneth George for the association of paganism and darkness with mission discourse in highland Sulawesi (1996, 37).

11 Alcoholic spirits appear again and again in the lists of commodities introduced to Aru through trade, notwithstanding the repeated remonstrances of colonial officials and other European visitors concerning their negative effects on the industry and temperament of the islanders (Bosscher 1853, 329; Brumond 1853, 293; van der Crab 1862, 86; de Hollander 1898, 521,523; Wallace 1962 [1869], 343–44). Despite the official attitude, the historic widespread use of alcohol in Aru is not surprising, given that alcohol was a primary means through which trade and, specifically, the Aruese indebtedness to traders were often stimulated in the islands. One Longgarese man confided in me that the desire for foreign *sopi* or distilled palm wine—also known as *arak*—was in fact the motivating force behind the migration of Bemunese ancestors from the Barakai interior to the coast in the early nineteenth century.

12 I was told that in the past participants and especially dancers at feasts that drew large numbers of people together displayed their emblems on plaited bands worn on the upper arms and around the calves, and great houses (B. *lev wawaru*) that were inhabited by members of an extended patrilineal clan boasted a carved effigy of the group's emblem under one of the corners of the elevated dwelling. Historically in Aru, Kei, and Tanimbar, collectivities actively maintained their distinct identities through the jealous preservation of exclusive rights to the designs that they conceived as their emblems. The MSC missionary Geurtjens, for example, observes that, in Kei, "chaque village, chaque famille a ses *poessaka* [heirloom objects] qu'elle défend avec un zèle jaloux. Lorsque le Gouvernement n'était pas encore établi ici, il y a une trentaine d'années, la seule imitation d'une ornamentation de barque ou de dessin dans une bannière etc. était un cas de guerre" (1910, 336). Writing in the 1880s about Aru, the Resident of Ambon, J. G. F. Riedel, claims that war ensues in the archipelago whenever a group, having usurped the designs of another, refuses to pay the fine demanded in compensation (1886, 260).

13 In the Netherlands East Indies, the openjas made its appearance in the 1920s and 1930s as a more casual alternative for men to the so-called *jas toetoep*, or "closed jacket" (Bronkhorst and Wils 1996, 13–25). Barakai islanders tended to identify Aruese who wore the openjas in old photographs as Protestant

converts from the island Trangan, where this religion arrived in the first quarter of the present century. Regarding pockets, Jean Gelman Taylor notes the disappearance of the umbrella of hereditary privilege (I. *payung*) from late nineteenth-century photographs of Javanese men and its replacement by the pocket watch as a new status symbol and marker of its owner's modernity (Taylor 1997, 100). Presumably, this object and its telltale chain would have drawn attention to its owner's pocket.

14   Indeed, the only time I saw a copy of the Qu'ran on the Backshore was in the context of a Thursday night ilmu session that was led by a Muslim man who worked on one of the local diving boats. The Qu'ran was used to assist in a divination.

15   This practice dates to the seventeenth century in the Netherlands East Indies and was, early on, central to voc policy in spice-producing areas like Ambon and the nearby Lease Islands (Chauvel 1990, 20). Its legacy in contemporary Indonesia is the forcible relocation of landless peasants, especially from Java to other parts of the archipelago—including, from the early 1990s, Aru, in the context of the government's so-called *transmigrasi* program.

16   "The Atjeh knot," a symbol of colonial abuse and excess if there ever was one, is so named for its widespread use during the wars between the Dutch and the Sultanate of Aceh in North Sumatra in the late nineteenth century. See also van der Veer 1996, 167–202.

17   To non-Dutch readers it may seem odd that van Baal, writing his memoirs in the 1980s, might feel the need to defend himself against suspicions that he might have anti-Catholic sentiments. It is really only since the 1960s that the Netherlands has become the highly secularized nation that it is today (in the common understanding of the term). Before this time, the rift between Protestants and Catholics ran deep, as evidenced, for instance, by the difference in naming of Protestant versus Catholic missions—in Dutch these are known as *zending* and *missie* respectively even though both mean the same, namely, "to send." During the time of the mass conversions in Aru in the 1970s, the competition for converts seemed to have been most fierce between the Protestants and the Catholics, causing one Dutch priest to characterize the conflicts as "miniature wars of religion" (D. *godsdienst oorlogjes*).

18   For an exemplary analysis of the materiality that inevitably accompanies missionization, see Comaroff and Comaroff 1991, 1997.

19   One of the tactics used by the district official at the time was to dismiss Aruese headmen who either refused to convert or, more often, to convert to the Protestant religion he himself represented.

20   Sol, 31 January 1971, msc archives.

21   Indeed, they were often quite disturbed. The missionaries I met were truly dedicated to their work and for a long time provided the only real health

care on the Backshore. See Kipp 1990 for a sensitive discussion of an early Dutch Protestant mission among the Karo in North Sumatra.

22 For a fascinating discussion of some of the dilemmas that the relationship between spirituality and materiality posed for Dutch orthodox Protestant missionaries in Sumba, see Keane 1996.

23 van Lith, 14 March 1968, MSC archives. St. Nicholas conjures for most Dutch today, as already in the 1970s, an image of holiday presents rather than piety, representing for these missionaries probably more than for most the perversion of religion by market-driven concerns.

24 van Lith, 17 June 1976, MSC archives.

4 Mothers of Pearl

1 In the mid-1980s one of Bemun's trading couples spent the off-season in Dobo. During the boom years of the late 1980s and early 1990s, both couples went on buying trips to Ujung Pandang and Surabaya, respectively, where wholesale merchandise is cheaper than in Dobo.

2 Divination, only practiced by men, is an informal affair held in the home of the person who requests it. Men who practice divination usually acquired the skill from an older male relative. The process refered to in the Barakai language as *eselal kowi*—something like "to divine from coffee"—consists of interpreting or "reading" the pattern left behind by coffee grinds on the bottom of a cup when the coffee is poured out into another container. The diviner often ties a kerchief around his head before beginning the process. With a cup of coffee supplied by his host, he then "reads" the grinds three times, pouring the coffee from one cup into another until he "discovers the path" or cause of the person's failure in diving, illness, or other affliction.

3 In his book on the history of the Newfoundland cod fishery, Gerald Sider argues similarly that the absence of developed agriculture among these fisherfolk is not adequately explained by the fact that they are fishing communities, but must be understood in relation to the hegemony of fishing interests over these settlers under socioeconomic circumstances in which viable alternatives to this form of livelihood are lacking (1986, 109).

4 The two seas distinguished as "drifting" and "ripe" on Barakai correspond to the Ambonese Malay *nep* and *sepring*, or in English ebb and flood or spring tide. The Malay terms clearly derive from the Dutch *eb* and *vloed* or *springvloed*.

5 The gendering of these distinctions is also common elsewhere in the Moluccas, for instance, in Tanimbar, where a dry ebb around noon is regarded as "male," while at its lowest point in the late afternoon, it is considered "female" (R. J. P. Mulders 1985, 11).

6 Thoha, "Maluku Tenggara, Maluku Sengsara," *Kompas*, 22 February 1987.

7   Liston P. Siregar and Mochtar Touwe, "Di Balik Kemilaunya Mutiara,"
    Tempo, 6 November 1993. In the same issue, see also Dwi Setyo Irawanto
    and Mochtar Touwe, "Suka Duka Sang Penyelam," about the "ups and
    downs" in the lives of divers. On June 21, 1994, the Indonesian Ministry of
    Information revoked the licenses of three popular news weeklies, including
    Tempo. For a detailed account of this incident as well as other actions taken
    against the press, see "Three Strikes against the Press," in *The Limits of
    Openness: Human Rights in Indonesia and East Timor* (New York: Human
    Rights Watch, 1994).

8   Specifically, the combination of having negligible debts with their trader
    and their own boat allowed these men some room in deciding where to
    trade their oysters. With considerable satisfaction the father recalled how
    his trader, on seeing him transact his produce on a pearl farm boat, had
    been hopping mad but at the same time helpless to do anything about it
    without a debt to fall back on. Presumably, the care this man and his
    brother took in instructing their sons how to manage their debts can be
    traced back to their own problems with indebtedness in the 1970s, when
    they were brought by their trader to court in Dobo. Following this incident,
    both men switched their affiliation from one to the other trader in the
    village and only recently, more than ten years later, had one of the men
    returned to his original trader. This move, in turn, was motivated by what
    was seen as a broken promise on the part of the other trader, who had
    commited himself to bringing wood for this man from Dobo for the con-
    struction of a boat and had consistently failed to do so.

9   Rarely, Barakai traders turned to a former military man, the so-called Ba-
    binsa posted in Longgar to help them enforce the payment of debts. Babinsa,
    or noncommissioned law enforcement officers affiliated with the civilian
    administration, are often placed in rural areas to "maintain order," which
    many, indeed, do despotically. Rather than dealing with this person, some
    traders preferred to take their debtors to court in Dobo, although this pro
    cess was inevitably more drawn out. The threat of force—whether of the
    Dobo court or of the Babinsa—though almost never called upon, hovers at
    the edge of the trader-diver relation. In the early 1980s, one of Bemun's trad-
    ers had taken several villagers to court in Dobo. Thereafter they switched
    their allegiance to the other trader, diving off of his boat and trading at his
    store. In 1994 one of the men who had been taken to court more than ten
    years before told me that he would have liked to return to his original trader
    but that "embarrassment" still kept him from doing so. On the traders' side
    of things, several confided to me that they either feared sorcery or allegedly
    had been sorcerized by Bemunese, thus demonstrating the power that those
    actually in power often project onto those beneath them (Taussig 1987).

10 The list below compares the prices of common store goods in Bemun and
    Dobo respectively in January 1994:

	Bemun	*Dobo*
rice (1 kilo)	Rp 900	Rp 800
sugar (1 kilo)	1,500	1,500
small box of tea	300	200
coffee (½ kilo)	2,000	1,500
bottle of sambal	2,000	1,500
Baygon repellent	1,000	600
Marie biscuits	500	400
one half plug of tobacco	1,750	1,500
rolling papers	100	50
Rinso soap	500	200
one case of tuak	40,000	24,000
one small bottle tuak	2,000	1,500
one large bottle tuak	4,000	3,000

11 To obtain cash, Barakai islanders sell, for instance, coconut oil they make or baskets of sago or garden produce (especially Mesiangese, who are the real gardeners on the island) to their fellow islanders and to the traders. They also sometimes catch fish for the latter. When large sums of money are needed, as for bridewealth, the men of a fam will dive together and pool the money they get for their shells or trepang to cover the costs of the marriage. Bridewealth on Barakai always consists of two parts; one part is paid in antique bronze gongs and the other is cash (see Spyer 1992).

12 A trader in one of the neighboring villages is said to have composed the song because he was upset that his deba-debas had accumulated such large debts. Presumably, their inability to pay these off had much to do with the crisis resulting from the pearl oyster disease and the drastically diminished returns of diving. Most of the women and men I knew were much amused by the song and delighted in reporting the considerable annoyance of the deba-debas they had witnessed when it was sung.

13 The expression derives from Victor Turner, who, however, takes it in a different direction than I do here (Turner 1967, 30).

14 While money-mindedness is a pervasive stereotype of ethnic Chinese in Indonesia, etiquette definitely is not. The latter association must therefore be seen as a development specific to Aru's Backshore, which follows from the traders' instantiation for Aruese of the values of modern urban life.

15 This intimacy is presumably the reason why it reflects poorly on a trades-woman when her anak piara carouses around after work, takes a lover, or becomes pregnant.

16 Although cash is usually paid for this work, it should be clear that these jobs, carried out for the traders and essential to the operation of the island stores, remain complementary to rather than competitive with trade and its debt system.

17 Following recent critiques, "experience" here is not taken as a baseline or zero-sum position where the truth of a given existence or the makeup, voice, and vision of the individual subject may be traced back to and thus explained, but rather as something that itself is continually and discursively constructed (Scott 1992; Steedly 1993; K. Stewart 1991).

18 Abu Sabuan's husband, Izkia Tebwayanan, first arrived at Barakai from Kei in 1959, when he was employed on a traders' junk that traveled around Aru picking up trade products and announcing its arrival to various coastal settlements with a gong.

19 Especially in Longgar and Apara, where, in contrast to Bemun's largely land-oriented cassowary performance, the rituals that open trade focus exclusively on the sea. In Bemun these songs are sung on other occasions like bridewealth negotiations and house raisings.

20 This assumption is not automatic but appears mediated by the age and all-around perceptions of the young diver—whether he is already approaching a state in which on land as well as under the sea he could in fact be married. When I asked regarding a young teenager, Bobi, whom public perception clearly did not yet associate with the possibility of marriage, whether having recently obtained his first shell, he now could also claim a "sea wife," the answers I received, while sometimes different, were consistently negative. Some divers said he was simply too young, others seeing no need for explanation responded flat out with a "not yet," while one insisted that since Bobi's shell had come from the "very edge" of the diving area rather than its "deeper" center, he as yet could not have a tie to a sea wife.

21 Although occasionally boats are built on Barakai, the bulk of local sailing craft are commissioned and bought in one of Aru's two main boat-building centers—on the western side of the archipelago in the villages of Feruni and Kalar-Kalar on Trangan Island or on its east coast in one of a chain of boat-building villages on Kobroor in central Aru.

22 On the few occasions that one of Bemun's traders allowed me to accompany his motorboat on a diving expedition (the other put me off with repeated excuses), it was clear to me that the day was recast as something out of the ordinary, as an outing with the overtones of a holiday. Backed by the members of my household, the tradeswoman insisted that I take a young girl along for "company," and she also prepared us a picnic lunch. Throughout the day I was encouraged by the men to fish, perhaps to diffuse the awkwardness of my presence as well as, undoubtedly, to provide a source of amusement for themselves.

23 As in other places, the Indonesian pas jalan along with the citizen's identity card, licenses, authorizations, and officially stamped letters can in Achille Mmembe's terms be seen as "amulets" necessary for moving around in the postcolony (Mmembe 1992, 19).

24 Among the Bimin Kuskusmin in Papua New Guinea, cowrie shells are

classified as male wealth that is explicitly identified with the vagina (Poole in Ardener 1987, 138). I only heard one such explicit association in Aru in the context of gossip about how a woman is said to have described herself to a lover.

25 The red hair of sea wives is often identified with a reddish brown seaweed that is known in the Barakai language as *mang*.

26 The most famous sea woman in Indonesia is Kangjeng Ratu Kidul, the spirit "Queen of the Southern Ocean" and consort of the successive dynasts of Mataram who realizes "the (erotic and other) potency of Javanese Kingship" (Florida 1992, 24). Seduction, wealth, and danger are also intertwined in the Mami Wata figures found in the great rivers and seas of West Africa as well as in Brazilian *garimpeiros'*, or goldseekers', tales of gold as a capricious femme fatale and a dangerous and alluring object of conquest for men (Meyer 1998; Slater 1994).

27 In the Tanimbar Islands, southwest of Aru, where prestations given as bridewealth to wifegivers follow a complicated, drawn-out trajectory, it is crucial that they travel a proper path. When prestations travel wrongly, a wifegiver who should have received a share of the woman's bridewealth but did not could justifiably say, "Some others might eat the bridewealth, but I eat the person." As McKinnon points out, "Instead of bridewealth acting as a substitute for the person, the person becomes a substitute for the bridewealth and sacrifices his or her life" (1991, 191). While both Tanimbarese and Aruese draw on a discourse of consumption to depict the possibilities and perils of the flow of bridewealth, they do so differently. Bridewealth turns back on a bride to "eat" her in Aru not when obligations to wifegivers remain unfulfilled but when their demands are excessive—something that underscores the difference between the pervasive hierarchy of Tanimbarese society and the more egalitarian Aru.

28 Several hours after he stepped ashore, Aluli entrusted the pearl to an older brother, after being refused by two older male relatives who claimed they feared the pearl's "heat."

29 The technical term for this fold is the "mantle." For a discussion of oyster anatomy, see Farn 1986, 22–31, and Taburiaux 1985, 103–5. The coffee table book *Pearls: Ornament and Obsession*, by Kristin Joyce and Shellei Addison (1993) gives a more general history of the pearl.

30 In my presence, the trader did spend a long time inspecting the pearl, and several days later I heard he had offered to buy it for half a million rupiah. I was unable to confirm this offer, and Aluli had by this time decided to keep it, imagining that the pearl might prove a formidable aid in his pencarian.

31 The profit a man makes on the sale of a pearl depends on its size and quality as well as on the splendor of the feast he provides for his companion divers, on the gifts he makes to his sisters, and on where he sells it. If the pearl remains undiscovered, a man may try to keep it in order to sell it for a better

price in Dobo, although concealment means running the risk that the pearl's heat will turn back on the diver and cause him illness. In 1994 a large, high-quality pearl sold on the Backshore for 100,000 to 125,000 rupiah and in Dobo sold for twice that amount. A dozen white plates, a pair of earrings, a necklace, a ring, and two bracelets cost approximately Rp 20,000; a meal of sweetened rice with coffee for twenty to twenty-five men, about Rp 6,000; leaving Rp 74,000 for the diver. Given, however, that alcohol should also be served on such occasions, that a "carton" in 1994 cost Rp 40,000 on Barakai, and that twenty-five Aruese men might in a night consume two cartons (not usually all paid for by the diver who found the pearl), a good, high-quality pearl would still provide some profit, although a "regular" (Rp 50,000), while requiring a less splendid output, would already bring in less.

32   I never heard of the opposite move being made in which, for instance, a diver would try to deceive his sea woman with offerings stolen from fellow divers rather than purchased by himself.

33   The significance of sugar in fostering harmony in social relations is most apparent when it is withheld. This situation occurs from time to time in the context of bridewealth deliberations, when the exchanges between a man's and a woman's peoples become especially bitter or heated. In such circumstances, the women of the host group (which depends on how the union between the man and the woman came about and thus varies) may choose to serve coffee without sugar to their guests or beverages without the sweet that should accompany it in such settings. Here, the bitter substance consumed by the guests captures the usually fleeting essence of their relation to the host group. As a direct breach of local standards of hospitality, it is an insult that further incites the guests.

34   This map of the Aru Islands was drawn up by the Dutch Hydrographic Service in 1893–94 and then again in 1909, and most recently has been reissued (unrevised) in 1983 by TNI-AL Jawatan Hidro-Oseanografi in Jakarta.

35   Such posts therefore go by two names on Barakai: *sir*, which refers to the wood from which such posts should be made, and *sabuan*, or "mooring post."

36   Among the Meratus of Kalimantan, *nabi* is a cover term for a wide range of spirits from the forty-one children of Adam and Tihawa (Eve) to the prophets linked by Meratus to all religions, including the ones that they themselves invent, and the guardian spirits of plant and animal species, also called *nabi* (Tsing 1993, 262–63).

37   The fact that the contemporary basis of the relations between Muslims and Barakai women and men is primarily nostalgic and that ties of debt and trade no longer bind them is not of negligible importance.

38   A central assumption here is the idea of the fetish as quintessentially a hybrid and border phenomenon. Following Pietz's painstaking genealogy

of the concept, the fetish not only emerges out of situations of cross-cultural encounter, but remains specific to such "border" zones (Pietz 1985, 1987, 1988). In this sense, fetishism demarcates a "space of cultural revolution" (1985, 11) or one that invites comparison between distinct social orders, possibilities, and schemes, and that, in so doing, also opens up the potential for social criticism. It is important to bear in mind the genealogy of fetishism, its "sinister pedigree" (1985, 5), as a derogatory term for the illusions of others, and thus the ethics of the term itself. At the same time, my approach here is influenced by recent work that rehabilitates the place of fetishism for social theory, seeing it no longer as misguided perception or frivolous "caprice" but, instead, as a reevaluation in social practice of the meaning of value itself (Apter 1991; Apter and Pietz 1993; Czetkovich 1992; Pinch 1998b; Spyer 1998a).

39   This word, which I only heard used in this context, derives from the Dutch *zwak* for "weak."

5 Prow and Stern

1   Dates and calendars play an important role in fostering the sense of synchronicity and the feeling on the part of a group of people of leading lives parallel to those of other people they have never met that is crucial to the formation of national consciousness. Benedict Anderson gives a wonderful example from Pramoedya Ananta Toer's *Bumi Manusia* (Earth of Mankind), where in the opening pages "the young nationalist hero muses that he was born on the same date as the future Queen Wilhelmina—31 August 1880. 'But while my island was wrapped in the darkness of night, her country was bathed in sun; and if her country was embraced by night's blackness, my island glittered in the equatorial noon'" (Anderson 1991, 188).

2   For an incisive reading of the process of elections in Indonesia, see Pemberton 1986.

3   As Pemberton points out, "The uncanny certainty of these [national election] successes is implicit in the government's campaign imperative to *mensukseskan* (to 'success' them) which means, in essence, to secure a victory already scored" (1994, 45)

4   The letter is written in a mix of Aru Malay and Barakai. To differentiate between them I italicize the phrases in Barakai that tend to refer to specific codified actions of Bemun's performance. Nonetheless, if this mix of languages can be considered an example of what linguists call code switching, it is clear that neither Aru Malay nor Barakai constitutes in and of itself a strict or highly circumscribed code. Nor, importantly, is this the way Barakai islanders normally speak. Instead, the code-switching here conveys

Gita's sense that a letter should properly be written in "Indonesian" whereas comments regarding Bemun's annual performance may only be stated in Barakai. At the same time, her writing, as opposed to speaking, of Barakai is the result of my own influence in recording what until my arrival to the island had been an unwritten language.

5   The Indonesian term *dinas* derives from the Dutch word for official service, *dienst,* and was used, among other things, to refer to the service performed by colonial bureaucrats.

6   As in Gita's letter, the Barakai term *momosim* and the Indonesian *adat* are regarded as synonymous, both being a gloss for custom and customary practices. Depending on which language they are speaking, Barakai islanders refer to offerings and dedications to ancestors or to the spirits of land and sea places as either *dai momosim* or *bikin adat*, that is, doing or carrying out momosim or adat. For Bemunese, who regard themselves as the sole claimants and practitioners of the cassowary celebration, the spirit Koder, or cassowary, distinguishes their community from others in Aru that also organize performances (dai momosim) to usher in the west monsoon. It is in this marked sense that Bemunese often prefer to designate their annual performance as "doing the cassowary" (B. *dai koder*), in this way differentiating their own momosim practices from those of their neighbors. Notwithstanding the adamancy with which this perception of Bemun's exclusiveness is maintained, an Indonesian anthropologist produced a B.A. thesis on a cassowary performance—which he calls Kudera— that is held in Kobadangar village on Baun Island north of Barakai (Purwadi 1980). I am grateful to G. G. Weix for seeking out this thesis and its author in the back streets of Legian, Bali.

7   Most, if not all, Barakai islanders are probably unaware of the existence of Beautiful Indonesia in Miniature Park. Except for Gita, who accompanied me on several trips to the provincial capital of Ambon, no Bemunese had ventured farther than the neighboring Kei Islands as of March 1988, and those that had traveled that far were relatively few. For many Barakai men a change in this regard resulted from the boom in shark fins, when they were often employed on boats that took them as far as Irian Jaya—but then usually only to relatively small coastal places like Kaimana. Before the early 1990s all adult men and women had, however, made at least one trip to Dobo, where they would either have watched television in the homes of traders or watched the television mounted on a post under an awning in Kampong Pisang ("Banana Village"), the Dobo settlement of Kei islanders where Bemunese otherwise reside when in the capital. Before 1993, when TV reception became possible on the Backshore and Bemun and the other Barakai villages received a television set from the government, it is in these settings that they might have seen the various "cultural" programs sponsered by TVRI. Barakai islanders are also aware of the annual adat dance

competitions held in the regency capital of Tual, in which representatives of the various southeast and southwest Moluccas participate. Many islanders also know that Aru's contribution is inevitably the bird of paradise dance (I. *tarian cenderawasih*). Some of the older islanders also know that the performance of such dances dates to the colonial period, when they were held in Dobo, as in other places in the Netherlands East Indies, on August 31 in honor of Queen Wilhelmina's birthday.

8　I have elsewhere characterized this process as "serialization" in order to foreground how the creation of homogeneously defined and bounded units such as adat dance but also more abstract categories as "religion" and "citizen" are, for the practical purposes of rule regarded as alike, interchangeable, and enumerable, as belonging to a series of a like sort (Spyer 1996b).

9　John Pemberton's wonderful discussion of Taman Mini Indonesia Indah, a chapter of his book *On the Subject of "Java"* that explores the appearance of order in contemporary Indonesia as an effect of the former Suharto regime's particular cultural politics, is the only full-fledged attempt I know of to analyze this national institution. Pemberton's insights regarding the recasting of tradition according to a provincial and hence state administrative mold are worth quoting at length: "The effects of Mini's continuous projection of recovered origins and timeless traditions reemerge most conspicuously in the culture park's twenty-six so-called customary houses (*rumah adat*), exhibition pavilions representing each of Indonesia's twenty-six provinces (before the annexation of East Timor). For the formal dedication of Mini in 1975, twenty-six governors attended, each attired in the 'customary regional costume' of his administrative territory regardless of his actual, most often Javanese, ethnic background. An East Javanese 'New Guinean' governor with a fur crown and large ornamental nose bone, sat, exemplifying diversity, alongside his fellow regional representatives" (Pemberton 1994, 157–58; cf. Anderson 1990, 152–93; Bowen 1991, 125–27).

10　James Siegel suggests how an Acehnese airplane dating from the Indonesian revolution and proudly donated by the province of Aceh to the Mini park in response to Mrs. Suharto's request for objects symbolizing the province disturbs the timeless past of an Indonesian heritage. Against the background of the museumized steady state of authenticity that characterizes the park, the Acehnese plane, fenced off from the other exhibits and only visible from Mini's overhead train, by having a particular history and anachronistic appearance in the setting of the park also has the capacity to bring the past actively into the present, thereby potentially setting off stories, stirring up idiosyncratic associations, and otherwise unsettling the "concrete ideology" of this miniature place. Greg Acciaioli argues, somewhat similarly, regarding Taman Mini Sulawesi that it undermines government intentions not only by referring to a geographic entity (the island of

Sulawesi) rather than the administrative unit of the province, but also in the historicity that it implies. The ruins of the Somba Opu fort, a main fort of the last independant Makassar sultanate, where archeological excavation is in progress and on which the park is built, constrain the location of adat houses, while graves of unknown soldiers to which offerings are made and sacred cannons from the original Makassar forces bring the past into association with the present in other ways (Acciaioli n.d.).

11   Beyond the Moluccas in other parts of eastern Indonesia, the topographical placement of a boat in an important site in village space indicates its coherence and efficacy for community understandings and endeavors (Adams 1974; Barraud 1985; Kana 1980; Pauwels 1990; van Dijk and de Jonge 1990; Visser 1989; Vroklage 1940). The eloquent testimony of the so-called ship cloths of south Sumatra (Gittinger 1979, 89–93; Barbier and Newton 1988, 234–48) suggests as well how the symbolic significance of the boat concept throughout the region outweighed and in some instances continues to outweigh any simple utilitarian function that boats fulfill for people. Notwithstanding the long-standing ubiquity of boat imagery across the archipelago, it is important to realize that geographical proximity to the sea in no way determines or necessarily motivates the elaboration of the boat within social or artistic forms (Barraud 1985, 117). Nor, indeed, do some of the people who employ boat imagery use boats or live from the sea (Kana 1980).

12   "Setting sail" and other forms of travel are a recurrent mode of framing performative action in eastern Indonesia. As Fox observes, "In eastern Indonesia a common metaphor for any elaborate sequence is that of the 'journey'—an interposed movement through time or space. This general metaphor is supported by numerous more specific metaphors: walking, climbing, soaring, diving, mounting ladders, following paths, riding horses, or setting sail" (1988, 21). The particular mode of travel may affect its meaning in yet other ways—the specifics of how the journey inscribes itself in time and space, or the perspective and particular subjectivity assumed by the travelers. For recent work on Indonesia that deals with shamanic journeying, see Atkinson 1989 and Tsing 1993.

13   Until recently Kei supplied many of the islands in the southeast Moluccas with boats, boat models, and more generally the knowledge of sophisticated woodworking techniques (Barraud 1979, 20–21; Brumond 1853, 286–87; Earl 1853, 103; Merton 1910, 134–35; van Hoëvell 1890, 37–38; Villiers 1981, 742). Older islanders still recall the seasonal visits of Keiese boat traders, who appeared on the Backshore during the west monsoon with a string of plank-built boats in tow. Additionally, at least a portion of the local supply of belan were probably built in Aru after Kei models from an early date. For Tanimbar, McKinnon mentions several plank-built boats, including one with the generic name *belan*, as variations on Kei prototypes (1988, 156).

14   *Bela*, or "friend-brother" alliances, do not have the same kind of social significance in Aru today as they seem to have had in the past, when they were characterized by reciprocal feasting and gift-giving (Riedel 1886, 200; cf. Brumond 1844, 263; de Hollander 1895, 526). In the past, communities associated as bela gave each other tusks, gongs, porcelain, and cloth as a "sign of friendship" (Riedel 1886, 260; cf. McKinnon 1991 on *kida bela* in Tanimbar). The term *bela* is related to a similar form of relationship known as *pela* that is prevalent in the central Moluccas and also of considerable importance among Ambonese resident in the Netherlands (Abdurachman 1981, 6–7; Bartels 1977).

15   The use of Kermode's idea of the "sense of an ending" to address the relation of the Prow and the Stern in Bemunese ritual practice is inspired by Elizabeth Traube's somewhat different use of this idea to talk about trunk-tip relations among Mambai peoples in East Timor (Traube 1989).

16   No indigenous names for months that presumably once existed are recalled today on Barakai. Islanders do, however, assimilate months to moons when speaking both Barakai and Aru Malay. Thus they speak of *olan eti, olan ru, olan lasi* or, in Aru Malay *bulan satu, bulan dua, bulan tiga,* or one/first month, two/second month, three/third month.

17   Spyer 1992 contains a brief hypothetical reconstruction of this intercalary process on Barakai, pp. 291–93. For an excellent and extensive discussion of so-called primitive calendars and a reconstruction of such a calendar on the Indonesian island of Sumba, see Hoskins 1993, 339–52.

18   Along with calendars, wall clocks have recently made a significant inroad on Aru's Backshore. In 1994 a wall clock was one of the most popular gifts that were given to couples when they raised a new home. One schoolteacher's house in Longgar boasted as many as eleven (see also Spyer 1996b).

19   The two-week upgrading courses that were required under Suharto for all civil servants below the rank of cabinet minister and focused exclusively on the state ideology of Pancasila were called P4, which is shorthand for Pedoman Penghayatan dan Pengamalan Pancasila, or Upgrading Course on the Directives for the Realization and Implementation of Pancasila. For a discussion of the P4 courses, see Morfit 1981.

20   Ward Keeler's insightful discussion of three village headman in Central Java of the late 1970s was helpful in understanding some of the problems that headmen under Suharto's development-oriented New Order often faced more generally. I draw here on his definition of modernist as both "modernizing," that is, concerned with the introduction and administration of government development programs, and "rationalizing," as in the process through which a village headman begins to shift from a more socially embedded understanding of his office to a more bureaucratically defined one (Keeler 1987, 85–108).

21 The Stern, who inherited the office from his father when the latter was too old to accompany the men on the cassowary hunt, is the oldest brother of three, the fourth and youngest having died when he was already an adult. In principle, the office of Stern will be passed by the current title holder to his younger brother, who, in turn, will eventually pass it on to his younger brother, the former village headman. Once the line of brothers is exhausted, the title should revert back to the eldest son of the eldest brother, that is, the eldest son of the current title holder (who actually seems the most likely to want to assume the office when his father becomes too old to continue in his function). Note that the conflict described by the Stern as "the ritual without an ending" pitted this man against his own brother, when the latter was Bemun's headman. Given that the village headman's pressures repeatedly put him at odds with the Prow and the Stern alike—both on different occasions and simultaneously—and that the two brothers generally get along and cooperate in numerous important matters, the fact of kinship was, I believe, largely irrelevant here. Moreover, unlike other parts of eastern Indonesia where rivalry tends to plague the relationships between elder and younger brothers (Fox 1980; McKinnon 1991; Schulte Nordholt 1971), such is not the case on Barakai Island. In part, this relative harmony among brothers may be due to the common exploitation of sago holdings by members of the same patrilineal group so that conflicts over groves tend to break out between fam, not within them, while the most important resources for the islanders—the reefs and deeps where they dive and collect sea products for trade—are held and exploited communally by the men and women of a village. Thus, conflicts over diving grounds and collection sites occur among the different Barakai communities and not within them.

22 "Western-style" is a gloss for a much more complex and hybrid form of fashion that I use only to indicate the gendered colonial-derived basic dress forms prescribed for women and men respectively: the skirts, blouses, and dresses of the former (although some older women prefer a sarong and kebaya combination), and the shorts and T-shirts worn by men and boys on a daily basis as well as the long trousers and shirts they wear on church holidays and official occasions. Barakai women pay much attention to the fashions worn by the Chinese tradeswomen; as of 1994 some of the younger women were beginning to wear the loose batik print skirt or shorts and blouse sets sold in Aru stores that were a common everyday form of attire among Backshore and Dobo tradeswomen.

23 Interestingly, su'buan adat, or "watchpost of adat," the term used by surrounding communities to refer to the role of guardian of adat practices assumed by a minority religious community in highland Sulawesi, is a cognate of the Barakai sabuan for "mooring post," which has become a privileged locus for assessing the state of Bemun's adat affairs (George 1996, 34).

6 The Cassowary's Play

1   In his sensitive study of contemporary headhunting ritual in upland Sula-
    wesi, Kenneth George comments similarly on the ambivalence villagers
    may experience when commenting on or performing traditional rites
    (1996, 102–3).

2   Derrida's discussion of the parergon emerged out of his reading of Kant's
    Critique of Judgement.

3   Known as *dag* in Barakai and *tuba* in Indonesian, this root is *Derris elliptica*
    Benth.

4   The roots are bundled by the men the day after they are collected and then
    left to soak in a small estuary not too far from Bemun for one night
    preceding the river performance. Soaking softens the roots so that they will
    easily release their poisonous sap.

5   In 1987, to everyone's surprise, the Prow "walked" immediately on the
    evening of the day on which the disappointing fish poisoning had been
    held. Usually, I was told, at least one day passes between this portion of the
    annual performance and the evening on which the men "speak" for the
    third and last time. Not only does this interval allow villagers to consume
    whatever fish may have been caught during the rite, but it also gives them
    time to visit the graves of their dead relatives before the cassowary hunt
    begins. One wonders, therefore, if the Prow's haste to "walk" was his own
    way of registering his disapproval over the meager fish catch and the river's
    chief, since Bemunese still had to wait the same amount of time—a mini-
    mum of one day on which the visits to graves took place—before the hunt
    could begin. In other words, his own remarked-upon haste did nothing to
    alter the rhythm of the performance itself.

6   Hoskins notes a similar transference between the success or failure of the
    collection of sea worms in the context of the "Kodi New Year" festivities on
    the Indonesian island of Sumba and that of the rice harvest (1993, 336).

7   Ilmu is regarded as "hot" (rara). Although it may provide its practitioners
    with wealth and power, its deployment comes with a cost that often ex-
    presses itself by taking the lives of close kin of the person who practices
    ilmu.

8   This prohibition on recording and photographing at any time of the per-
    formance except immediately before dawn, right before the cassowary is
    "killed" for the last time on the concluding night of the performance,
    applied during both successive years in which I participated. At this point
    in the performance, the community has already begun the process of open-
    ing itself again to a larger malayu world, having ritually washed their hands
    earlier in the day and thereby relaxed some of the bans and prohibitions in
    force. Many, however, were skeptical that my recordings and photo taking
    would have any results. Several mentioned a tradesman who had once

unsuccessfully tried to photograph the cassowary effigy. Most, including the Stern, claimed that the cassowary was both too ethereal and too refined to be captured on film, while the heat that both he and the performance more generally produce and generate would more likely than not burn the film roll up in the camera. No one was surprised, therefore, when the first roll of film indeed failed. When in 1994 I returned to Aru with some successful pictures of the effigy that I had made in 1987, the Stern simply nodded and said "they agreed"—by whom he meant the guardian spirits of his community's annual performance. Hence the photo in this chapter.

9 Although Bemunese do not themselves describe their annual performance as a process of turning inwards and backwards, I use this characterization here because it captures well the introspective mood that takes hold of many villagers, the effect of the severing of ties with the malayu as introducing a distinction between an "inside" gwerka and an "outside malayu, and the sense of an Aru past as set off from and prior to a Malay present.

10 During the performances of 1986 and 1987 in which I participated, the only persons who chose to opt out of the performance as a whole were Bemunese women married to men from Kei, although in some cases and in some years Keiese resident in the village and married to Bemunese would participate in the cassowary celebration. Some women chose to participate without their husbands, while others would not participate but nonetheless joined in the dancing on the last night of the performance when the village was also open to spectators from the neighboring Barakai communities. As for Keiese women married to Bemunese men, they would almost always participate with their husbands in the performance.

11 Except in cases of old age or illness, deciding to "gather palm fronds" or, rather, taking a decision one way or the other, is a serious matter. Although in both 1986 and 1987 a number of men were forced to "gather palm fronds" for what seemed a trivial reason—the lack of a fishing spear—this does not mean that no perceived difference exists for Bemunese between participation and nonparticipation or, more precisely, that true participation is not regarded as having an important efficacy both for the community and for the individual participant. Thus, if the fish poisoning imposes the ban of the sea and sets the conditions for the arrival of the cassowary, it is also held to affect the pencarian of those who participate and, notably, of the men. It follows that the concrete details of each man's participation in the annual performance (if a man speared a wild boar, got burned by the fires, was wounded by another man, and so on) can be scrutinized, evaluated, and mined, on the one hand, for their predictive power over what the coming year will bring and, on the other, for post hoc explanations of pencarian-related events in this man's life and in those of his family. For instance, a week or so before the 1987 performance, I heard the headman's wife berate her husband, saying that he had gathered palm fronds for too many years

and that it was having a negative effect on his pencarian. One of the reasons, I believe, that the headman chose to spend the day in Longgar during the fish poisoning is that, more than any other portion of Bemun's annual performance, the fish poisoning contains practices that would be condemned as backward and primitive by government officials and other residents in the capital Dobo. The choice of whether to "gather palm fronds" or not should not be made lightly: once spoken aloud, a person's decision is held to be irreversible. When several weeks before the performance in 1986 a teenage boy complained to his mother that his loincloth was too short and he would need another for this year's celebration, his mother replied that he could at least wear it on the fish poisoning. The boy retorted, angrily, that in that case he would "gather palm fronds" this year. His mother and older sister both shook their heads at this rash assertion, knowing that he would regret it when he watched his friends departing in loincloths for the river, as indeed he did.

12   Following Comaroff and Comaroff, the implications of actual bodily experience for imaging and acting on the forces of history are crucial (1992, 72).

13   Both the name *gar* and the miniature size and simplicity of this betel basket contrast with the larger, intricately decorated betel baskets (*sevlaan*) that Wallace praised more than one hundred years ago (1962 [1869], 356).

14   A lengthier treatment of the Stern's accounting of the "sins" of his fellow villagers is included in my discussion of the role of numbers and seriality in Bemun's conversion to Catholicism; see Spyer 1996b.

15   There are, however, several occasions beyond the performance when special behavior marked as lul may be deliberately imposed. The most common occurs when a man or woman places a "ban" on the physical person of a child who is given his or her name at birth. Already by virtue of sharing a name, Barakai islanders attribute a certain affinity to namesakes (*temun*) as well as a sense of comparability, which, however, never seems to be elaborated in propositional statements concerning shared physical characteristics, personality traits, destinies, or the like. When infants are named for relatives in the grandparental generation, this practice augments the identification between alternate generations that is already implied in the use of the reciprocal term *abu* between grandparents and grandchildren. When an older person who is not a grandparent decides to observe a ban regarding the physical person of his or her namesake until some future, unspecified moment, then the affinity contained in the sharing of a name becomes a powerful and efficacious bond. This efficacy rests in the hands of the older person, who establishes the precise moment to lift the ban by laying her hands on her younger namesake. At such time, she pools small contributions from close kin and selects an article of clothing to concretize the more personal dimension of the "payment" she makes for "touching the namesake." After a period of avoidance that can last as much as the first ten years of a child's life, the lifting of the ban by the physical laying on of hands

suggests the same idea of implicit blessing as when a child is named for a grandparent.

16 Although Bemunese speak of the ban of the sea as ensuing from the fish poisoning, its full force is not felt until the cassowary is in the village and his celebration begins in earnest. During the one or two days that usually fall between the poisoning and the hunt, villagers do not refrain from eating saltwater fish, from sailing their boats to the neighboring Barakai communities to stock up on additional supplies and to collect relatives who want to participate in the feast, or from making trips to the beach to bail out and secure their boats before the hunt begins. But still there are limits to the types of engagement that Bemunese can enjoy with the sea following the fish poisoning or more precisely to the marked malayu activity of pencarian. A woman who spent the afternoon following the 1987 fish poisoning thigh-deep in the sea gathering eucheuma seaweed to help defray the costs of the feast was, for instance, severely criticized by members of her own family, who said they feared repercussions from the spirits.

17 The Barakai word *tabol*, which I translate as "game," refers, as in English, both to the animals hunted in the forest and to the meat that these animals provide.

18 Visibility is a crucial aspect of this process, as I discovered to my discomfort when, owing to a bout of conjunctivitis during the 1986 performance, I tried to substitute eyeglasses for my usual contact lenses. While presumably both of these objects would be classified as malayu, only the former, being visible, were prohibitively so and hence momosim.

19 Since the first fam said to have arrived on Barakai has died out, the Sister's Children today all trace themselves to one of three women in the third ascending generation who represented the last members of the now extinct fam Walwl. As already noted, the Prow is also selected from the fam that first settled on the island, while the Stern comes from the fam held to be the latecomer.

20 Men's and women's loincloths differ in appearance as they also did at the turn of the century (chapter 2) and have distinct names, respectively *gom* and *roro*. Loincloths of women are simple affairs consisting only of a narrow piece of cloth between the legs suspended from a cord around the waist and remain unseen today. Those worn by men are long pieces of cloth edged on either end with a colored band of a different fabric. Once wrapped around the loins, the two ends are left to dangle freely and play about the thighs of the hunters.

21 Given the ban of the sea (and of its products) that is in force during the cassowary celebration, it is noteworthy that the pendants are carved from pearl shell and that the patterning of the beads is described as "strips of fish cut lengthwise." These were in fact the only reference to the sea or the products of pencarian that I could discover in the context of the celebration. A remark made by my assistant when she was helping me translate the

cassowary's song is perhaps telling in this regard. Although some others later challenged her interpretation of this part of the song, she claimed that one of the song's refrains evoked the green turtle found in the seas around Barakai and appreciated by traders and Aruese alike for its meat and eggs. As an explanation for this inclusion, Gita explained at the time that things of the land always contain a bit of the sea within themselves and vice versa. This view provides an interesting twist on the assertion that I mentioned earlier that the two, by contrast, "never mix" and suggests that this relationship as well as that of malayu and gwerka allow for a number of different and divergent interpretations.

22   Some men also make offerings at the small altar in the adat house that is associated with the former village site of the Bemunese, Wanusumor. Both the house and the office pertaining to Wanusumor belong to the fam Jonjonler. Simply referred to as "the middle," owing to its approximate location between the houses of the Prow and the Stern, this house—apart from the offerings that some men choose to make there at this time of year—plays no part in community affairs. Nonetheless, since the Jonjonler ancestor Gwadaur is rumored to have been a great war leader, men besides this man's descendants may deem it wise to offer at this altar. Bemunese, especially men, occasionally describe the hunt as a "war" waged against game animals.

23   Apart from men or adolescent boys belonging to the fam of the Prow or the Stern, who should gravitate respectively toward their kinsman at the front or rear of the line, and the Sister's Children, who position themselves immediately after the Prow, all others assume a place in the line arbitrarily. The only exceptions are the participants from the neighboring communities, who are assigned a place at the extreme rear of the formation directly in front of the Stern.

24   During both years in which I participated in the performance, I only saw the men's game played by boys. It is unlikely that even in the past adult men would have engaged in this game with much frequency. Unlike the women, who sometimes spend almost the entire day in such play, the men can only have enjoyed their game in the short interval between their return from the forest and the evening meal, a time when many prefer to rest.

25   Similarly, Janet Hoskins mentions a game that is traditionally associated with the annual sea worm festivities in Kodi, West Sumba, and that may not be played in the period preceding the arrival of the worms (1993, 92),

26   Since all of these games provoke laughter and ululation, there is a sense in which the enforcement of silence when the men are in the forest refers primarily to the interior of the house. The same idea seems to be implied in a remark of Abu Meme, who noted to me that she always steps out of her house to pound coffee when the men are in the forest.

27   *Koal* derives from *dakoal*, "to hunt or track game."

28   "*Our* ancestors" merges in significance and is often used interchangeably with the spirit guardians who watch over the complex of adat or momosim

practices that constitute and empower Bemun as a distinct community in relation to its neighbors.

29 Reassuringly, I was told that this kind of accident would only occur if the hunter or the man felled had committed a serious transgression such as sleeping with a woman while the celebration was under way.

30 On the relationship between palms and cassowaries in neighboring New Guinea, see Gell 1975.

31 In both 1986 and 1987 two of these men belonged to the Sister's Children, another was a Longgarese who had married into Bemun, while two others were sons of the Stern. Although one of the Stern's sons always wore the effigy first, villagers denied any special importance to this occurrence and claimed that it was so only because this man was so adept at the game of hide and seek that begins the nightly feasting. Nonetheless, this initial association with the fam that provides the official who represents "the ending" at this time of year seems to prefigure the ending that awaits the cassowary at each night's conclusion.

32 The "coming to life" of such material effigies often hinges on a critical detail. In the case of the *malangan* of New Ireland, the addition of the "eye," which allows the image to look back at the viewer, brings the malangan to life (Kuchler 1988, 631).

33 The cassowary's master's decision of when to end the nightly feasting is necessarily swayed by the crowd, which may protest if they feel he wants to kill the effigy too swiftly.

34 If a kajinwaten is killed by the hunters in the forest, then a second "killing" will not take place in the village that day, although it will on every other day of the performance that a real cassowary is not taken.

35 Reid notes the early importance throughout Southeast Asia of dance as a means of communicating with spirits and gods and of encouraging their attendance at feasts (1988, 203).

36 A similar dance performed by Tanimbarese women is called "to dance like frigate birds" (McKinnon 1983). Von Rosenberg writes that the Aruese bird of prey *nawai* corresponds to both *Halieaetus leucogaster* and the less common *Haliastur leucosternum* (1867, 356).

37 The village headman held the task of singing at the conclusion of the nightly festivities and notably when the cassowary was killed. The headman had a fine singing voice and denied that there was any other reason why he rather than any other man in the village should sing the final lead. At the same time, he confided that, since he took over this task, numerous cassowaries had been killed during the hunt.

38 One woman gave a slightly different interpretation of the third stanza, "the cassowary drinks palm wine, he drinks water," tracing it back to the structure of bans and prohibitions in place during the performance. Taken together the drinking of water and palm wine indexed, in her view, the ban on "touching water" as well as its acknowledged transgression in the expression

"she/he drinks palmwine." This view discloses a transgressive dimension to the cassowary himself and one that ultimately motivates his killing and exile from the human community. A Longgarese man provided a disparaging reading of this same stanza, claiming that the Bemunese song mentions palm wine because it was the desire for foreign spirits and especially sopi that in the early nineteenth century motivated the migration of Bemunese ancestors from the island's interior and their resettlement on the coast.

39 See Keane 1997a and 1997b on the problematic tendency to privilege the semantic over the pragmatic and context-bound when analyzing ritual speech.

40 By calling the "long thoughts" of Bemunese women and men personal and biographical, I do not suggest that they somehow lie beyond the larger, more encompassing, and shared "social frames of memory" specific to Aru's Backshore. As Halbwachs and others since him have argued, memories are always socially constituted (Halbwachs 1952 [1925]). That this is so is especially clear in the case of Bemun's annual performance, where the personal memories of women and men are both subsumed and elaborated under the specific and exclusive form of "long thoughts" within the context of the larger process of memory work and mourning that characterizes the annual performance as a whole.

41 As on previous nights the effigy—still containing the cassowary's master—was hoisted onto a pole supported by two men, and with the crowd of ululating, "barking," and wailing men, women, and children in hot pursuit rushed off to the enclosure at the Front of the Path. There the men lay the cassowary on the ground and gestured as if incising his chest to divide the spirit's meat among the living. At this, the cassowary's master stepped out of the effigy and hung this third and last "skin" of the 1987 performance alongside the others from the previous nights. On the final night, Bemunese linger around the Front of the Path and talk quietly in the village pathways. Some drift back to their houses to rest, but most await their first bath since the hunt began before going home to sleep. The Stern, who "bathes first" and thereby lifts the prohibition on "touching water" imposed at the outset of the performance, usually sets off fairly quickly for the village water source. Somewhat later the Stern's wife follows suit when she is satisfied that most of Bemun's men have bathed.

42 The four directions are north (*medemar*), west (*awar*), south (*trangan*), and east (*sumor*).

7 The Women's Share

1 Not surprisingly, slippage in the opposite direction, from adat to agama, also often occurs. Thus, Bemunese often construe their obligations to and

exchanges with the Catholic church in adat terms, that is, following a strict reciprocity logic. In 1987, for instance, a wooden plaque with a crude skull and bones and the words *sasi gereja* on it was affixed to a mango tree in the approximate center of Bemun. Having paid a sum of money to the church with the specific aim of garnering protection for his tree, the owner was assured that if some person stole his mangos, God would be sure to retaliate—hence the sign complete with skull and bones reading "church sanction."

2   This association is further enabled by the way in which "baptism" is construed in the Barakai language. Thus, when Bemunese claim that the cassowary was baptized first in their community, they say "the cassowary bathed first" (B. *koder artur nal mon*).

3   The phenomenon of constructing parallelisms that frequently lend themselves to temporalization crops up widely in the literature on conversion (cf. Hoskins 1987). Graham gives a wonderful example from Flores in which the "new" religion is more or less spliced onto something configured as the "old" indigenous religion, or the so-called *agama asli*, conceived as "analogous to the biblical Old Testament and the knowledge of Christ it contains" (Graham n.d.). This temporalization informed the organization of a procession that in tracing a trajectory from the site of the demolished temple of the "old indigenous religion" to the Catholic church enacted the supposed transition from the "old" to the "new," from a "before" to an "after."

4   Indeed, Bemunese who spoke of their cassowary celebration as their own agama tended to lower their voices when doing so. What they meant was not their former "old" religion but their own, legitimate, claim to having a religion that they had inherited from their ancestors as opposed to one imported from elsewhere. In contrast to other parts of Indonesia, where minority groups have successfully managed to have their traditional religion officially recognized by the government—for instance, the Kaharingen religion practiced by peoples in Kalimantan and the *uluk to dolo* of the Toraja peoples of Sulawesi—such was never an option in Aru. With the hindsight of knowledge brought to these islands by the recent introduction of national television, some Bemunese wondered why their own choice of agama had been so restricted—why, more precisely, unlike themselves, the Balinese, as they see it, were permitted to remain "Hindu," a term that in Aru applies to what on certain limited occasions these islanders conceive of as their former religion.

5   After giving birth, women are considered to be cool. Therefore, in the first weeks after birth, a fire is kept constantly burning near the woman and her newborn.

6   Stories, rumors, and criticism of the Prow and his family underscore the substantive connection between this official's home and the Sea House of the Land. In 1988, for instance, when the mooring post was toppled by a

Longgarese belan, the Prow's house became an object of scrutiny and criticism. Some women I spoke to about the felled post recalled that, before the Prow built himself a cement house, the hunters would lay their spears on the ends of the floor posts that jutted out from under the Prow's raised dwelling when they returned from the forest during the cassowary hunt. As with many other actions in this context, the men, according to the women, did so with an eye toward their own pencarian. The women went on to explain that the ends of the floor posts of the Sea House of the Land are encrusted with oysters, which they added accounts for the strict prohibition against crawling under houses—to fetch, for instance, something that has fallen from above—during the performance. Currently, however, several women complained, only the rear of the house—raised several feet off the ground and constructed of the same *sir* wood as the post—conforms to the requirements of an adat house and thus to the Sea House of the Land. One woman added as well that, while the construction of this back kitchen area was itself fine, its location was at fault. What she described as the momosim part of the Prow's house should have been the more important front and public part of this adat official's home rather than its devalued rear, where the bulk of women's activities, especially cooking and socializing, take place. Summing up the entire discussion, another woman commented on how the pencarian of neighboring Mesiang had declined dramatically when the village had tried to make do with a cement adat house. Instead of beds full of oysters, Mesiangese divers had only encountered banks of sand. It was not until a proper raised house again replaced the cement one, she added, that Mesiang's pencarian took an equally dramatic turn for the better, pointing to the abundance of trepang found in its seas.

7   The mooring post's food comprises four times the contents of the earthenware sago mold (B. *taukor kau*) and four coconuts (B. *ar kai*) as well as an earthenware water jug filled with water. Sago flour is baked in the five-slotted mold four times, thus yielding a total of twenty square cakes. These cakes are stacked, tied with rattan cord to form a tall packet and then placed in a woven basket that is commonly used for storing sago flour. Women claimed that when the mooring post topples and triggers a longer, more elaborate version of the cassowary performance, the food prepared for the post is somewhat different: eight coconuts are readied instead of four, while a number of new items supplement the packet of sago cakes. The senior woman of the Sister's Children who prepares the sago cakes also boils four bunches of bananas (B. *ken okau*) together in an earthenware wok. Another senior woman belonging to this group husks and cleans so-called Aru rice on a mat spread at the base of the ladder leading into the Prow's house. The husks may not fall on the ground. The rice is subsequently cooked with grated coconut and molded together on a plate into a tall mountain. The fact that the falling of the post compels the preparation of a greater quantity

of more elaborate food suggests that the food is seen as a source of sustenance for the mooring post itself.

8   The Barakai rendering of *kenangan* falls somewhere between the Indonesian word that covers souvenir, keepsake, memento, remembrances, ideals of the past (*kenang-kenangan*), and the verb recall (*mengkenangkan*) (see also Echols and Shadily 1989).

Works Cited

Abdurachman, Paramita R. 1981. *New Winds, New Faces, New Forces (Ambon Island)*. Jakarta: Lembaga Ilmu Kebudayaan Nasional LIPI.

Abu-Lughod, Lila. 1990. The Romance of Resistance: Tracing Transformations of Power through Bedouin Women. *American Ethnologist* 17:41–55.

Acciaioli, Greg. 1996. Pavilions and Posters: Showcasing Diversity and Development in Contemporary Indonesia. *Eikon* 1:27–42.

———. n.d. A Tale of Two *Taman* (-*Mini*): National and Local Representations of Regional Identity in Contemporary Indonesia. Paper presented at the Center for Asian Studies, University of Amsterdam, April 8, 1997.

Adams, Kathleen M. 1998. More than an ethnic marker: Toraja art as identity negotiator. *American Ethnologist* 25(3):327–51.

Adams, M.J. 1974. Symbols of the Organized Community in East Sumba, Indonesia. *Bijdragen tot de Taal-, Land- en Volkenkunde* 130:324–47.

Anderson, Benedict. 1990. *Language and Power: Exploring Political Cultures in Indonesia*. Ithaca, N.Y.: Cornell University Press.

———. 1991. *Imagined Communities: Reflections on the Origin and Spread of Nationalism*. London: Verso.

Appadurai, Arjun. 1981. The Past as a Scarce Resource. *Man*, n.s, 16:201–19.

———. 1986. Introduction: Commodities and the Politics of Value. In *The Social Life of Things: Commodities in Cultural Perspective*, ed. Arjun Appadurai, pp. 3–63. Cambridge: Cambridge University Press.

———. 1988. Putting Hierarchy in Its Place. *Cultural Anthropology* 3 (1):6–49.

———. 1996. *Modernity at Large: Cultural Dimensions of Globalization*. Public Worlds, vol. 1. Minneapolis: University of Minnesota Press.

Apter, Emily. 1991. *Feminizing the Fetish: Psychoanalysis and Narrative Obsession in Turn-of-the-Century France*. Ithaca, N.Y.: Cornell University Press.

Apter, Emily, and William Pietz. 1993. *Fetishism as Cultural Discourse*. Ithaca, N.Y.: Cornell University Press.

Ardener, Shirley. 1987. A Note on Gender Iconography: The Vagina. In *The Cultural Construction of Sexuality*, ed. P. Caplan, pp. 111–42. Baltimore, Md.: Johns Hopkins University Press.

Asad, Talal. 1993. *Genealogies of Religion: Discipline and Reasons of Power in Christianity and Islam*. Baltimore, Md.: Johns Hopkins University Press.

Atkinson, Jane M. 1989. *The Art and Politics of Wana Shamanship*. Berkeley: University of California Press.

Barbier, Jean Paul, and Douglas Newton. 1988. *Islands and Ancestors: Indigenous Styles of Southeast Asia*. New York: Metropolitan Museum of Art.

Barraud, Cécile. 1979. *Tanebar-Evav: Une société de maisons tournée vers le large*. Cambridge: Cambridge University Press.

——. 1985. The Sailing-Boat: Circulation and Values in the Kei Islands, Indonesia. In *Contexts and Levels: Anthropological Issues on Hierarchy*, ed. R. H. Barnes, Daniel de Coppet, and R. J. Parkin, pp. 117–30. Oxford: JASO.

Bartels, D. 1977. Guarding the Invisible Mountain: Intervillage Alliances, Religious Syncretism and Ethnic Identity among Ambonese Christians and Moslems in the Moluccas. Ph.D. dissertation, Cornell University.

Barthes, Roland. 1967. *Système de la mode*. Paris: Seuil.

Beekman, E. M. 1988. *Fugitive Dreams: An Anthology of Dutch Colonial Literature*. Amherst, Mass.: University of Massachusetts Press.

Bell, Catherine. 1992. *Ritual Theory, Ritual Practice*. Oxford: Oxford University Press.

Benjamin, Walter. 1969. *Illuminations*. Ed. and introd. Hannah Arendt, trans. Harry Zohn. New York: Shocken.

Beversluis, A. J., and A. H. C. Gieben. 1929. *Het gouvernement der Molukken*. Weltevreden: Landsdrukkerij.

Bhabha, Homi K. 1989. Location, Intervention, Incommensurability: A Conversation with Homi Bhabha. *Emergences* 1 (1): 63–88.

——. 1994. Of Mimicry and Man: The Ambivalence of Colonial Discourse. In *The Location of Culture*, pp. 85–92. London: Routledge.

Bickmore, A. S. 1868. *Travels in the East Indian Archipelago*. London: John Murray.

Bik, A. J. 1928 [1824]. *Dagverhaal eener reis, gedaan in het Jaar 1824 tot Nadere Verkenning der Eilanden Keffing, Goram, Groot- en Klein Kei en de Aroe Eilanden*. Leiden: A. W. Sijthoff.

Bleeker, P. 1856. *Reis door de Minahassa en de Moluksche Archipel in 1855*. 2 vols. Batavia: Lange and Co.

Blussé, Leonard. 1991. The Role of Indonesian Chinese in Shaping Modern Indonesian Life: A Conference in Retrospect. *Indonesia* (special issue on the Role of the Indonesian Chinese in Shaping Modern Indonesian Life): 1–11.

Boon, James A. 1985. Anthropology and Degeneration: Birds, Words, and Orang-utans. In *Degeneration: The Dark Side of Progress*, ed. J. Edward Chamberlin and Sander L. Gilman, pp. 24–48. New York: Columbia University Press.

Bosscher, C. 1853. Staat aantoonende de voornaamste eilanden der Aroe Groep, benevens de voornaamste negorijen en het aantal van hare bewoners en huizen, in 1850. *Tijdschrift van Indische taal-, land- en volkenkunde* 1:327–31.

Bourdieu, Pierre. 1984. *Distinction: A Social Critique of the Judgment of Taste*. Trans. Richard Nice. Cambridge, Mass.: Harvard University Press.

Bowen, John R. 1991. *Sumatran Politics and Poetics: Gayo History, 1900–1989*. New Haven: Yale University Press.

Brenner, Suzanne April. 1998. *The Domestication of Desire: Women, Wealth, and Modernity in Java*. Princeton, N.J.: Princeton University Press.

Bronkhorst, Dorine, and Esther Wils. 1996. *Tropen Echt: Indische en Europese kleding in Nederlands-Indië*. The Hague: Stichting Tong Tong.

Brown, Peter. 1981. *The Cult of the Saints: Its Rise and Function in Latin Christianity*. Chicago: Chicago University Press.

Brumond, J. F. G. 1844. Proeve over de Aroe Taal. *Tijdschrift voor Nederlandsch-Indië* 6 (2):321–40.

——. 1853. Aanteekeningen gehouden op eene reis in het oosterlijk gedeelte van den Indischen Archipel. *Tijdschrift voor Nederlandsch-Indië* 7 (2): 69–89, 251–99.

Calvino, Italo. 1972. *Invisible Cities*. Trans. William Weaver. San Diego: Harcourt Brace Jovanovich.

Campione, Adele. 1989. *Women's Hats*. Milan: Be-ma Editrice.

Cayley-Webster, H. 1898. *Through New Guinea and the Cannibal Countries*. London: T. Fisher Unwin.

Chauvel, Richard. 1990. *Nationalists, Soldiers and Separatists*. Leiden: KITLV Press.

Clarence-Smith, William Gervase. 1998. The Economic Role of the Arab Community in Maluku, 1816–1940. *Indonesia and the Malay World* 26 (4): 32–49.

Clifford, James, and George E. Marcus. 1986. *Writing Culture: The Poetics and Politics of Ethnography*. Berkeley: University of California Press.

Cohn, Bernard S. 1989. Cloth, Clothes, and Colonialism: India in the Nineteenth Century. In *Cloth and Human Experience*, ed. Annette B. Weiner and Jane Schneider, pp. 303–53. Washington, D.C.: Smithsonian Institution Press.

Colley, Linda. 1992. *Britons: Forging the Nation, 1707–1837*. New Haven: Yale University Press.

Collins, James T. 1983. Linguistic Research in Maluku: A Report of Recent Field Work. *Oceanic Linguistics* 21 (1/2): 73–146.

——. 1996. Etymology and the History of Malay: Dutch Words. Paper presented at the workshop Malay Studies from Dutch Sources, Kuala Lumpur, November 1996.

Comaroff, John L., and Jean Comaroff. 1991. *Of Revelation and Revolution: Christianity, Colonialism, and Consciousness in South Africa*. Vol. 1. Chicago: University of Chicago Press.

——. 1992. *Ethnography and the Historical Imagination*. Boulder: Westview Press.

——. 1997. *Of Revelation and Revolution: Christianity, Colonialism, and Consciousness in South Africa*. Vol. 2. Chicago: University of Chicago Press.

"Comité 100 jaar MSC" of the Dutch Province. 1954. *Memoriale: Hundred Years of MSC All Over the World*. Tilburg: Mission House MSC.

Compost, Alain. 1980. *Pilot Survey of the Exploitation of Dugong and Sea Turtles in the Aru Islands*. Indonesia: Yayasan Hijau.

Coolhaas, W. Ph. 1960–1979. *Generale missiven van gouverneurs-generaal en raden aan Heren XVII der Vereenigde Oostindische Compagnie.* 7 vols. The Hague: Martinus Nijhoff.

Corbin, Alain. 1990. Backstage. In *A History of Private Life*, vol. 4: *From the Fires of Revolution to the Great War*, ed. Phillipe Ariès and George Duby, pp. 451–667. Cambridge: The Belknap Press of Harvard University Press.

Corpus Diplomaticum. 1907–1955 [1596–1799]. *Corpus Diplomaticum Neerlando-Indicum.* 6 vols. The Hague: Martinus Nijhoff.

Corrigan, Philip, and Derek Sayer. 1985. *The Great Arch: English State Formation as Cultural Revolution.* Oxford: Basil Blackwell.

Coward, Rosalind. 1983. *Patriarchal Precedents: Sexuality and Social Relations.* London: Routledge and Kegan Paul.

Cribb, Robert. 1997. Paradijsvogels op Nieuw-Guinea: Een pootloos modeartikel. *Spiegel historiael* 32 (10/11): 456–60.

——. 1998. Birds of Paradise and Environmental Politics in Colonial Indonesia, 1895–1931. In *Paper Landscapes: Explorations in the Environmental History of Indonesia*, ed. Peter Boomgaard, Freek Colombijn, and David Henley, pp. 379–408. Leiden: KITLV Press.

Curtin, Philip D. 1984. *Cross-Cultural Trade in World History.* Cambridge: Cambridge University Press.

Czetkovich, Ann. 1992. *Mixed Feelings: Feminism, Mass Culture, and Sensationalism.* New Brunswick, N.J.: Rutgers University Press.

Darwin, Charles E. 1979 [1859]. *On the Origin of Species by Means of Natural Selection, or the Preservation of Favoured Races in the Struggle for Life.* New York: Avenel Books (reprint ed.).

de Bougainville, Louis-Antoine. 1982 [1771]. *Voyage autour du monde par la frégate La Boudeuse et la flûte L'étoile.* Paris: Gallimard.

de Certeau, Michel. 1984. *The Practice of Everyday Life.* Berkeley: University of California Press.

——. 1986. *Heterologies: Discourse of the Other.* Trans. Brian Massumi. Minneapolis: University of Minnesota Press.

——. 1988. *The Writing of History.* Trans. Tom Conley. New York: Columbia University Press.

de Hollander, J. J. 1895. *Handleiding bij de beoefening der land- en volkenkunde van Nederlandsch Oost-Indië.* 2 vols. Breda: van Broese.

Derrida, Jacques. 1982. Signature Event Context. In *Margins of Philosophy.* Trans. Alan Bass, pp. 307–30. Chicago: University of Chicago Press.

——. 1988. *Limited Inc.* Trans. Samuel Weber and Jeffrey Mehlman. Evanston, Ill.: Northwestern University Press.

——. 1994. *Specters of Marx: The State of the Debt, the Work of Mourning, and the New International.* Trans. Peggy Kamuf. New York: Routledge.

Descombes, Vincent. 1980. *Modern French Philosophy.* Trans. L. Scott-Fox and J. M. Harding. Cambridge: Cambridge University Press.

de Vries, J. H. 1921. Godsdienstige Gebruiken en Christelijke Overblijfselen in de Residentie Amboina. *Nederlandsch-Indië oud en nieuw* 6:111–23.

Dirks, Nicholas B. 1990. History as a Sign of the Modern. *Public Culture* 2 (2): 25–32.

Djajadiningrat-Nieuwenhuis, Madelon. 1987. Ibuism and Priyayization: Path to Power? In *Indonesian Women in Focus: Past and Present Notions*, ed. Elsbeth Locher-Scholten and Anke Niehof, pp. 43–51. Dordrecht: Foris.

Drabbe, P. 1940. *Het Leven van den Tanémbarees: Ethnografische studie over het Tanémbareesche volk. Internationales archiv für ethnographie* 38, supplement. Leiden: E. J. Brill.

Earl, George Windsor. 1853. *The Native Races of the Indian Archipelago: Papuans.* London: Hippolyte Baillière.

Echols, John M., and Hassan Shadily. 1989. *An Indonesian-English Dictionary.* Ed. John U. Wolff and James T. Collins, in cooperation with Hassan Shadily. Ithaca, N.Y.: Cornell University Press.

Ellen, Roy F. 1986. Conundrums about Panjandrums: On the Use of Titles in the Relations of Political Subordination in the Moluccas and along the Papuan Coast. *Indonesia* 41:47–62.

——. 1988. Ritual, Identity and the Management of Interethnic Relations on Seram. In *Time Past, Time Present, Time Future: Perspectives on Indonesian Culture*, ed. Henri J. M. Claessen and David S. Moyer, pp. 117–35. Dordrecht: Foris Publications.

Fabian, Johannes. 1983. *Time and the Other: How Anthropology Makes Its Object.* New York: Columbia University Press.

Farn, Alexander E. 1986. *Pearls: Natural, Cultured, and Imitation.* London: Butterworths.

Florida, Nancy. 1992. The Badhaya Katawang: A Translation of the Song of Kangjeng Ratu Kidul. *Indonesia* 53:21–32.

Forbes, Anna. 1987 [1887]. *Unbeaten Tracks in Islands of the Far East: Experiences of a Naturalist's Wife in the 1880s.* Singapore: Oxford University Press.

Foucault, Michel. 1973. *The Birth of the Clinic: An Archaeology of Medical Perception.* Trans. A. M. Sheridan Smith. London: Tavistock Publications.

——. 1977. *Discipline and Punish: The Birth of the Prison.* Trans. Alan Sheridan. London: Allen Lane.

——. 1988. The Battle for Chastity. In *Politics, Philosophy, Culture: Interviews and Other Writings, 1977–1984*, pp. 227–41. New York: Routledge, Chapman and Hall.

——. 1990. *The History of Sexuality*, vol. 1: *An Introduction.* New York: Vintage Books.

Foulcher, Keith. 1990. The Construction of an Indonesian National Culture: Patterns of Hegemony and Resistance. In *State and Civil Society in Indonesia*, ed. Arief Budiman, pp. 301–20. Melbourne: Centre of Southeast Asian Studies.

Fox, James J. 1971. Sister's Child as Plant: Metaphors in an Idiom of Consanguinity. In *Rethinking Kinship and Marriage*, ed. R. Needham, pp. 219–52. Association of Social Anthropologists Monograph 11. London: Tavistock Publications.

——. 1988. *To Speak in Pairs: Essays on the Ritual Languages of Eastern Indonesia.* Cambridge: Cambridge University Press.

——, ed. 1980. *The Flow of Life: Essays on Eastern Indonesia.* Cambridge: Harvard University Press.

Freud, Sigmund. 1955 [1919]. The "Uncanny". In *The Standard Edition of the Complete Psychological Works of Sigmund Freud,* vol. 17, ed. James Strachey, pp. 217–52. London: Hogarth Press.

——. 1961 [1927]. Fetishism. In *The Standard Edition of the Complete Psychological Works of Sigmund Freud,* vol. 21, ed. James Strachey, pp. 152–57. London: Hogarth Press.

Gaines, Jane. 1990. Introduction: Fabricating the Female Body. In *Fabrications: Costume and the Female Body,* ed. Jane Gaines and Charlotte Herzog, pp. 1–27. New York: Routledge.

Garber, Marjorie. 1992. *Vested Interests: Cross-Dressing and Cultural Anxiety.* New York: Routledge.

Geertz, Clifford. 1990. "Popular Art" and the Javanese Tradition. *Indonesia* 50 (twenty-fifth anniversary issue), 77–94.

Gell, Alfred. 1975. *Metamorphosis of the Cassowaries: Umeda Society, Language, and Ritual.* London: Athlone Press.

George, Kenneth M. 1996. *Showing Signs of Violence: The Cultural Politics of a Twentieth-Century Headhunting Ritual.* Berkeley: University of California Press.

Geurtjens, P. H. 1910. Le cérémonial des voyages aux îles Kei. *Anthropos* 5:334–58.

Gilloch, Graeme. 1996. *Myth and Metropolis: Walter Benjamin and the City.* Cambridge: Polity Press.

Gittinger, Mattiebelle. 1979. *Splendid Symbols: Textiles and Traditions in Indonesia.* Washington, D.C.: Textile Museum.

Gluckman, Max. 1963. *Order and Rebellion in Tribal Africa.* Glencoe, Ill.: Free Press.

Graham, Penelope. n.d. Moralities in Conflict: Forging Minority Identities within the Indonesian State. Paper presented at the meetings of the European Association of Social Anthropologists, Oslo, Norway, June 1994.

Granta. 1998. *The Sea.* No. 61.

Greenblatt, Stephen. 1991. *Marvelous Possessions: The Wonder of the New World.* Chicago: University of Chicago Press.

Gupta, Akhil, and James Ferguson. 1992. Beyond "Culture": Space, Identity, and the Politics of Difference. In *Space, Identity, and the Politics of Difference,* ed. James Ferguson and Akhil Gupta. Theme issue, *Cultural Anthropology* 7 (1): 6–23.

Halbwachs, M. 1952 [1925]. *Les cadres sociaux de la mémoire.* Paris: Presses Universitaires de France.

Hanna, Willard A. 1978. *Indonesian Banda: Colonialism and Its Aftermath in the Nutmeg Islands.* Philadelphia: Institute for Human Issues.

Haraway, Donna J. 1991. *Simians, Cyborgs, and Women: The Reinvention of Nature.* New York: Routledge.

Hatley, Barbara. 1993. Constructions of "Tradition" in New Order Indonesian Theater. In *Culture and Society in New Order Indonesia*, ed. Virginia Matheson Hooker, pp. 48–69. Oxford: Oxford University Press.

Heryanto, Ariel. 1988. The Development of "Development." Trans. Nancy Lutz. *Indonesia* 46 (October): 1–24.

Hobsbawm, Eric J. 1983. Introduction: Inventing Traditions. In *The Invention of Tradition*, ed. Eric J. Hobsbawm and Terence Ranger, pp. 1–14. Cambridge: Cambridge University Press.

Hoskins, Janet. 1987. Entering the Bitter House: Spirit Worship and Conversion in West Sumba. In *Indonesian Religions in Transition*, ed. Rita Smith Kipp and Susan Rodgers, pp. 136–60. Tucson: University of Arizona Press.

——. 1993. *The Play of Time: Kodi Perspectives on Calenders, History, and Exchange*. Berkeley: University of California Press.

Hughes, Jock. 1987. The Languages of Kei, Tanimbar and Aru: A Lexicostatistic Classification. In *Miscellaneous Studies of Indonesian and Other Languages in Indonesia*, part 10, ed. Soenjono Dardjowidjojo. Jakarta: Badan Penyelenggara Seri NUSA.

Hugh-Jones, Stephen. 1992. Yesterday's Luxuries, Tomorrow's Necessities: Business and Barter in Northwest Amazonia. In *Barter, Exchange and Value: An Anthropological Approach*, ed. Caroline Humphrey and Stephen Hugh-Jones, pp. 42–74. Cambridge: Cambridge University Press.

Humphrey, Caroline and Stephen Hugh-Jones. 1992. Introduction: Barter, Exchange and Value. In *Barter, Exchange and Value: An Anthropological Approach*, ed. Caroline Humphrey and Stephen Hugh-Jones, pp. 1–20. Cambridge: Cambridge University Press.

Indische Gids. 1893a. De expeditie naar de Aroe-eilanden. 15 (1): 862–72.

——. 1893b. Hoe men in 1881 een woelgeest op de Aroe-eilanden tot rede bracht. 15 (2): 1247–1249.

Ivy, Marilyn. 1995. *Discourse of the Vanishing: Modernity, Phantasm, Japan*. Chicago: University of Chicago Press.

Joyce, Kristin and Shellei Addison. 1993. *Pearls: Ornament and Obsession*. New York: Simon and Schuster.

Kana, N. L. 1980. The Order and Significance of the Savunese House. In *The Flow of Life: Essays on Eastern Indonesian Culture*, ed. James J. Fox, pp. 221–30. Cambridge Mass.: Harvard University Press.

Kantorowicz, Ernst H. 1957. *The King's Two Bodies: A Study in Medieval Political Theology*. Princeton, N.J.: Princeton University Press.

Kartomi, Margaret J. 1993. Revival of Feudal Music, Dance, and Ritual in the Former "Spice Islands" of Ternate and Tidore. In *Culture and Society in New Order Indonesia*, ed. Virginia Matheson Hooker, pp. 193–210. Oxford: Oxford University Press.

Keane, Webb. 1995. The Spoken House: Text, Act, and Object in Eastern Indonesian Exchange. *Man*, n.s., 29:605–29.

——. 1996. Materialism, Missionaries, and Modern Subjects in Colonial Indonesia. In *Conversion to Modernities: The Globalization of Christianity*, ed. Peter van der Veer, pp. 137–70. New York: Routledge.

———. 1997a. Knowing One's Place: National Language and the Idea of the Local in Eastern Indonesia. *Cultural Anthropology* 12 (1): 37–63.

———. 1997b. *Signs of Recognition: Powers and Hazards of Representation in an Indonesian Society*. Berkeley: University of California Press.

———. forthcoming. Money Is No Object: Materiality, Desire, and Modernity in an Indonesian Society. In *Regimes of Value: Materiality and Modernity*, ed. Fred R. Myers.

Keeler, Ward. 1987. *Javanese Shadow Plays, Javanese Selves*. Princeton, N.J.: Princeton University Press.

Kenji, Tsuchiya, and James Siegel. 1990. Invincible Kitsch, or as Tourists in the Age of Des Alwi. *Indonesia* 50:61–76.

Kermode, Frank. 1966. *The Sense of an Ending: Studies in the Theory of Fiction*. Oxford: Oxford University Press.

Kipp, Rita Smith. 1990. *The Early Years of a Dutch Colonial Mission: The Karo Field*. Ann Arbor: University of Michigan Press.

Kipp, Rita Smith, and Susan Rodgers. 1987. Introduction: Indonesian Religions in Society. In *Indonesian Religions in Transition*, ed. Rita Smith Kipp and Susan Rodgers, pp. 1–31. Tucson: University of Arizona Press.

Kolff, D. H. 1840. *Voyages . . . through the Southern and Little Known Parts of the Moluccan Archipelago, and along the Previously Unknown Southern Coast of New Guinea . . . 1825–1826*. London: James Maddon and Co.

Koloniaal Verslag. 1893. The Hague: Algemeene Landsdrukkerij.

Kopytoff, Igor. 1986. The Cultural Biography of Things: Commoditization as Process. In *The Social Life of Things: Commodities in Cultural Perspective*, ed. Arjun Appadurai, pp. 64–91. Cambridge: Cambridge University Press.

Kracauer, Siegfried. 1995. *The Mass Ornament: Weimar Essays*. Trans., ed., and introd. Thomas Y. Levin. Cambridge: Harvard University Press.

Kuchler, S. 1988. Malangan: Objects, Sacrifice, and the Production of Memory. *American Ethnologist* 14 (4): 625–37.

Lach, Donald F. 1965. *Southeast Asia in the Eyes of Europe: The Sixteenth Century*. Chicago: University of Chicago Press.

Lears, Jackson. 1994. *Fables of Abundance: A Cultural History of Advertising in America*. New York: Basic Books.

Lévi-Strauss, Claude. 1950. Introduction à l'oeuvre de Marcel Mauss. In *Marcel Mauss: Sociologie et anthropologie*, pp. ix-lii. Paris: Presses Universitaires de France.

———. 1966. *The Savage Mind*. Trans. George M. Weidenfeld and Nicolson Ltd. Chicago: University of Chicago Press.

Lindsay, Timothy C. 1993. Concrete Ideology: Taste, Tradition, and the Javanese Past in New Order Public Space. In *Culture and Society in New Order Indonesia*, ed. Virginia Matheson Hooker, pp. 166–82. Oxford: Oxford University Press.

Lowenthal, David. 1985. *The Past Is a Foreign Country*. Cambridge: Cambridge University Press.

MacKnight, Charles Campbell. 1976. *The Voyage to Marege: Macassan Trepangers in Northern Australia*. Carlton: Melbourne University Press.

Maier, H. M. J. 1991. From Heteroglossia to Polyglossia: The Creation of Malay and Dutch in the Indies. *Indonesia* 50 (special issue): 37–65.

Mani, Lata. 1992. Cultural Theory, Colonial Texts: Reading Eyewitness Accounts of Widow Burning. In *Cultural Studies*, ed. Lawrence Grossberg, Cary Nelson, and Paula Treichler, pp. 392–408. London: Routledge.

Marin, Louis. 1988. *Portrait of the King*. Minneapolis: University of Minnesota Press.

Martin, Emily. 1992. The End of the Body? American Ethnological Society Distinguished Lecture, 1990. *American Ethnologist* 19 (1): 121–40.

Marx, Karl. 1967 [1867]. *Capital*. Vol. 1. New York: International Publishers.

Mauss, Marcel. 1967 [1925]. *The Gift: Forms and Functions of Exchange in Archaic Societies*. Trans. Ian Cunnison. New York: W. W. Norton and Company.

McKendrick, Neil. 1982a. Introduction. In *The Birth of a Consumer Society: The Commercialization of Eighteenth-Century England*, ed. Neil McKendrick, John Brewer, and J. H. Plumb, pp. 1–8. London: Europa Publications Limited.

——. 1982b. Part I: Commercialization and the Economy. In *The Birth of a Consumer Society: The Commercialization of Eighteenth-century England*, ed. Neil McKendrick, John Brewer, and J. H. Plumb, pp. 9–196. London: Europa Publications Limited.

McKinnon, Susan. 1983. Hierarchy, Alliance, and Exchange in the Tanimbar Islands. Ph D. dissertation, University of Chicago.

——. 1988. Tanimbar Boats. In *Islands and Ancestors: Indigenous Styles of Southeast Asia*, ed. Jean Paul Barbier and Douglas Newton, pp. 152–69. New York: The Metropolitan Museum of Art.

——. 1991. *From a Shattered Sun: Hierarchy, Gender, and Alliance in the Tanimbar Islands*. Madison: University of Wisconsin Press.

Meilinck-Roelofsz, M.A.P. 1962. *Asian Trade and European Influence between 1500 and 1630*. The Hague: Martinus Nijhoff.

Merton, Hugo. 1910. *Forschungsreise in den südöstlichen Molukken (Aru- und Kei Inseln)*. Frankfurt A.M.: Senckenbergischen Naturforschenden Gesellschaft.

Merwin, W. S. 1994. *Travel Poems by W. S. Merwin*. New York: Alfred A. Knopf.

Meyer, Birgit. 1998. Commodities and the Power of Prayer: Pentacostalist Attitudes towards Consumption in Contemporary Ghana. *Development and Change* 29 (4): 751–76.

Mmembe, Achille. 1992. Provisional Notes on the Postcolony. *Africa* 62 (1): 3–37.

Morfit, Michael. 1981. Pancasila: The Indonesian State Ideology According to the New Order Government. *Asian Survey* 21:838–51.

Mrázek, Rudolf. 1997. Indonesian Dandy: The Politics of Clothes in the Late Colonial Period, 1893–1942. In *Outward Appearances: Dressing State and Society in Indonesia*, ed. Henk Schulte Nordholt, pp. 117–50. Leiden: KITLV Press.

Mukerji, Chandra. 1983. *From Graven Images: Patterns of Modern Materialism.* New York: Columbia University Press.

Mulders, R. J. P. 1985. Fishery in Connexion with the Village Organisation at the Tanimbar Archipelago. Unpublished manuscript.

Munn, Nancy D. 1986. *The Fame of Gawa: A Symbolic Study of Value Transformation in a Massim (Papua New Guinea) Society.* Cambridge: Cambridge University Press.

———. 1992. The Cultural Anthropology of Time: A Critical Essay. *Annual Review of Anthropology* 21:93–123.

Murra, John. 1989. Cloth and Its Function in the Inka State. In *Cloth and Human Experience,* ed. Annette B. Weiner and Jane Schneider, pp. 275–302. Washington, D. C.: Smithsonian Institution Press.

Nieuwenhuys, Rob. 1988. *Met vreemde ogen: Tempo doeloe—een verzonken wereld. Fotografische documenten uit het oude Indië, 1870–1920.* Amsterdam: Em. Querido.

Onvlee, L. 1977. The Significance of Livestock on Sumba. In *The Flow of Life: Essays on Eastern Indonesian Culture,* ed. James J. Fox, pp. 195–207. Cambridge, Mass.: Harvard University Press.

Ortner, Sherry B. 1985. Theory in Anthropology since the Sixties. *Comparative Studies in Society and History* 26 (1):126–66.

Osseweijer, Manon. 1997. "We Wander in Our Ancestors' Yard": Sea Cucumber Gathering in the Aru Archipelago, Indonesia. Paper presented at the East-West Environmental Workshop on Local Knowledge, Canterbury 1997.

Parry, J., and M. Bloch, eds. 1989. *Money and the Morality of Exchange.* Cambridge: Cambridge University Press.

Pauwels, Simone. 1990. From Hursu Ribon's "Three Hearth Stones" to Metanleru's "Sailing Boat": A Ritual after the Harvest. *Bijdragen tot de Taal-, Land- en Volkenkunde* 146 (1): 21–34.

Pels, Peter. 1998. The Spirit of Matter: On Fetish, Rarity, Fact, and Fancy. In *Border Fetishisms: Material Objects in Unstable Spaces,* ed. Patricia Spyer, pp. 91–121. New York: Routledge.

Pemberton, John. 1986. Notes on the 1982 General Election in Solo. *Indonesia* 46:1–22.

———. 1994. *On the Subject of "Java."* Ithaca, N.Y.: Cornell University Press.

Perniola, Mario. 1989. Between Clothing and Nudity. In *Fragments for a History of the Human Body,* part 2, ed. Michel Feher, with Ramona Naddaff and Nadia Tazi, pp. 236–65. New York: Urzone Inc.

Pietz, William. 1985. The Problem of the Fetish, I. *Res* 9:5–17.

———. 1987. The Problem of the Fetish, II. *Res* 13:23–45.

———. 1988. The Problem of the Fetish, IIIa. *Res* 16:105–23.

Pinch, Adela. 1998. Stealing Happiness: Shoplifting in Early-Nineteenth-Century England. In *Border Fetishisms: Material Objects in Unstable Places,* ed. Patricia Spyer, pp. 122–49. New York: Routledge.

———. 1998b. Rubber Bands and Old Ladies. In *In Near Ruins: Cultural Theory at the End of the Century*, ed. Nicholas B. Dirks, pp. 147–71. Minneapolis: University of Minnesota Press.

Platenkamp, J. D. M. 1988. Tobelo: Ideas and Values of a North Moluccan Society. Ph.D. dissertation, Leiden University.

Pleyte, C. J. M. 1893. *Bijdrage tot de kennis der ethnographie van de Zuidwester- en Zuidooster-Eilanden*. Leiden: E. J. Brill.

Post, Peter. 1991. Japanse bedrijvigheid in Indonesië, 1868–1924: Structurele elementen van Japan's economische expansie in Zuid-Oost Azië. Ph.D. dissertation, Vrije Universiteit Amsterdam.

Pratt, Mary Louise. 1992. *Imperial Eyes: Travel Writing and Transculturation*. New York: Routledge.

Purcell, Rosamund Wolff, and Stephen Jay Gould. 1992. *Finders, Keepers: Eight Collectors*. London: Hutchinson Radius.

Purwadi. 1980. "Kudera": Upacara Menjelang Berburu di Desa Kobadangar, Kecamatan Pulau-Pulau Aru, Kabupaten Maluku Tenggara. B.A. thesis, Fakultas Sastra Universitas Padjadjaran, Bandung.

Quammen, David. 1993. Trinket from Aru: Window-shopping in the Markets of Paradise. *Outside*, September, 35–40.

——. 1996. *The Song of the Dodo: Island Biogeography in an Age of Extinction*. New York: Scribner.

Rafael, Vincente L. 1993. *Contracting Colonialism: Translation and Christian Conversion in Tagalog Society under Early Spanish Rule*. Durham, N.C.: Duke University Press.

Ranger, Terence. 1983. The Invention of Tradition in Colonial Africa. In *The Invention of Tradition*, ed. Eric Hobsbawn and Terence Ranger, pp. 211–62. Cambridge: Cambridge University Press.

Reid, Anthony. 1988. *Southeast Asia in the Age of Commerce, 1450–1680: The Lands below the Winds*. Vol. 1. New Haven: Yale University Press.

Riedel, J.G.F. 1886. *De Sluik- en kroesharige rassen tusschen Selebes en Papua*. The Hague: Nijhoff.

Rutherford, Danilyn. 1996. Of Birds and Gifts: Reviving Tradition on an Indonesian Frontier. *Cultural Anthropology* 11 (4): 577–616.

Sahlins, Marshall. 1972. *Stone Age Economics*. Chicago: Aldine-Atherton.

——. 1985. *Islands of History*. Chicago: University of Chicago Press.

——. 1994. Cosmologies of Capitalism: The Transpacific Sector of "The World System." In *Culture, Power, History*, ed. Nicholas Dirks, Geoff Eley, and Sherry Ortner, pp. 412–57. Princeton, N.J.: Princeton University Press.

Savage, V. R. 1984. *Western Impressions of Nature and Landscape in Southeast Asia*. Singapore: Singapore University Press.

Scheurs MSC, P. G. H. 1992. *Terug in het erfgoed van Franciscus Xaverius: Het herstel van de katholieke missie in Maluku, 1886–1960*. Tilburg: Missiehuis MSC.

Schieffelin, Edward L. 1976. *The Sorrow of the Lonely and the Burning of the Dancers*. New York: St. Martin's Press.

Schneider, Jane, and Annette B. Weiner. 1989. Introduction. In *Cloth and Human Experience*, ed. Annette B. Weiner and Jane Schneider, pp. 1–29. Washington, D.C.: Smithsonian Institution Press.

Schulte Nordholt, Henk. 1997. Introduction. In *Outward Appearances: Dressing State and Society in Indonesia*, ed. Henk Schulte Nordholt, pp. 1–37. Leiden: KITLV Press.

Schulte Nordholt, H. G. 1971. *The Political System of the Atoni of Timor*. The Hague: Martinus Nijhoff.

Scott, James C. 1985. *Weapons of the Weak: Everyday Forms of Peasant Resistance*. New Haven, Ct.: Yale University Press.

Scott, Joan W. 1986. Gender: A Useful Category of Historical Analysis. *American Historical Review* 91 (5): 1053–75.

———. 1992. Experience. In *Feminists Theorize the Political*, ed. Judith Butler and Joan W. Scott, pp. 22–40. New York: Routledge.

Sears, Laurie J., ed. 1996. *Fantasizing the Feminine in Indonesia*. Durham, N.C.: Duke University Press.

Seremetakis, C. Nadia. 1994. The Memory of the Senses, Part I: Marks of the Transitory. In *The Senses Still: Perception and Memory as Material Culture in Modernity*, ed. C. Nadia Seremetakis, pp. 1–18. Chicago: University of Chicago Press.

Shell, Marc. 1982. *Money, Language, and Thought: Literary and Philosophic Economies from the Medieval to the Modern Era*. Berkeley: University of California Press.

———. 1992. Money and Art: The Issue of Representation in Commerce and Culture. *Regional Review* 2 (4): 20–24.

Sider, Gerald M. 1986. *Culture and Class in Anthropology and History: A Newfoundland Illustration*. Cambridge: Cambridge University Press.

Siegel, James T. 1997. *Fetish, Recognition, Revolution*. Princeton, N.J.: Princeton University Press.

Slater, Candace. 1994. "All That Glitters": Contemporary Amazonian Gold Miners' Tales. *Comparative Studies in Society and History* 36 (4): 720–42.

Smith, Adam. 1976 [1904]. *An Inquiry into the Nature and Causes of the Wealth of Nations*. Chicago: University of Chicago Press.

Sommer, Doris. 1991. *Foundational Fictions: The National Romances of Latin America*. Berkeley: University of California Press.

Sperling, Irene. 1936. Beiträge zur Länderkunde von Niederländisch-Neuguinea: Das Hinterland von Merauke mit der Frederik-Hendrik-Insel und die Aroe-Inseln. *Frankfurter geographische Hefte* 10 (1): 88–132.

Spyer, Patricia. 1992. The Memory of Trade: Circulation, Autochthony, and the Past in the Aru Islands (Eastern Indonesia). Ph.D. dissertation, University of Chicago.

———. 1996a. Diversity with a Difference: *Adat* and the New Order in Aru (Eastern Indonesia). *Cultural Anthropology* 11 (1): 25–50.

———. 1996b. Serial Conversion/Conversion to Seriality: Religion, State, and Number in Aru, Eastern Indonesia. In *Conversion to Modernities: The Globalization of Christianity*, ed. Peter van der Veer, pp. 171–98. New York: Routledge.

——. 1997. The Eroticism of Debt: Pearldivers, Traders, and Sea Wives in the Aru Islands, Eastern Indonesia. *American Ethnologist* 24 (3): 515–38.

——. 1998a. Introduction. In *Border Fetishisms: Material Objects in Unstable Spaces*, ed. Patricia Spyer, pp. 1–11. New York: Routledge.

——. 1998b. The Tooth of Time, or Taking a Look at the "Look" of Clothing in Late-Nineteenth-Century Aru. In *Border Fetishisms: Material Objects in Unstable Spaces*, ed. Patricia Spyer, pp. 150–82. New York: Routledge.

——. 1999. What's in a pocket? Religion and the formation of a pagan elsewhere in Aru, Eastern Indonesia. In *De bindkracht der dingen*, ed. Hans Harber and Sjaak Koenis. Special Issue, *Tijdschrift voor Empirische Filosofie* 23: 37–49.

Stallybrass, Peter. 1993. Worn Worlds: Clothes, Mourning, and the Life of Things. *Yale Review* 81 (2): 35–50.

——. 1998. Marx's Coat. In *Border Fetishisms: Material Objects in Unstable Spaces*, ed. Patricia Spyer, pp. 183–207. New York: Routledge.

Stallybrass, Peter, and Allon White. 1986. *The Politics and Poetics of Transgression*. Ithaca, N.Y.: Cornell University Press.

Stapel, F. W. 1943. *De Oostindische Compagnie en Australie*. Amsterdam: P. N. van Kampen en Zoon.

Steedly, Mary Margaret. 1993. *Hanging without a Rope: Narrative Experience in Colonial and Postcolonial Karoland*. Princeton, N.J.: Princeton University Press.

Stewart, Kathleen. 1990. Backtalking the Wilderness: "Appalachian" Engenderings. In *Uncertain Terms: Negotiating Gender in American Culture*, ed. Faye Ginsburg and Anna Lowenhaupt Tsing, pp. 43–56. Boston: Beacon Press.

——. 1991. On the Politics of Cultural Theory: A Case for "Contaminated" Cultural Critique. *Social Research* 15 (2): 395–412.

Stewart, Susan. 1984. *On Longing: Narratives of the Miniature, the Gigantic, the Souvenir, the Collection*. Baltimore, Md.: Johns Hopkins University Press.

Stoler, Ann L. 1992. Sexual Affronts and Racial Frontiers: European Identities and the Cultural Politics of Exclusion in Colonial Southeast Asia. *Comparative Studies in Society and History* 34 (3): 514–51.

——. 1995. *Race and the Education of Desire*. Durham, N.C.: Duke University Press.

Strathern, Marilyn. 1984. Marriage Exchanges: A Melanesian Comment. *Annual Review of Anthropology* 13:41–73.

——. 1988. *The Gender of the Gift: Problems with Women and Problems with Society in Melanesia*. Berkeley: University of California Press.

Suryakusuma, Julia I. 1996. The State and Sexuality in New Order Indonesia. In *Fantasizing the Feminine in Indonesia*, ed. Laurie J. Sears, pp. 92–119. Durham, N.C.: Duke University Press.

Swadling, Pamela. 1996. *Plumes from Paradise: Trade Cycles in Outer Southeast Asia and Their Impact on New Guinea and Nearby Islands until 1920*. With

Contributions by Roy Wagner and Billai Laba. Papua New Guinea Museum, Boroko.

Taburiaux, Jean. 1985. *Pearls: Their Origin, Treatment and Identification*. Trans. David Ceriog-Hughes. Radnor, Pa.: Chilton Book Company.

Tambiah, S.J. 1968. The Magical Power of Words. *Man*, n.s., 3:175–208.

———. 1984. *The Buddhist Saints of the Forest and the Cult of the Amulets*. Cambridge: Cambridge University Press.

Tan, Mély G. 1991. The Social and Cultural Dimensions of the Role of Ethnic Chinese in Indonesian Society. In *The Role of the Indonesian Chinese in Shaping Modern Indonesian Life*, ed. Leonard Blussé, pp. 113–25. *Indonesia* (special issue) on the Role of the Indonesian Chinese in Shaping Modern Indonesian Life): 113–25.

Taussig, Michael. 1980. *The Devil and Commodity Fetishism in South America*. Chapel Hill: University of North Carolina Press.

———. 1987. *Shamanism, Colonialism, and the Wild Man*. Chicago: University of Chicago Press.

———. 1993. *Mimesis and Alterity: A Particular History of the Senses*. New York: Routledge.

———. 1995. The Sun Gives without Receiving: An Old Story. *Comparative Studies in Society and History* 37 (2): 368–98.

———. 1998. The Beach: A Fantasy. Paper presented at the conference "Fantasy Spaces" at the University of Amsterdam, August 1998.

Taylor, Jean Gelman. 1983. *The Social World of Batavia: European and Eurasian in Dutch Asia*. Madison: University of Wisconsin Press.

———. 1997. Costume and Gender in Colonial Java, 1800–1940. In *Outward Appearances: Dressing State and Society in Indonesia*, ed. Henk Schulte Nordholt, pp. 85–116. Leiden: KITLV Press.

Thomas, Nicholas. 1989. *Out of Time: History and Evolution in Anthropological Discourse*. Cambridge: Cambridge University Press.

———. 1991. *Entangled Objects: Exchange, Material Culture, and Colonialism in the Pacific*. Cambridge, Mass.: Harvard University Press.

———. 1992. Politicised Values: The Cultural Dynamics of Peripheral Exchange. In *Barter, Exchange and Value: An Anthropological Approach*, ed. Caroline Humphrey and Stephen Hugh-Jones, pp. 21–41. Cambridge: Cambridge University Press.

Tillema, H. F. 1926. *Zonder tropen geen Europa!* Bloemendaal: Tillema.

Toer, Pramoedya Ananta. 1981. *This Earth of Mankind: A Novel*. Trans. and intro. Max Lane. Ringwood: Penguin Books Australia.

Traube, Elizabeth. 1986. *Cosmology and Social Life: Ritual Exchange among the Mambai of East Timor*. Chicago: University of Chicago Press.

———. 1989. Obligations to the Source: Complementarity and Hierarchy in an Eastern Indonesian Society. In *The Attraction of Opposites: Thought and Society in the Dualistic Mode*, ed. David Maybury-Lewis and Uri Almagor, pp. 321–44. Ann Arbor: University of Michigan Press.

Tsing, Anna Lowenhaupt. 1990. Gender and Performance in Meratus Dispute Settlement. In *Power and Difference: Gender in Island Southeast Asia*, ed. Jane Monnig Atkinson and Shelley Errington, pp. 95–125. Stanford, Calif.: Stanford University Press.

———. 1993. *In the Realm of the Diamond Queen: Marginality in an Out-of-the-Way Place*. Princeton, N.J.: Princeton University Press.

Turner, Terence S. 1980. The Social Skin. In *Not Work Alone*, ed. J. Cherfas and R. Lewin, pp. 112–40. London: Temple Smith.

Turner, Victor. 1967. *The Forest of Symbols*. Ithaca, N.Y.: Cornell University Press.

Valeri, Valerio. 1980. Notes on the Meaning of Marriage Prestations among the Huaulu of Seram. In *The Flow of Life: Essays on Eastern Indonesia*, ed. James J. Fox, pp. 178–92. Cambridge, Mass.: Harvard University Press.

———. 1985. *Kingship and Sacrifice: Ritual and Society in Ancient Hawaii*. Trans. Paula Wissing. Chicago: Chicago University Press.

van Baal, J. 1985. *Ontglipt Verleden: Tot 1947 Indisch bestuursambtenaar in vrede en oorlog*. Franeker: T. Wever.

van der Crab, P. 1862. *De Moluksche Eilanden: Reis van Z. E. den Gouverneur-Generaal Charles Ferdinand Pahud, door den Molukschen Archipel*. Batavia: Lange and Co.

van der Veer, Peter. 1996. *Modern oriëntalisme: Essays over de westerse beschavingsdrang*. Amsterdam: Meulenhoff.

van Dijk, Toos and Nico de Jonge. 1990. After Sunshine comes Rain: A Comparative Analysis of Fertility Rituals in Marsela and Luang, South-East Moluccas. *Bijdragen tot de taal-, land- en volkenkunde* 146(1): 3–20. Special issue on Rituals and Socio-Cosmic Order in Eastern Indonesian Societies. Part II, Maluku. Edited by C. Barrand and J. D. M. Platenkamp.

van Doorn, J. A. A. 1994. *De laatste eeuw van Indië: Ontwikkeling en ondergang van een koloniaal project*. Amsterdam: Bert Bakker.

van Doren, J. B. J. 1854. *Fragmenten uit de reizen in den Indischen Archipel*. Part 1. Amsterdam: J. D. Sybrandi.

van Eijbergen, H. C. 1866. Verslag eener reis naar de Aroe- en Key Eilanden in de maand Junij, 1862. *Tijdschrift voor Indischen Taal-, Land- en Volkenkunde* 14:220–72.

van Hoëvell, G. W. W. C. Baron. 1890. De Aroe-Eilanden, geographisch, ethnographisch en commercieel. *Tijdschrift van Taal, Land en Volkenkunde* 32:1–45.

van Kol, H. 1903. *Uit onze koloniën: Uitvoerig reisverhaal*. Leiden: A. W. Sijthoff.

van Leur, J. C. 1955. *Indonesian Trade and Society*. The Hague: W. van Hoeve, Ltd.

van Weerdenburg MSC, H. n.d. MSC. Tilburg: Missiehuis MSC.

van Wouden, F. A. E. 1968 [1935]. *Types of Social Structure in Eastern Indonesia*. Trans. R. Needham. KITLV Translation Series, vol. 2. The Hague: Martinus Nijhoff.

Vernant, Jean-Pierre. 1991. From the "Presentification" of the Invisible to the Imitation of Appearance. In *Mortals and Immortals: Collected Essays*, ed. Froma I. Zeitlin, pp. 151–63. Princeton, N.J.: Princeton University Press.

Veth, Peter, et al. n.d. Bridging Sunda and Sahul: Archeological Survey and Excavation in the Aru Islands, Maluku. Unpublished manuscript.

Vickers, Adrian, ed. 1996. *Being Modern in Bali: Image and Change.* New Haven, Conn.: Yale University South Asian Studies.

Villiers, John. 1981. Trade and Society in the Banda Islands in the Sixteenth Century. *Modern Asian Studies* 15 (4): 723–50.

Visser, Leontine E. 1989. *My Rice Field Is My Child.* Dordrecht: Foris.

Volkman, Toby Alice. 1990. Visions and Revisions: Toraja Culture and the Tourist Gaze. *American Ethnologist* 17 (1): 91–110.

———. 1994. Our Garden Is the Sea: Contingency and Improvisation in Mandar Women's Work. *American Ethnologist* 21 (3): 564–85.

von Rosenberg, C. B. H. 1867. *Reis naar de Zuidoostereilanden, gedaan in 1865 op last der regering van Nederlandsch-Indië.* The Hague: Martinus Nijhoff.

Vroklage, B. A. G. 1940. De prauw in culturen van Flores. *Cultureel Indië* 2:193–204.

Wallace, Alfred Russell. 1962 [1869]. *The Malay Archipelago.* New York: Dover Publications.

Weber, Max. 1930. *The Protestant Ethic and the Spirit of Capitalism.* London: George Allen and Unwin.

Weber, Samuel. 1991. *Return to Freud: Jacques Lacan's Dislocation of Psychoanalysis.* Trans. Michael Levine. Cambridge: Cambridge University Press.

———. 1996. *Mass Mediauras: Form Technics Media.* Stanford, Calif.: Stanford University Press.

Wilentz, Sean. 1985. *Rites of Power,* ed. Sean Wilentz. Philadelphia: University of Pennsylvania Press.

Wurffbain, Johann Sigmund. 1931. *Reise nach den Molukken und Vorder-Indien I: 1632–1638* and *II: 1638–1646.* In *Reisebeschreibungen von Deutschen Beamten und Kriegsleuten im Dienst der Niederländischen West- und Ost-Indischen Kompagnien 1602–1797.* The Hague: Martinus Nijhoff.

Xenos, Nicholas. 1989. *Scarcity and Modernity.* London: Routledge.

Young, Robert. 1990. *White Mythologies: Writing History and the West.* New York: Routledge.

Žižek, Slavoj. 1994. *The Metastases of Enjoyment: Six Essays on Woman and Causality.* London: Verso.

Archive and Manuscript Collections

ARA. Algemeen Rijksarchief (General State Archive), Ministerie van Koloniën (Ministry of Colonies), The Hague. Series consulted include Mailrapporten, Memorie van Overgave.

MSC. Missionaires du Sacré Coeur. Archives belonging to the Dutch branch of this order: Missionarissen van het Heilig Hart. Housed in MSC Mission House, Tilburg, the Netherlands, and at the Bishopric Ambon, Indonesia.

Index

Abu Lughod, Lila, 7
Abu Magar, 103, 129
Abu Matagwa, 140
Abu Meme, 269
Abu Sabuan, 80–86, 96, 106, 260, 279;
dream of cassowary doubles, 254–
259, 287; dream of oysters, 252. See
also *Sejara:* of great ship
Adat, xii, 6, 32; *agama* and, 223, 228,
256–257, 324 n.1; authority and,
191–192; casting off of practices of,
90, 181, 200; *dinas* and, 164, 194–
197; men's preeminence in, 90, 173,
233, 260, 285, 287; *momosim* and,
313 n.6; New Order and, 164, 194–
197
Agama. See *Adat;* New Order;
Religion
Agar-agar. See Trade products
Agency, 132, 135, 158, 159, 176. *See also*
Ancestors; Pearl oysters
Alcohol: cassowary ritual and, 183,
222, 226, 240–241, 248; trade and,
16, 35, 48, 89, 304 n.11
Ama Tiong, 75
Ambon and Ambonese, 55, 61, 72,
100–101, 134, 288
Ancestors, 204–205; agency of, 106,
173, 174, 239, 252; anger of, 163, 190;
fish poisoning and, 221–222; informing of, 210, 225; mythic diaspora of Karang-Enu, 178; origins
and, 177, 195. *See also* Cassowary
ritual; Mimesis
Anderson, Benedict, 45, 166, 228,
293 n.3, 312 n.1

Anthropology, 143, 285. *See also* Ritual
Apara, xviii, 107, 114, 222, 229; miniature sea house of, 180–181; settlement history of, 294 n.10. *See also*
Barakai Island
Appadurai, Arjun, x, 6, 80, 143, 291, 292
Arabs. *See* Traders
Aru, xi, 47; ambivalence toward, 6, 32,
65, 99; as backward, xiv, 32, 67;
colonial mapping of, 98; egalitarianism of, 150, 310 n.27; elsewhere, 4,
6, 29–30, 32, 36, 66–67, 86, 99, 106,
169, 202, 215, 276; fauna of, 42; government officials in, 72; *gwerka lir,*
xxiii–xxiv, 203, 212; imports and
exports, 48–49; language in, xxiii–
xxiv; in national media, 120–122; as
nature, 52; sense of lack and, 65–66,
291; the work of, 117
Aru and Malay: difference of, xiv, 37,
88, 108, 170, 212–214, 218, 283–285;
elsewheres, ix, 4, 6–8, 29–30, 36–
37, 99, 168, 290–292; emblems of,
36; as work of Aru versus work of
sea, 117
Aruese: as backward, 5–6, 132, 200,
216, 257; savvy trade attitude of, 33–
34, 123
Asad, Talal, 161

Baadilla, Sech Said. *See* Pearl-diving
companies
Backshore, xi, 28, 37–40, 53, 109, 200;
and Frontshore, 5–6; rebellions of,
12–13, 16, 55, 98, 155–156. *See also*
Barakai Island; Frontshore

Patricia Spyer is a lecturer at the Research Centre Religion and Society, University of Amsterdam, and editor of *Border Fetishisms: Material Objects in Unstable Places.*

Library of Congress Cataloging-in-Publication Data

Spyer, Patricia
The memory of trade: modernity's entanglements on an Eastern Indonesian island / Patricia Spyer.
p. cm.
Includes bibliographical references and index.
ISBN 0-8223-2405-9 (cloth : alk. paper). — ISBN 0-8223-2441-5 (paper : alk. paper)
1. Aru Islands (Indonesia)—Social life and customs.   2. Economic anthropology—Indonesia—Aru Islands.   3. Aru Islands (Indonesia)—Commerce—History.   I. Title.
DS647.A78S69 2000
959.8'5—dc21   99-37251